ANTHROPOLOGY

ANTHROPOLOGY

Ramnath Sharma
Rajendra K. Sharma

ATLANTIC
PUBLISHERS & DISTRIBUTORS (P) LTD

Published by

ATLANTIC

PUBLISHERS & DISTRIBUTORS (P) LTD

7/22, Ansari Road, Darya Ganj,
New Delhi-110002
Phones : +91-11-40775252, 23273880, 23275880, 23280451
Fax : +91-11-23285873
Web : www.atlanticbooks.com
E-mail : orders@atlanticbooks.com

Branch Office
5, Nallathambi Street, Wallajah Road,
Chennai-600002
Phones : +91-44-64611085, 32413319
E-mail : chennai@atlanticbooks.com

Printed in India at Glorious Printers, A-13, D.S.I.D.C.,
Jhilmil Industrial Area, Delhi-110095

PREFACE

This comprehensive textbook on Anthropology. It cover's the following papers taught to M.A. (Sociology) and M.A. (Anthropology) at Indian Universities:

1. Physical Anthropology
2. Cultural Anthropology
3. Social Anthropology
4. General Anthropology
5. Anthropology and Indian Tribes
6. Comparative Sociology.

This book also covers courses prescribed in Anthropology for P.C.S. and I.A.S. examinations. The material for this book has been collected from authentic sources : works of eminent anthropologists, reports of researches on Indian tribes and Government data published in various books, reports and journals. The subject matter has been divided into four parts which includes the following:

Part A. General Anthropology : 1. Introduction to Anthropology; 2. Anthropology in India; 3. Relationship with Other Social Sciences; 4. Anthropological Methods.

Part B. Physical Anthropology : 5. Introduction to Physical Anthropology; 6. Anthropology; 7. Race and Racism; 8. Criteria of Racial Classification; 9. Classification of Race; 10. Racial Groups in the World; 11. Races of Asia; 12. Races in India.

Part C. Cultural Anthropology: 13. Introduction to Cultural Anthropology; 14. Pre-historic Culture; 15. Growth of Civilisations.

Part D. Social Anthropology : 16. Introduction to Social Anthropology; 17. Basic Concepts of Social Anthropology; 18. Researches of Radcliffe-Brown; 19. Researches of Bronislaw Malinowski ; 20. Primitive Social Organisation; 21. Kinship; 22. Family; 23. Marriage; 24. Status of Women; 25. Avoidance and Joking Relationship; 26. Youth Dormitories; 27. Economy; 28. Religion and Magic; 29. Language; 30. Art, Mythology and Culture; 31. Legends; 32. Government and Law; 33. Justice and Punishment; 34. Criminal Tribes; 35. Tribal Problems and Welfare.

At the end of the book Objective Questions Bank has been given particularly for those readers who are appearing at P.C.S. or I.A.S. examination. Selected Bibliography has been divided into two classes. While the first includes books on General Anthropology, the second is a comprehensive list of books published on Tribal Studies in India. This will be particularly useful for researchers working in the field of tribal studies.

Thus, this book has been prepared as an ideal textbook for the students of Indian Universities and aspirants for success in I.A.S. and P.C.S. Besides, it will serve as a reference book for every one connected with Anthropology : Teachers, Researchers and Field workers. Suggestions for improvement are solicited from indulgent readers.

RAM NATH SHARMA
RAJENDRA K. SHARMA

CONTENTS

PART A — GENERAL ANTHROPOLOGY

1

Introduction to Anthropology

Anthropology is the scientific study of man, especially his origin, development, races, customs and beliefs. In the broadest sense Anthropology is the study of all aspects of Man, including the sociology of "primitive" peoples.

Man has inherited and acquired attributes. The inherited traits are the potential bodily forms, passed on by genes and the acquired traits as some forms of bodily growth, moulded by lack of nutrition or disease and cultural features passed on by imitation. These classes are unrelated and independent, both in nature and distribution so that to use any features for deduction, its class must be recognized.

We gather knowledge about the origin, evolution and antiquity of man primarily from fossil remains. Man is a mammal who has evolved from ape-like ancestors common to himself and the anthropoid apes some 5,00,000 years ago.

Man distinguishes himself from all the animal kingdom by his unique ability to think out his future and make anticipatory acts to ward off evil and also his ability to use tools. He is the only creature capable of language and transferring his experiences from generation to generation by folklore and legends. This helps him to build up a useful and serviceable store of knowledge. He has discovered fire and put it to great use. Beginning as a hunter and gatherer roaming all over and leading a precarious life, he has learnt the art of animal husbandry and agriculture. This allowed him to set up settlements and begin the civilizing process.

Evolution led to the development of different types of men and of these all have become extinct except the *Homo Sapiens*. Evolution also led to differences within species and this is an ongoing process. An example is differences in skin colour which are due to the amount of pigment (melanin) present. In hot countries, individuals with a quantity sufficient to protect them from harmful effects of the actinic rays of the sun are best able to survive in tropical areas, and so pass on the beneficial character.

Man has been classified into biological groups as Cancasoid, Mongoloid, Negroid and Australoid, each called race on account of sets of differences in bodily features and measurements between them. But these groups merge into each other because the features are widely and independently spread among them. Barring the primitives of Andaman and Nicobar Islands there are no specimen of pure race today. The relative superiority of any race over others is now regarded as a myth by knowledgeable persons. For example, often cultural characters are confused with biological characters, and people are described as a race who speak the same type of language, Indo-Germanic, English or groups like tribes as gypsies.

Culture — the beliefs, practices and artifacts of man — may be studied by History, Sociology and Economics as a living pattern specific to particular space-time.

Earlier anthropologists like Frazer (1854-1941), Morgan (1818-1881), E.B. Tylor (1832-1917) and Wester Marck studied mainly the origin and history of cultures, institutions and customs. Heavily under the spell of Darwinian theory of evolution they tried to work out elaborate hypothetical stages of evolution for cultural features such as marriage, group loyalty, gregariousness and means of collecting food.

Now it is a moot point whether the culture spreads through evolution or diffusion. Elliot-Smith-Perry hypothesized that civilization spread from Egypt but the recent archaeological studies have exploded this hypothesis. According to Gordon Childe, agriculture started and spread from the Near East about 8,000 years ago and this induced settlements and the beginning of civilization. For more than 5,00,000 years human existence was limited to the life of nomads who led an economy characterized by hunting, food gathering and fishing. Settled life and surplus food permitted man to develop urban life, with substantial habitation and beginning of the industries of pottery, metal work and trade. However, if the duration of man's evolution, now estimated at 17,50,000 years, is likened to a single year, then the earliest of the recorded civilization began after 5 P.M. on December 30. Put otherwise 289/290th of man's existence has been uncivilized.

The anthropological researches have paved ways and means for integrating agricultural societies with industrial civilization and tribal welfare without destroying their cultural identity. Now-a-days the so-called primitive tribes can derive the benefits of modern technology and still not lose their ethnicity. That is, the rich cultural diversity can be preserved in spite of technological invasion. The tribals can now get full benefits of civilization without losing their virtue and identity. The culture of each social groups is an inter-weaved pattern of ideas, practices and industry each performing a function in the whole and each dependent upon others. The surviving beliefs and customs like tolemism and exogamy which appear incomprehensible if viewed out of context have value and significance related to other items of culture. The great anthropological scholar B. Malinowski (1884-1942) pioneered the concept of "functionalism" which necessitated detailed recording of day-to-day life of communities and their geographical environments.

The religion and ideology are basic to any culture. The cohesion among various members of society is achieved through this multi-faceted pattern and provides mystical support to the laws of society and its moral code is sustained by loyalty to tradition and ideology. This alone enables men to face crises let loose by fickle nature. Hence, the value of magic, birth customs and couvade (widespread birth custom of primitive in which the father retires to bed alone after the birth of the child to avoid any action that might spiritually be detrimental to the baby) as well as various beliefs and rites connected with the disposal of dead which compensate for the emotional blow of death and consequent economic upset.

DIVISIONS OF ANTHROPOLOGY

Anthropology has been divided into two main branches : physical anthropology and cultural anthropology. These two main branches have been again, sub-divided into several other branches which have been given in the following chart:

CLASSIFICATION OF ANTHROPOLOGICAL SCIENCE

ANTHROPOLOGY

Physical Anthropology | Cultural Anthropology

Human Genetics | Human Palaeontology | Ethnology | Anthropometry | Biometry

Prehistoric Archaeology | Social Anthropology

Linton's Classification of Anthropology[1]

Physical Anthropology | Cultural Anthropoloy

Human Palaeontology | Somatology | Archaeology | Ethnology Linguistics

Piddington's Classification of Anthropology[2]

Physical Anthropology | Cultural Anthropology

Human Genetics | Anthropometry or Somatology | Prehistoric Anthropology | Social Anthropology

1. Linton, R., *The Study of Man*, p. 2.
2. Piddington, R., *An Introduction to Social Anthropology*, Oliver and Boyd, London (1952), p. 2.

DEFINITION OF ANTHROPOLOGY

1. *The Concise Oxford Dictionary*. "Study of mankind especially of its societies and customs; study of structure and evolution of man as an animal."

2. *Herskovits*. "Anthropology may be defined as the measurement of human beings."

3. *Jocobs and Stern*. "Anthropology is the scientific study of the physical, social and cultural development and behaviour of human beings since their appearance on this earth."

4. *Kroeber*. "Anthropology is the science of man." The term anthropology has been derived from two terms : *Anthropos* meaning man and *logos* meaning knowledge. Thus, anthropology is the knowledge of man.

5. *Boas*. "Anthropology deals with man as social being."

SCOPE OF ANTHROPOLOGY

A. Physical Anthropology

Physical anthropology studies human body, genetics and the status of man among living beings. In the words of J. E. Manchip White, "Physical anthropology is the study of bodily appearance of man."[3] According to Hoebel, "Physical anthropology is therefore, the study of the physical characteristics of the human race as such."[4] M. J. Herskovits has written in *Man and His Works*, "Physical Anthropology is, in essence, human biology"[5] Piddington, in his book, *An Introduction to Social Anthropology*, defined Physical Anthropology in these words: "Physical Anthropology is concerned with the bodily characteristics of man."[6] Thus, the subject matter of Physical Anthropology includes the study of human genetics, human palaeontology, ethnic characteristics, anthropometric and biometric measurements, etc. Manchip White has classified Physical Anthropology into search for human genesis and the distribution of human races on earth. According to Herskovits, in Physical Anthropology, we study the nature of distinctions among human races, the process of transference of physical characteristics from one generation to another, origin, development and degeneration of the human being and the influence of natural matter on the study of Physical Anthropology in the classification and characteristics of human races. This requires description and measurement of physical characteristics which is now the special field of Anthropometry or Somatology. The study of races requires the study of human genetics. Another important field of study in Physical Anthropology is the process of human evolution which shows how human body has evolved through different stages. Thus, Physical Anthropology

3. White, J.E.M., *Anthropology*, p. 17.
4. Hoebel, E.A., *Man in the Primitive World*, p. 2.
5. Herskovits, M.J., *Man and His Works*, p. 3.
6. Piddington, R., *An Introduction to Social Anthropology* (1953), p. 2.

has now been divided into the following five branches according to the specialization of study:

1. Human Genetics. Human genetics is the branch of physical anthropology which studies the genesis of man. In the words of E. C. Colin, "Genetics is that branch of biology which deals with the laws or principles of heredity and variations as observed in plants, in animals and in man."[7] Human genetics is the study of human heredity. It studies the human physical characteristics that are transmitted through heredity from generation to generation.

2. Human Palaeontology. Human Palaeontology studies the old human skeletons of different stages. It also studies the history of earth evolution. According to Webester's New International Dictionary, "Human Palaeontology is the science that deals with life of the past geographical periods. It is based on the study of the fossil remains of organisms."[8] Thus, it has traced the evolution of man. This, in its turn, has thrown much light on primitive man. The study of fossil man and the process of evolution has been possible by it.

3. Ethnology. Ethnology studies human races. In the words of S. C. Dube, "Ethnology is a comparative study of the races and cultures of mankind in their different aspects."[9] Ethnology classifies human races and studies their physical characteristics. Ethnology is based upon anthropometry and biometrics, since both measure racial characteristics.

4. Anthropometry. According to Herskovits, "Anthropometry may be defined as the measurement of human being."[10] Anthropologists have decided certain definite traits by the measurement of which human races may be classified. Anthropometry, again, has been classified into two branches, the study of the physical structures of living human beings and the study of human fossils. For example, anthropologists have fixed upon traits like length and breadth of head, length and breadth of nose, etc., which may be measured. Still other traits cannot be measured but only observed and described, such as the colour and texture of skin, eyes, hair, etc.

5. Biometry. In the words of Charles Winick, "Biometry is the statistical analysis of biological studies specially as applied to such areas as disease, birth, growth and death."[11] Thus, biometry is the statistical study of biological characteristics.

B. Cultural Anthropology

Cultural anthropology, as is clear by the nomenclature, studies human cultures. To carry on his personal and social life man invents some sort of

---

7. Colin, E.C., *Elements of Genetics* (1956), p. xiii.
8. *Webster's New International Dictionary*, p. 1550.
9. Dube, S.C., *Anthropology* (1952), p. 2.
10. Herskovits in his article "Anthropology" in *Encyclopedia of Social Sciences*, Vol. II, p. iii.
11. Winick, C., *Dictionary of Anthropology*, p. 70.

system, develops and establishes it. This total system is culture. It is social heritage. It is, however, not transmitted through heredity. It is learned through imitation, experience and understanding. In the words of E. A Hoebel, "Culture is the sum total of learned behaviour patterns."[12] Defining culture, Herskovits has written, "Culture is the learned portion of human behaviour."[13] Each society has its own culture which embodies social experience of ages. Thus, culture is embedded in society. Culture, however, transcends the individual. It controls individual's behaviour and moulds it. It includes customs and traditions, social organization, procedures of activities, moral fabric, system of values, science, art, religion, literature and all that man has developed through experience of ages. In brief, it is the total way of living.

Thus, cultural anthropology studies human customs, mores, traditions, social life, religion, art, science, literature and economic and political organization. In the words of Beals and Hoizer, "Cultural anthropology studies the origins and history of man's culture, their evolution and development, and the structure and functioning of human culture in every place and time."[14] According to E. A. Hoebel, "The phase of anthropology that devotes its attention to the customs of mankind is called cultural anthropology."[15]

Cultural anthropology has been divided into the following two classes :

1. Prehistoric Archaeology. Literally speaking, archaeology is the study of ancient time. Thus, it studies ancient things. In the words of Beals and Hoizer, "Archaeology or prehistory deals primarily with ancient cultures and with past phases of modern civilization. It attempts to reconstruct the cultural forms of the past and to trace their growth and development to Anthropology."[16] Thus, it is clear that archaeology studies the ancient history which has no written records. Things and articles discovered by archaeological excavations give us an idea about the culture of the people using them. For example, excavations have led to the evidence of the existence of the ancient Indian culture of Harappa and Mohenjodaro. Archaeology also helps in reconstruction of the social, economic and political organizations of these cultures. It records cultural successes of a particular era and also area of its expansion.

2. Social Anthropology. Social anthropology as is clear by the nomenclature, studies social organization and social institutions. In the words of Charles Winick, "Social anthropology is the study of social behaviour especially from the point of view of the systematic comparative study of social forms and institutions."[17] According to R. Firth, "One of the broadest way of defining

12. Hoebel, E.A., *Man in the Primitive World*, p. 4.
13. Herskovits, *Man and His Works* (1952), p. 3.
14. Beals and Hoizer, *Introduction to Anthropology*, p. 8.
15. Hoebel, E.A., *Man in the Primitive World* (1949), p. 4.
16. Beals and Hoizer, *Introduction to Anthropology* (1956), p. 9.
17. Winick, C., *Dictionary of Anthropology*, p. 21.

social anthropology is to say that it studies human social processes comparatively."[18]

Physical anthropology and cultural anthropology are closely related. Different branches of physical anthropology have close bearing upon the study of social anthropology, a branch of cultural anthropology. Again archaeology has been helpful in the study of various branches of physical anthropology. Majumdar and Madan have rightly pointed out, "Prehistory would lose its human touch, if it neglected the study of the types of prehistoric men, who were responsible for the various prehistoric industries."[19]

APPLICATIONS OF ANTHROPOLOGY

Although no scientist today has any doubt in the application of anthropology in the field of social sciences, yet about fifty years ago, scholars were unware of its practical usage. The study of primitive societies is not the gift of the 20th century. Even in the 11th century, political philosophers had studied the nature of the state in the domain of nature. For this, they studied primitive institutions. Besides this, the travellers and explorers studied the life of the primitive men in different countries they visited and wrote in detail about the subject. But their viewpoint was not scientific. They studied the primitive man only out of curiosity, though their study had been highly advantageous in so far as it created an interest in such a study.

Application in Administration

As a result of the industrial revolution, the production of different commodities in some of the Western countries increased rapidly and there arose a necessity of exploring new markets for them as well as to secure the supply of the raw materials at a cheap price. The agents of different companies, therefore, took sail to Asia, Africa and to many other countries in the Far East to explore suitable markets for the sale of European products and also to secure a supply of raw materials at a cheap rate. With the business point of view many European companies began to dominate the people of Africa, Asia and Far Eastern countries which ultimately resulted in the birth of colonialism and imperialism. But they very well knew that in order to stabilize their domination over the people of any new country, a knowledge of the social and religious customs of the people there was necessary, without which no effective control over them was possible. It was mainly with this point of view that the East India Company had to study the Indian society before the British rule in India could be established. An interesting example of how far the study of a particular human society is a pre-requisite condition for establishing domination over it is given by D.N. Majumdar in his book entitled *An Introduction to Social Anthropology*.[20]

---

18. Firth, R., *Elements of Social Organisation* (1951), p. 2.
19. Majumdar, D.N. and T.N. Madan, *An Introduction to Social Anthropology*, Bombay, Asia, 1957, p. 3.
20. *Op. cit.*, pp. 38-39.

Among the Oraon people in India, every village has its own flag and whenever the people of different villages get an opportunity to meet at some common place or join a dancing group known as "Yatra", the people of each village carry the flag of their village in front of them. Once a contractor had to build a railway bridge in the Oraon area. On one side of the bridge there lay a Hindu village and on the other side there was an Oraon village. It was a common belief among the people that the river over which the bridge was to be constructed, was haunted by evil spirits, because on two previous occasions, when a bridge was constructed, it was demolished by the spirits. The contractor, therefore, made a plan to propitiate the gods of both the Hindu and the Oraon villages. He got a temple repaired in the Hindu village. To the people of the Oraon village he presented a flag with a railway engine painted on it. With this new flag in their possession, the people declared themselves more powerful than the people of other Oraon villages. Upon this, the people of some other village, who wanted to increase their strength, made a still bigger flag of their own with a railway train painted on the flag which they carried ahead in the annual procession. The people who had received the flag from the contractor, now felt highly dissatisfied. It led to a free fight between the two parties on the Yatra occasion, as a result of which two persons lost their lives and many others were wounded. The police confiscated the new flag. Many people were prosecuted and some were placed behind the bars. When the time for the next annual meet came, the district magistrate, as a precaution against a quarrel, took the help of Sarat Chandra Roy, an Indian anthropologist. Sarat Chandra Roy made a flag with an aeroplane painted on it and handed it to the people who had carried a flag with a railway train painted on it on the previous occasion. Roy explained to the leaders of the village that the sign of an aeroplane was better than that of a railway train. The people felt satisfied with the new flag and gave up their intention to carry the unauthorized flag with a railway train painted on it. In this way the trouble, which even the strictest police action on the occasion of the earlier Yatra could not stop, was now easily avoided by the help of an anthropologist. This clearly proves the fruitfulness of the application of anthropology in administration.

There is yet another example of the application of anthropology in a tribal quarrel of Ashanti in Africa. The people of this tribe lived on the western coast of Africa. Among them the king sat on an ordinary stool but rested his arms on another gold plated stool which was supposed as something come from heaven. It was considered to be the abode of the whole tribe and for that reason the stool was regarded as holy and powerful. Whenever the people of that tribe needed to collect their full strength to face some common danger, the king used lo sit on the stool three times. This golden stool was never allowed to be put on the bare ground. They spread an elephant skin under it and covered the skin with special kind of cloth. In the year 1896, their British rulers tried to take possession of this golden stool, because by doing so, they thought they would be able to keep control over the natives. Ashanti people were strongly opposed to this attempt of their rulers and they concealed the golden stool somewhere. In 1921, they examined the stool and found that the gold which covered the stool was removed and sold. They were much enraged and demanded that the offenders be killed. This episode could become the cause of a fight between the British and the Ashanti people, but due to the interference of Captain Rattray, a British anthropologist, a fight was averted. It is clear from both the examples given above that social anthropology can be of great help in matters of administration. This is the reason why every candidate for the British colonial service had to first study anthropology.

Utility for Christian Missionaries

Besides the British rulers, the Christian missionaries also showed special keenness for the study of the primitive societies in India. All along the course of establishment of colonial rule in Asia, Africa and other Far Eastern countries. by the people of the Western countries, the Christian missionaries kept pouring into these countries and tried to convert the natives to the Christian fold. It was possible only when they could create respect and faith for them in the local people and they did not lag behind in the matter. They minutely studied the social and religious institutions of the local tribes and lived amidst them. It gave them a chance of participant observation and they wrote and published important accounts of their study of different primitive societies. Many missionaries opened schools in numerous areas of primitive tribes in India; they opened schools for their education; they lent money to the people and, above all, they learnt their language in order to know their customs and to do some work of social service among them. Their main purpose behind all this was to spread Christian religion. The harm and benefit done to tribesmen in this connection will be discussed later in this book. It is sufficient to know at this stage that it was due to their study of social anthropology that the Christian missionaries could succeed in their missionary work. It is, thus, clear that they could not succeed without the help of social anthropology.

It was after the written accounts of the travellers of distant countries and the missionaries, that the early anthropologists, Tylor and Morgan, wrote on anthropology using the scientific method. It was also influenced by the evolutionist ideology of Darwin and the positivist philosophy of Auguste Comte. Thus, applied anthropology emerged in the 20th century, although the first magazine on the subject was published in 1941.

Along with the British, the American administrators also took help of social anthropology in their rule over the natives. Attempts were made in the United States of America for the safety of the primitives called the Red Indians and, to work in this direction, help was taken from anthropologists. Mexico and other Latin American countries followed the example of the United States of America. On the other side, the French and the Dutch, who established their colonies in Asia, Africa and the Far East, were constantly engaged in imparting anthropological training to their workers.

Importance in Modern India

After the independence of the country, the study of social anthropology has gradually been on the increase in the Indian universities. It has many practical advantages, some of which are given below:

1. As a remedy for ethnocentrism. According to Dr. M. N. Srinivas, social anthropology removes ethnocentrism through a comparative study of different civilized and primitive societies.

2. Scientific viewpoint towards social problems. Social anthropology helps in comparative study of social relations in different societies and of different events in one and the same society. It removes partiality in social problems and other preconceptions and imparts a scientific viewpoint.

3. Help in solving problems. It is clear that social anthropology will also prove helpful in solving problems. For example, social anthropology can help in solving the problems arising from the relation between man and woman. As Raymond Firth has said, "Social anthropology aims at a reasoned comparative analysis of how people behave in social circumstances."[21]

4. Help in understanding the primitive societies. As laid down in *Encyclopaedia Britannica*, "Social anthropology is one of the social sciences engaged in the comparative study of human societies." This comparative study is of special advantage in understanding primitive societies and evaluating their institutions, art and literature, etc. This knowledge can be of great help to us in understanding the problems of primitive societies and solutions, according to their cultural ideology, can be easily obtained.

5. As a remedy against all kinds of social prejudices. Social anthropology helps in removing all sorts of social prejudices. It removes prejudiced attitude of civilized society towards a primitive society and that of an individual of one society towards an individual of another society, because a comparative study of anthropology helps in understanding the differences caused among different cultures in relation to their institutions, customs, traditions, etc. It goes to form an advanced and a liberal attitude towards domestic, economic and political institutions. It also removes vanity in relation to language.

The above mentioned discussion about the importance of social anthropology clearly proves the importance of its study in modern India. Modern India is a progressive country. Along with the progress of civilized people in India, attention has to be paid to the progress of primitive tribes. The study of social anthropology is very helpful in that respect. It will help the workers in tribal areas in understanding the life, culture and society of the tribes and enable them to solve their problems. In the same manner, social anthropology will be helpful in understanding and solving the problems of civilized society. It will also help in ending the great struggle going on in India today on the question of language as well as in expanding the scientific outlook regarding the language

---

21. Firth, R., *Elements of Social Organization* (1951), p. 1.

question. To be brief, the study of social anthropology will be helpful in removing the various prejudices and in evolving a liberal and scientific viewpoint in all the social, cultural, economic and political fields in modern India.

SCOPE OF APPLIED ANTHROPOLOGY

A constant evolution in the field of social anthropology has been witnessed after the Second Word War and anthropologists have given important assistance in solving many problems of human relations. American anthropologists greatly helped in winning the war, as has been elaborately described by Claude Kluckhohn. Anthropologists did a creditable work in training soldiers belonging to primitive tribes, in the department of administration, in economic war boards, in military governments and in the unification of the military services as well as in war information, problems of raising moral standards of the citizens and obtaining their co-operation. Even in the Korean War in the 20th century, the American government received great help from anthropologists.

Use in Peace Period

Besides the war period, anthropologists have given important help in the peace period also and it signifies the usefulness of anthropology. Anthropologists have studied human problems resulting from the technological changes in backward areas. They have studied the evolution of ethnography and comparative aspect which has helped in the solution of social problems. Anthropological studies have made it definite that no mental characteristics are either joined to any special tribe or depend only on the racial applications. Anthropologists have also carried on experiments about Serology which are found useful in the field of medical science. They have studied the relation between employees and employers in order to reduce the different group tensions. Anthropologists have studied the patterns of values and inclinations to control the population trends, food habits and social changes. In this way anthropologists have helped in the control and cure of many diseases of social relations.

Study of National Character

The application of anthropology in different fields of human life has constantly been on the increase in the 20th century. It is clear from a survey of the evolution of anthropology. About fifty years ago, Franz Boas published a book, *Anthropology and Modern Life*, to describe the contribution of Anthropology in modern life. In this book, the writer has conveyed an important piece of information as furnished by anthropology regarding hereditary factor in crimes, racial importance and contribution of education in human society. The point of view of Boas has created a practical viewpoint towards anthropology in America. Similarly, Malinowski and other functionalists in Britain created through their attempts a practical viewpoint towards anthropology. Malinowski gave a functional definition to culture, according to which culture helps man in his social and biological existence. According to Radcliffe Brown, culture helps in maintaining the existence of the whole human society. Its importance lies in its usefulness. It is thus clear that the science of anthropology, which studies culture. is not only a pure science but also a practical one. Anthropology is a branch of humanity. Raymond Firth has gone so far as to call anthropology a science of social engineering. He has attached great importance to the safety of primitive society from destruction likely to result from its association with civilized society. According to him, anthropology fills the gap between primitive and modern society.

In this way, a social anthropologist plays the part of a doctor more than that of an engineer. An anthropologist is a social doctor with social medicine as his field of operation. He defines the social diseases and gives methods of their cure. Although it is true that due to the importance attached to cultural variety these days, an arrangement of common culture for all people is not possible, yet the help of the anthropologist in policy framing cannot be overestimated.

S. F. Nadel, a social anthropologist. has laid great stress on the practical aspect of anthropology. He says that anthropology does not only help us in understanding primitive as well as prehistoric societies but also helps us in solving the problems of our own period. As has already been said, anthropology proved useful in the rule over the colonies. On the other hand, it has helped in forming a liberal outlook towards different cultures, because, in fact, the different cultures present different solutions of the total problems of man and we can accept any one of the solutions by discussing advantages and disadvantages of these different solutions. The life of any one generation is not so long as to enable it to reach the correct alternative by trying all kinds of alternatives about family, marriage, education and other institutions of the same kind. The best way for this is to study the different forms of advantages and disadvantages and their results found in different cultures of these institutions through anthropological study. From this, it will be easy to know the form which should be given to any social institution in order to build a particular society. For example, of all the alternatives about the relation between men and woman, each alternative is sure to be sound in one culture or the other. We can know the result of an alternative of a particular kind of relationship between man and woman from the study of the results of that alternative. In this way, by studying relations between man and woman in different cultures, we can know, for the desired end, how to control relations between man and woman in the kind of society we want. It will definitely save much of our time and labour as well as protect us from the danger involved in making experiments. Therefore, the social structure of societies, possessing ancient cultural inheritance, is stronger than that of other societies lacking in such inheritance. It is specially true in India. We cannot solve our problems by blindly following any one culture, ancient or modern, Eastern or Western. For that we will have to discuss the various alternatives through an impartial study of anthropology and action may be taken only in the light of such a study.

MISUSE OF ANTHROPOLOGY

It does not follow from the above discussion that social anthropology has not been misused. Many a time, things are done with a scientific outlook as a mere show. For example, the white people in South Africa have long been practising a racial policy based on colour in the name of anthropology. Here it should be the duty of the anthropologist to expose such false claims. Anthropology faces a double danger, one from the politicians and the other from the scholars who treat anthropology purely as a theoretical science. As a matter of fact, no science lies in its usefulness and anthropology is no exception to this rule. On the one hand, anthropology studies different cultures and social institutions and on the other hand it evaluates and gives decisions. It can help in framing policies.

BRIGHT FUTURE OF APPLIED ANTHROPOLOGY

The future of applied anthropology is bright. Its use in reforming the primitive societies is quite clear. On the other hand, its importance in economic and political fields has been proved. Anthropologists have been of constant help in solving tribal problems in India after independence. Anthropologists can render important help in evaluating different national plans. For example, anthropological studies can be helpful in evaluating the success of family planning, cooperative movements and community planning. etc., and also in suggesting various ways for their success. Besides this, anthropology can also help in solving problems of labour, adult and child criminology and in other social problems like those of increasing population, industry and rural life. In brief, anthropological researches provide the viewpoint which is helpful in the investigation of relations, unity and progress in every aspect of human relations. Thus, the usefulness of anthropology is proved everywhere.

2

Anthropology in India

Attempts have been made to review the growth of anthropology in India by S.C. Roy, D.N. Majumdar, G.S. Dube, N.K. Bose, L.P. Vidyarthi and Surjeet Sinha, etc. In 1921, S.C. Roy presented a bibliogrpahy of the publications of tribal and caste studies in India. 25 years later Majumdar reviewed the development of anthroplogy in India. G.S. Ghurye reviewed the development of anthropology in Bombay in a volume published by UNESCO in 1956. S.C. Dube presented a review in the proceedings of the fourth International Congress of Anthropology and Ethnological Sciences, in 1952 in Vienna. In 1962, he presented another title *Anthropology in India,* published in D.N. Majumdar commemoration volume. N.K. Bose prepared a small booklet on this issue entitled *Fifty Years of Science in India, Progress of Anthropology and Archaeology*, published by Indian Science Congress Association, Calcutta in 1963. L.P. Vidyarthi reviewed the growth of social anthropological research a thorough and the latest review of the growth of social anthropological research a thorough and the latest review of the growth of Indian anthropology in his book entitled *Rise of Anthropolgy in India,* a social science orientation, Vol. I, *The Tribal Dimensions,* published in 1978.

The growth of Indian anthropology has been divided into different periods by the above mentioned and other notable anthropologists in a slightly different way. According to S.C. Roy, the growth of anthropology in India can be classified in terms of the sources of publications such as magazines, handbooks and monograms, etc. and also in terms of the nationality of the authors. According to S.C. Dube, this growth can be classified in three phases :

(1) Compilation and publication of volumes on tribes and castes.

(2) Detailed monographic studies of individual tribes mostly based upon personal observation.

(3) Quantitative advancement and qualitative achievement.

N.K. Bose divides the growth of anthropology in India into the following three phases:

(1) Encyclopaedia of tribes and castes.

(2) Descriptive monographs.

(3) Analytical studies of village, marriage and family, caste and civilization, etc.

D.N. Majumdar divided the growth of anthropological researches in India into the following three historical periods:

(1) Formulation phase (1774-1911),

(2) Constructive phase (1912-1937),

(3) Critical phase (1938 to present day).

According to L.P. Vidyarthi, the constructive period started around 1920 with the opening of the Department of Anthropolgy in Calcutta with R. Chandra as its head and the starting of Indian Journal of Anthropology by S.C. Roy in 1921. In the critical period Indian and British Anthropologists met together on the occasion of Silver Jubilee of the Indian Science Congress at Lahore. D.N. Majumdar published a problem-oriented monograph on the tribe published under the title *A Tribe in Transition : A Study in Culture Patterns,* published by Longman's Green and Co., London in 1937. This constitutes the start of what Majumdar calls critical periods in the growth of Indian anthropology. This period had the initiation of American collaboration with Lucknow University in anthropological studies. Oscar Lewis came to India as a consultant to the Central Ministry of Community Development, to carry on anthropological studies on a large scale. Another significant outsider to help in this growth was Morris Opler. Some noted Indian anthropologists like S.C. Dube also visited academic anthropological institutions in America. An important publication of this period was *Religion and Society among the Coorgs of South India* by M.N. Sriniwas, published by Oxford University Press in 1952. Thus, the critical period was also called analytical period by some anthropologists including L.P. Vidyarthi. In short, the growth of anthropology in India can be briefly summarized as follows:

1. The beginning, formative period. In 1774, Sir William Jones started Asiatic Society of Bengal as its founder president, to study nature and man in India. Since then the British administrators, missionaries, travellers and anthropologists studied Indian tribes and published their accounts in the Journal of Asiatic Society of Bengal (1784), Indian Antiquary (1872), Journal of Bihar and Orissa Research Society (1915), and Man in India (1921). Accounts were also published in a series of districts Gazetteer, hand-hooks and monograms on tribes. Data were collected on the tribes during the census in 1931 and 1941. Important contribution in this direction was made by scholarly British administrators such as Risley, Dalton, O'Malley, Russel, Thurston and Crooks, Cambell, Latham and Risley published general books on Indian ethnology. These were followed by detailed accounts of specific tribes by Briggs, Shakespear, Gurdel, Mills, Parry and Grigson, in the following important works :

(1) R.G. Latham, *Ethnography of India,* London, Voorst, viii + 375 pp., 1859.

(2) H.H. Risley, *Tribes and Castes of Bengal,* Calcutta (1891).

(3) George W. Briggs, *The Chamars,* Calcutta Association Press, Russel Street, Calcutta, 1920.

(4) J. Shakespear, *The Lushai Kuki Clans,* London, MacMillan & Co., 1912.

(5) P.R.T. Gurden, *The Khasi*, London, MacMillan & Co., 1912.

(6) J.P. Mills, *The Lhota Naga*, London, MacMillan & Co., 1922 and *The Rengma Naga,* London, MacMillan & Co., 1937.

(7) N.E. Parry, *The Lakhers,* London, MacMillan & Co., 1932.

(8) W.V. Grigson, *The Maria Gonds of Bastar,* Oxford University Press, London, 1938.

Some missionaries also made important ethnographic and linguistic studies. Among these were P.O. Bodding and J. Hoffman, W.H.R. Rivers published an important work, *The Todas,* in 1906 published by MacMillan and Co., London in 1911, G.G. Saligmann and B.G. Saligmann published an important work entitled *The Veddas of Ceylone,* in 1911 by Cambridge University Press.

2. Constructive period. In 1919, Social Anthropology was included in the curricula of Bombay University in Sociology. In 1921, Department of Anthropology was started at Calcutta University. These centres started anthropological research to which important contributions were made by the following scholars and their publications.

(1) A.R. Radcliffe Brown, *The Andaman Islanders : A Study in Social Anthropology,* Cambridge University Press, The Free Press, Glencoe, Illinois, 1922.

(2) J.H. Hutton, "*Census of India*", Vol. 1, India, Simla, Government of India Press, Part III-B, Ethnographic Notes, 1931.

(3) S.C. Roy: *(a) Mundas and Their Country,* Calcutta City Book Society, 1912, *(b) The Oraons of Chhota Nagpur,* Ranchi, Author, Bar Library 1915. *(c) The Birhor, a Little Known Jungle Tribe of Chhota Nagpur,* Man in India Office, Church Road, Ranchi, 1925, *(d) Oraon Religion and Customs,* Ranchi, Man in India Office, 1928, *(e) The Hill Bhuinyas of Orissa,* Ranchi, Man in India Office, 1935, and *(f) The Kharia,* Vol. I & II (with R.C. Roy), Ranchi, Man in India Office, 1937.

(4) G.S. Ghurye : (a) "A Note on Cross Cousin Marriage and Rural Organization Kathiawar", *Journal of University of Bombay,* Vol. 5, Part 1, pp. 88-90, 1943, (b) "Social Change in Maharashtra", Part I, *Sociological Bulletin,* Vol. 1, (c) "Social Changes in Maharashtra", Part II, *Ibid.*

(5) K.P. Chattopadhyay : (a) "An Essay on the History of Mewar Culture", *Journal and Proceedings of Asiatic Society of Bengal* (New Series), Vol. XXIII, No. 3, 1925 and (b) "Some Malayalam kinship terms", *Man in India,* Vol. II, No. 2, 1922.

(6) M.N. Srinivas : (a) Marriage and Family in Mysore, Bombay, 1942, and (b) The Social Organization of South India (note), *Man,* Vol. 46, No. 86, 1946.

(7) D.N. Majumdar : *A Tribe in Transition : A Study in Culture Patterns,* London, Longmans, Green & Co., 1937.

(8) Iravati Karve : Kinship Terminology and 'Kinship Uses of the Maratha Country', *Bulletin of the Deccan College Research Institute,* Vol. 2-4, pp. 327-89, 1940.

Among others who made important contribution to the growth of anthropology in India, the most notable were the studies of the following :

P.N. Mishra, L.K.A. Iyer, K.P. Chattopadhyaya, T.C. Das and D.N. Majumdar in the East and North India, and G.S. Ghurye, Iravati Karve, L.K. Ananthakrishna Iyer and A. Aiyappan in the West and South India. All these scholars stimulated anthropological research and publication of articles, monographs and books. In 1938, a joint session of the Indian Science Congress Association and the British Association, reviewed the progress of anthropology in India. This was the first review of the anthropological researches in India. Among the most notable contribution made to anthropology during this period the works of D.N. Majumdar, M.N. Srinivas and N.K. Bose may be noted. D.N. Majumdar published from Lucknow in 1950, *The Affairs of a Tribe : A Study of Tribal Dynamics.* In 1942, M.N. Srinivas published his work, *Marriage and Family in Mysore.* An important contribution was made by N.K. Bose in his paper Hindu Method of Tribal Absorption, published by *Cultural Anthropology,* in 1941. The following may be noted as important additions to the anthropological literature published during the period :

(1) Verrier Elwin : (a) *The Baiga,* London, Johan Murry, 1939, *(b) The Agaria,* O.U.P., 1943, *(c) Maria, Murder and Suicide*, O.U.P., 1943, *(d) The Muria and Their Ghotul,* Geoggery Cambridge, O.U.P., 1947, *(e) Religion of an Indian Tribe,* Oxford University Press, 1955.

(2) C. Von Furer-Haimendorf : *(a) The Chenchus, Jungle Folk of the Deccan*, London, MacMillan & Co., 1942, *(b) The Tribal Population of Hyderabad.* Hyderabad Revenue Department Census, 1945, *(c) The Reddis of the Bison Hills : A Study in Acculturation* (in collaboration with Elizabeth von Furer Haimendorf) in two volumes, London, MacMillan & Co., 1945, *(d)* "The Agriculture and Land Tenure among the Apa Tanis," *Man in India*, Vol. 26, 1946, pp. 181-95 and "Notes on Tribal Justice among the Apa Tanis", *Man in India,* Vol. 29, 1946.

(3) G.W. Briggs, *The Chamars,* Calcutta Association Press, Russel Street, Calcutta, 1926.

(4) L.K. Ananthakrishna Iyer, "The Kahars of Mysore", *Man in India,* Vol. 9, 1929.

(5) J.H. Hutton, *Caste in India,* Cambridge University Press, 1946.

Summing up the development of anthropology in India during the constructive period, L.P. Vidyarthi has rightly remarked, "Thus, Indian anthropology which was born and brought up under the predominant influence of the British, matured during the constructive phase on the lines of British anthropology. During this period, except a few studies of Indian institutions like Caste, the tribal studies continued to be the exclusive field of study by the enlightened British scholars, administrators, missionaries and later by the British and Indian anthropologists till the end of the forties of this century. On the lines of anthropology taught at that time at Cambridge, Oxford, and London, Indian anthropology was characterized by ethnological and monographic studies with a special emphasis on researches in kinship and social organization.

3. Analytical Period, 1950. After Second World War some eminent American anthropologists including Morris Opeler of Cornell University, Oscar Lewis of University of Illionis, David Mandelbaum of the University of California and others came to India and conducted many important studies in rural and tribal areas. Besides, important rural studies were made by M.N. Sriniwas, Iravati Karve, S.C. Dube and D.N. Majumdar among others. The following are the notable contributions to the growth of anthropology in India during this period :

(1) M.N. Srinivas, *Religion and Society among the Coorgs of South India*, Oxford University Press, 1952.

(2) Iravati Karve, *Kinship Organization in India,* Poona, Deccan College (first edition), 1953.

(3) S.K. Srivastva, "The Tharu : A Study in Cultural Dynamics", Agra, Agra University Press, 1958.

(4) D.N. Majumdar, *"Himalayan Polyandry",* Bombay, Asia Publishing House, 1963.

(5) Burling, "*Rengsanggri,*" Philadelphia, University of Pennsylvania Press, 1963.

(6) C. Von Furer-Haimendorf, *The Konyak Nagas,* London Oxford University Press, 1969.

(7) L.P. Vidyarthi, *The Maler : A Study in Nature-Man-Spirit Complex of a Hill Tribe,* Calcutta, Bookland Private Limited, 1963.

(8) Edward J. Jay, *A Tribal Village in Middle India,* Calcutta Anthropological Survey of India, 1970.

(9) D.P. Sinha, *Culture Change in an Inter-Tribal Market,* Bombay, Asia Publishing House, 1968.

(10) Sachchidananda, *Culture Change in Tribal Bihar*, Calcutta, Bookland Private Limited, 1964.

(11) B.N. Sahay, *Dynamics of Leadership,* New Delhi, Book Hive, 1968.

(12) A.B. Saran, *"Murder and Suicide Among the Two Tribes of Bihar"*, New Delhi, National Publishing House, 1975.

(13) P.K. Bhowmick, *The Lodhas of West Bengal : A Socio-Economic Study,* Calcutta, Punthi Pustak, 1963.

(14) F.G. Bailey, Tribe, Caste and Nation, Bombay, Oxford University Press, 1960.

(15) G.S. Ghurye, *The Scheduled Tribes,* Bombay, Popular Book Depot, 1960.

(16) P.G. Shah, *Tribal Life in Gujarat,* Bombay, Gujarat Research Society, 1964.

(17) L.N. Chapekar, *The Thakurs of Sahadri*, Bombay, O.U.P., 1960.

(18) P.G. Shah, *Tribal Life in Gujarat,* Bombay, Gujarat Research Society, 1964.

(19) Y.V.S. Nath, *The Bhils of Ratanmal,* Baroda, M.S. University of Baroda, 1960.

(20) Ehrenfel, *Kadar of Cochin,* Madras, University of Madras, 1952.

(21) P.K. Mishra, *Nomads in Mysore City,* Calcutta, Anthropological Survey of India, 1971.

(22) G.M. Carstairs, *The Twice-Born,* London, The Hogarth Press, 1957.

(23) Oscar Lewis, *Group Dynamics in a North Indian Village,* Delhi, Planning Commission, 1954.

(24) H.S. Dhillon, *Leadership and Groups in a South Indian Village,* New Delhi, Planning Commission, 1955.

(25) S.C. Dube (ed.), *Emerging Patterns of Rural Leadership in Southern Asia,* Hyderabad, National Institute of Community Development, 1965.

(26) Rajni Kothari (ed.), *"Caste in Indian Politics,"* New Delhi, Orient Longmans Ltd., 1970.

(27) L.P. Vidyarthi, *Dynamics of Tribal Leadership in Bihar,* Allahabad, Kitab Mahal, 1976.

(28) D.N. Majumdar, *Affairs of a Tribe : A Study in Tribal Dynamics,* Lucknow, Universal, 1950.

(29) Verrier Elwin, *Religion of an Indian Tribe,* London, Oxford University Press, 1955.

(30) L.P. Vidyarthi, *Aspects of Religion in Indian Society*, Meerut, Kedar Nath Ramnath, 1961.

(31) E.B. Harper, *Religion in South Asia,* Seattle, University of Washington Press, 1964.

(32) L.P. Vidyarthi, *Sacred Complex of Hindu Gaya,* Bombay, Asia Publishing House, 1961.

(33) M. Jha, *Sacred Complex of Janakpur,* Allahabad, United Publishers, 1971.

(34) L.P. Vidyarthi and M. Jha (eds.), *Sacred Complex of India,* Ranchi, Council and Cultural Research, Bihar, 1974.

(35) S. Narayan, *Sacred Complex of Deoghar,* Ph.D. Thesis submitted to Ranchi University, Ranchi, 1973.

Among the important seminars conducted and published during this period are : *Urgent Researches in Social Anthropology and Tribal Situation in India* published by Indian Institute of Advanced Study, Simla. Numerous papers have been published by Anthropologists in India concerning: (a) change leading to tribal identity, integration, vanishing culture and planning, (b) emergence of industrial anthropology, (c) increased emphasis on tribal demography, and (d) integrated study of tribal regions. Important contribution has been made to Action Research, Socio-Psychological Research, Folklore Researches, Studies of Power Structure and Leadership and Anthropology of Religion. To conclude in the words of L.P. Vidyarthi, "The journey of Indian anthropology still continues. It has gone much ahead under the influence of and in collaboration with the British and American anthropologists. Of course, in a broader perspective, they will continue to influence the Indian social science for some more time. Science knows no barrier and the science of man in Indian will continue to collaborate and learn in the fields of theory and methods of social research from the other scientifically advanced countries of the world."

3

Relationship with other Social Sciences

STATUS OF ANTHROPOLOGY AMONG SCIENCES

Whether anthropology should be included among physical sciences or among social sciences is the subject on which anthropologists differ. Under the influence of evolutionism, anthropology had no such problem in the beginning and it was considered a natural science. According to his opinion, man is a part of nature and social laws are similar to natural law. But, on the other hand, German idealistic thinkers regarded human life and Nature as two separate things and refused to accept human life as part of natural life. It has not been clear about so many modern anthropologists whether they regard anthropology as a natural science or a social science. For example, Malinowski, an anthropologist, on the one hand, refers to new psychological reactions being at the root of the man's cultural attempt and on the other hand, regards anthropology as a branch of natural sciences. His whole working principle was an attempt to make use of the naturalist philosophy of John Dewey and others in the field of social sciences. According to him, culture is a means to satisfy bio-psychological needs of man. In this way, according to Malinowski, anthropology stands in between natural and social sciences. But other anthropologists do not present such a viewpoint. Radcliffe Brown, Nadel and other anthropologists regard anthropology as a natural science which studies through the modes of natural sciences. According to these anthropologists, the work of anthropology is not to give a detailed description about some special culture, but to give a comparative analysis of different cultures and to frame social laws about the origin and change of human society through that analysis. According to these anthropologists there are some such patterns in the social life of many which do not undergo any change with a change in place and time, and the work of the anthropologist is to discover laws about them. On the other hand, according to Kroeber, Bidni and Evans Pritchard, culture and nature are different things and have no real unity in them. According to this theory, anthropology is a branch of History. As a matter of fact, both these viewpoints about the relation of anthropology and other sciences are still accepted in different branches of anthropology. While, on the one hand, the methods of science are owned in physical anthropology, on the other hand, along with these methods, the methods of history and aesthetics are also owned and their examples are found in the writings of Evans Pritchard and R. Benedict. Redfield says that holiest tendencies are on the increase in anthropology, man is being studied on different levels of culture and interest in the study of values and personality is increasing. All these tendencies show that in future anthropology will come closer to social science in comparison to natural sciences.

The place of anthropology in social sciences is clear from the above discussion. Different social sciences study the different aspects of man and society in different ways. Anthropology is the science of man. It is a study of human nature. It studies human behaviour in every time and place and in different cultures. It studies man everywhere on earth. It studies man in both the periods, historic and prehistoric. It studies man on all levels, civilized and uncivilized. In the words of Herskovites, anthropology is a science of man and his actions. It studies the origin and evolution of man from material, cultural and social points of view. In this way, different fields of anthropology study man in different aspects. It is clear that the anthropologist gets important help from sociology, psychology, history, linguistics, logic, economics and many other social sciences.

Anthropology is the most general science. It studies all aspects of man. The order to have a holistic conception of man we must examine physical, social, cultural, political and ideological aspects of his person. Man is on the one side distinguished from animals on account of his physical features, highly evolved sensory and nervous apparatus and on the other side he is alone in making use of language, establishing at traditional structure of beliefs and ideology. He is also a myth-maker as well as most sophisticated innovator of techniques of controlling his environment and aspire for superhuman status, and an effort to transcend his limitations. Thus, anthropology is closely related to almost all the physical, biological and natural sciences as well as with history, culture and religion. The theory of evolution was in main responsible for the development of anthropology. Therefore, it is dependent upon geology, archaeology, biological as well as medical sciences. This primarily accounts for Physical Anthropology. The Cultural Anthropology on the other hand bends upon historical, social sciences as well as Humanities. Below we shall very briefly examine its links to various sciences. The science whose maturation is a *sine qua non* for the growth and development of Anthropology are Geology, Archaeology, Palaeontology, Biology, and various medical sciences. Pertinently Beals and Hoijer observe that to some sciences Anthropology is related in the sense that it could not itself have developed until the above-mentioned sciences had achieved a certain stage of maturity. For example, until Geology had provided a chronology or time sequence with which to measure it, the antiquity and origin of man could not be established. Similarity Palaeontology and Biology had to develop techniques sophisticated enough to relate man and other animals. The ancestry of man could be determined upon maturation of the above to sciences. Another science vital in linking man and animal is archaeology.

ARCHAEOLOGY AND ANTHROPOLOGY

The stratigraphic methods of Geology to determine the relative age of layers of material deposition in fixing the relative time of different cultures. The archaeologist deals with relatively other spans of time than the geologists sciences but also make solid contribution to them. Such type of relationship subsist biology, humanities and social sciences. Biology and Anthropology have enjoyed closest links for a very long time. The evolutionary concepts are useful in the development of cultural anthropology. But sometimes cultural patterns modify biological relationships. As an eminent scientist has observed, ''Although biological concepts are no longer employed in cultural anthropology, and understanding of man's biology is essential to understanding his culture. For a fairly long time anthropology and biology have worked hand-in-glove and made mutually beneficial contributions. Biology influences culture. Few decades back the theory of evolution had assumed the pivotal place in the thinking of man. The idea that what appears later is superior and progressive and that man is slowly moving toward becoming overman or superman and that the nature will unravel all into secrets and man would conquer evil in nature and the civilization would become a state of bliss and peace. Even today transgenic engineering is assuring us an infinitely long life. The average age in Japan today is 80 plus and zest in life is becoming broader as well as deep. He deals with the subject matter both intensively and extensively compared to more general approach of Geology. The archaeologist, however, relies exclusively upon geologist and palaeontologist to fix eras.

GEOLOGY, PALAEONTOLOGY AND ANTHROPOLOGY

The Physical Anthropologist, is indebted to Geologist and Palaeontologist to establish age of specimens of prehistoric man. The successful resolution of the problems of evolution depends upon precise dating of fossils. The Physical Anthropologist uses taxonomical techniques of biologists and also leans heavily upon anatomy and embryology and genetics. Mineralogist physical and Chemist also help in studying the manufacturing techniques and analysis of the materials used by prehistoric man. Indeed all scientific disciplines help in one way or the other in acquiring in-depth knowledge of prehistoric man and his habitats.

Another type of relationship between Anthropology is not one-sided but two way traffic. In this class of relationship Anthropology does not merely follow other into medical research in order to increase man's pleasure naturally as well as mechanically. Culture is more than a biological phenomenon, but society apparently attempts to heighten man's biologic and psychologic satisfaction. Man's new found happiness is in turn modifying biological operations. The study of culture and the study of human biology are constantly inter-related.

ANTHROPOLOGY AND HISTORY

As has been said earlier, some anthropologists regard anthropology as a branch of history. Human being is born in a natural way, but social life is not the product of nature. Social level is different from biological level. It is true that human nature is such that human beings have to live in united groups, but human nature does not decide the cultural level of society. It does not decide what to eat and how to eat, what dress to put on and how will it be put on, how many times and how to marry or what shall be our viewpoint towards natural powers. In other words, culture of a particular society is not the product of human nature. The structure of society has no natural order like that of the structure of solar system or atom. Society is a web of social relations supplied by history and are united among them by moral values. The forces of nature have no hand in keeping them united. In this way, society is a social and moral order and sociology, which studies it, is a social science. It is a part of Humanities. Anthropologists have been doing the work of social reformation. It cannot be inferred from this discussion that anthropology has no relation with natural sciences but only this much can be said that anthropology and history are closely related. History and anthropology are both related to human actions. Social anthropology discusses human actions which cause social events. History presents a description of these events. Social anthropology studies the origin of civilization and culture and processes of evolution. etc. On the other hand, history studies particular civilization or culture on the basis of a particular period. In brief, the relation between anthropology and history can be comprehended from the following table:

ANTHROPOLOGY AND HISTORY

Anthropology	History
Similarities:	
1. Anthropology studies the past.	1. History describes human actions.
2. Anthropology studies ancient things.	2. Anthropology makes history.
Differences:	
1. Anthropology also studies the physical aspects of man along with social aspect.	1. History has no interest in the physical aspect of man.
2. The viewpoint of anthropology is anthropological.	2. The viewpoint of history is historical.
3. Anthropology is mainly related to human culture.	3. History is mainly related to political events.

ANTHROPOLOGY AND SOCIOLOGY

Relation of Anthropology and Sociology

Sociology studies human behaviour in groups. It is a science of societies. Anthropology is a science of man and studies human behaviour in social surroundings. Thus, it is clear that the subject matter of sociology and anthropology is common to a great extent. In fact, no special difference in these two sciences was recognized in the beginning of the 20th century. The idea of recognizing them as two separate sciences is comparatively new. Sociology and anthropology have very much influenced each other. For example, the ideology of Durkheim, a sociologist, has greatly influenced the doctrines of anthropologists like Malinowski and Radcliffe Brown. Hoebel has stated very clearly. 'Sociology and Social Anthropology, in their broadest senses, are one and the same.''[1] The subject matter of social anthropology, which is one of the two main branches of anthropology, is so much similar to the subject matter of sociology that many scientists have regarded it as a branch of sociology. Evans Pritchard has written, 'Social anthropology can, therefore, be regarded as a branch of sociological studies, that branch which chiefly devotes itself to the primitive societies.''[2]

Scholars have also laid stress on the relation of sociology with social anthropology. Kroeber has gone so far as to call sociology and anthropology as twin sisters. Robert Redfield writes: ''Viewing the whole United States, one sees that the relations between sociology and anthropology are closer than those between anthropology and political science, this is partly due to greater similarity in ways of work.''[3]

Utility of Anthropological Researches for Sociology

Discoveries in different branches of anthropology have thrown a new light on the principles of sociology. Social anthropology as a branch of anthropology is nearest to sociology. Its aim is to study human behaviour in social surroundings. Many of its discoveries have thrown new light on several subjects of sociology. Sociology has taken the ideas of cultural field, cultural apparatus, interdependent tools, cultural lagging, etc. from social anthropology, and have developed them further.

The important discoveries of famous anthropologists like Ralph Linton and Abraham Kardiner have greatly influenced sociology. Both these anthropologists have discovered that there is a basic personality type in every society which is created by cultural influence on an individual from the very childhood. This basic personality type is different because of a difference in cultural influences.

Kardiner has written about Alorese, an Indonesian Negro tribe, that in their society, the basic personality type is a mistrustful, doubting, quarrelsome, coward and exploited individual, whereas in our own society, such an individual will be considered mentally diseased and unnatural. According to Ralph Linton, the same anxiety and ritual taboos and rules are found about food articles among the people of Markeses island in Pacific Ocean as are found in our society about sex matters. It is clear from these discoveries that every society

1. Hoebel, E.A., *Man in the Primitive World*, p. 6.
2. Evans Pritchard, *Social Anthropology*, p. 12.
3. Robert Redfield in his article, ''Relation of Anthropology to the Social Sciences and Humanities'' in A.L. Kroeber's *Anthropology Today*, pp. 7-9.

has its own culture and the individual character of its people undergoes a change according to that culture from the very childhood.

The discoveries of Malinowski, a British Anthropologist, have proved very important in sociology. The applied viewpoint of the study of culture is a special contribution to sociology by Malinowski. According to it, culture should be studied with the viewpoint of its usefulness for man. The discoveries of Ruth Benedict have been very helpful in studying various sociological problems about national character.

Besides social anthropology, the various discoveries of physical anthropology have also exerted great influence on various problems of sociology. In the book entitled *Anthropology and the Modern Life,* Franz Boas has given a detailed description of this influence playing an important part in turning an individual into a criminal. It has been proved from ethnological discoveries of Franz Boas and Otto Klineberg that physical characteristics have nothing to do with the mental special features and that the influence of environment is the chief cause of mental differences. Anthropology has also helped sociology by disproving the ideas of racism. The discoveries of anthropology have proved that no race today can claim purity or superiority over other races.

In this way, the discoveries of anthropology have proved very useful for sociology. Maclver and many other sociologists have attached great importance to this contribution of anthropology.

Difference Between Anthropology and Sociology

In the modern age, anthropology and sociology have developed so much that to know their differences is more necessary than to know their relations. The main differences between these two sciences are given below:

(1) Difference in scope. The scope of sociology and social anthropology is different. Social anthropology studies primitive society whereas sociology studies modern society. Social anthropology studies all the social, economic, political and cultural sides. Sociology studies the social relations and social interactions. In this way, the study of sociology is more particular and that of anthropology more general.

(2) Difference of Object. A sociologist also suggests means for improvement along with his study, whereas an anthropologist is more neutral and does not offer any suggestions.

(3) Difference in methods of study. The methods of study of sociologist and social anthropologist are different. Social anthropologist specially uses applied methods. One method of this kind is participant observation according to which, the anthropologist himself goes to live in that society which he has to study. On the other hand, the chief methods of sociology depend on survey and statistics.

(4) Difference in viewpoint. Sociological viewpoint is different from anthropological viewpoint. One is particular and the other is general. One is the viewpoint of a specialist and the other viewpoint is that of a scientist. One is actuated by a desire to improve and the other is neutral.

Sociology and social anthropology and their decisions can be of important help for human well-being. For example, they help uprooting the dangerous elements like racialism and colour discriminations. They can create a sense of tolerance towards the members of other societies, institutions and cultures and they can also help in understanding and solving social, economic and political problems. For example, anthropological study will be of great help in finding out means for the welfare of different tribes and primitive societies in India.

ANTHROPOLOGY AND PSYCHOLOGY

Psychology is the science of human behaviour. Anthropology studies man in all places and times. In this way, both are closely related. Psychology is really the science of human experience and behaviour. It studies man's behaviour in relation to environment. Anthropology is also a comparative and analytic study of human behaviour and experiences. Both of them observe human behaviour and common principles are evolved on that basis. Both of them carry on minute analysis of human nature. Both of them try to define man's social behaviour. Both are complementary to each other. Whereas on one side a psychological knowledge helps an anthropologist in understanding the root causes of human behaviour in different cultures, on the other side anthropological studies help the psychologist in calculating the influence of cultural environment of human behaviour.

Help of Anthropological Studies in Psychology

In modern times, the various anthropological studies have rendered important help in the field of psychology. By studying different primitive cultures, anthropologists have shown how human behaviour differs in different cultural environments. Every culture has its special method of social control which has an important influence on the personality of its members. For example, there has been a great disturbance in the adjustment of adolescence due to great restraint on the mutual relations among the individuals of different sexes in civilized societies. It has been found through anthropological studies that such changes are nowhere to be seen in many primitive societies. For example, as in civilized societies, there is no restriction of any kind among the natives of Samoa island and therefore an adult becomes self-reliant very early. In India, as compared to Hindu society, it is easier for adolescents of tribal society to become adult due to increased sex education and decreased restrictions. In this way, psychologists learn from psychological studies the changes which can be seen in human personality and behaviour as a result of cultural changes. Remember that nothing can be known in this field on the basis of application, because cultural environments, specially in group form, cannot be created in an artificial way. In order to elicit the importance of the contribution of social anthropology, in the field of psychology, only one example is enough. In modern age, anthropological discoveries have proved that different personalities are developed under different environments and that difference of sex has very little influence. The famous anthropologist, Margaret Mead, studied the cultures of three primitive tribes of Arapesh, Mundugumor and Tchambuli in New Guinea. In Arapesh tribe, no difference was found in the personalities of men and women. Both were equally found to be cooperating and serviceable. In Mundugumor tribe, men and women were both found to be cruel and aggressive. A difference was, no doubt, marked in the personalities of men and women of Tchambuli tribe. From this Margaret Mead concluded that the evolution of personality depends on cultural environment.

The closest relation between psychology and anthropology is seen in the relation between the main branches, social psychology and cultural anthropology. In social psychology, individual behaviour is studied under social environments. Social anthropology also studies human society, social institutions and groups. Explaining their relation, the famous anthropologist, Hoebel writes, "The anthropologist concentrates chiefly on the society of primitive people and the sociologist concentrates on our contemporary civilization. The social psychologist roams happily between them manipulating his tests and measurements."

Difference Between Anthropology and Psychology

In spite of the above-mentioned close relation, the difference between anthropology and psychology should not be forgotten. In brief, the chief difference between them is given below:

1. Psychology studies individual human behaviour whereas anthropology studies not an individual but the whole of mankind.

2. Psychology studies individual behaviour in social environments whereas social anthropology studies groups of individuals.

3. Psychology and anthropology both study man but the viewpoint of both of them is different.

4. Whereas some methods of observation are commonly employed in both of these sciences, some methods of psychology — for example, the introspection method — are not used in anthropology.

5. Psychology and anthropology both have an important place in social sciences. A successful knowledge of human behaviour is obtained from both of them. Different researches have influenced each other in the field of both of them. In studying man, help from both of them is unavoidable.

4

Anthropological Methods

The main methods of anthropology are :

1. Method of Participant Observation,
2. Historical Method,
3. Comparative Method,
4. Functional Method.

PARTICIPANT OBSERVATION METHOD

What is Participant Observation?

Participant observation, as is clear from its very name, is that observation of social events in which the observer takes part in the social events. In the words of Goode and Hatt, "This procedure is used when the investigator can so disguise himself as to be accepted as a member of the group."[1] In this way, the investigator lives like an ordinary member of the social group. In the words of Young, "The participant observer, using non-controlled observation, generally lives or otherwise shares in the life of the group which he is studying."[2] An example of such participant study is the study of the people of London by Charles Booth, study of Cornville Social and Athletic Club by Wm. F. Whyte and the study of the Russian Molokan group by P.V. Young. It is through such studies that the famous social anthropologists like Margaret Mead, Malinowski and Abraham Kardiner have carried out important studies of many primitive societies. As Lundberg has written, "In this application of the technique it is essential to realise that it is not only the investigator himself but also the members of the group being studied who are to regard him as a participant." It is thus clear that so long as the members of the group do not accept the investigator as a member of their group, participant observation will not be possible. In her study of Molokan group, P.V. Young has written in details how she could not, in the beginning, gain their confidence but how, in the end, she

1. Goode, W.J. and P.K. Hatt, *Methods in Social Research*, McGraw Hill Book Co., New York (1952), p. 121.
2. Young, P.V., *Scientific Social Surveys and Research*, p. 159.

could gain the confidence of their men and woman, young and old, through her cleverness and power of understanding by avoiding all kinds of discussions with them and by treating them sympathetically and it was only then that she was welcomed among them as a respectable scientist. After she got a place in the group, her work was easy because the people of the group themselves began to invite her on various occasions. She could thus carry on a close, real and minute study of their behaviour in every field. It is necessary for participant observation that the members of the group do not doubt in any way the object of the investigator. Its success depends on the cleverness and personality of the investigator.

Advantages of Participant Observation

The following advantages can be easily seen in the participant observation method :

1. Observation of natural behaviour. Since the participant investigator is himself a member of the group, he can observe the natural behaviour of the group members in various fields. This is not possible for a non-participant investigator because people do not behave in a natural way in his presence.

2. Close contact with the group members. By being a group member, by sharing their happiness and sorrows and by participating in their various social programmes and customs, the investigator comes in very close contact with the group members. This helps him in his minute study of their behaviour.

3. Insight in behaviour. To obtain insight in the behaviour of any group, it is necessary to participate in the group life. It is because of this that the various anthropologists have studied the life conditions of primitive societies by living in those societies. Only those, who themselves go to these primitive habitations and live among the inhabitants can present the most scientific study of these primitive people. It is only by participating in the group life that an investigator can understand the inclinations, problems, difficulties and the ideas of the group members in their different activities. He cannot gain this insight by keeping himself outside the group.

4. Convenience of discussion. In order to know many things about the social events, it is necessary to discuss with the people whose social events are being studied. If the investigator is familiar with these people he can go deep into various factors concerning their social life through a discussion with them at a convenient time. A non-participant investigator has no such convenience. People mostly do not have trust in him and they cannot therefore discuss with him frankly.

Limitations of Participant Observation

In spite of the aforesaid qualities, the participant observation method lacks in those qualities which are found in non-participant observation. In brief the main limitations in participant observation are given below:

1. Lack of Scientific approach. Since the participant investigator also takes part emotionally in the activities of the Group under research, his observation therefore is not objective because he becomes a member of the group and thus cannot remain a neutral observer. After becoming a member of the group, he begins to like many of the group activities and does not see any evil even when there are some evils in them. But this drawback in participant observation method is not an unavoidable difficulty. As a matter of fact, if you pay necessary attention, you can understand that after becoming a member of the group, it is necessary that neutrality and a scientific outlook of the investigator come to an end. Participant investigators like Margaret Mead and Malinowski, are able to maintain their scientific neutrality even when they take part in group activities. Thus, it is not a valid objection against participant observation.

2. Partiality due to social situation. Some people have raised the objection against participant observation method that since the investigator, in this method, obtains a special social status in the group under study, his behaviour with the people, according to his own social status, becomes partial. His viewpoint, thérefore, does not remain scientific. Like the first objection, this second objection against participant observation also does not appear to be valid. Acceptance of a social position does not necessarily lead to a partial behaviour but, on the other hand, social position can be advantageous if the investigator can know many such facts about the social life of the group which cannot be known from outside.

3. Lack of importance of various events. Some people think that since a participant investigator takes an active part in the group lifes he finds many such ordinary and unimportant things which can appear important to the man who sees things from outside. The objection may be correct in certain circumstances, but if the investigator is wide awake, he can know its importance by attending to small things of group life. There is yet another advantage from this. It can help the participant investigator in knowing the real importance of group life when the man who looks from outside may attach unnecessary importance to anything. Many things, which appear important from outside, are not important from the viewpoint of the members. On the other hand many things which appear unimportant from outside have an important place in the life of the group. In this connection, only the man, who takes part in the life of the group, can decide.

4. Narrow field of experience. Another objection against participant investigation is that it limits the investigator's scope of experience because by taking a social place in the group, he develops close contact with some people and keeps away from others. The objection commonly appears to be correct in certain circumstances. But the experienced investigators, even when they are taking part in group life, do not take part in party politics or discussion of any kind and therefore are never so close to a group as to become enemies of other groups or to keep away.

5. Entanglement in party politics and quarrels. There is another objection raised against participant investigation that it gets the investigator entangled in party politics and quarrels because he has to side with one party or other according to his position and this is likely to sidetrack the original aim of investigation. This objection can apply to only those investigators who come in so close a contact with group life as to forget the original aim of the investigation. If they do not forget that they have entered the group life with the sole object of investigating its different aspects, they can keep aloof from all quarrels and party politics. It is true that the work is difficult and the investigator often gets entagled in many quarrels against his wishes. But if an attempt is made, these difficulties can be overcome.

6. Limit of participant investigation. There are some aspects of group life in which participant investigation is not possible. For example, to take part in groups of thieves, dacoits and criminals may be regarded as immoral. This objection against participant investigation shows its limits. It is true that in many cases, participant investigation is not possible and in such circumstances the investigator has to feel satisfied with non-participant investigation alone.

The above objections raised against participant investigation make it clear that, like other methods, it has also its limits and disadvantages but the disadvantages have been greatly exaggerated. If due attention is not paid to them, a good number of aforesaid evils will be found in those investigators who, being participants, forget the very rule of investigation. In fact even when he is taking part in the group activities, the investigator maintains his special position and differs from other members of the group. An investigator therefore should not behave like other members who are entangled in party politics and are partial and selfish. It is true that by participating in group life he acquires a special social position, but this social position, first of all should be the position of a social scientist, because in the group life, an investigator is first an investigator and then anything else. When people come to know that he is a social scientist their respect for him and their familiarity with him do not grow less, but on the other hand, he is often called upon as an expert to solve many quarrels and difficulties which arise in the group. While maintaining his position as a social scientist and while at the same time participating in the group life, a participant investigator can escape the above evils and can discover such minute things which a non-participant investigator cannot know. Therefore, although we have to be content with non-participant investigation alone in certain fields, yet in most of the situations, participant investigation is better than non-participant investigation to investigate the social events.

HISTORICAL METHOD

In the modern age, many anthropologists have studied the various social institutions through historical method. The famous book, *History of Human Marriage*, written by Westermarck, is an excellent example of this and contains a historical study of the gradual evolution of the institution of marriage. The influence of biological principle of evolution on the same is clear.

What is historical method? The influence of the philosophy of history and the biological principle of evolution on the authors, who have used this method in the field of anthropology, is very distinct. In this the origins of social institutions, societies and cultures are discovered and the positions of evolution are shown. It studies special social institutions in the background of the whole human history. August Comte, Herbert Spencer and Hobhouse have studied the main institutions of society in the background of the whole human history.

Many scholars have opposed this application of the principle of evolution to the field of social events. According to them, all these works, based on historical method, were merely historical descriptions. In the 18th and 19th centuries due to the triumph of evolutionism in scientific fields, it was used even in defining sociological events. In the modern period the use of historical method is made for the study of special historical events in the field of anthropology, because it is clear that various social events take place after their origin from different sources and following different lines of evolution. The attempt of filling social events into a preplanned frame of evolutionary principle is not quite correct because it leads to an artificial definition of a natural phenomenon. It does not mean that such studies are not important or offer no contribution to anthropology. Such studies have furnished important knowledge about social changes.

Example of Molokan Group

From the example of the study of the Russian Molokan Group, P. V. Young has shown the great importance of the study of historical matter in social investigation. It will be proper to give here a brief description of Young's study. Only the elders of Molokan group could give a real account of the various events of the evolution of the group culture, but this account alone was not enough for social investigation, because an investigator has also to know other relations among the events besides artistic relation. In other words, along with a serial study of the social events, he has also to discover cause-effect relationship among them. The members of Molokan group, who lived in Los Angles thought that the origin of their community lay in Russian religious persecution. They knew that a long time ago their ancestors had been targets of Russian religious persecution and had undergone great tortures. The young men of the group said that they were highly moved by the great tortures meted out to their ancestors. Their ancestors had fought a fierce battle against the Russian conservative Church and the State. This made it clear that Molokanism was not a mere system of ideas. It was also a way of life, a philosophy. In this community, communal emotions were very sharp and it was because of this that a cultural reawakening could be seen among the people or the third generation of Molokan community born in America. Young saw that it was necessary to know the history of Russian religious discrimination in order to examine the accounts given by the members of the Molokan group and to gain a wide outlook of the whole situation. Young came to know, through study, that it all happened in the 18th century. Molokan community was the creation of such a religious movement which moved not only the Russian empire but many other countries of western Europe as well.

From the study of Russian religious discrimination, the question of cause-effect sequence in it was raised. How did the Russian farmers under Czar raise their voice against the conservative Church was the question. What were the situations which caused the rebellion? It was known from a historical study that the movement against Russian religious discrimination began about fifty years after the establishment of slave system in Russia. Then the effect of slavery on the farmers' conditions and their attitudes was studied. From this, it was known that the slaves rebelled against the State which gave the masters a right to confiscate the property of the slaves. They rebelled against the society which acted according to that right. In this way, the rebellion was historic and deep-rooted. A disorganization in the Russian social, political and economic administration had already begun before the establishment of the farmer-slave system. The masses had lost their patience and considered the Church to be the cause of their troubles. These were the causes which gave birth to an unprecedented religious and social movement. Even the greatest punishments such as fines, imprisonment and exile could not stop the members of the movement from coming still closer to one another and created in them a great faith and unity for their own religious principles.

The historical accounts of the Russian religious discrimination have thrown light on the causes of Molokan group. The fire of communalism had made the farmer hard like steel. The personality of a member of the Molokan group could not be known only through the study of this community because there were other forces influencing it. For example, another community named Dukhobor also came into existence along with it. The principles of both of these were different. Both of them were attached to their different impressions. Both of them presented a new way for salvation and gave new definition of divine law.

From historical study, P.V. Young concluded that the present form of Molokanism was different from its belief and actions in 18th and 19th centuries. Besides this, Russian Molokanism was different from American Molokanism in the 19th and 20th centuries. In this way, economic, religious, political and social evolution of a period of 300 years was studied for an assessment of Molokan individuality and social institutions. It was clear from this historical study that Molokan community started with some definite religious and social principles. It was not only a religious community. Its members had employed all their means, the whole of their determination and their entire strength for the achievement of one ideal which had become a centre of light for their lives. The members of this group thus wanted to live within their community and therefore they had created means of protection against reaction of assimilation into American culture. In this reaction a struggle between religious and secular institutions could be seen. A historical study gradually showed the causes of reawakening in the group. This community could not be studied without the study of its cultural background and historical evolution. In the words of

P. V. Young, "The historical accounts provided a frame of reference, a point of view of the social and cultural soil in which Molokanism as a unique way of life had its inception."

The above example, given by P.V. Young, about the contribution of historical account in social investigation may serve as an inducement for some people to raise the objection that too much time and force is spent in historical study. But, if looked attentively no investigator, who has to go down deep in any social field, can do without its historical study. The further he proceeds with his study, the wider becomes the field of knowledge that opens before him and thus he goes on without worrying about the time that the study may take. The present social event takes a new shape in the light of a historical study which helps in understanding many new things. To understand any aspect in the study of any group, investigation in its past historical shape becomes necessary.

COMPARATIVE METHOD

Durkheim was the first to explain comparative method in the study of social events most clearly in his book entitled, *The Rules of Sociological Methods.* According to Durkheim, social explanation is given through the establishment of cause-effect relationship. in order to show that one social event is the cause of another social event, such events, wherein two events are present or absent together, will be studied. In this way, we can know how far one event depends on the other.

Comparative method has been successfully applied in many studies in the field of anthropology. Hobhouse, Wheeler and Ginsberg studied main social institutions in primitive societies. Economic organizations in primitive societies were differentiated and then the reaction of the difference among economic organizations on social standardization was discovered.

Criticizing the comparative method, Radcliffe-Brown has written, "The comparative methods alone give you nothing. Nothing will grow out of the ground unless you put seeds into it. The comparative method is one way of testing hypotheses." It is clear from the criticism of the comparative method that formation of a clear hypothesis is necessary before applying the comparative method. Whether the hypothesis is true or not is proved through comparative studies. There is no use applying this method in the absence of a hypothesis. There is another limit to the application of comparative method. A comparison among all societies, through this method is difficult. A comparative study of special social institutions in one and the same society is easier.

FUNCTIONAL METHOD

The application of the functional method in the study of anthropological events is based on the fundamental acknowledgement that society is like a biological organization wherein different social institutions work differently. Herbert Spencer has applied this method in his book entitled, *Principles of*

Sociology, but the best examples of its application are found in Durkheim's works *The Division of Labour in Society* and *The Rules of Sociological Method*. Durkheim has regarded the relation of social institutions with the needs of social individual as the function of social institution. He has shown difference between normal and pathological function of an institution.

Functional method in anthropology is the creation of reactions of the evolutionary methods. These anthropologists criticized the application of comparative and historical methods in anthropology. According to them, the principle of evolution cannot present a scientific definition of the whole social history of man. But the functional method was criticized because its original recognition was not satisfactory. As a matter of fact, there are many such differences between society and biological organization on the basis of which it can be said that society is not an organic structure. While the parts of an animal body do not have independent control and life, individuals of a society do have their independent control and life. While the body regulates the functions of its organs in an animal, it is not so in society. Even then, in the field of social anthropology, functional method has been applied in important studies of the functions of various social institutions in primitive society. Many important studies of the village communities have been done through the help of this method. Malinowski's studies are worth mentioning in this connection. But Malinowski's recognition of the functional integration in various parts of society, as in animals, has been criticized. This recognition of Malinowski created difficulty in explaining social changes in society. The modern anthropologists, therefore, regard the application of functional method as proper only in a limited field and many precautions are considered necessary in applying this method. In this connection, the suggestions of R. K. Merton are important. Merton differentiated between function and dysfunction and between manifest and latent functions. He drew attention to the fact that there are many functions of social institutions and one or other of these functions may be more important and, for the discovery of which, historical and comparative studies may prove to be more useful. In the words of Bottomore, "What is most valuable in the functionalist approach is the greater emphasis and clarity given to the simple idea that in every particular society the different social activities are interconnected. It still remains to discover, however, in each case which activities are related and how they are related."

PART B — PHYSICAL ANTHROPOLOGY

5

Introduction to Physical Anthropology

Physical anthropology studies the man as animal. Two diverse methods are employed for this study though both have identical purpose. First is the study of man through evolutionary process and the second is the study of human populations. The methodology employed, though different, the results of each are complementary to the other. Both approaches centre about the basic theme of *human variations* and understanding the ways and means of human adaptation.

Darwin's theory of evolution which is based on the twin concepts of "natural selection" and "survival of the fittest" has had such favourable impact upon human imagination that the evolution of man from the lower forms of life was blindly acquiesced in and taken to be an axiomatic and gospel truth. Hence, the science of biology was seen to be the natural path to understand man. Therefore, anthropologists concentrated on the history of man's physical characteristics and the nature of life itself. The science of archaeology and geology were thoroughly used to fish out the early traces of human life and were compared *inter se* and with modern man.

If, before 1859, Western civilization found its intellectual continuity in the Biblican doctrine, after 1859, it found its new continuity in the doctrine of evolution. A doctrine is only seized upon in that fashion when it supplies some great need, emotional as well as intellectual, in the life of man. Darwin's theory supplied the end for a new philosophy of life. It not only afforded a new vista of human development, but also provided a new justification of world progress in terms of Western civilization. The evolution of man was seen as an infinite progression, from lower forms to the higher with civilization to the representative of the high form in evolutionary scale. But more than that, the Darwinian theory of natural re-election became synonymous with advance. Since all life was a struggle for existence, the fittest who survived were *ipso facto* superior.

In our search for sterling human traits that aid survival, we wish to know how a particular trait becomes widespread, and why and how in some instances it disappears. We also examine how a trait or cluster of traits among a particular population fares when these come into contact with diverse groups. Though, there are some wide gaps in our historical understanding of physical human traits we do know when and where earliest human beings appeared. How the early man looked and how did it resemble or differ from each other and we learn also how the physical characteristics of man changed during his time on earth.

Physical anthropology is keenly interested in learning early forms of man and his closer relatives among apes and monkeys. Though, there are controversies among scholars regarding various fossils, the main outlines of human evolutionary process are well established. Behavioural studies of the higher animals are beginning to yield clues regarding origin of human behaviour. Though, the qualitative differences in behaviour between modern and primitive men are great, the broad principles are well-established.

In the basic structure men of today are quite similar to each other in spite of external physical differences. Man of today belong to a Single Species of *Homo Sapiens*, though in prehistoric times there were numerous other species. If we peep into classical pre-history we find a large span of time when no anthropoid or man-like creature existed. Therefore, it is abundantly clear that man of today has emerged from earlier non-human forms. According to Beals and Hoizer, "The study of processes whereby man developed from his non-human ancestors and the continuing process of change still slowly altering his bodily form is also the part of physical anthropology. From such studies we learn how men gradually became different from the other animals and assumed the bodily characteristics which mark them today. We also learn how men diversified themselves, and something of the factors responsible for the infinite variety of human forms."

Men not only interact with each other but also interact with nature including sea, air, land and many other physical features. No study of man would be complete which overlooked his relationship *in toto* with the environment. It is extremely vital concern of physical anthropology to know how the environment affects man's structure. It is the influence of environment that accounts for the diversity of human forms. For example, the people of cold climates are hard working whereas warmer climes induce laziness. The hill people are sturdy and fair-complexioned; they are usually of tall stature. But the people of plains are swarthy and short. Negroid people generally excel in athletics and games and are more virile than white races.

According to Beals and Hoizer, "An important and relatively new part of physical anthropology is the study of actual process by which changes occur. An older phase of this subject included the study of the development of the human being from conception of adulthood and the effect of differing environmental conditions on this development." The modern phase of this subject is human genetics, the study of the mechanism of heredity, the ways in which heredity is modified and man's attempts at adaptation to new conditions.

Population analysis has contributed a great deal to material conducive to advances in genetics and heredity. Man does not live in a vacuum, he is basically a gregarious creature and he belongs to a family, tribe or nation. He is constantly interacting with other members of his community and indirectly with foreign people. The intensity of proximity and distance from other community members and diverse group determine the pace of his physical and structural change. The people who mix with many diverse peoples grow and evolve fast whereas isolated individuals stagnate or change very slowly. Physical anthropology examines whether interbreeding leads to radical changes in man and whether there is any relationship between physical type, temperament, intelligence, aptitudes or behaviour in general.

Physical anthropology is closely related to geology and archaeology. It uses anthropology (measurement of size and weight of cranium, cephalic index, etc.) pigmentation, that is variation in the colour of hair, skin and eyes, to establish racial features. It also makes physiometric observations to cover a diversity of phenomenon like colour, blindness, ability to taste phenylthiocarbamide (a chemical substance) and finger prints whose variation is entirely or almost entirely hereditary, to character like heat and cold tolerance and physiological adaptations to high altitude whose state is very largely a function of the environment in which an individual is living. Physical anthropology also divides people according to their blood groups (A, B, AB or O) because this sheds ample light on the inheritance of physical characters. Haemoglobin and other serological studies are also examined to reveal patterns of heredity and genes.

HISTORICAL DEVELOPMENT

Ever since antiquity man has evinced an interest to know his roots and home. He has made efforts of some kind to trace his origin and define his culture. Much of this interest among the non-literate societies has taken recourse to imagination. He has waved interesting myths and legends for this. Myths explain a number of the features of his culture — discovery of fire, invention of useful tools and technique of growing food.

The Greeks have left a record of man's discovery of fire, agriculture as also the account of the life and culture of their neighbours. Herodotus studied the life style of Egyptians and Scythians and also proposed a theory concerning the origin of language.

Though, the impetus for a full-fledged science was provided by the doctrine of evolution, a body of anthropological facts started accumulation from the fifteenth century when travellers, missionaries and soldiers started recording quite precisely the manners and customs of people abroad whom they visited and lived with. Much of their observations were subjective and reflected their own bias, nevertheless the materials so collected formed the stepping stone of the proper science of anthropology.

In the middle of 19th century, a number of skeletal remains and flint implements were found at various places in the world. Many scholars took deep interest in them and this stimulated geological and paleontological research. The doctrine of evolution overwhelmed the curiosity of scientists and set afire an adventure into the strange and mysterious. Everything was brought under scientific scrutiny and even the *Bible*, which had provided the mystic basis of Western civilization, was brought under it. The ancient aeons of the earth's past soon disclosed themselves in geological formation and structure. The rapid mutations of the modern world revealed themselves in social science and historical theory. The idea of movement and change become an obsession.

To a French scholar, Boucher de Perthes, goes the credit of establishing for the first time the existence of man in Europe during the Ice age. He discovered stone tools in some valley sand and loose rounded fragments of rocks as early as 1830 and in 1847-1864 published his discoveries in a number of booklets. However, at his death his works were withdrawn from sale by the decision of his family and it was not until 1900 that his pioneering work received due recognition. In 1865, Sir John Lubbock first established the distinction between old and new Stone Ages.

The first direct evidence of Fossil Man, the Neanderthal man, was made in Germany in 1856. This material provided a sound basis of the sciences of Archaeology and Physical Anthropology. Though as early as 1750, Linnaeus had evolved the conception of four races of mankind — European white, Asiatic yellow, American red and African black — there was great accumulation of archaeological data between 1860 and 1890. In 1865, E.B. Tylor of England published a major anthropological treatise *Primitive Culture*, followed by L.H. Morgan's *Ancient Society* in 1877.

These scholars defined Anthropology as a natural science, concerned with pre-historic people as well as the culture of contemporary non-literate people called primitives or tribals. Modern anthropology, both physical and cultural, begins in 20th century.

Greek and Roman Thought

The idea of human origin and evolution occurred to some of the ancient Greek and Roman thinkers.

1. Herodotus. In the writings of Herodotus (484-425 B.C.) we come across description of skulls of the inhabitants of Greece, Egypt, Asia Minor, Libya, Scythia, etc. He demonstrated that the skull wall was thicker in the Egyptians and thinner in the Persians. According to him these differences were due to influence of environment.

2. Hippocrates. Hippocrates (460-377 B.C.) laid more emphasis on environment to explain differences in physical features among different populations. He demonstrated the differences in physical features between the inhabitants of the hills and of the plains. He was in favour of inheritance of acquired characters.

3. Aristotle. Aristotle's (384-322 B.C.) works provides us with many useful and interesting anthropological information on heredity, growth, distribution of body, hair, body proportions in children, human brain, skull, biped, nature of man and so forth. He observed the comparative characters of man and other animals. According to him man is the most complete animal in all its parts. He marked the peculiar characteristics of man. On the basis of those he gave man a special place among the animals. He is considered as the first authority to use the word anthropology.

4. Galen. Galen (A.D. 131-200) dissected animals of different kinds including apes to study muscles, nerves, development of photos, etc. At that time dissection of the human body was prohibited. Galen, however, got opportunities to study human skeletons. He observed that the apes were the closest kins of man. He found that the apes resembled man most closely in viscera, muscles, arteries, nerves, bones. etc.

After this period of about one thousand years less importance was given to the study of the natural history of man. It almost lost its identity as an independent discipline. Man became a subject of study of the historians, philosophers, physicians, and naturalists.

Emperor of Germany

In 1240, Emperor Frederick II of Germany passed a regulation that a student studying medicine must dissect a human body once during his course of study. But nobody paid any attention to this for another one hundred years.

Thirteenth Century

During the period between 1306 and 1315 to Italian Physician Mundinus (1270-1326) dissected two human bodies, when the need of dissecting human body in medical science was gradually realized.

Sixteenth Century Thought

1. Vesalius. Vesalius (1514-1564) was a renowned anatomist of the sixteenth century. His observations on anatomical characters and descriptions of the structure of the human body contributed considerably towards the growth and development of physical anthropology at a later stage. He noted that the skull of Greeks and Turks was globular, that of the Belgians was oblong and the skull of Germans were rounded with a flat accept. Thus, he may be considered as a pioneer in racial craniology.

2. Koyter. Koyter (1534-1600) was another scientist of the sixteenth century who made special study of the foetus and child.

Scientists of Seventeenth Century

Of the scientists of the seventeenth century who made notable contributions towards the understanding of physical aspects of man, mention may be made of Tyson (1650-1708). Garengeot (1688-1708) and John Ray (1628-1705), Tyson made a comparative study of the anatomical characters of apes and man, while

Garengeot studies the anatomy of the muscular system of man in comparison to other animals, like dog.

Eighteenth Century Scientists

Carl Linnaeus (1707-1778), Count de Buffon (1707-1788) and J.F. Blumenbach (1753-1840) were three renowned scholars of the eighteenth century, who made notable contribution to physical anthropology.

1. Linnaeus. Linnaeus was professor of botany in the University at Upsala, Sweeden. His famous book, *The Systema Naturae,* was first published in 1735. He started systematization and classification of plants and animals introducing binary nomenclature, whereby each plant and animal was assigned a genus name and a species name. He called man by the name Homo Sapiens, Homo being the genus and sapiens the species.

2. Buffon. Buffon may be regarded as the founder of anthropology. He was the first to outline the great divisions of anthropology. According to him with an anthropological approach man may be studied : (i) in general as a natural history subject throughout the ages, (ii) in groups, *i.e.,* races — their origin, description and admixture, (iii) to compare physical chacteristics of man and other animals, and (iv) to trace man's origin and to place him in the animal kingdom. Thus, Buffon studied man as species. His method was followed by others. His works indicate that the concept of evolution occurred to him though he could not develop his idea of evolution. At one stage he himself contradicted his own evolutionary concept. This was because he did not like to defy Church which was very much against evolutionary thoughts.

3. Blumenbach. Blumenbach has been considered to be the father of physical anthropology. In the eighteenth century anthropology meant description of the body and soul. Blumenbach used the word anthropology to denote physical anthropology. He looked at the variation in physical features observed in different population groups. He made a systematic study to classify mankind into different groups on the basis of craniological materials.

Contribution by Explorers

In this connection it may be mentioned that several explorers of the period between the twelfth and eighteenth centuries travelled through different parts of the globe and thereby came in contact with the autocthonous inhabitants of several countries. Most of them kept record of their experiences of meeting divergent peoples belonging to different regions. Through their writings it was possible to know the physical features of various types of man. These helped a lot in identifying and classifying human groups.

4. Vesalius. Though Blumenbach is called the real father of craniology, the first scientific data on anthropological craniology comes from the sixteenth century when Vesalius made comparison of cranial form of different peoples like Greek, Turk and German.

5. Spieghel. One of the first attempts at craniometry was made by Spieghel (1578-1625). He measured four diameters of skull, namely, facial, transverse, vertical and oblique. According to the relationship among these four diameters he attempted to classify the various skulls.

6. Daubenton. Buffon's collaborator Daubenton (1716-1800) applied craniometric method to study cranial characteristics. He observed the position of the foramen magnum which varies between posterior and interior sides of the skull in different animals including man. He devised a technique to measure an angle to determine the inclination.

7. Camper. Camper (1722-1789) developed projection to obtain craniometric data on skull.

8. Hoeven. Hoeven (1801-1868) used eleven measurements to study human cranium.

9. Retzius. Retzious (1796-1860) established relationship between cranial length and breadth by calculating length-breadth cranial index.

10. Karl von Baer. Following Retzius, Karl von Baer calculated length-height cranial index.

Craniometry

In this way, craniometry was developed by different scientists from the middle of nineteenth century. Of them the names of Paul Broca (1824-1880), A.de Quatrefages (1810-1892) and Virchow (1821-1902) must be mentioned.

Theories of Evolution of Man

Following R.S. Lull the theories concerning evolution of man may be grouped under four heads: (i) Theory of eternity of the present conditions, (ii) Theory of special creation, (iii) Theory of catastrophism, (iv) Theory of organic evolution.

1. Theory of Eternity. Those who advocate theory of eternity of the present condition believe that the universe with its organism was there and it will be there without any change. This idea was, however, shared by a handful of men of science.

2. Theory of Special Creation. The Christian church authorities were the chief supporters of the theory of special creation. St. Augustine (A.D. 354-430) maintained that God created Adam and Eve about 6,000 years ago and that all human beings were descended from Adam and Eve. Archbishop Ussher (1581-1656) went one step further to calculate the ages of the generations after Adam and to arrive at the conclusion that Adam and Eve were created in 4004 B.C. Lightfoot even gave the exact date and time of creation of man — 9 A.M. on 23rd October, 4004 B.C.

According to this theory, the world was created in six days. On the first day, the earth was created. On the third day, animal and plant kingdoms showed their appearance. By the fifth and sixth day all the creatures were created. Among the foremost defenders of the theory of special creation, the name of Father Suarez (1548-1617) may be mentioned. Until the eighteenth century this sort of idea of special creation was hardly challenged.

During the eighteenth century, fossil remains of several extinct animals were discovered from different parts of Europe. In some cases human remains were associated with those fossil remains. Along with remains of an elephant like creature a worked flint tool was discovered from gravel deposits near London in 1715. In 1771, human remains along with cave bear remains were collected in Germany. In 1797, hand axes were found along with remains of extinct animals. The geologists also started collecting new information on the geological strata. Thus, paleontology and geology made a rapid progress. More and more was learned about these.

3. Catastrophism. In the early nineteenth century the theory of Catastrophism was put forward mainly upheld by Georges Cuvier (1769-1832). According to this theory the earth had periodically experienced natural calamity like floods, volcanic eruptions. As a result of this sort of disasters the organisms were extinguished. After the disasters new forms came to replace the previous forms. Thus, Cuvier rejected the theories of continuous evolution. According to him each time that the earth settled down after catastrophe, new animals appeared. In the beginning, there were corels, molluses and crustaceans and then came plants. After that fish and reptiles emerged and finally, birds and mammal appeared. Man appeared after the last geological revolution. That was about 6,000 years ago. Thus, in the theory of catastrophism one finds a compromise between the findings on the growing knowledge of paleontology and geology on the one hand and the conservative biblical thoughts on the other.

4. Theory of Organic Evolution :

(i) *Greek and Roman Thinkers.* The idea of evolution is found in the works of the ancient Greeks and Romans. Thales of Miletus (636-546 B.C.), a Greek scholar looked for beginning of life in the blue water of the Agean Sea. He considered water as the mother of life, wherefrom life originated. He suggested that man had evolved from fish which came out of water and developed in land. Empedocles (490-430 B.C.) considered the remains of fossilized hippopotamus as the remains of extinct giants from which later on other types of animals developed. Herodotus attempted evolutionary interpretations to explain the variations in cranial characters of the Egyptians and Persians. Hippocrates' works also indicate that he could think of some sort of evolutionary mechanism. Aristotle also conceived of evolution. He thought of a gradual progress from plants to animals and then to man. He suggested that organisms had certain inborn power to adapt themselves to the environment. As a result an organism makes a progress. However, he could not explain the facts scientifically, as he had no clear understanding of the subject. Lucretius (99-55 B.C.), a

Roman philosopher advanced a scheme of both biological and cultural evolution of man. Thus, even before the beginning of the Christian era evolutionary concepts were conceived.

(ii) *During Middle Ages.* During the Middle Ages and at the beginning of the modern era, several scientists and thinkers contributed their shares by throwing some light on the subject of evolution. Edward Tyson, after comparing the anatomy of a pygmy with that of a monkey, an ape and a man came to the conclusion that the pygmy was intermediate between ape and man. Carl Linnaeus grouped man along with apes on the basis of close physical similarity between them. He, however, did not think of their common ancestry or evolution. Buffon's idea on evolution has already been referred to. Robert Hooks (1635-1703) suggested that the earth's past can be revealed by the fossil remains. Leibniz (1646-1716) said that men were linked to the animals, which in turn were connected with the plants, and these with the fossils. Thus, in the works of both these scholars evolutionary tendency of organisms was suggested.

In this connection we must consider the works of several scholars including Monboddo (1714-1790), Charles Bonnet (1720-1793), Goethe (1749-1832), Immanuel Kant (1724-1804), Schopenhauer (1788-1860), Charles Lyell (1797-1875), Karl vol Baer (1792-1876), Erasmus Darwin (1731-1802), etc.

(iii) *Origin of Species.* In the works of Monboddo, a suggestion on the origin of species and the evolution of man is found. Bonnet prepared a continuous scale beginning with minerals and ending with man including numerous intermediary forms. Goethe's works include so much of evolution that by some he was considered as a predecessor of Darwin. Kant suggested that perhaps man was descended from the monkey. Erasmus Darwin outlined his ideas of heredity, natural selection and evolution in one of his books.

(iv) *Lamarck.* The French naturalist Lamarck (1744-1829) was one of the forerunners who presented evolutionary concept. He expressed his views concerning evolutionary concept. He expressed his views concerning evolution in one of his works in 1800. He believed in the inheritance of acquired characters. Evolution was the result of the adaptation of organisms to environment. The adapted characters were transmitted from parents to offsprings. When more number of characters were acquired in this way, the species was transformed to a new one. The transformation took place because of use or disuse of certain bodily parts of an organism to adapt to a particular environment. For example, giraffe acquired elongated neck, because of continuous stretching of neck to reach leaves of tall trees; the webbed feet of birds are to live in an aquatic environment; certain ducks cannot fly because of disuse of wings.

Human Evolution

As regards evolution, Lamarck wrote that, "Let us assume that a certain quandrumanous race which was highly perfected should lose the habit, acquired through environmental necessity or by any other cause, of climbing trees and grasping the branches with the feet as well as the hands. If the individuals of this race, for a series of generations, should be obliged to sue their feet exclusively for walking purposes and should cease to use their hands as feet such quadraumana would undoubtedly be transformed eventually into bimana and their toes would no longer be separated or supposable since their feet would only be utilized for walking." Similar explanation was given for erect posture, decrease of prognathism, reduction of mandible, etc.

(v) *Charles Darwin*. Charles Darwin (1809-1882) published his work, *The Origins of Species by Means of Natural Selection* in 1859. Here he detailed his concept of evolution in general and also the concept of natural selection which helped to cause evolutionary changes. This may be considered as the turning point in the thinking of evolution. Again in 1871 his work. *The Descent of Man* came to light. In this book he outlined the evolution of man. He based his arguments about human evolution not only on the fossil remains of early types of man, which were found in Europe, but also on comparative anatomical data.

Natural Selection

Darwin observed that in spite of the tendency of organisms to increase in geometrical ratio, species generally have fairly constant populations. Their numbers are held in check by struggle for existence. In the course of struggle individuals of an organism having certain favourable variations survive and they reproduce, while those with unfavourable traits disappear. The favourable ones are selected by Nature. This is Darwin's natural selection.

Genetic Studies

But Darwin could not explain how new variations rise in an organism. That was later explained by geneticists. Darwin founded the concept of natural selection and evolution, while the science of genetics was founded by Gregor Mendel (1822-1884). The development of genetics has helped to explain many facts which could not be done during the time of Darwin of course. Mendel reported his works in 1865, but his works remained unnoticed till 1900, sixteen years after Mendel's death, when the science of genetics was born. Otherwise, Darwin perhaps could have attempted to explain certain ideas developed by him.

Criticism of Darwin

Darwin's theory was criticized by some and appreciated by others. Among the adherents of Darwinism of the nineteenth century mention may be made of

Thomas Huxley, Lyell, Wallace, Wiesmann, Haeckel, Carl Vogt, Edmand Perrier, etc. They tried to develop the Darwinian idea in their own ways.

Neo-Darwinism

Subsequently, Darwin's idea was modified by some scientists. They attempted to rejuvenate Darwinism, which led to new trend called, neo-Darwinism. Wiesmann was one of the leading exponents of this new trend.

Darwinianism and Genetics

In modern times scientists are trying to synthesize the Darwinian concept and the knowledge gathered from the rapid development of the science of genetics to understand the basic biological facts and the physical bases of evolution in natural selection.

SCOPE OF PHYSICAL ANTHROPOLOGY

Physical Anthropology is concerned with man as a physical organism in time and space. 'Time' means the stages of development of man in the process of evolution during different periods of time. 'Space' refers to the differentiation of physical types in modern man living in different parts of the globe. Thus, physical anthropology focuses human evolution and human variation.

Human Evolution

Man was not created by God or any other agency in a day or a short span of time. He had to pass through various stages of evolution to attain the present human status. Scholars unearthed, collected, and studied the paleontological or fossil remains of our ancestors and their collaterals, to seek answers to the question : What are the stages of evolution at which time and stage the human line bifurcated from the common stem; what are the physical features of the early huminoids and hominids; where did they live, etc.

1. Australopithecus. In this stage one finds different varieties of creatures, the good representatives of which were unearthed in some parts of Africa. Some of them were the true tool makers and tool users. Man is the only animal having the ability of manufacturing and using tools. This is one of the characteristics which distinguishes man from other animals.

2. Homo erectus. Man is the only animal capable of standing erect on two feet in the truest sense of the term. Bipedal locomotion is a distinguishing feature of man. The fossil remains of the representatives of this stage have been discovered from different parts of Asia, Europe and Africa. Some of the famous discoveries are : Pithecanthropus crectus or Java man, Sinanthropus pekinensis or Pekin man and Homo Heidelbergensis or Heidelberg man.

3. Neanderthal man. The true representatives of the various types of Neanderthal race mostly lived in Europe, West Asia and North Africa.

4. Homo sapiens.

PROCESS OF EVOLUTION

The aim of studying the evolution of man is not only to establish the different stages during the evolutionary process but also to understand its mechanism. Scientists like Lamarck and Darwin put forward their theories of evolution. Lamarck laid more stress on the use and disuse of bodily parts and inheritance of acquired characters. Darwin tried to explain the process by 'natural selection' that is, selection of certain varieties by Nature. But there were many questions which the earlier scientists could not answer. Today with the advent of science we have come across several new schools of thought throwing light on the concept of evolution, such as Neo-Darwinism and New-Lamarckism.

MAN'S POSITION IN ANIMAL KINGDOM

Man is a vertebrate. Of the vertebrates, man belongs to the Mammalian group, which again comprises several orders. The primate is one such order to which man belongs. This order includes besides man, the monkeys and apes. Out of the four apes, the gorilla and chimpanzee are more akin to man. Next to them stand the other two apes, orang and gibbon which are followed by the catarrhine monkeys.

Perspective of Primate Study

Physical anthropologists are interested in studying the primates, the close relatives of man, from following different angles for different reasons :

1. The study of fossil primates in relation to geological and temporal sequence. This helps in understanding the evolutionary stages.

2. The comparative anatomical study of the living primates. Anatomical features include bone, morphological features, blood chemistry, dermatoglyphic traits and the like.

3. The study of primate behaviour in their natural surroundings.

4. The experimental study of apes and monkeys in the laboratory. This is to understand certain fundamental aspects of man and these animals.

UTILITY OF PRIMATOLOGY

An important aspect of physical anthropology, this sort of study on the primates held in understanding the nature and degree of relationships between man and other members of the primate. This relationship is not accidental but to common ancestry. It has already been stated that there exists a very close relationship between man and chimpanzee. They have similar type of blood, suffer from the same type of disease and so forth. Therefore, experiments could be carried on chimpanzee to understand certain fundamental aspects of man.

Primate Paleontology

As is evidenced by the numerous fossil remains, man did not acquire his present characteristics in a day but through ages by a process of gradual development from his non-human ancestors. Proper understanding of primate paleontology requires some knowledge of stratigraphical geology and the various geological eras and periods, that is, geochronology. Nobody can deny the effect of environment on man. The knowledge of geoecology is to be acquired to understand the influence of environment on man, prehistoric as well as modern.

Study of Human Variation

The study of human variation is a principal focus of physical anthropology. 'Scientists are generally agreed that all men living today belong to a single species, Homo sapiens, and that all men are derived from a common stock'. Therefore, any man from any part of the globe can marry any woman of any part. From the biological point of view such union is viable and hence can produce fertile children. But though all men belong to the same species, remarkable variations in respect of physical features are observed among different populations. Some populations are woolly haired, others have straight hair, some are dark-skinned, while others have lighter skin. Then there are differences in nose form, head form, face form, stature, blood types and many other such traits. Hence, nobody can deny that this single species comprises several types on varieties of population.

THE RACES

Varieties of Races

On the basis of variation and similarity with regard to physical features, physical anthropologists have divided mankind into certain smaller groups, called the races. There are three major races of man, *viz.*, Negroid, Caucasoid and Mongoloid. Some like to add one more, the Australoid. Others want to include the Australoid under the Caucasoid giving a name, the Archaic Caucasoid. Each of the major races is again divided and sub-divided into smaller groups.

The Concept of Race

The concept of race may be regarded as a classificatory device to provide a frame within which different population groups may systematically be arranged. In anthropology one can define race as 'a population characterized by some concentrations' relative as to the frequency and distribution, of genes of physical characters, which appear, fluctuate, often disappear in the course of time by 'geographic and/or cultural isolation'. The hereditary physical traits determine the membership in a race hence nationality, language or religion are not necessarily connected with race. However, these factors sometimes help in maintaining the distinctiveness of a racial group by way of isolation.

Racial Characteristics

Some of the physical features of races are easily distinguishable with naked eye, while others require scientific measurements.

1. Somatoscopy. Skin colour, hair colour, eye colour, face form, nose form, lip, etc., are observable characters. This sort of scientific observation of the bodily part is known as somatoscopy.

2. Anthropometry. Measurements on the different parts of the body, taken in anthropology, are called anthropometry.

3. Somatometry. Measurements are taken on the body of living persons, when it is called somatometry.

4. Craniometry. Creniometry is the measurement on the skull.

5. Osteometry. It deals with the measurements on bone other than that of skull. The earlier physical anthropologists were mainly concerned with this sort of observations and body measurements in order to classify the human types and write racial histories. But now they are also interested in distribution of blood types such as ABO, MN, Rh and the like, and other biochemical factors.

Occurrence of certain hereditary abnormalities, such as hemophilia, sickle-cell anaemia, colour blindness in different populations is also a subject matter of physical anthropology. Physical anthropologists make attempt to learn the relative susceptibility or immunity of different populations to different diseases.

Causes of Localization

People used to cold climate do not like to migrate to hot region. Hill people prefer to live in the hills. Sea coast dwellers enjoy living in the coastal area. Is there any biological reason behind it? Are the people biologically adapted to a particular environment? These questions are to be answered by physical anthropologists.

Study of Human Growth

The study of growth and its related problems is one of the important aspects of physical anthropology. They prepare growth curves, growth standards and find out the reasons for normal and retarded growth. Their findings are fruitfully utilized to build a healthy nation. The children are the future of a nation. Their good health is a national wealth. So every possible care should be taken so that the children become healthy. There should be normal growth and development of the children. The growth is dependent on several factors, which could be placed under two broad headings — heredity and environment. Environment includes a large number of variables like climate, attitude, food, socio-economic condition, etc.

Demography

Demography also attracts attention of physical anthropologists. It is directly related to fertility and mortality. Both these two are greatly influenced by a host of factors in heredity and environment. These physical anthropologists are directly concerned with different facets of demography. The fertile period is between menarchy and menopause. The age at menarchy and that at menopause may vary from population to population effecting demographic structure. So is mortality. Physical anthropologists are to give the answer about what are the factors behind these phenomena?

Human Genetics

The trend of physical anthropological research has remarkably changed during the last 25 years. The subject has made a rapid progress and has expanded greatly exploring more diversified fields. Now more emphasis is given on human genetics, a major branch of physical anthropology. Physical anthropologists are now trained in specialized laboratory techniques.

The existence of human variations is a well established fact. One population varies from another with regard to physical traits which are determined by heredity. Then there are individual variations. No two persons are exactly alike. Again similarities among closely related persons are observed. Why these variations and similarities?

Two brothers born of the same parents may have opposite characters. One may be tall, light skinned and of normal health. The other may be short, dark and have very bad health. Why is it so? Some people are easily susceptible to certain diseases and others are not. Certain diseases are not curable. Are the mental traits affected by heredity or by environment? The answers these sort of questions are found out by physical anthropologists studying human genetics.

APPLIED PHYSICAL ANTHROPOLOGY

Like all other branches of science, physical anthropology has also two aspects — theoretical and applied. What is 'applied'? A dictionary definition of applied is, using and adapting abstract principles and theory in connection, with concrete problems especially with a utilitarian aim. Hence, it is important to know the abstract and theoretical principles of physical anthropology, only when the acquired knowledge could meaningfully be utilized.

1. Racism. Physical anthropologists subscribe to the view that there is no superior or inferior race in the biological sense. Racial prejudice is not inherited. It is the culture or the society which makes a man prejudiced. If this is taught properly to the people, tension will be much released and peace and harmony will prevail.

2. Industry. Physical anthropologists have made notable contribution to various industries by supplying them the information on body size and proportions. But that has become such a common place even that nobody bothers to give due credits to the physical anthropologists.

3. Army. Application of physical anthropology in the armed service is a well accepted fact. Physical anthropologists are appointed in defence services. They help in space travel projects also by providing necessary information on the need of placement of the equipments according to the body size and proportion of the space travellers to minimize the cost and labour.

4. Medicine. The role of physical anthropologists in the various aspects of medicine and public welfare projects are obvious.

5. Penology. Physical anthropological knowledge has been used since long past in criminology and penology.

6. Medico-Legal Application. Medico-legal application of physical anthropology is as well known fact.

7. Genetic Counselling. Genetic counselling gradually become more popular in many advanced countries.

8. Education. Pedagogical anthropology is directly concerned with education in various educational fields, physical anthropological findings are fully utilized in many advanced countries.

The physical anthropologist must remember that man is always depandent on his environment. Environment does not include geographical conditions like temperature, humidity, rainfall, soil only, but social, religious, cultural and various other factors also. In each of these factors again a large number of variables are involved. One cannot overlook man's relationships, in past as well as present and in all places, with the environment. Therefore, man must be studied in relation to his environment, both social and physical.

6

Anthropometry

Both individuals and populations of individuals vary in their size and shape. Anthropometry represents the different measuring techniques, usually made with calipers, which are used to analyse this physical variation as it occurs both in the living body and in the skeleton. From the early 19th century anthropometry has been a mainstay of physical anthropology. Particular atention has been devoted to the skeleton, since one of the main problems has been in establishing the evolutionary descent of the different races and skeletal remains constitute the most direct evidence of earlier populations. Many measurements have been devised, but the ones most commonly taken are of stature, head length and head breadth. For many years the latter two were especially favoured and used to calculate the cranial index (on the skull) or the cephalic index (on the living) by expressing the breadth as a percentage of the length. Long heads, with low cephalic indices (below 75) are termed dolichocephalic, while round heads with high indices (above 81) are termed brachycephalic. The intermediates are said to be mesocrephalic.

DIFFERING FEATURES

Anthropometric features vary widely among the world's populations. Thus, hiel the Nilotes of the Sudan have an average stature of 1.78m, the African Pygmies average only 1.36m. There is little systematic pattern in the geographical distribution of stature itself, but it is a component determining the relationship between body volume and skin surface area, which shows a very distinct distribution. In people in cold regions, skin surface area is low in relation to volume whereas in hot regions it tends to be high. This is explained by the need to conserve body heat in Arctice environments and to dissipate heat in the tropics. Because he follows this pattern man is said to observe the ecological rules of Bergmann and Allen. The causes for the variation in head shapes are not known, though there is evidence that brachycephaly has been increasing in frequency since Upper Palaeolithic times. Now-a-days, dolichocephalic heads are prevalent among Australian Aborigines while brachycephaly is extremely prevalent among mongoloid peoples.

Although there is a heritable component to most anthropometric variation, the nature of the environment in which an individual grows and develops can also be important. This has been shown by comparing migrants to new environments and their offspring, with parental populations.

PIGMENTATION

Variation in the colour of hair, skin and eyes is mainly due to differences in the amount and distribution of the black, pigment melanin, which even causes the "blueness" of eyes when overlain with unpigmented tissues which diffract light. The variation typically has a strong hereditary component, especially in eyes, but immediate environmental experience can have an important effect, as for example, in skin tanning on exposure to ultra-violet radiation. Traditionally, colour differences were described either in subjective terms or else by reference to matching standards. Both procedures presented serious limitations in reliability and in comparability of results. Recent years have withnesed the sue of much more satisfactory objective procedures, involving spectrophoto meters in hair and skin colour studies. These instruments record the percentage of light of a number of known specified wavelengths reflected from a surface relative to the reflectance from a pure white surface. In general, the darker the specimen, say of hair, the lower the percentage of light which it reflects. Using such instrument, precise and reliable quantitative estimations of hair and skin colour are possible and the genetic basis of the traits may be clarified and comprehended. There is some evidence that the skin colour differences between Europeans and Africans are due to three or four pairs of major genes. Dark skins confer advantages in sunny areas, since they protect the body against the harmful effects of ultra-violet tradition, minimising sunburn and the incidence of skin cancer. Light skins are advantageous in cloudy areas with low insolation, since they facilitate the body's synthesis of Vitamin D, thus reducing the incidence of rickets. The correlation between dark pigmentation and higher levels of solar radiation is high, but it is impossible to state how much of the geographical distribution of skin colour mirrors the spread of dark — and light — skinned peoples from one or two source and how much of the patterning is due to independent adaptations in many human groups in the past.

PHYSIOMETRIC OBSERVATIONS

These cover a diversity of pheomena, ranging from characters like colour blindness, ability to taste phenylthiocarbamide and fingerprints, whose variation is entirely or almost entirely hereditary, to characters like heat and cold tolerance and physiological adaptations to high altitude whose state is very largely a function of the environment in which an individual is living.

1. Colour Blindness. Red green colour blindness is a sex-linked recessive character; males being far more commonly affected than females. Within Britain percentages of colour-blind males (which represents the frequency of this colour blind gene) range from 5.4 in N.E. Scotland to 9·5 in S.W. England. Traditional societies, and particularly those still practising a hunter gatherer economy, show much lower frequencies, and it may be presumed that colour blindness is a severe handicap under such a life-style. It has, in fact, been shown that red-green colour blind individuals have difficulty in following a blood spoor on grass.

2. The tasting of P.T.C. It is controlled by two genes T and t, the former being dominant. TT and Tt individuals normally experience a bitter taste sensation when they sip P.T.C. solution; it individuals either cannot taste the substance at all or else only in very strong concentrations. The tt individuals are termed Non-tasters; TT and Tt individuals are termed Tasters. High frequencies of Non-tasters (exceeding 38%) occur in part of Wales and Orkney, while low values (approximately 24%) occur in North Lancashire and Northumberland. A clue to the selective significance of this trait is provided by the excess of Non-tasters among individuals with nodular goitres (thyroid abnormalities). Non-European populations usually have lower percentages of Non-tasters than the British figures quoted. Thus, for example, the Jivaro Indians in the Amazonian lowlands of Ecuador contain are but 1-2% of Non-tasters, as do the Chinese and many African Negro groups.

3. Finger-prints. These are one form of dermatoglyphic variation which also occurs on the palms of the hands, the soles of the feet and the toes. They arise as a series for epidermal ridges which form patterns on the surface of the stratum comeum of the skin. There is a strong genetic determination of these patterns, but the practice mode of inheritance is not known. Nor is it known why individuals and populations show this variation, or indeed why different patterns are found on the different fingers. In some pathologies, however, *e.g.*, Down's syndrome, there is marked abnormality of the dermatoglyphics.

4. Variation in Adaptations. The physiological variations in heat, cold and atitude adaptation tells us little or nothing about race, but thus human beings may help to explain why man has been able to colonise every type of terrestrial environment on earth.

BLOOD GROUPS

Attributes of the blood have increasingly been used in anthropological genetics because their mode of inheritance is relatively simple. One such set of attributes comprises the blood groups, which are complex chemical substances found in the wall of the red blood cell. These substances are antigenic and can be detected through their reactions with antibodies. A number of quite different blood group systems are now known. The first to be discovered, and still the most important in blood transfusion, is the ABO system. Whereas the antibodies to the other systems are only obtainable through immunisations, those to the ABO system are naturally occurring in human blood serum. The ABO system basically involves three genes, A,B and O (though there are sub-types of A). Every individual inherits two of these genes from parents, and so the genotype (genetic constitution) must be one of the following: AA, AO, BB, BO, AB, or OO. O is recessive to both A and B, and thus there are four possible pheno types (genetic constitutions detectable by blood grouping) : A, B, AB and O.

The ABO genes constitute a polymorphic system, that is several genes occur with frequencies such that the least frequent of them occurs with a frequency exceeding that due to mutation alone. Certain selective advantages and disadvantages of the ABO genes in human population are known. Thus, stomach cancers are more frequent among individuals of group A than they are in the population at large. Again, duodenal ulcers are almost 40% more common among persons of blood group O than in individuals of the other ABO groups.

Both on a global and on a local scale, the ABO genes display marked racial variation. Within Britain A varies from 31 to 53%, increasing in frequency from North to South; O varies from 38 to 54%, increasing in frequency from South to North. B shows less variation, though it is most prevalent in the celtic areas. The regional fluctuations are not random but systematic and statistically highly significant despite the enormous migration within Britain during the last few hundred years, which might well have masked or minimised the underlying variability.

Globally, the ABO variation is also striking. Thus, the percentage of the blood group B exceeds 30 among the mongoloids of Central and East Asia, but the B gene is virtually absent in the Australian Aborigines, the American Indians and in the Basques. Many Amerindian tribes are 100% O; some others have very high A frequencies.

The Rhesus blood group system is more complicated. It involves a number of closely linked genes. One pair of genes in this series determines whether an individual is rhesus Positive, Rh+ (DD or Dd), or rhesus negative, Rh – (dd). The system is important in pregnancy, since if a mother is Rh – and her baby Rh+, any blood of the baby which crosses into the mother's blood stream can lead her to synthesise anti-Rh+ antibody. This will then cross the placenta and cause the baby's blood to haemolise; a condition known as crythroblastos foetalis and often fatal. First pregnancies are rarely affected, but subsequent ones often are, though in the last decade effective treatment has been discovered. Prior to this there was strong natural selection against the Dd, heterozygote which should lead to the least frequent of the two genes in a population being eliminated. Nevertheless, many populations are polymorphic for these rhesus characteristics. In many parts of North-West Europe and Africa the Rh– frequency is around 15%, and among the Basques it rises towards 40%. It is absent, however, from Amerindians, Australian Aborigines and most Eastern Asians.

An examination of the occurrence of the M and N genes for the MNS blood group system shows that most populations have an M frequency of 0.5-0.6. However, a higher frequency is found among North-East Asia; while N is higher in Australian Aborigines, New Guineans and Melanesians. In fact, there is a gradient of genes frequency known as a cline, around the Pacific. On the other hand, the S-linked gene is very rare among the aboriginal people of Australia, but it occurs at a frequency of some 20% in the native population of New Guinea.

Anthropologically, the Diego system is of special interest, because it indicates affinity between Amerindian populations and the peoples of Eastern Asia. Other blood group systems include Kell, Duffy, Kidd, Lutheran, P, Xg — the last of these being a sex-linked character.

HAEMOGLOBIN

Haemoglobin, the red respiratory pigment of the red blood cell, exists in alternative forms in man, and these are genetically controlled. The frequencies of some of the genes which control haemoglobins vary markedly among human population. The principal technique used to show variant haemoglobins electrophoresis — the movement of charged particles in an electric field.

Normal human haemoglobin comprises two different haemoglobins, A and A2. An interesting variant of A is haemoglobins S. This may be indicated by electrophoresis and also by a sickling test. Red cells containing haemoglobin S placed in an Oxygen-free atmosphere assume sickle shapes. It should be noted that major advances have recently been made in the treatment of sickle-cell disease which give ground for very much increased optimism. Some abnormal haemoglobins including S, E and C have high frequencies and their existence, since all of them are deleterious to some extent, provides opportunities for viewing the action of natural selection and gene flow in human populations. Haemoglobin S reaches very high frequencies among some populations in southern Asia and particularly in much of tropical Africa (10-40%). Haemoglobin C is most prevalent in northern Ghana and contiguous areas, while Haemoglobin E is found principally in South East Asia, with frequencies as high as 27% in Kampuchea.

Homogygous SS individuals have a reduced life expectancy and without compensatory mechanisms the gene would eventually be lost apart from new mutations, were it not for some compensatory mechanism. This is possibly through positive selection in favour of A individuals who are more resistant to and so protected from falciparum malaria. Again AS females might be more fertile than AA females in certain populations, and this again would help to maintain the high S frequencies.

In addition to the genes which affect the chemical structure of the protein chains in haemoglobin, there are others which determine the rate of synthesis of those chains. These are the so-called thalassemia genes, and some of them also reach polymorphic proportions despite disadvantage in the homozygous state. Cooley's anaemia, which is common in certain Mediterranean countries, is an example. It would appear that this variation is also due to malaria; in Sardinia, Cooley's anaemia is confined to low land villages and does not occur in the mountains, where anopheline mosquitoes cannot breed.

OTHER SEROLOGICAL ATTRIBUTES

In addition to the blood groups and haemoglobin examples, many other polymorphisms are now known from human blood, and all of these show variation between populations as well as within them. In the serum of the blood are found the haptoglobins (protein that bind the haemoglobin of old and broken down red blood cells), transferrins (proteins in the blood sera used in transporting iron within the body) and the Gm groups (inherited variety within the structure of antibody molecules). The white blood cells carry the HLa antigens, so important in tissue and organ transplantation, and within the red blood cells a large number of genetically determined differences in enzyme structure have been discovered; examples include phosphoglumutase, adenylate kinase, acid phosphatase and glucose-6-phosphate dehydrogenase (which is particularly interesting, since it is a sex-linked character which, like the haemoglobins, appears to be important in resistence to malaria).

The extent of this variety is remarkable. It is now estimated that the average individual is heterozygous at 16% of his geneticloci (*i.e.*, sites of the genes). Taking the very conservative estimate that there are only 50,000 genes in man (a gene for this purpose being defined as a segment of DNA coding for a protein), this means that on an average 8,000 geneoloci carry different genes. With this level of variety the probability of two individuals being genetically alike, apart from idential twins, is astronomically low.

Analysing the causes for this incredible genetic variety is one of the central problems in anthropological genetics today. The factors which can determine the frequency of genes in populations are mutation, natural selection, movement and gene flow, genetic drift and founder effects. Further differences between populations will only arise if they are to some extent geographically or socio-culturally isolated from each other. Gene mutation is a point change in the DNA code, and it constitutes the most fundamental factor acting upon gene frequencies. The mutation rate, or the rate of this alteration in the basic chemical structure of the gene, is evidently the same in all human populations. Whether or not a new gene remains in the population after its initial appearance depends upon the action of other evolutionary agencies. Thus, for example, natural selection, is an environment force that promotes the reproduction of certain members of the population who carry certain genes, at the expense of all the other members. Natural selection favours those genes which place their possessors at a reproductive advantage and tend to eliminate those genes that place the individual at an initial or long-term disadvantage. An example as simple as the amount of melanin present in the skin is entirely appropriate. High melanin concentrations inhibit the natural production of Vitamin D by irradiation, and thus bring about Vitamin D deficiency, rickets and subsequent pelvic disproportions, which may adversely interfere with pregnancy and a normal delivery.

Without doubt many of the characteristics used to identify groups of people or races have come into being through the forces of natural selection. A population whose members have shared the same gene pool for many generations and, who are all descendants of common ancestry, have more than likely occupied the same geographical area and have thus responded to same environment for a long period of time. If the environment has changed over the generations it may be assumed that natural selection has been at work, retaining some mutations, eliminating others and in any event changing the gene frequencies. Thus, many genes now in the pool of a particular population were established through natural selection many generations ago. Unfavourable genes in an individual cannot be modified or corrected, and it is unlikely, especially if their effects are major, that they will be transmitted to the next generation. Rather, carriers of these in-built genetic errors will have a lower probability of reproducing than those without them, so that the next generation will have a higher proportion of individuals without the genetic defects and the generation following than an even higher proportion and so on. Population survival depending on genetic adaptation can only be effected through differential reproduction of genetically different individuals over the course of a number of generations.

The physical constitution of a population can also be influenced by gene flow which occurs when genes are transferred from one population to another. The carriers of these genes may arrive in great numbers and inundate the previously existing gene pool. On the other hand, the rate of genetic transfer may be slow but persistent over a protracted period. It is very unlikely that any human population even remains totally genetically isolated over many generations despite geographical and/or socio-cultural barriers.

Recently there has been a striking increase in mobility, almost world-wide. Movement is the great homogenising force in evolution, for, although it increases the variety within populations, it decreases the differences between populations. And the bicycle as well as the motor car and aeroplane can be shown to have had an effect. Racial and social barriers are also breaking down; in Brazil, for example, almost half the genes in the so-called Black group are of European origin, and in American Blacks the proportion is nearly a quarter.

Unless mutation, natural selection and gene flow are operating on a population, the gene frequencies within it will remain unchanged through successive generations, at least in large populations. On small populations, on the other hand, the situation prevailing during most of man's evolution, the genetic state of affairs is quite different, since the changes of gene frequencies may have nothing to do with selective advantages and disadvantages. In such populations the gene frequencies may oscillate due to random factors, such as the greater fertility, by chance, of one or two females, or disaster killing many men from one kin group, and the like. Similarly, only a small and unrepresentative sample of people may be involved in the founding of a new population. When this happens the genetic difference is said to have arisen from "founder effect". In this context, it is necessary to refer to the effective size of a population, that is, the percentage of the total population actually carrying out reproduction. In any human population many individuals are either too old or too young to be involved in reproduction, and many, who are of the appropriate biological and cultural age, may not be reproducing. It has, for instance, been estimated that about 60% of the population of the U.S.A. will reproduce the entire next generation. In hunter-gatherer and simple agricultural societies the effective populations frequently below 100, and drift can produce marked changes in gene frequency in a single generation. Whether or not it does act, however, depends also on whether the genetic alternatives affect the probabilities of survival and reproduction, *i.e.*, whether there is any natural selection. There is much debate at the moment on the extent to which neutral genes occur.

7

Race and Racism

The greater the currency given to the word 'race' in scientific, political and literary texts, greater is the latitude within which its meaning is interpreted. Politicians and the common people are small fry when compared with scientists who have persisted in using the term most confusingly and unscientifically. The term race has been used in a variety of differing senses, some of the following being the more important usages :

1. Particular colour. Many scientists have used the term to denote the classification of human beings on the basis of skin's colour such as black, white, yellow races, etc.

2. Physiological characteristics. The term race is also used for physiological recognition of the individual, such as Negro, European, etc. Of these all have special physiological characteristics.

3. Specific linguistic group. The term has also been employed by some scientists to denote specific linguistic groups such as Aryans, Dravidians, etc. In such groups, each has its own particular language.

4. Human characteristics. The most comprehensive sense in which the term race has been used is when it is employed to denote the entire human race. When compared with other beings in the animal kingdom, man is found to possess certain characteristic features that serve to distinguish him from the animals. It is to indicate this difference that an individual is designated the member of human race.

In addition to the more important usages of the term, race is also utilized to denote the offspring of a particular couple and their subsequent offspring in the generations to come. But a scientific analysis would end in serious confusion if the most important term used by it is open to so many different interpretations. Hence, the need to define the word race and to limit its use to only one particular concept.

Biological Interpretation

The first person to introduce the biological interpretation of the term 'race' to the annals of scientific literature was Buffoon. Huxley, too, used the term in its biological connotation. Explaining race, MacIver and Page elaborated it as a group that differs from other classes or human group by virtue of some specific physiological characteristics that are found uniformly within that group, the cause of this difference being hereditary. In this way, according to biological interpretation all the big human groups that claim superiority over other human groups because of their physiological characteristics are races. Such human groups also evolve a consciousness of race. This explanation of race is also biological.

But the biological interpretation of the term race is not adequate. The conception of race held by the biologists underwent a serious modification by Mendel's researches in the nineteenth century. Modern biology does not admit any pure race. It is incorrect to attribute race to heredity, because races have been largely inter-mixed, besides which geographic and other conditions have exercised considerable influence. Anthropological investigations prove that excessive inter-mixing has left no pure race and neither is there any actual basis of any consciousness of race.

Genetic Interpretation

The term is now-a-days used in its genetic sense, in addition to the traditional biological sense. According to Penniman, race is a genetic class in which there are many indefinite and mutually related genetic characteristics, by means of which it can be distinguished from other classes and on the basis of which the conditions of continuous separation among its offspring and future generations of continuous separation among its offsprings and future generation can be distinguished. In this way, race is a group of individuals who possess some similar genotypes and some general physiological characteristics on the basis of which one race may be distinguished from another. The characteristics that serve to distinguish one race from another may not necessarily be possessed by each and every member of the race. All the children of the same parents may not resemble their parents much but they resemble them more than can any other children. This is due to the genotypes that are transferred to the children from their parents.

On 18th July 1950, in a statement issued by UNESCO, it was decided to replace the word race by the term ethnic group. The original suggestion for the use of this term came from Julian Huxley, who did not subscribe to the biological concept of race. According to him, "It would be highly desirable if we could banish the question begging term race from all discussions of human affairs and substitute the non-committal phrase Ethnic."[1] Lapiere, Dawson and Gettys have also approved of the idea and have used the word. Its use is further endorsed by MacIver and Page.

And this insistence on the part of Julian Huxley is well directed. In the present day, there is no such thing as a pure race. In their treatise, *We Europeans*,

1. Huxley, J., *Concept of Race*, Harper's Magazine, Vol. 170 (1935), pp. 617-18.

Haddon and Carr Sanders have proved that there is no nation in Europe that can boast of a pure race. The concept of race has come in for some bitter criticism at the hands of M.F. Ashley, in an essay *Man's Most Dangerous Myth : The Fallacy of Race,* published by Columbia University. In his work, *The Study of Man,* Ralph Linton has written that only that race can maintain its purity whose women are so ugly and disgusting that they cannot entice men of other races to steal them, or the men of the race are so effiminate that they cannot steal women of other races, or if no other race invades the residence of this race. Hence, it is useless and unjustified to divide the human community into different races because there is no race anywhere. And it is actually true that it would be more accurate and appropriate to use the term ethnic group instead of race.

Conclusions of UNESCO

The different definition of race strike a note of discord and there is no one opinion expressed in them. Experiencing this difficulty, UNESCO arranged a conference of some prominent sociologists, anthropologists and psychologists in order to determine a single concept of race. The conference gave the following judgments concerning race :

1. Fundamentally the entire human species has one origin and all men are homo-sapiens.

2. Types of group such as national, religious, geographical, cultural, linguistic, etc., are all entirely unconnected with and unrelated to race. These groups do not give an indication of any race.

3. The difference found to exist between the physical characteristics of men is due both to heredity and to environment. Difference hereby arise due to the processes known as mutation and in-breeding.

4. Distinctions can be made between different races on the basis of differences in physical characteristics but not on the basis of cultural traits.

5. Some races make claims of purity but this is not true. Today, pure races cannot be found anywhere in the world. The process of mixing of races originated long back.

6. Human races can be classified, but these classifications are based solely on physical traits. They have no relation of any kind with mental or intellectual superiority or inferiority.

7. The inner capacity for the development of mind and culture is found equally in every race. Hence, distinctions between races cannot be based on cultural differences or level of intelligence. Intelligent people are to be found in all races.

8. It is possible that in one nation the degree of racial difference may be greater while in another nation it may be of lesser degree.

9. Evidence in support of the fact that the race has no important effect on

the social and cultural difference between various human groups has been found in historical and sociological studies. By no stretch of imagination can one conceive of any relation between racial and social changes.

10. That from the biological viewpoint, mixing of races is deleterious, is an essentially incorrect and invalid belief.

To conclude, the race is a group of inter-marrying people who are born of common ancestors, possess similar physical traits and a 'we feelings'. In-breeding renders physical characteristics of the race permanent and due to them one race may be distinguished from another. One major cause of in-breeding is geographical separation. Besides geographical isolation, a race originates due to mutation, migration, selection and adaptation also.

View of Hooton

According to Hooton, race is a "Great division of mankind, the members of which, though individually varying, are characterized as a group by certain combinations of morphological and metrical features, principally, non-adaptive, which have been derived from their common descent." Hotton has differentiated into primary and secondary races according to their mode of formation :

1. Primary races. These are "differentiated by early geographical and genetic isolation, by loss of some genes and fixation of others, by mutations, by in-breeding, and by selection."

2. Secondary races. These are formed by the stabilization of blends of two or more primary races."

Montague's View

Montague has given the genetical definition of a race. According to him, "Race is a population which differs in the frequency of some gene or genes, which is actually exchanging or capable of exchanging genes across whatever boundaries separate it from other populations of the species." In other words one man define race in an anthropological sense as "a population characterized by some concentrations, relative as to the frequency and distribution of genes or physical characters, which appear, fluctuate, and often disappear in the course of time by means of geographical and/or cultural isolation." The concept of race may be regarded as a classificatory device to provide a frame within which the different population groups may be systematically arranged.

Some Related Facts

While dealing with the definition of race one should bear in mind a few related facts. National, religious, cultural and geographical groups should not be confused with racial groups. For example, the Indians do not form a race. The Persians or the Germans are national groups. The Jews also do not form a race. They constitute a religious group like the Buddhists or the Protestants. In the anthropological sense the Dravidians or the Aryans also do not constitute race as these are only linguistic groups. Thus, a student of anthropology should be cautious in applying the term race to a particular group of people, because its use in referring to above mentioned groups may lead to a serious error.

Hybridization

The skeletal materials belonging to different periods collected from various regions of the world suggest that hybridization among different human populations has been taking place since long past. Even now race mixture is an ongoing process. The races have got admixtured. Hybridization is one of the factors for race formation and at the same time it plays role in extinction or absorption of racial groups. Therefore, one can say there was never a pure race of man and at present also there is no pure race. The concept of so-called 'pure' race is based on wrong information. Again one does not have any evidence to say that from the biological point of view rate mixture produces bad results.

While classifying human races most of the anthropologists do not consider the mental characteristics. As Klinberg has very aptly stated, "The scientist knows no relation between race and psychology." The concept of racial 'superiority' and 'inferiority' has created many problems in human society. The scientists have not accepted the view that certain races are 'superior' and others are 'inferior'.

CULTURE AND SOCIETY

Man is a social animal possessing culture. His way of life and general behaviour is determined by three factors. Firstly, his instinct which is part of his biological heritage; secondly, his personal experience and thirdly, what he learns from other members of the same group. The experience and the knowledge so acquired can be conveyed through language from generation to generation. The end result of all these thus develops into a 'culture'. As a member of the society man learns this culture. Therefore, culture is what a man does following the prescribed norm of the society. The way of life, the general behaviour and the like must have sanction of the society so that it may be considered as a part of the culture of the society. In the words of Ralph Linton, culture is 'a configuration' of learned behaviour and results of behaviour whose component elements are shared and transmitted by the members of a particular society.

A society is a group of individuals. The group may be small or large and the individuals may be related by different ways depending on many factors. The members of the society share the basic conditions of a common lice. They maintain social relations on various planes. The society transmits the cultural components of that society to the new generation. Thus, culture is transmitted through society and learnt by a member of the society. Therefore, it cannot exist or continue without society which provides the base. Thus, culture is a social legacy, while a race is a biological legacy.

RACE AND CULTURE

Now let us see if there is any relation between race and culture and if each of the various ethnic groups inclines to develop a peculiar culture of its own. Today it has been accepted that hereditary physical differences do not bring about differences in culture between the peoples. For example, Egyptian civilization started in the Neolithic age and lasted till the third century of the present era when Christianity spread over the country. The excavated materials suggest that the Neolithic culture of Egypt is the contribution of the Hamitic people. On the other hand from the beginning of the dynastic epoch one finds entirely different racial strains in addition to the earlier one. The Hyksos, the Libyans the Assyrians and the Persians came to Egypt at different intervals of time and thereby contributed various strains to the population. They were in regular intercourse with the neighbouring countries of the Near East.

Take another example. The Tungus conquered China and established a dynasty in the middle of the seventeenth century. They ruled the country at a period when a great civilization flourished. Later, the Tungus were overthrown and China favoured to go for a republic. Then, the process of socialization started and one finds a different culture in modern China.

What about the modern Scandinavian who are now a peace loving people? Are they not descendants of the Vikings who terrorized the area at one time ?

All these examples clearly suggest that the components of a culture are not due to single race. At the same time, a particular race does not necessarily practice a single culture. For example, language and religion are two major aspects of culture. We cannot conceive of an 'Aryan race' though there was an Aryan language, which is the ancestor of many languages including Ancient Greek, Latin, Sanskrit and the majority of the languages spoken in Europe today. These languages are spoken by various peoples belonging to different ethnic groups and having different cultures.

The Jews are also wrongly considered to form a race. They are not physical anthropologically recognizable, though very often one speaks of a so-called Jewish type. In respect of physical characters the Jews are undistinguishable from Germany. Nazis had to use badges to distinguish themselves from the Jews. They had to adopt the religious criterion in order to locate a Jew, as the Jews do not form a racial group but a religious one or at most a cultural group.

Meaning of Cultural Variation

Cultural variation from population to population, from society to society, does not necessarily mean superiority or inferiority of culture. The past history of a people is reflected through culture. Cultural variations may be due to several factors like their acquired experience, their scales of values. Ancient Hindus attached more values to self-control and mediation. Tibetans give more importance to the monastic life than to military organization. The Americans and Europeans are more materialistic. These may be termed as cultural specialization or 'the focus of the culture'. No culture is absolutely free from any kind of defect. In certain aspects a culture may be more complex or developed than others but in other aspects it may be defective. For example, the American

Indians had highly developed social organization. The Mayas had the concept of zero independently of the Arabs, even at a time when they had no knowledge of iron, wheel or draft animals. The Chinese created a great civilization at a time when they did not know the use of dung in agriculture. The Polynesians had a very rich mythology. The Negroes made a notable contribution to arts, but in other respects they were lagging-behind.

CULTURAL HIERARCHY

The concept of cultural hierarchy is the outcome of one's subjective analysis of the whole situation. If an element of a culture does not fit into one's cultural perspective it very often appear to be absurd. This sometimes leads to the idea of cultural superiority. Western civilization spread to different parts of the globe with the migration of the Western stock. The Western people met the natives, who had cultures quite different from their own. They looked down on the native culture. They imposed their own culture on them because they thought that their culture was superior. This is a wrong conception. Each culture has its own values and functions.

ENVIRONMENTAL FACTORS

We cannot ignore the environmental factors. Geographical isolation is a big hindrance to cultural growth and development. Deserts and thick jungles kept African Negroes out of contact with culture centres of Asia and Europe. Other peoples remained ignorant of the cultural development in Negro Africa. Contact with other people provides opportunities to accumulate experience. The civilizations of Egypt, Mesopotamia, Greek and China did not develop in isolation. To quote the celebrated anthropologist Franz Boas, "The history of mankind proves that advances of culture depend upon the opportunities presented to a social group to learn from the experience of their neighbours."

Cultural traits but not the racial strains can be acquired by one in his own life time. For example, certain populations of North-East India, have adopted Western culture. Their cultural behaviour may mislead one, but not their physical appearance. However, admixture at the biological level bring changes in the Racial types also. Racial traits are also changeable like cultural traits though the mechanism of change is not the same.

RACE AND RACISM

Homo sapiens comprise a number of races, each of which differs from the others in the relative frequency of certain heritable traits. Scientists are interested in the study of nature and extent of such variations and similarities among the various racial groups. They try to account for such inequality of human races. This sort of scientific and objective type of study of different aspects of race is entirely different from racism. Racists look at the races from a different angle of view. As Jaun Comas puts it, "Racism involves the assertion that inequality is absolute and unconditional, *i.e.*, that a race is inherently and by its very nature superior or inferior to others quite independently of the physical conditions of its habitat and of social factors." Racists believe that certain races are underdeveloped and are as such inferior to the others.

In the *Old Testament* one may come across mention of inborn inequality between individuals and groups alike. The famous Greek philosopher Aristotle was of the opinion that some peoples are by nature free from birth while others slaves. On the other hand, Cicero believed that, "Men differ in knowledge, but all are equal in ability to learn; there is no race, which guided by reason cannot obtain virtue." In human groups of different races one finds differing cultures and physiological characteristics. And usually, they marry within their own group. All these factors lead to the creation of a 'we feeling' in them, which gives rise to social consciousness. From the scientific viewpoint theory of race has been proved weak. Hoebel has rightly written that, "There is no such thing as pure race on the face of the globe today, whether there were pure races in the pre-historic past we do not know. That there never will be a pure race in the future is a certainty."[2] On similar lines, any definite correlation between physical characteristics and mental abilities has also been disproved by modern studies. For example, the idea that there is specific correlation between brains and the shape of the head has been disproved. But then, it was only on the basis of race distinction that Hitler managed to arouse a tremendous social consciousness in the people of his country in whom it took such a strong hold that it has not been completely wiped out even today.

In fact, the concept of race continues from generation to generation. Even today, it would not be difficult to locate some people in India who believe in the purity and superiority of the Aryan race. In Hindus inter-marriage between people of different castes is forbidden only because of this race distinction. The idea of race has a direct and strong influence on the behaviour of the individual. In India, the Arya Samaj has made efforts to revive the ancient Aryan culture, inspired by the notion of Aryan superiority, be it true or a fallacious concept.

The relation between the nation of race and social consciousness can be easily understood by the example of Negros who live in the Western countries. It is because of racial discrimination, though unconstitutional, that Negroes are deprived of their fundamental rights such as the use of Hotels, Restaurants and Schools. In certain places they have even no right to vote and to occupy any responsible position in the government institutions. In this way, one finds serious and important differences, in the living standards, facilities, privileges, etc., of the whites and the blacks on the basis of race. It is undeniable that this distinction and discrimination does not lessen whatever truth there is in race but it does influence the personalities and social institutions of the whites and the blacks. Both of the two groups look upon themselves as belonging to different races, and the social consciousness that they develop conforms to this notion of basic differences.

---

2. Hoebel, *Man in the Primitive World*, p. 73.

In this way, then, even though the concept of race lacks any scientific basis, it plays an important role in developing social consciousness.

ARYANISM

William Jones was the first person to extract the word Arya from its Sanskrit background and introduce it to the European languages where Aryan came to denote all Aryan languages. Later on, Max Muller used this same term for a specific group of languages. Max Muller's investigations proved that with the exception of Bask, Magyar and Finnish languages, all other European languages belong to the family of Sanskrit of India and the language of Iran. These languages were then given the name Aryan or Indo-European languages. One the basis of this similarity of languages, the existence of a common race was imagined which was called the Arya race. This theory was given its scientific form in Count Joseph De Gobineau's essay, *The Inequality of Human Races*. This essay was an attempt to prove and to establish the superiority of the Aryan race. It was elevated to its highest pinnacle by Lapouge. Indians, Greeks and Romans who spoke the Aryan languages in the past gave rise to the most highly evolved cultures and civilizations. In the following centuries, the European Aryan races made great scientific progress, on the basis of which it was believed that the rise of civilization is particularly related to the Aryan race. No two races are identical in respect of qualities, and neither are the equal. It is the Aryan race that can develop the best civilization. In this way, the object of Aryanism was the deficiation of the ancestors and the establishment of the superiority of particular race.

NORDICISM

In Europe every country did its best to modify Aryanism and to assimilate it into its own national history. Nordicism is also one form of it. It was called Teutonicism in Germany, Anglo-Saxonism in England and Gallicism in France. Nordicism aimed at the emancipation and praise of the culture qualities of the extinct Nordic race. According to it, only the Nordic race is capable of ruling the world. It is the most superior in civilization. It is also the most superior in physiological and mental characteristics. It is the race that will prove to be the strongest and the best equipped to face the struggle of life. According to Nordicism, the race lose their power of generating a civilization when they intermix and a threat to civilization becomes imminent. The actual or real Aryan race is represented by the Dolichocephalic or white-skinned, tall and long-headed people. They were called Nordic because they lived in North Nord. All the best artists, philosophers and politicans of ancient Greece and Rome were claimed lo be Nordic. It was said that all the great historic figures, beginning with Jesus Christ, Mohammed, right down to Changez Khan, had Nordic blood in their veins. The Nazis went a step further and declared the Teutonic race, among all the Nordic races, as the most superior and accomplished race in the world. After 1933, when Hitler had come into power Nordicism was at its prime, with the result that it led to the complete extermination and mass eradication of millions of Jews. In 1938, when Mussolini signed a treaty with Hitler, he thought it fit to declare that the Italians were the only true Aryans. In his work *'Foundations of the Nineteenth Century'*, Houstan Steward Chamberlain staunchly supported the inseparability of the Aryan and Teutonic races. This principle had been further elaborated by Stoddard in his book *The Rising Tide of Coloured and Racial Realities in Europe.*

Is the White Race Superior to Other Races?

Scientific investigations have finally and conclusively rejected the myth of the superiority of the white race. The following arguments are advanced to establish that the white race is not superior to the other races:

1. White race is not mentally superior. Modern scientific tests have established that no race is superior of any other in respect of mental ability. In his *Scientific Aspects of the Race Problem,* Klinberg, in the essay entitled 'Mental Testing in Racial and National Groups', has proved the thesis that difference in the intelligence quotient obtained by intelligence tests is due to environmental differences rather than the result of racial difference. The intelligence quotient of a nine year old Negro girl was found to be 200, twice the normal or average. Similarly, it was found that the intelligence quotient of North American Negroes was higher than that of the Negroes settled in the Southern countries because there were better educational facilities in the North. The intelligence quotients of the American Indians and the ordinary Americans were found to differ because of the dissimilar environment.

2. White race is not superior in culture. The proponents of Nordicism and Aryanism assume one or the other European race to be the most superior and then they believe it to be the founder of all the cultures of the world, but history provides the evidence of the fact that at a time when the European races were still in the barbaric stage, the civilization of India and China was at its zenith, and things such as dynamite, paper and the magnetic needle had been invented. Hence, the principle of the cultural superiority of any race is completely at variance with historical facts.

3. No race can claim purity. Modern scientific discoveries have deprived the idea of pure blood of its last vestige of respect. All races are found to possess the same blood groups. Blood has no relation with heredity, and the concept of superiority of blood is a mere figment of imagination. There is no pure race in the world today. In India one finds a mixture of the Negroid, proto-Australoid, Mediterranean, Dravida, Mongol, Iranian, Shak, Kushan, Pahalava, Hun, Arabic, Moghul, Afghan and East European races. Despite the tremendous disturbances on the basis of colour distinctions, there is considerable mixing of the white and dark skinned races in the U.S.A.

From the above arguments it is evident that the white race is in no way superior to other races in respect of intellectual or cultural attainments.

Fallacies of Racism

Hence, racism is unjustified. The principle of racism is faulty in many respects, the main ones being the following :

1. Confusing race with culture. In these theories, culture has been confused with race. It has also been assumed in these theories that the emancipation or downfall of culture is dependent exclusively upon race. This assumption has no logical ground. In fact, race does not influence culture or civilization. The same race sometimes reaches the pinnacle or its civilization and cultural development while at other times it falls back completely, and culture and civilization are lost. This cycle of rise and fall in culture can be seen in the cultural history of the Indo-Aryan race and in the rise and fall of the Arabian culture. Racial elements play little or no part in this rise or fall. In fact, race is neither the basis of culture nor one of its more important factors. Culture is a social phenomenon while race is a physiological or biological factor. The elements of culture are poetry, art, philosophy, customs, institutions, languages, etc., none of which is concerned with racial elements. Culture spreads through cultural contact but race cannot spread in a different area without actual crossing.

2. Interpreting language as a characteristic of race. Another defect in these principles is that language is treated as a characteristic of race. In fact, language and race have no relation. It is improper to imagine that the Aryan languages would be spoken exclusively by the Aryan race or those with Aryan blood. Despite the fact that English is an Aryan language, there are approximately twelve million Negroes in America who speak no language other than English. History records repeated incidents in which the victorious nation foisted its own language upon the vanquished people. There are also incidents in which it is the victor who had adopted the language of the vanquished nations. The truth of the matter lies in the fact that language is a part of culture and it can be learnt by any individuals of any race. It cannot be associated with race.

3. Identifying race with nationality. In these views, race has been identified with nationality. Race and nation are two different and distinct concepts. According to Huxley and Huddon, nationality is specific aspects of the development of classes among men. Many different racial elements can be admixed in the organization of a nation. In an entire nation, There can be only one racial element, and there can also be numerous racial elements resulting from their mixture. Race can be physical or material element of the nation. Nation is a social concept while race is a genetic concept. Nation has a geographical limit while race has no specific limits. Nation is created with a view to attaining some definite purposes. The creation of the race is the outcome of natural processes. Nation is subjective; it is impossible without a national psychological oneness. Race is objective since it is based on common physiological characteristics. Briefly, nation and race are not attributes of one another.

4. Imagination of a pure race. These principles also imagine the existence of a pure race a concept that is entirely unrealistic. In fact, there is no pure race such as the Nordic or any other race. In his book *We Europeans,* Car Sanders Huxley and Huddon have proved that there is no European nation in which there is any pure race. There is not race that can scientifically be proved pure.

Briefly, then, the principle of racism is completely lacking in any rational basis. The civilizations of ancient Egypt, Cambodia, China, Mesopotamia and Mexico were evolved neither by the Nordics nor by the Aryans. Two thousand years ago when the Nordic race had yet to cross the barbaric stage the great civilization of Rome was at the height of its development. And in the most advanced nations of the modern world France, America, Germany and Italy, Britain and India, there has been almost a complete mixing of the various human groups. In the modern age no scientist worth the name accepts the validity of the concept of race which is a harmful and baseless principle.

Admixture of Races

Racists are opposed to racial admixture in order to keep the racial groups in pure state. But race crossing has been taking place from the prehistoric past. As such there is no so-called 'pure race' today, all are more or less admixtured groups. At one time it was thought that blood is the carrier of hereditary traits. But now blood has nothing to do with hereditary transmission, it has been realized that children's blood may be different from the parents.

Very ably summing up certain facts as regarding race crossing Juan Comas has stated that miscegeneration process starts since the dawn of human life. It helps in producing a greater somatic and psychic variability. New genetic combinations emerge as a result of race mixture. In biological sense miscegeneration is neither good nor bad. Its effect is dependent on various aspects of the populations involved in this process. It is demonstrable that, "The great majority of areas of high civilization are inhabited by obviously cross-bred group. Thus, the idea of the inferiority or superiority of the cross-breeds is not tenable."

Colour of skin is another factor which is very much associated with racism. The racists consider the white people superior. Coloured people are inferior to them. This conception is meaningless. Physical characters including the brain of the whites and coloured people were studied by many doctors and anthropologists. It has been found that a brain of a coloured man is indistinguishable from that of a white one. The weight or volume of brain has nothing to do with the intellectual attainment of an individual or a group though whites are different from the coloured, as regards physical traits the differences do not mean superiority or inferiority.

In discussing racism two populations are very often referred. One is Jew and the other is Aryan. The Aryans are considered to be superior people. The Nazi regime of Germany wanted to exterminate the entire Jew population of Germany to constitute a superior pure Aryan race. However, the Jews do not form a racial group. They are racially heterogeneous. For example, the Jews of

Spanish origin are dolichocephalic, whereas the Jews of Russian origin are brachycephalic. The 'Jewish race' is a misnomer. Jews form a cultural group, on the other hand, the Aryan is a linguistic group. Max Muller has rightly staled that, "To me an enthologist who speaks of Aryan race, Aryan blood, Aryan eyes and hair, is as great sinner as a linguist who speaks of a dolichocephalic dictionary or a brachycephalic grammar."

In this way, it will be demonstrable that racial prejudice is based on certain wrong conceptions. The concept of purity of blood and of the inferiority of cross-breeds is a myth. So is the colour prejudice. Racism is based on certain dangerous myths. Nobody should encourage this sort of subjective assessment of racial group.

FORMATION OF RACIAL GROUPS

Race formation is a complex process in which the following factors are involved:

1. Mutation. It is important process by which different forms of characters are produced. Mutation be defined as the sudden though permanent change in a particular gene producing a new form of an old character. As soon as a new mutant gene appears, it multiplies from one generation to another and becomes a distinctive characteristic of the particular population, provided other conditions are favourable.

2. Adaptive Genes. Some genes are more adaptive than others to certain conditions of life. For example, skin colour and nose form are adaptive characters having selected value. With a few exception, dark-skinned people are concentrated in the regions of hot moist climatic conditions, while concentration of the light-skinned people may be seen in cold dry climatic regions. This is so because dark skin protects the body from the actinic rays of the sun. On the other hand, white skin is the best for keeping the heat of the body. Similarly broad noses and narrow noses have selective values. Broad-nosed Negroes can easily inhale hot air without causing harm to their systems. In cold dry country where cold air is injurious, a narrow nose is required to make the inhaled cold air warm while passing through the nose.

3. Natural Selection. Suppose the earliest men had light skin colour. As a result of mutation appeared some more colours, say, dark or yellow skin. As dark skin has some advantages over other shades of skin in hot moist climatic region, for example, in equatorial Africa, that colour adapted itself to that particular environment, or in other words, it was selected by Nature. This is the process of *Natural Selection.* The advantageous genes multiply more rapidly than the disadvantageous genes as the latter are eliminated by Nature. Thus, that particular group of people will form a dark-skinned population. Under different sets of conditions, other shades of skin colour were selected by Nature. In the same manner different hereditary characters became distinctive features of the different population.

This is how mutation and selection the two main biological processes worked in the early development of races. Another process sometimes works in shaping a particular combination of genes. This is *accidental or chance fluctuations* or accidental loss or fixation of gene of genes, or *genetic drift*. This is more effective in a partially or fully isolated small population than in a larger one where it is of limited importance. In this process, increase or decrease of the frequency of a gene in a certain population does not depend upon advantageous or disadvantageous conditions of life in a particular locality. It happens merely as an accident of chance. The different frequencies of gene for tasting or not tasting PTC in different populations are a good example of accidental fluctuation on genes.

4. The fourth factor is migration. It has played an important role in racial differentiation. It helped in isolation and also in hybridization or mixing of different populations. Groups of people migrated in different directions from the common centre, and became isolated from one another.

5. Isolation. Isolation, geographical or social, is considered to be a great race-maker. The above-mentioned biological processes more particularly selection and genetic drift, act properly only when a particular population is isolated from the neighbouring populations. Otherwise in a certain populations mutation may produce new characters, out of which, say, one will be selected by Nature. Suppose that character is blue eye. Before blue eye becomes the distinctive character of that population some genes responsible for brown eye may also be introduced into that population by others, if the former one is not an isolated group. This process of adding of new genes may be continued, resulting in different shades of eye colour, none being distinctive of the population. Similarly, accidental fluctuation of gene will not be able to produce a new distinctive genetic character, if the population is not isolated.

People migrated in groups, where new traits appeared through mutation. Being selected by Nature some of the traits became adaptive to particular sets of conditions of life thus forming new gene pools. As the isolation became greater and inter-marriage between the groups less possible, the new genes multiplied themselves. These were transmitted from generation to generation by the process of heredity resulting in new racial groups.

6. Hybridization. Hybridization of mixing of different populations may also lead to the formation of new races. For example, the Anglo-Indians have been formed by the intermixture of Europeans and Indians. The mingling of Americans and Negroes has produced a new racial population. This process of race-making is still going on. Isolation plays the most important part in hybridization.

7. Sexual selection. By sexual selection is meant the process of selecting mates on the basis of some preferred qualities. In course of time the sexually preferred type would become the dominant variety of the population. For example, in a population where brown eye-colour was preferred to blue colour, the blue coloured individuals would get lesser and lesser number of mates. Ultimately the gene for blue eye might be eliminated by this process. Or the blue-eyed would marry blue-eyed and the brown-eyed would marry brown-eyed. In that case two distinct types would be formed. Such a sexual selection is in process in America where the dark Negro males prefer females with lighter complexion.

8. Social selection. Social selection may be defined as the method of regulation of marriage between artificially divided socially approved groups within a population. It helps in isolating mechanism. In course of time it results in considerable modifications in a population.

8

Criteria of Racial Classification

Racial Criteria

Racial classifications are made on the basis of certain genetic traits referred to as racial criteria. The racial criteria should fulfil certain requirements. Boyd suggested following important requirements which should be satisfied by criteria chosen for racial classification :

1. Objective. A Criterion must be objective, so that different investigators do not show individual variation in identifying and classifying the concerned traits.

2. Non-adaptive. A criterion should be non-adaptive, so that natural selection cannot play effective role.

3. Unmodified. A criterion should not be modified to a large extent by environmental factor.

4. Not subject to high mutation. A criterion should not be subject to a high rate of mutation, so that the nature of the trait does not alter frequently, otherwise the frequency of the trait in a population may show considerable variation from time to time.

5. Controlled by known genetic mechanism. A criterion should be controlled by a known genetic mechanism. It is always better if the mechanism is simple.

Categories of Criteria

The criteria chosen for human classification may be divided into three different categories as follows:

1. Common variable characters. The heredity mechanism of these is not simple and therefore not very perfectly known. For example, skin colour, nose form, face, etc. Some of these characters are noted by visual observation such as hair colour, nasal bridge, etc. Some others are observed with the help of instruments. For example, cross-section of hair is observed under microscope. Still other require careful measurements by instruments, specially devised for the purpose.

2. Common physiological characters. The genetic process of these traits are quite well known. Some of these traits are ABO blood group, MN blood type, etc.

3. Rare genetic characters. Test reaction to phenyl-thio-carbomide (PTC), colour blindness, abnormal traits of human blood, etc., are rare genetic characters which occur in low frequencies.

Important characters used for racial determination:

(1) Skin colour

(2) Hair

(3) Head form

(4) Face

(5) Nose

(6) Eye

(7) Stature

(8) Blood Groups

(9) Dermatoglyphics.

SKIN COLOUR

Broadly speaking, three shades of skin colour are found in man; the following classification may be made on that basis:

(i) *Leucoderms or white-skinned people.* It does not include Europeans only. It also includes most of the Western Asiatics, North Africans and Polynesians, where skin colour varies from pinkish white to tawny-white or light brown. Within this group the brown-skinned peoples are also included such as Hamites Indo-Dravidians, etc.

(ii) *Xanthoderms of yellow-skinned people.* Asiatic Mongoloids are the best representatives of this class where a yellowish tinge is always present in the skin colour. Besides them some Amerinds, Bushmen and Hottentots also show a yellowish touch in their skin colours.

(iii) *Melanoderms of black-skinned people.* The Negroids fall in this division. Some are really black, others are dark chocolate brown, some others again show variations in colour. Papuans, Melanesians, pre-Dravidians, Australians, etc., may also be included in this group.

Causes and Value of Skin Colour

Putting in one group does not necessarily mean any genetic relationship. For example, though Australian aborigines and African Negroes may have similar skin colour they are not in any way nearer to one another than either is to the leucoderms or xanthoderms.

In the deeper layer of the epidermis lie various granules which make the skin pigmented. Thus, the colour of skin varies with the varying frequencies of the granules. These variations protect the melanoderms from the actinic rays of the sun and the leucoderms from cold. In the Old World, at least in the northern hemisphere but not in the New World, a concentration of the darker skinned people is seen in the equatorial regions, while the fairer peoples live away from it. However, this association of various shades of skin with geographic and climatic conditions should not be generalised. For example, the dark-skinned Negroes of Congo basin, pale yellow-skinned Punan of Borneo and cinnamon-coloured people of Amazon Valley live under more or less similar geographical conditions.

Sunlight and specially ultra-violet rays have direct effect on skin colour. When sun-rays are allowed to fall directly on the skin, the epidermal cells get stimulated to produce more granules, making the skin more pigmented, Therefore, many people believe that Negroes acquired their skin colour from the inherent effect of hot sun. However, that was not the case. One can assume that the earliest men had neither black nor white skin but of intermediate shade that may be brown or yellow-brown. At this state the genes for skin colour were changed by mutation producing varieties of skin colour. Those who were best protected from the sun-rays were selected by nature and thus, gradually became dominant and outlived the rest. Sexual selection also played its role to accelerate the process, which ultimately made that particular group of people black-skinned. As this phenomenon happened in other parts of the world, other colours were also produced.

HAIR

According to some anthropologists, the most convenient and striking character which provides the basis for a primary classification of present day races, is hair. The following characteristics of hair are worth considering :

(1) ***Form***. The characteristics types with numerous intermediaries of hair forms are recognized. They are the following:

(i) *Leiotrichous or smooth form.* It may again be divided into : (a) *stretched* — hair is usually straight, coarse and stiff; (b) *smooth* — hair is thinner and soft; (c) *flat wavy* — hair with a tendency to become wavy. Mongoloid races are remarkable for this type of hair.

(ii) *Cymotrichous or wavy form.* This form is characteristics of many peoples of Western Asia, North-Eastern Africa, Europe, etc. In other words, the members of the White race (*e.g.* Mediterranean, Alpine, Nordic, etc.) show this type of hair. This type occurs in secondary races of hybridized origin also. Wavy form may be: (a) *broad wavy* — waves are broad and lie in one plane; (b) *narrow wavy* — short, strongly curved waves lying in one plane; (c) *curly* — large spirals, no lying in one plane.

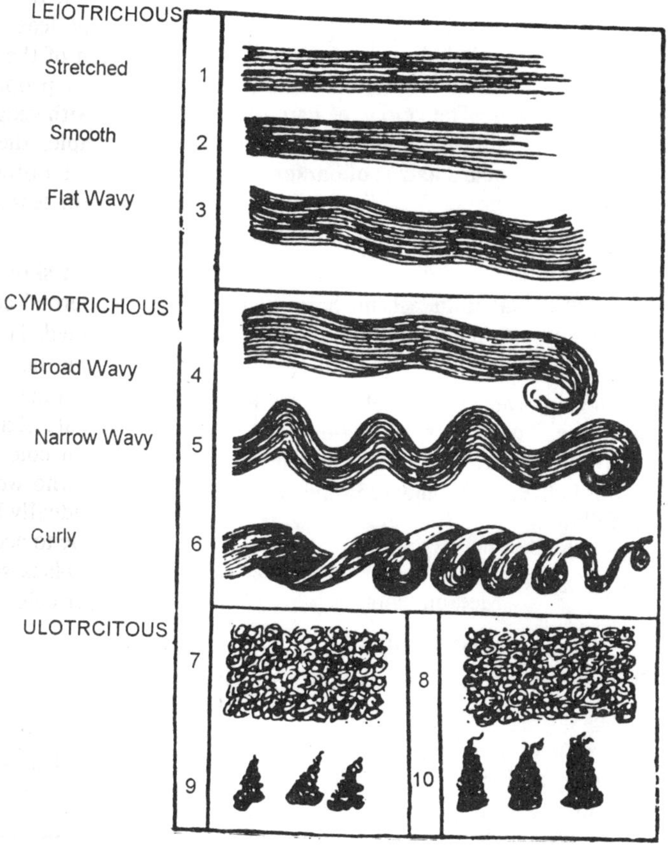

Fig. 8.1. Hair Form

(iii) *Ulotrichous of woolly form*. Negroes, Negrillos, Negritos, Papuans, Melanesians, Bushmen, etc., possess Ulotrichous hair. This type shows a considerable range of variation, *e.g.* — (a) frizzly hair with short, deep waves which does not form a complete spiral. Frizzly hair is longer than woolly hair. (b) *Filfil,* the so-called pepper-corn hair of the Bushmen where small knots of thick rolled hairs appear to be separated by bare spaces.

Ulotrichous hair is seen under warm moist climatic conditions; leiotrichous under dry cold conditions and cymotrichous under the intermediate conditions. Thus, climatic conditions have some indirect influence on the character of the hair.

There may be some relationship between curvature of hair and head on moisture. Some scholars suppose that Negroid hair is an adaptation to the moist tropical country. Here, it may be pointed out that Mongoloids of the tropical region do not show ulotrichous hair. Again, white people living in tropical zones do not appear to produce more curved hair.

(2) ***Colour of hair***. The colour of hair shows a wide range of variation specially in Europe and parts of Northern Asia. For example among the Mediterraneans hair is of darker colour while in Northern Europe it is lighter ranging from light brown to reddish colour. Dark hair is common everywhere. It may show brownish or reddish tinge in some parts.

Environmental influence on hair colour does not seem remarkable. Change in colour with age is an important phenomenon which should be noted.

(3) ***Texture of hair.*** Texture of hair may be — (i) coarse, (ii) medium, or (iii) fine. For proper estimation of thickness of hair a microscopic study should be made. Garn found that thickness of human hair varies between 25μ and 125μ and he made an arbitrary classification as follows:

Fine hair	— 56μ
Medium hair	57—84.μ
Coarse hair	85μ+

The Chinese and the Japanese, two members of the Mongoloid race possess coarse hair. The Whites show medium hair.

(4) ***Quantity of hair***. The quantity of hair is described as (i) scanty medium, and (ii) rich body hair and beard and moustache are also noted in observing quantity of head hair. Hair are sparsely distributed in face and body in Mongoloids and Negroids. White races show rich quantity of body and face hair.

(5) ***Hair whorl.*** The whorls on the occiput of the head are also observed. The whorls may be of two types — clockwise, and anti-clockwise. Usually, one whorl occurs but double whorls are also not very rare. Three or more whorls are found very rarely. As regards inheritance of this character the clockwise hair is dominant over anti-clockwise.

(6) ***Cross-section of hair***. Two types of cross-section of human head hair are so far known. They are (i) circular and oval, or (ii) elliptical. Circular cross-section is usually met with the Mongoloids possessing straight hair while oval type occurs in the ulotrichous hair of Negroids and in the other form of hair.

Considerable value attributed to the cross-section of hair as a racial criterion has been rejected as the recent studies have shown that both oval or circular cross-section may occur in the same head.

(7) ***Other hair characters.*** To these it may be added that the weight of hair, the longitudinal study of hair characters and some other characters are also taken into consideration in studying hair as a racial criterion.

HEAD FORM

Head Index. No part of the human body has been so thoroughly studied by anthropologists as the head. Head is readily measurable. It is relatively independent of environmental fluctuations. Hence, it is a very important character which can be used as a racial criterion. When looked at from above the skull presents varieties of contour like oval, pentagonal, long, narrow, etc. These descriptions of head are not suitable for comparison and statistical treatment. Therefore, the head is measured and the index is calculated. Index is the ratio of the maximum breadth to the maximum length, the latter being taken as 100. Accordingly, the head is classified into (i) dolichocephalic (narrow), (ii) mesocephalic (medium), and (iii) brachycephalic (broad) groups. Measurements are taken on the head of the living as well as on the skull. In the former the ratio is termed the cephalic index (C.I.) while in the latter the cranial index (C.I.). The index is roughly two units higher on the head of the living than on the skull.

Meaning of Index

Thus, the cranial or cephalic index does not give any idea of the contour or real form of the skull; it merely expresses the relation of the breadth to the length.

$$\text{Length — Breadth Index (C.I.)} = \frac{\text{Breadth of Head} \times 100}{\text{Length of Head}}$$

Classification of Head Form

According to Martin, Head form may be classified as follows :

1.	Hyperdolichocephalic (very long and narrow)	— 69.9
2.	Dolichocephalic (long and narrow)	70.0 — 75.9
3.	Mesocephalic (medium)	76.0 — 80.9
4.	Brachycephalic (short or broad)	81.0 — 85.5
5.	Hyperbrachycephalic (very short and broad)	85.6 —

Calculation of Head Form

The height of head is also measured to find out its relations to the length and the breadth, which are expressed in the length-height and breadth-height indices respectively. According to Martin, the classification of head in respect of these two indices are as follows :

1. $$\text{Length-Height Index} = \frac{\text{Auricular Head Height} \times 100}{\text{Head Length}}$$

Classes	Ranges
(i) Chamaeocephal	— 57.6
(ii) Orthocephal	57.7 — 62.5
(iii) Hypsicephal	62.6 —

2. Breadth-Height Index = $\frac{\text{Auricular Head Height} \times 100}{\text{Head Length}}$

Classes	*Ranges*
(i) Tapeinocephal	— 78.9
(ii) Metriocephal	79.0 — 84.9
(iii) Acrocephal	85.0 —

Ranging from very long to very broad head form occurs in all the three primary races, namely, Mongoloid, Negroid and Caucasoid. However, it is seen that in Mongoloids dolichocephaly is comparativey rare. In Negroids brachycephaly is comparatively rare. In Caucasoids none of the head forms appear to be very predominant.

Human knowledge of palaeontology and available data suggest that early man was generally dolichocephalic. Brachycephaly developed later as a result of repeated mutations and various other factors.

Mendelian Law

As regards its hereditary nature, it has been stated that the development of the shape of the skull is controlled by the Mendelian laws of inheritance. However, the process is complicated as various factors are involved in the characterization of the skull.

Modification of Head Form

Head form is modified to some extent by some environmental factors. For example, as is evident from artificial deformation of the head practised by some American Indian tribal folks prolonged pressure by means of a special device may result into a permanent change in the shape of the head. Malnutrition may also bring some changes in the form of the head, as has been shown by Prof. A. Ivanovsky's works among some populations of Southern Russia.

Dr. H.L. Shapiro found that among the Hawiian-born offspring of Japanese immigrants the head became shorter and broader. Boas found modifications in the head form of the children of European immigrants into the United States. It is believed that head form is related to stature at least in part. Sexual variation is another factor which is also to be considered.

Head Height

As regards head height it is difficult to get accurate measurement of it in the living. It shows a wide range of individual variations. Apart from these, available data on height indices are too meagre and incomplete to come to any definite conclusion as regards its importance as a racial criterion.

FACE

Shape of the Face. The shape of the face is generally described as oval, round, square or pentagonal, but it is better expressed in terms of the relation of the breadth of the face to its length. The length is measured from nasion (upper end of internasal stature where it meets the frontal bone) to gnathion (lowest point of the mandible in the median plane). The greatest breadth is obtained across the check bones.

Facial Index. The facial index is the length expressed as a percentage of the breadth. The facial index tells us whether the face is broad, medium or narrow. A classification is given below:

$$\text{Morphological Facial Index} = \frac{\text{Morphological Facial Length} \times 100}{\text{Bizygomatic Breadth}}$$

(1) Hyper euryprosopic (very broad face)	...		— 78.9
(2) Euryprosopic (broad face)	...	— 79.0	— 83.9
(3) Mesoprosopic (medium face)	...	— 84.0	— 87.9
(4) Leptoprosopic (narrow face)	...	— 88.0	— 92.9
(5) Hyper leptoprosopic (very narrow face)	...	— 93.0	

Face and Cranium

1. Harmonic. A broad face is usually associated with broad cranium. Similarly, a narrow face is associated with a long narrow cranium. When this condition is fulfilled a skull is termed harmonic. But this is not always the case, as is seen among the Armenoids, who possess long and relatively narrow faces, associated with short and relatively broad cranium. A similar combination of face and cranium is found among the French Basques also.

2. Disharmonic. On the other hand, a long head and broad face occur in Cro-Magnon type and among the Eskimos. This condition is described as disharmonic.

Prognathism.

Prognathism is the protrusion of the jaw. When the face does not show any protusion it is called orthognathism. Prognathism is present in marked degree among the Negroes and Australians. They also usually exhibit projection of the alveolar margins of the upper and lower jaws which is termed *alveolar prognathism.* The other type is *called facial prognathism.* There may be little or no facial prognathism among most of the Mongoloids and some white peoples, but they show slight or moderate of alveolar prognathism.

Value of facial Index

Though, the face is considered to be a racial criterion it cannot always be used extensively for purposes of racial discrimination, as the facial index is affected by some factors, such as sex, age, function, etc. Females almost invariably possess shorter and comparatively broader faces than the males of the same ethnic group.

Causes of Variation

Facial index shows considerable variation along with the changes of age. Again functional variation is also to some extent responsible for various type of face. Apart from these, hereditary nature of the different forms of face, *e.g.*, short, broad, long, narrow, etc., is also not perfectly known.

NOSE

Forms of Nose. The nose is important criterion used for purposes of racial classification. It is very complicated in the living beings as its various parts are to be simply described in the absence of any practicable method of measurement. The different parts, generally noted, are : the root of nose which may be broad or narrow. The bridge may be low (platyopic), medium (mesopic) or broad (prosopic). When seen in profile the nasal root may be depressed or otherwise. Depression may be shallow, medium or deep. The bridge is that portion of nose, which extends from below the nasion to the tip of the nose. The bridge, in profile, may be straight, concave, convex, or concavoconvex. The tip of the nose may be bluntly rounded or sharply pointed, thick or thin. The nasal septum may be horizontal, directed downwards or directed upwards. Again the alae of nose may be thin and compressed, broad and flaring or intermediate.

Nasal Index

The proportion of the nose, particularly its breadth in relation to its length, is found out by actual measurements. In the living person the length of nose measured from the nasion (point where the internasal suture meets the frontal bone) to the subnasale (meeting point of the septum and the upper lip). In the nasal index, the breadth is expressed as a percentage of the length. Again on the skull the length is measured from the nasion to the naso-spinale (the point where a line drawn tangent of the two lateral curves of the lower margin of the aperture crossing the median line). The greatest breadth is measured at right angle to the median plane, within the lateral margins of the nasal aperture.

Classification of Nasal Index

As the two nasal indices do not correspond closely to one another, they are only relatively comparable.

$$\textit{Nasal Index} = \frac{\text{Nasal breadth} \times 100}{\text{Nasal length}}$$

Classification (of living) on skull

(1) Hyperleptorrhine (Very narrow nose)	...	— 54.9	
(2) Leptorrhine (Narrow nose)	...	55.0 — 69.9	— 47

(3) Mesorrhine (Medium nose)	...	70.0 — 84.9	47 — 51
(4) Platyrrhine or Chamaerrhine (Broad nose)	...	85.0 — 99.9	51 — 58
(5) Hyperplatyrrhine (Very broad nose)	...	100.0—	

The native Australians have markedly platyrrhine nose. The Negro nose is also broad and short. Among the various Mongoloid peoples, the nasal index is frequently mesorrhine. Leptorrhine nose is characteristics of the Caucasoid peoples of Asia, North Africa and Europe. Haddon writes, "Speaking generally, the leucoderms are Leptorrhine, the xanthoderms mesorrhine (but the Eskimos are Leptorrhine) and the melanoderms platyrrhine." For example, it may be stated that the general Negro nose is short and very broad with a slightly depressed root, straight or concave bridge, thick bulbous tip and very thick, flaring alae. The Australian nose differs from the Negro type in having more deeply depressed root. The typical Mediterranean nose is leptorrhine, with a bridge which is straight and of medium height; the root is rather narrow, the wings compressed or of medium spread. The Nordic nose is higher, longer and narrower with pinched wings.

Wide Range of Sexual Variation

The nasal index shows a wide range of sexual variation. The females show a tendency to have broader and shorter nose than the males of the same people. Age is another factor to be noted as almost all children are platyrrhine but they become less so, or more Leptorrhine with age.

Role of Natural Selection

Many anthropologists believe that natural selection has an important part to play in narrowing or widening nasal apertures. The people with broad nose and wide nostrils who live under hot moist conditions, can snuff great quantities of comparatively warm and moist air without causing any harm to the linings of the respiratory organs. On the other hand, in dry cold country a high narrow nose charged with blood is required to warm the inhaled air as it passes through. Thus, the Arctic Eskimos have very Leptorrhine nose while the equatorial Negroes possess very platyrrhine nose.

Effect of Climate

Thompson and Buxton have shown that there is a very close relation between the average nasal index of a particular group of people and the average temperatures and average relatives humidities of that particular place where live. Of course, there are always some exceptions.

Hereditary Impact

As regards the hereditary nature of the different characters of nose it is stated that the data available are not adequate to give any conclusive remarks on the subject.

EYE

Hooton has distinguished only two sharply contrasted varieties of eyes in modern man — the Mongoloid eye and the non-Mongoloid eye.

1. **The Mongoloid Eye.** In typical Mongoloid eye the palpebral fissure is oblique, the outer angle being higher than the inner angle. The slit or opening of the eye is narrow. The inner epicanthus (epicanthic) or complete Mongoloid fold is present in varying degrees of development.

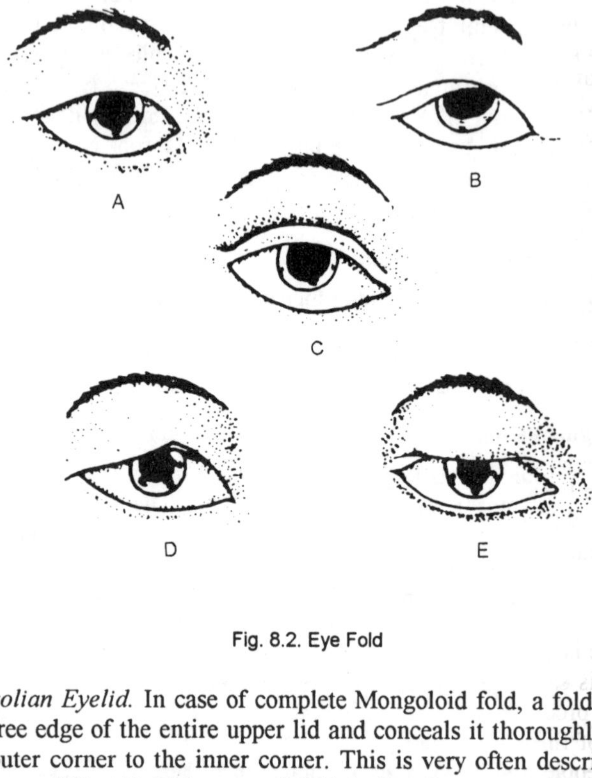

Fig. 8.2. Eye Fold

Mongolian Eyelid. In case of complete Mongoloid fold, a fold skin hangs over the free edge of the entire upper lid and conceals it thoroughly extending from its outer corner to the inner corner. This is very often described as 'the Mongolian eyelid'. (A) This type of fold is found to occur in different age groups, *i.e.*, in the young, the middle-aged and the old.

Mongoloid Fold. A very common variety of eye fold is inner epicanthus or epicanthic or simply ''Mongoloid fold'' where the fold covers the free edge of the inner angle of the eye and may extend on to the cheek. This inner epicanthus starts on the inner or medial part of the upper lid. This type of fold is very common in infants and children and also in the females. Thus, it shows variations with age and sex (B).

External Epicanthus. Another variety of eye-fold is the external epicanthus. It starts on the middle part of the upper lid and extends below the outer portion of the upper lid covering the outer corner of the eye. It is observed more frequently in the middle-aged and elderly adult males (D).

Sometimes a fold of skin hangs over the middle part of the upper lid covering the edge of that region. This type of fold is termed as median or cover fold. In this case both inner and outer corners of eye remain uncovered (E).

Detailed studies on the occurrence and nature of eye-fold have shown that it may be divided into a number of divisions and sub-divisions besides the four main varieties described above.

As the name implies 'the Mongoloid eye' is found among the Mongoloid peoples and peoples having Mongoloid admixture. Typical characteristic of it is shown in varying degree by the different Mongoloid peoples. It is believed that complete Mongoloid or inner epicanthic fold has some Mongoloid racial significance, while the two other varieties appear to be associated with age factor.

The eye-fold is occasionally present in some African Negroes, specially in the Bushment and Hottentots also.

2. Non-Monogoloid Eye. The typical 'non-Mongoloid eye' is wide open and straight. The eye-fold is not observed. This is found to occur in the members of the white racial stock (C).

PIGMENTATION OF IRIS

The pigmentation of the iris is also an important feature noted for racial study. It shows a wide range of variation. It may be black, darkbrown, light brown, blue brown, grey brown, green brown, blue or gray. Greatest range of variation is observed among the leucoderms. The Negroids and the Mongoloids generally show dark brown iris.

STATURE

Stature is an important variable character. It deserves careful consideration because it is said that environment has an obvious effect on stature. Different results are produced under varied environmental conditions. An unfavourable condition of life may temporarily make a people undeveloped. But the same group of people may show increase in stature when subjected to improved and favourable conditions as has been seen in the case of Limousine district of France and the Yupa Indians of Venezuela. Martin has demonstrated that the German youth showed stunted stature being undernourished during First World War and post-War periods. Thus, stature is notably influenced by general nutritive conditions and the internal secretions of some glands like pituitary, thymus and gonads. Experiments on animals have revealed that unequal body size are found when the animals are treated under different conditions. This may be also applicable to man.

In his study of Japanese immigrants into Hawaii Shapiro has found an increase of stature under different environmental conditions. Among the Kannikars, Thurston found that the stature increased in the case of domesticated Kannikars as compared from that of the jungle Kannikars. Sarkar noticed an increase of stature from the Hill Male stage to the Plains Males. A similar increase of stature was seen among the Garos. The Plains Garos are taller than the Hill Garos. Torday found that certain Congo pygmies left their forest country and led a settled life practising agriculture. After two generations they became significantly taller. Torday thinks that free air, sunshine and regular life are the main factors to bring about changes in stature.

Role of Environment

It is seen that when other conditions are not unfavourable and open wandering habit makes people taller. On the other hand stunted stature is met with among the peoples in infertile, heavy forest or excessively cold country whose life is hard. Much has been said against these views also.

Role of Heredity

The above facts do not necessarily means that environment is the only controlling factor, and heredity has no role to play. In the same place two peoples with variable statures, may live side by side like the tall Norwegians and the short Lapps in the north of Scandinavia. Various studies on race-crossing and other things have shown the role of heredity in producing different types of stature. The inheritance of stature follows the general Mendelian rule. Thus, it is believed that stature is dependent upon an association of paratypical (environmental) and diotypical (hereditary) factor. It should be borne in mind that every case must be taken by itself.

Despite these variations, stature is also employed to characterise various ethnic groups. Stature, however, shows a considerable range of variation among the same group of people within certain limits. For example, a group characterized by short stature, may include some tall stature persons also and *vice versa*.

Scales of Classification

The scales used by different authorities are as follows for classification of stature.

1. Topinard's Scale

(i)	Pygmy	... ...	50.0 cm.	
(ii)	Short	... ...	150.0 — 160.0 cm.	(59—62 in)
(iii)	Under average	... ...	160.0 — 165.0 cm.	(63—65 in.)
(iv)	Above average	... ...	165.0 — 170.0 cm.	(65—67 in.)
(v)	High	... ...	170.0 +	(67 +)

Thus, according to Topinard, the average stature of man is 16 5 cm. (5 ft. 5 in.).

2. Haddon's Scale

(i)	Pygmy	148.0 cm.
(ii)	Short	148.0 — 158.0 cm.
(iii)	Medium	158.0 — 168.0 cm.
(iv)	Tall	168.0 — 172.0 cm.
(v)	Very Tall	172.0

3. Martin's Scale

(i)	Pygmy	— 129.9 cm.
(ii)	Very Short	130.0 — 149.9 cm.
(iii)	Short	150.0 — 159.0 cm.
(iv)	Below medium	160.0 — 163.9 cm.
(v)	Medium	164.0 — 166.9 cm.
(vi)	Above medium	167.0 — 169.9 cm.
(vii)	Tall	170.0 — 179.9 cm.
(viii)	Very Tall	180.0 — 199.0 cm.
(ix)	Giant	200.0 +

Martin's classification is in general use.

1. Tall Stature. It is characteristic of Sikhs and Rajputs of India and also of the North-Western Europeans. It is also found in other parts of Europe and among the Northern Chinese. Nilotic Negroes and Patagonians are also tall people.

2. Medium Stature. Mediterraneans, Alpines, Armenoids, Dravidians, Ainus are some of the medium stature peoples. Some Mongoloids, *e.g.*, Eskimos also fall into this group.

3. Short Stature. Veddas, Kadars, Melanesians are short in stature. The shortest groups of mankind, that is, pygmies are represented by Andamanese, Aeta, Tapiro, Negrilloes like Akka, Ba Twa, Ba Mbute, etc.

This does not mean that all the tall races or all the pgymy races are genetically related to one another. They may not have any genealogical relationship.

BLOOD-GROUPS

A new approach to classify human races is based on some normal physiological characters determined by certain easily defined genes whose genetic behaviour is well known. The classic example of such character is blood-groups.

DERMATOGLYPHICS MEANING

The human body is covered with hairs and sebaceous (oil) glands except the palmar and planter regions which are continuously corrugated with narrow ridges. The ridges make certain patterns. Dermatogyphics (*derma, skin + glyhic,* carve) is the study of the ridge patterns of the skin of the fingers, palms, toes and soles.

Dermatoglyphic Patterns

Dermatoglyphic patterns have long since been used for various purposes for their permanency and unchangeability throughout life. From the time of their formation in the foetus to the final disintegration of the skin after death the patterns remain unchanged. Of course, the ridges may be worn out and thus become invisible owing to various reasons.

Uses of Dermatoglyphic Traits

Ever since the beginning of the Christian era finger patterns have been used for personal identification. Yet systematic scientific studies started from the end of the nineteenth century. Uses of Dermatoglyphic traits are manifold. However, the anthropologists are more concerned in establishing variations in respect of traits among different human populations. They are also interested in the study of dermatoglyphics in the context of twin diagnosis, paternity diagnosis, primatology, etc.

Dermatoglyphics fulfil many of the conditions laid down by Boyd for a good racial criterion.

Effect of Environment and Heredity

Dermatoglyphic traits are not modified by environmental factors as they are non-adaptive. They are not subjected to a high rate of mutation. They are identifiable without any subjective bias. However, the genetic process of Dermatoglyphic traits is complex and is not perfectly known.

Ridges and patterns of the finger, palms, toes and soles are studied from different angles applying various methods.

Finger patterns

Henry has classified the various finger patterns into four main types. These are : (i) arches, (ii) loops, (iii) true whorls, and (iv) composites. The composites form a heterogeneous assemblage of patterns. Again Galton have identified three types : arches, loops and whorls. A loop may be open to the ulnar side or to the radial side and accordingly it is termed as ulnar or radial loop. The classic and widely used notation is A = arches; Lr = radial loops; Lu = ulnar loops; and W = whorls. The whorls possess two triradii, while only one trirradius is present in loops. On the other hand triradius is absent in arches. Thus, generally speaking, the patterns may be identified from the occurrence of triradius.

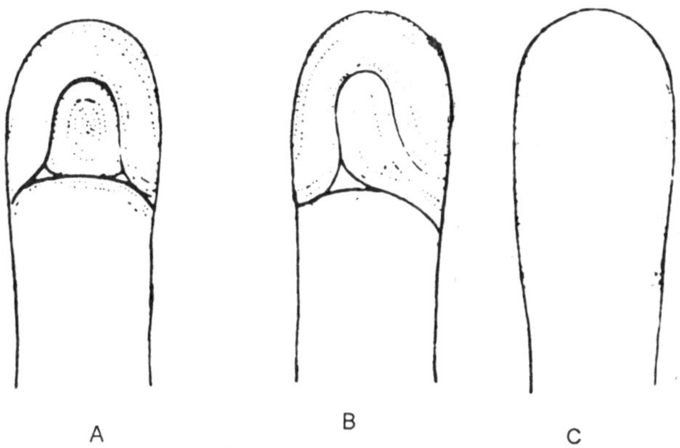

Fig. 8.3. Finger Patterns

In general, loops are more frequent than whorls. Arches are found in small numbers. Again, of the two types of loops, ulnar loop is much more frequent than radial loops.

As shown in the Table below finger patterns exhibit racial variation:

	Population	Whorls %	Loops %	Arches %
1.	Mongoloid	40 to 50	50 to 60	1 to 2
2.	Caucasoid	20 to 30	60 to 70	4 to 7
3.	Negroid	30	50 to 60	6 to 7

Thus, whorls are most frequent among the Mongoloid population and less among the Caucasoid population. Loops appear most frequently among the Caucasoid groups while among the Mongoloid and Negroid groups these are found in equal frequencies. Arches appear in very small number in the Mongoloid but are most frequent in the Negroid. The position of the Caucasoid is intermediate.

Indices of Finger Patterns

Usually three indices are calculated on the basis of the frequency distribution of the different finger patterns. These are as follows :

(1) Furuhata's Index $= \frac{\text{Whorls} \times 100}{\text{Loops}}$

(2) Dankmeijer's Index $= \frac{\text{Arches} \times 100}{\text{Whorls}}$

(3) Pattern Intensity Index $= \frac{2 \times \text{Whorls} + \text{Loops}}{n}$

n being the total number of subjects.

***Palm* (Main Line Formula) :**

At the bases of the digits II, III, IV and V four digital triradii are located as shown in the 21.4 Finger. These are called a, b, c and d in radio-ulnar sequence. For the purpose of formation of palmar main lines the palm is divided into 13 regions and each region is given a symbol or number. The proxima radiant of a digital triradius is directed toward the interior of the palm. This radiant line is fully traced to find out in which region of the palm it ends and accordingly the symbol of termination is determined. This line is called a palmar main line. In this way four main lines can be obtained. These four main lines are named A, B, C and D. The symbols of the four termination regions of the four main lines give the main line formula. The formula is recorded in the order of D, C, B and A.

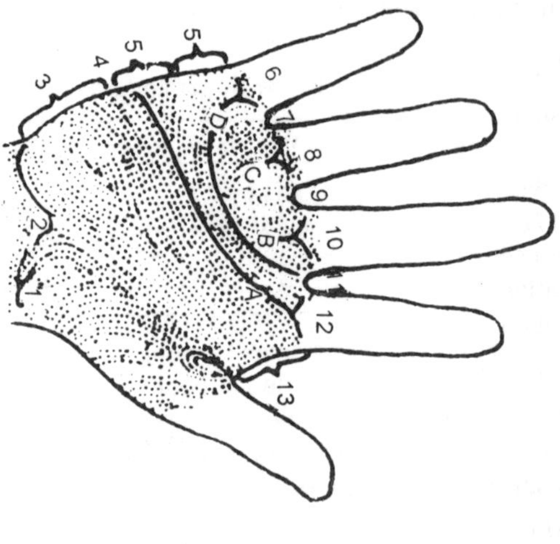

Fig. 8.4. Palm

The following three formulae are frequently observed in man : 11.9.7-, 9.7.5. and 7.5.5.-, It should be noted in this connection that the main line A is not usually considered in finding out population variations. According to Wilder the 11.9.7.- is the European formula and the 7.5.5.- the Negro formula.

9

Classification of Race

Ancient References

In 200 B.C. the Chinese distinguished five human groups according to colour. The Egyptian royal tombs of the XVII of the XXI dynasties exhibit human figures painted by using different colours to represent four human groups. In ancient Sanskrit literature one finds description of physical features of some human population groups. The dark complexioned Nishadas (Australoids) were distinguished from the yellow-coloured Kiratas (Indo-Mongoloids). These two were again differentiated from the light-coloured Indo-Aryans. All these suggest that variations among populations with regard to certain physical feature were marked by the people of very early time as well.

First Classification

Bernier travelled who through the Old World, classified the people he met during his journey in 1684. This may be considered as the first attempt to classify human races.

In 1721, Bradley made another attempt to classify the human races. But Carl Linnaeus, a Swedish naturalist, was the first to make a systematic classification of the human species, Homo sapiens into four varieties. This classification is based on some mental traits and not on physical characteristics.

H. americanus (American Indian) : These are tenacious, contented and free. They are ruled by custom.

H. europaeus. These are characterized by light, lively and inventive nature. They are ruled by rites.

H. asiaticus. These are stern, haughty and stingy. They are ruled by opinion.

H. afer (African). These are cunning, slow and negligent by nature. They are ruled by caprice.

Classification by Blumenbach

In 1775, Blumenbach, a German scientist, recognized five varieties of man. These were as follows :

1. Caucasian or white. These include, Europeans, except the Laplanders and Finns. This type is met with in North Africa and also in Western Asia as far as the Ganges.

2. Mongolian or Yellow. These include Finns and Laplanders of Europe, Eskimos of America, the inhabitants of Asia, except those included among the Caucasians.

3. Ethiopian or Black. These include rest of inhabitants of Africa not included in the Caucasians.

4. American or Red. These are the people of America other than the Eskimos.

5. Malayan or Brown. These are the inhabitants of the Pacific.

Each of these varieties was called a 'race', a term first coined by Buffon, a French scientist. Blumenbach's classification is mainly based on a single trait, the skin colour.

Other Classifications

1. Pickering. In 1848, Pickering identified eleven human races.

2. Huxley. In 1870, Huxley proposed a classification of mankind including five principal races divided into fourteen secondary races.

3. Topinard. Topinard (1885), Quatrafages (1889) and Hacckal-Muller (1870) also attempted to make racial classifications. But their classifications show only slight modification of the classification made by Huxley.

4. Deniker. In course of time, more and more characteristics and new methods were employed in classifying human races, as a result of which more number of races and sub-races were distinguished. In 1889, Deniker proposed to divide mankind into twenty-nine races according to hair form, with nose form and skin colour as secondary traits.

5. Hooton. In 1931, American anthropologist, Hooton recognized three primary races — White (Caucasoid), Negroid and Mongoloid, with several secondary, composite and sub-races. In 1947, however, he modified his classification.

6. Eickstedt. According to German anthropologist Eickstedt there are three basic races. These are Europoid, Mongoloid and Negroid with eighteen 'sub-races', three 'collateral races', eleven 'collateral sub-races' and three 'intermediate forms'.

7. Dixon. In 1923, Dixon employed three indices, namely, cephalic index, length-height index, and nasal index, to classify human races.

8. Haddon. In 1925, Haddon used hair form as a primary character and stature, cephalic index and nasal index as secondary traits to propose his classification of races.

9. Montandon. In 1933, Montandon recognized five races, namely,

Pygmoid, Negroid, Veddoid-Australoid, Mongoloid and Europoid, with twenty sub-races.

10. Lester and Millot. In 1936, Lester and Millot made four groups of mankind, namely, Pygmy Black, Yellow and White, with twenty races.

11. Vallois. In 1948, the famous French anthropologist Vallois proposed a classification showing four major races, namely, Australoid, Black, Yellow and White, each having certain sub-races.

12. Coon, Garn, and Birdsall. In 1950, Coon, Garn and Birdsall set-up six 'putative stocks', *viz.*, Negroid, Mongoloid, White, Australoid, American Indian and Polynesian with thirty different races.

13. Biasutti. In 1959, Biasutti recognized four sub-species, sixteen primary races and fifty-two secondary races.

Three Major Races

Thus, it appears that several classifications have been proposed by different anthropologists at different times. However, in general we can say that there are three major races. Negroid (Black), Caucasoid (White) and Mongoloid (Yellow). Some anthropologists add one more and that is Australoid thereby making four major races. Others propose to include the Australoid under Caucasoids giving a name Archaic Caucasoid.

The above mentioned classifications were made on the basis of the criteria of the first category. Some anthropologists attempted to classify human races on the basis of gene frequencies, that means, using the criterion of the second category.

14. Ottenberg. Ottenberg was the first to attempt at a racial classification based on blood groups of the ABO system. In 1925, he divided mankind into the following six principal groups :

(i) *European.* Norwegian, Germans, Italians, English, French, Swedes, Greeks, North American of Anglo-Saxon origin, etc.

(ii) *Intermediate.* Russians, Arabs, Turks, Armenians, Polish Jews, etc.

(iii) *Hunan.* Japanese, Southern Chinese, Rumanian, Jews, Hangarians.

(iv) *Hindu-Manchu.* Manchu, Koreans, Northern Chinese, Gypsies, Ainus, Hindus.

(v) *Afro-Malaysian.* Negroes, Malayans, Americans, etc.

(vi) *Pacific-American.* Amerindians, Icelanders, Australian Aborigines.

15. Snyder. Snyder was in favour of splitting the Pacific-American group of Ottenberg into two groups — one Pacific-American and the other members of the Pacific-American group.

16. Lahovary (1949). Lahovary proposed the following classification based on the M and N genes, besides ABO blood group system. He occasionally used other blood factors also. He distinguished the following eight groups of people :

(1) European, (2) Mediterranean, (3) Mongolian, (4) African, (5) Indonesian, (6) American-Indian, (7) Oceanic, (8) Australian.

17. Weiner (1946 and 1948). Weiner put forward another classification on the basis of ABO blood group, MN blood type and RH blood factor as follows :

(i) *Caucasoid group.* About 20 to 25 per cent A2 M gene slightly more than N. *Rh* negative in highest frequency.

(ii) *Negroid group.* A2 relatively high. M slightly more than N, *Rh* negative moderate frequency. *Rh* gene frequency very high.

(iii) *Mongoloid group.* A2 almost absent *Rh* negative rare.

(iv) *Asiatic sub-group.* M slightly more than N as in Caucasoid and Negroid.

(v) *Pacific Islands and Australia.* N much more than M.

(vi) *Americans and Eskimos.* M much more than N.

18. Boyd. In 1950, Boyd proposed following classification taking into account ABO, MN and *Rh* factors.

(i) *Early European group* (Hypothetical. Perhaps almost absence of B. A2 frequently relative high, so also *Rh1*. Frequency of N perhaps slightly more than in present day Europeans. *Rh* negative very high over 30%.

(ii) *European or Caucasoid group.* Next to Early European highest frequency of *Rh* negative. *Rh1* and A2 relatively high.

(iii) *African or Negroid group.* High frequency of B and A2 and also *Rh* positive. M and N normal. High incidence of *Rho, Rh* negative moderate.

(iv) *Asiatic or Mongoloid group.* High B and A1. Low A2 and *Rh* negative. M and N normal.

(v) *American Indian group.* B and *Rh* negative almost absent. N very low. A2 absent. A variable.

(vi) *Australoid group.* A2 and *Rh* negative absent. N high. A1 high.

In 1958, Boyd modified his classification. He made six groups comprising thirteen races as follows:

(i) European group. (1) Early Europeans, (2) Lapps, (3) North-west European, (4) Eastern and Central Europeans, and (5) Mediterraneans.

(ii) *African group.* (6) The African races, excluding inhabitants of North Africa, which belong to European group.

(iii) *Asian group.* (7) The Asian races, (8) Indo-Dravidian.

(iv) *American group.* (9) American Indians.

(v) *Pacific group.* (10) Indonesian race, (11) Melanesian race, and (12) Polynesian race.

(vi) *Australian group.* (13) Australian aborigines.

While classifying races one should remember that it is not proper to classify human groups on the basis of single criterion only, as the populations or races differ from each other in respect of a cluster of physical traits or genes.

Physical Characteristics of the Three Major Races of Man

Characters	*Caucasoid*	*Negroid*	*Mongoloid*
Skin colour	Light reddish white to olive brown. Some are brown.	Brown to brown-black. Some are yellow-brown.	Light yellow to yellow-brown. Some are reddish brown.
Head hair	Light blond to dark brown in colour. Fine to medium in texture. Straight to wavy in form.	Brown-black in colour. Coarse in texture. Curly to frizzly or woolly in form.	Brown to brown black in colour. Coarse in texture. Straight in form.
Body hair : quantity	Moderate to profuse.	Slight	Sparsely distributed.
Eye	Colour is light blue to dark brown.	Brown to brown black	Brown to dark brown. Mongoloid eye fold is very often present.
Head form	Dolichocephalic to brachycephalic. Height is medium to very high.	Predominantly dolichocephalic. Height is low to medium.	Predominantly brachycephalic. Height is medium.
Face	Narrow to medium broad.	Medium broad to narrow. Prognathism is very often present.	Medium broad to very broad. Cheek-bones are high and flat.
Nose	Leptorrhine to mesorrhine. Usually bridge is high.	Platyrrhine. Usually bridge is low.	Mesorrhine to playtyrrhine. Usually bridge is low to medium.
Stature	Medium to tall.	Very short to tall.	Medium to short.
ABO blood group	Relatively high incidence of A2.	Relatively high incidence of A2. Comparatively high incidence B.	High incidence of A1. Very low frequency of A2.
Rh factor	Highest frequency of *Rh* negative.	Moderate frequency of *Rh* negative.	*Rh* negative is rare.

10

Racial Groups in the World

Different anthropologists have proposed different classifications of mankind. However, there are three major races of man, Negroid, Caucasoid and Mongoloid. Some anthropologists call the Australoids separate major racial group. In that case there are four major races. Anthropologists agreed that each of the major races can be divided into certain groups and sub-groups.

1. NEGROID

Physical Characteristics

Negroids have hair on the head have woolly or frizzly. The colour of hair is black. The skin colour is dark-brown to black, and sometimes yellowish-brown. The nose is broad and flat, its bridge and root are usually low and broad. The eyes are dark brown to black in colour. The lips are thick and everted. The ears are small with little or no lobe. The facial prognathism is often marked. The head is predominantly long with protruding occiput and rounded head. The brow ridges are small.

Classification

The Negroids have been divided into (1) African Negro (Ulotrichi African of Haddon), and (2) Oceanic Negro (Ulotrichi Orientals of Haddon).

1. African Negro. These Negroids include the following main groups (i) True Negroes, (ii) Nilotic Negroes or Nilote, (iii) Bantu-speaking Negroid or 'Bantu', (iv) Bushmen Hottentot, (v) Negrillo.

(i) *True Negroes.* Their physical characters are : short-legged and long-armed dark brown or black skin colour; woolly hair; tall stature (average height 5' 8" or 173 cm.); platyrrhine nose; dolichocephalic head (C.I. 73-75) with often bulging forehead and prognathous face; thick lips which are often everted.

The True Negroes are distributed in West Africa, and in Guinea coast.

Forest Negroes, who inhabit the region extending from the Senegal River in the West to Sudan, Uganda and Northern Rhodesia, differ from the True Negroes, in being shorter (average stature 5' 5" or 165 cm.) and having coarse features in face and body. Then nose is very broad, its root is low and the bridge flat. Check bones are prominent, face is markedly prognathous, chin is retreating and lips are markedly everted.

(ii) *Nilotic Negroes or Nilotes.* Their physical characters include very dark colour; very tall stature (average 5' 10" or 178 cm.): slim figure; long-legged; dolichocephalic head (C.I. 71-74; woolly hair; nose less playtyrrhine than the True Negroes; facial prognathism less marked and lips less thick and everted than in the True Negroes; retreating forehead.

The Nilotes are referred to as Negroids as some of the Nilotic Negroes, *e.g.*, the Shilluk, the Dinka, the Kavirondo and others show certain Hamitic or Ethiopian elements which suggest an infusion of hamitic traits into these peoples.

The Nilotic Negroes are distributed in the region of Upper Nile Valley and Eastern Sudan.

(iii) *Bantu speaking Negroid or 'Bantu'.* These include the numerous Bantu speaking peoples of Central and Southern Africa are ethnic groups that constitute this division have not yet been definitely ascertained. They have wide range of variations in respect of different physical characters which may be described as follows: Dark chocolate skin colour varying from yellowish brown to black, Negro characteristics hair stature above average, being 5' 6" or 167 cm; head typically dolichocephalic, though mesocephalic heads are also met with. The mesocephalic group is characterized by shorter stature; less dark skin colour, flatter forehead; less marked prognathism and generally narrower and more prominent nose than in true Negroes.

Bantu-speaking peoples are essentially Negroes, though they are mixed up with Hamitic, Negrillo and Bushmen-Hottentot elements.

(iv) *Bushmen-Hottentot.* The Bushmen and the Hottentot are more or less the same people, having very little differences in respect of physical characters. In culture, however, they are somewhat different from one another. The Hottentot are known as the Khoi Khoi and the Bushmen the Khuai or San. Though, formerly they occupied the greater part of South Africa the Bushmen are mainly confined to the Kalahari desert. The Hottentot are found in South-West Africa.

The physical characters of the Bushmen-Hottentot are as follows : short head half lightly coils up to spiral knots leaving bare spaces between them, termed as Pepper-corn; black hair colour; sparse or absent; beard and body hair light to brownish skin colour in Bushmen and light reddish yellow in Hottentot; dark brown to black; eye colour. The Hottentot, (5' 3" or 160 cm.) are slightly taller than the Bushmen (4' 11" or 145 cm.); Amae Bushmen head is dolichocephalic and high among Hottentot it is low mesocephalic. In Bushmen Parietal bosses are more marked and occiput is less protruding than in Hottentot. In the Bushmen face is shorter, squarer, often orthogonathous while in the Hottentot it is more elongated triangular and somewhat prognathous. In both cheek bones very prominent; chin small; bulbous forehead with little developed brow ridges; ears frequently lobeless; lips usually thick platyrrhine nose with very broad, flat root, low and broad bridge; concave profile and thick tip, eyes narrow and slanting with internal epicanthous; hands and feet small. Steatopygia (immense deposit of fat in the buttocks) is more pronounced in Hottentot women than in Bushmen women.

(v) *Negrillo (African pygmy)*. The Negrillos are very short in stature. Their average height is 4' 6" or 136 cm. They have short trunk, short legs and long arms; Steatopygea is occasionally present in women. Their head is mesocephalic (C.I. 79.0), face usually proganthic; chin narrow and weak; lips full but not everted; nose very flat and broad; the wings very broad and high; hair on head very short, woolly in form, dark rusty brown in colour; hair on body yellowish, brown hair on armpits and black on pubis, skin colour yellowish light brown or reddish yellow, sometimes very dark.

The Negrillos are represented by the Akka, Ba Twa, Ba Mbute, etc. inhabit Equatorial forests of Congo region.

Pygmy-statured peoples, commonly known as the pygmies are found in different parts of the globe, *e.g.*, Congo region of Equatorial Africa, Malay Peninsula, Sumatra, Andaman Islands, Philippine, New Guinea, etc. They may be grouped into three classes according to their geographical distribution : (1) African Pygmy of Negrillo, (2) Oceanic, and (3) Asiatic Pygmy. Oceanic and Asiatic Pygmy are known Negrito.

2. Oceanic Negro. This sub-division of the Negroids includes (i) the Negritos, both Asiatic and Oceanic, and (ii) Melanesia and Papuans.

(i) *Negritos*. The Andamanese, Semang, Aeta, Tapiro are the important representatives of the Negritos. Of these while the first three belong to Asiatic Pygmy group the Tapiro is member of the Oceanic Pygmies.

(ii) *Andamanese*. The Andamanese have very short stature. Their (average height is 4' 10" or 148 cm.). They have small brachycephalic head (C. I. 83); straight nose, sunken at the root, well proportioned body with small hands, face broad at the molar region, jaws not projecting and the lips full but not everted. Their skin colour varies from bronze to sooty black. Body hair is scanty or absent, head hair short, coloured black with a reddish tinge and woolly in form.

Andamanese inhabit the Andaman Islands.

(iii) *Semang*. Their average height is 5' or 152 cm. They are well-proportioned, with sturdy built body mesocephalic head (C.I. 79. 0); round face, short flattened very broad nose (N. I. 97.0) usually not thick lips; upper jaw not much projecting, skin colour dark chocolate brown, head hair short, coloured black with the reddish tinge and woolly in the form; face and body hair scanty.

The Semangs live in the central region of the Malay peninsula and in East Sumatra.

(iv) *Aeta.* The Aeta are of an average height of 146 cm. or 4' 9". They are brachycephalic (C. I. 82.0); with very short broad and flat nose (N. I. 102); lips moderately thick, skin colour sooty brown, hair colour dark brown to black from frizzly; hair on face and body frequently abundant.

They are inhabitants of Philippine Island.

(v) *Tapiro.* The average height of the Tapiro is 4' 9" or 146 cm. Their baody is muscular, head mesocephalic (C.I. 79.5); nose short, straight and medium in breadth; upper lip deep and convex; head hair black, woolly and short; face and body hair abundant; skin colour yellowish brown.

They live in New Guinea.

Hooton has distinguished two morphological types of Negritos, namely, infantile and adultform.

Some scholars believed that the Pygmies of the different parts of the globe are genetically interrelated and form a common Pygmy race from various branches of a common older racial stock. But current researches show that there is nothing like a Pygmy race. Pygmy formation is ascribed to several environmental factors. They neither belong to the same stock nor to the branches of a common stock.

(vi) *Papuans.* The Papuans have typically dolichocephalic head, which is high with and narrow retreating forehead. They have heavy and continuous brow ridges and prognathic face, broad nose nasal root depressed; convex profile with thick lip, variable stature but usually medium, average being 5' 6" or 168 cm.; skin colour dark chocolate or sooty brown; hair black, somewhat frizzly, facial hair abundant, hair colour often dark brown or reddish brown than dead black.

The Papuans are distributed in New Guinea and other islands of Melanesia.

(vii) *Melanesians.* Their stature is variable — short or medium; head form also variable (C.I. 67.85) generally dolichocephalic but mesocephaly and brachycephaly also occur. Forehead is rounded, wider and lower, browridges less developed than in the Papuans, nose is platyrrhine, more so than in the Papuans; nasal root deeply depressed, straight or concave profile, thick lip, hair usually frizzly, but sometimes curly or even wavy; hair on face and body usually scanty, skin colour dark chocolate, sometimes copper-coloured, sometimes very dark.

The Melanesians are distributed in some coastal parts of New Guniea and the neighbouring islands in Fiji, Admiralty Island, New Caledonia, etc.

II. MONGOLOID

Physical Characteristics

Physical characteristics of the Monoloids are black, straight, coarse head hair; yellow or yellow-brown skin colour; scanty body and facial hair; broad flat face with prominent cheek bones; oblique eye with narrow slit-like opening and internal epicanthic fold or total Mongoloid fold, etc.

Classification

The Mongoloids may be sub-divided into four main sub-divisions on the basis of their geographical distribution : (1) The Classic or Central Mongoloid, (2) The Arctic or Northern Mongoloid or Eskimoids, (3) The Southern or Indo-Malayan Mongoloids, and (4) The American Indians.

1. Classic or Central Mongoloid. These are characterized by the generally brachycephalic head (C.I. 85.0) through mesocephalic and dolichocephalic heads are also met with: projecting, occiput rounded and of medium height forehead nose very low root but no nasal depression; low bridge medium in breadth; profile variable but usually straight or concave; the alae of the nostrils of medium spread, cheek bones very strongly developed, projecting laterally and forward, the skin colour yellow or yellow brown, head hair straight, black and coarse, hairs sparsely distributed in the body and face, eye colour is medium to dark brown, obliquely set; opening is narrow, slitlike; internal epicanthic or complete Mongoloid fold is present.

Classic or Central Mongoloid are found in Sibesia and Amur river district; sporadically in Northern China, Mongolia and Tibet. They are represented in : Mongoloid tribes like Buriat, Konyak, Goldi, Gilyak, etc.; Tibetans; some Northern Chinese, etc.

2. The Arctic or Eskimoid. Eskimoid are characterized by straight, black hair, yellowish skin colour, large broad flat face with prominent cheek bones; narrow prominent nose; remarkably small hands, feet large trunks and relatively short legs, black very often straight eyes; complete epicanthic fold, variable stature and head form. The Western Eskimos (168 cm.) are taller than the Alaskan Eskimos (163.8 cm.). As regards head form the Eastern Aleutian Eskimo (C.I. 84.6), and the Kuskokwin Eskimo (C.I. 81.50) are brachycephalic while the Greenland Eskimo (C.I. 76.8) and the Arctic Eskimo (C.I. 78.6) are mesocephalic.

The Eskimoids are distributed in Northern Asia, the Arctic coast of North America, Greenland, Labrador and Western Alaska represented by the Eskimo, Chukchi, Kamtchadales, Yakuts, Samoyedes, etc.

3. Indonesian-Malay Mongoloid. A large number of Mongoloid peoples shows a considerably Caucasoid elements. Negroid elements too are met with throughout Southern Asia. They are known as the Indonesian-Malay Mongoloids. Two types are distinguished in this group : Malay type and Indonesian type.

(i) *Malay type*. Their average stature is 5' 2" or 158 cm.; head brachycephalic (C.I. 85.0); browridges of medium development; nose usually mesorrhine and sometimes platyrrhine; hair straight; coloured black but with occasional reddish tinge; face and body hair scanty; skin colour light yellow brown to dark yellow brown; eye colour medium to dark brown or almost black; internal epicanthic fold present; face short, broad with prominent cheek bones.

Malay type is distributed in Southern China, Indo-China, Burma, Thailand, Malay Peninsula, Dutch East Indies, the Philippines, Japan, etc. The Japanese mostly belong to the Malayan type.

(ii) *Indonesian type or Nesiot*. The Indonesians are slanderer and slightly shorter (5' 1" or 155 cm.) than the Malay. They are mesocephalic (C. I. 78.5), though dolichocephaly also occurs. Their nose is narrower, higher and longer and the face is narrower, longer and more oval than the Malay type. The internal epicanthic fold is also less frequent. Their hair colour is black with occasional reddish tint; hair form usually slightly wavy, skin colour light red to medium brown.

The Mongoloid influence appears to be more strongly marked in the Malay type than in the Indonesian type. The Indonesian type is found in Southern China, Indo-China, Burma, Thailand, the interior of the Malay Archipelago, etc.

4. The American Indian or the Amerindian. Though, data on the physical anthropology of the American Indians are not adequate for a scientific sub-division of these peoples, it appears that the American Indians are predominantly Mongoloid. However, some non-Mongoloid racial strains like Caucasoid, Australoid and very small Negriloid elements, have entered into these populations. Hence, diversic types are distinguishable among them; but they exhibit a certain basic homogeneity of characters distributed in different parts of North, Middle, and South America.

Basic Common Traits

The basic common traits are : of Amerindians black rarely dark hair is coarse, straight and sometimes slightly wavy; hair sparsely distributed in body and face; skin colour varying from yellow brown to red brown; eye-colour dark brown to black; complete Mongoloid fold almost absent, internal epicnathic fold frequently present in women and children but rare in males; external epicnathic fold common; face broad with typical Mongoloid cheek bones; chin more prominent than in typical Mongoloid; face exhibiting medium prognathism; lips thiner; shovel-shaped incisors strongly developed browridges and glabellar portions forehead slopes more than in typical Mongoloid. Nose very long predominantly mesorrhine; bridge usually high and convex, tip of medium thickness, stature variable and head form of two types dolicho-mesocephalic and brachycephalic.

Classification of Amerindians

(i) *Dolicho-Mesocephals — Palaeo-Amerind* (or Lagoa Santa type of Brazil, Ecuador Officio). They form an archaic South American race with very dolichcephal small skulls; high vaulted, hypiscranial; faces longer and narrower, possibly more reddish brown than yellow brown skin colour and black wavy hair.

Some of living representatives of these peoples are Botocudo, Buru, etc. Some members of these types are found in the Eastern United States and Canada with sporadic distribution in many parts of America.

(ii) *Northern-Amerind.* These include the American Indians of the plains and of the northern and eastern Woodlands. They are characterized by tall stature (161-175 cm.) dolichocephalic or mesocephalic head (C.I. 73-75) with a tendency towards brachycephaly in the West; yellow brown skin colour; straight hair, coloured black; large, flat oval face; straight or convex nose, etc.

(iii) *Brachycephals — Neo-Amerind.* Their physical characters are: short to tall stature (155-178 cm.); brachycephalic head, straight or concave nose; face broader and relatively shorter than in dolichocephals; straight black hair, yellow brown skin colour.

Neo-Amerind are distributed in South America, Central America and the North American Plateaux.

(iv) *Tehuelche.* They are a very tall people (173-183) with brachycephalic head (C. I. 85), square broad face; brownish skin colour and straight black hair. They live in Patagonia. Possibly the Onas of Teirra deal Fuego form a branch of the Tehuelche.

(v) *North-West Coast Amerind.* In them the colour of skin and hair is lighter than in other Northern Amerinds. They are of medium stature, with long arms and short body. They are allied to the natives of North-East Asia. Two types are distinguished in this group : Northern type and Southern type, of which the former is taller than the latter. They possess concave or straight nose, broad face with moderate height while in the latter, very often convex and high nose and face of great height.

They inhabit the North-West coast of North America.

III. CAUCASOID

The Caucasoids include numerous ethnic groups with diverse racial elements and a wide range of variation in respect of many characters. Their general characteristics are — Skin : white, olive, all shades of brown and sometimes dark brown; Hair: variable in form ranging from falt wavy to various degrees of curliness, usually wavy hair; hair colour of lighter shades, rarely dead black; hair texture rarely coarse, usually medium to fine; body and face hair usually moderate or abundant head form variable ranging from dolichocephalic to brachycephalic; nose leptorrhine to mesorrhine, never platyrrhine; high nasal bridge face with prognathism usually absent; cheek bones generally not prominent, thin lips; chin pronounced or medium in development: forehead comparatively high; eyes colour not black but of lighter shades.

A large number of ethnic groups come under this division of mankind of which the following are the most representative type :

1. Mediterranean. As the name implies, these inhabit the Mediterranean shores though at present they have migrated in all directions as far as India. They are widely distributed in Protugal, Spain, France, Italy, Greece, Turkey and parts of North Africa, also in Arabia, Iran, Afghanistan, Pakistan and India. All members of the Mediterranean exhibit some remarkable common characters. However, three sub-types are distinguished among them. These are Classic Mediterranean Atlanto-Mediterranean and Indo-Afghan Mediterranean.

(i) *Classic Mediterranean* (Basic Mediterranean or Indo-Insular). Their physical characters are — light brown of tawny white skin colour, hair wavy or even curly black, head dolichocephalic and mesocephalic, cephalic index ranging from 73 to 76. Nose leptorrhine, usually straight with medium thick tip, face narrow and oval with pointed chin, eyes usually dark, slender and somewhat delicately built body and medium stature.

This type is found in the whole of Mediterranean basin Portugal. Spain, France, Italy, etc. It is sporadically distributed in eastern, central and north-western Europe. In North Africa it is seen among the Egyptians, the Berbers of Morocco and also in Arabia. The basic Jewish population of Palestine also form a part of this type.

(ii) *Atlanto-Mediterranean* (*or Littoral*). They are characterized by generally darker skin colour, usually very wavy or curly and very dark hair; dolichocephalic or mesocephalic head with retreating forehead and usually well-developed brow ridges, nose straight and of medium height and breadth, the root being usually deep, face long, cheek-bones and slightly prominent. They are usually tall, but medium stature also frequently occurs. They are more robustly built than the Classic Mediterranean.

This type is found in the population of North Africa, in Iraq, Palestine, parts of Arabia and the Eastern Balkans. It also occurs in small numbers in the British Isles, Spain and Portugal.

(iii) *Indo-Afghan (or Irano-Afghan)*. Their physical characters include very light brown, skin colour black and wavy; hair on head usually abundant; body and facial hair dolicho-mesocephalic (C. I. 71-77) and high head, finely cut, leptorrhine nose; straight or convex bridge long and narrow face, eyes dark in colour variable stature, tall to medium (161-178 cm.) slightly built body, etc.

Indo Afgans are distributed in Iraq, Iran, Afghanistan, Baluchistan, North-West India and Pakistan.

2. Nordic. The Scandinavians are considered to be the typical representatives, common in the Baltic region, Northern Germany, Northern France, parts of Netherlands and Belgium, British Island, etc. Its sporadic occurrence is observed in various parts of Europe. It forms an important chunk in the United States and some British colonies.

These are characterized by florid or reddish-white skin colour. Hair slightly wavy, rarely curly in form; hair colour variable, reddish brown, very light brown, ash brown, golden brown, etc.; hair texture fine to medium; body and facial hair sparse or medium long mesocephalic (C. I. 76-79) and finely arched prominent, long narrow and usually straight; nose long, narrow face with bones strongly developed, brow ridges moderately developed, chin prominent; lips thin or medium, eye colour blue or grey, stature tall, average height being 172 cm. or 5' 8".

3. Alpine. Their physical characters are : olive or brunette white or bronze skin colour. Hair colour medium brown or dark brown; rarely black; hair abundantly distributed over the body and face; hair texture medium to fine; hair form wavy; head brachycephalic (C.I. 85) and high with somewhat curved occiput and wide high forehead, nose leptorrhine and often mesorrhine with straight or slightly convex nasal profile and short thick fleshy tip, face more or less round or oval; brow ridges moderately or strongly developed; chin well developed; prognathism absent, eyes straight, dark brown or medium brown occasionally blue in colour; stature medium to shorts; average height being about 165 cm. or 5' 5". Their body is thick set and short.

Concentration of the Alpines may be seen in Central Europe along a line extending from France to the Urals. They are found in the Balkans, Denmark, Norway, Northern Italy in the mountains of Asia Minor, etc. They are sporadically distributed throughout Europe. They show a good deal of admixture with two other racial types — Nordics and Mediterraneans.

The Beaker-Folk. The Beaker-Folk formerly known as "Round-barrow men", "Bronze Age men", etc., are regarded as a cross between Alpines and Nordics. The Beaker-folk are distributed in the region extending from Central Spain to Central Europe, in England and Scotland, and sporadically in most Central and Western European countries. Their physical characters may be summarized as florid skin, wavy hair form, skin colour often fair and reddish, head is large, brachycephalic (C.I. 81), glabellar region prominent; brow ridges well developed. Occiput flattened is long, narrow and prominent — leptorrhine those face long and narrow with somewhat prominent malar regions, large jaw and square chin, eye colour blue or blue-grey, stature very tall; and other characteristics robust and muscular body.

4. East Baltic. Their skin colour is generally tawny white or creamy white and hair colour light-ash blond or ash brown, rarely reddish; form usually straight, sometimes wavy; texture medium to coarse; facial hair moderately developed; body hair usually sparse; head broad — brachycephalic, forehead is high and broad; occiput is rather flat; face square in form; cheek bones prominent; angles of the lower jaws square, chin well developed, jaw heavy; brow ridges of medium development. Nose prominent, mesorrhine in profile and convex sometimes straight; bridge low; wings broad; tip snubbed; eye colour light blue or grey. Their stature is variable short and medium predominant, with thick set body.

They are concentrated in North-Eastern Germany, Poland, Baltic States, Russia, Finland, etc.

5. Dinaric (Adratic or Illyrian). Their skin colour is variable — usually lighter brunette. Other characteristics are : hair form straight to wavy, sometimes curly; hair colour medium brown to dark brown, occasionally lighter shades also occur, texture medium: face and body hair abundant, head brachycephalic, very high; extremely flat occiput; forehead sloping; brow ridges well developed; nose narrow — leptorrhine, nasal profile is straight or convex; tip is usually fleshy. It is larger and narrower than in the Armenoid. Their face is longer and narrower with deeper, heavier and more projecting chin than that of the Armenoids. Their lips are of medium fullness — thinner than in the Armenoids. Their eye colour is brown or lighter. They are tall statured people with average height of 172 cm. or 5' 8".

They are distributed in Dinaric Alps region in Yugoslavia, Albania, Austrian Tyrol and Sporadically in Central Europe. They show some social element o Alpine, Armenoid, Nordic, Atlanto-Mediterranean and possibly also of Indo Afghan.

6. Armenoid. The Armenoid have a considerable amount of Classic Mediterranean, Alpine, Nordic, Indo-Afghan racial elements in them. They have olive or tawny white skin colour. Other characteristics are : hair colou dark brown to black, usually wavy to curly in form, roughly straight; textur coarse to medium; abundant hair on face and body; eye-brows thick, speciall in males. Their head is broad — brachycephalic; high hypsicephalic with vertical occiput, with a high, sloping forehead. Their nose is prominen leptorrhine; root is high and broad; bridge in profile is usually convex: tip i depressed and fleshy. Their face is long and narrow; cheek-bones rather we developed; chin of medium prominence; lips moderately thick and full. Statu is medium to tall, average height being 167 cm. or 5' 6". Their body is heavil built with a tendency to obesity.

They are concentrated in Turkey, Syria and Palestine, Iraq, Iran and Balka countries. Their typical representatives are ancient Hittites.

7. Keltic. Their distinguishing characteristics are : pale white skin colour medium to dark brown or red and rarely black in colour; hair usually wavy or curly, rarely straight hair form mesocephalic, head long,. narrow, and high — leptorrhine, nose whose profile is straight or convex, face is long and narrow; cheek bones compressed; eye colour blue or grey and tall stature.

These are distributed in Iceland, Scotland and Wales with sporadic occurrence in England and many parts of Western Europe.

8. Lapp. Their physical characteristics are : skin colour varying from grayish yellow to yellowish brown, sometimes light, hair colour usually dark brown of black; form usually straight or slightly wavy; body and facial hair sparse brachycephalic (C.I. 84.6); head mesorrhine nose; nasal profile concave; tip very often snubbed, face moderately broad and remarkably short, cheek-bones moderately prominent with forward projection; forehead narrow; brow ridges faintly developed; face showing little or no prognathism; lips of medium thickness; eye colour variable; occasionally present Mongoloid fold, short stature average, height being 5' 3" or 159 cm.

The Lapps are distributed in Northern Scandinavia, Sweden, Northern Finland, Norway and north-western region of Russia. They have mixed-up with Swedes, Finns, Norwegians, Russians, Samoyedes, etc. Though, they exhibit some common characters by which they may be regarded as a separate ethnic group. Some of the Lapps are classified with the Mongoloids, though, they appear to be more Caucasoid than Mongoloid.

9. Indo-Dravidian (Dravidian). The Indo-Dravidians are predominantly Caucasoid. Among them is seen an admixture of Classic Mediterranean and Australoid (Veddoid). Their characteristics are : skin colour varying from light brown to dark brown, hair usually black and slightly wavy, occasionally tending towards curly, head hair plentiful; body and face hair sparse to medium, head dolichocephalic (C.I. 73.76); forehead usually rounded, nose mesorrhine (N.I. less than 77); somewhat depressed at the root; usually straight in profile; bridge moderately high; tip of medium thickness, face narrow and of medium length; little or no prognathism and brow ridges moderately developed. The Indo-Dravidians are a medium-statured people, average height being 164 cm. or 5' 4". They are concentrated in South India and Central India.

10. Polynesian. The Polynesians are a composite race. They are essentially a white people but they have mixed with Mongoloid and Negroid peoples. Their characteristics are : skin colour varies from light brown to yellow brown, hair colour dark brown to black; form usually wavy, sometimes straight, rarely curly, body and facial hair sparse, predominantly brachycephalic (C. I. 82.6) head but delichocephaly and mesocephaly also occur; forehead high slightly sloping and narrow; flat occiput nose prominent, somewhat broad at the wings; root usually slightly depressed, nasal profile sometimes convex but very often straight; nasal tip thick; face long and broad; cheek bones prominent; brow ridges moderately developed; chin well developed; lips of medium fullness; eye colour varying from medium to dark brown; Mongoloid fold rarely occurring, stature tall, average height about 178 cm. or 5' 8" and muscular body built.

The Polynesians live in Polynesian Islands of the Pacific, *e.g.*, New Zealand, Friendly Islands, Samoa, Society, Marquesas, Hawaii.

11. Ainus. The Ainus represent a very ancient stock of Japan. They are predominantly Caucasoid, but a considerable amount of Mongoloid admixture is seen among them. As they closely resemble the Australian aborigines in respect of many characters, some writers incline to include them with the Australoid or Archaic Caucasoid group.

Their physical characteristics are : skin colour light brownish white, hair colour is dark brown to black; hair form wavy, abundant rather excessive hair on body and face (referred as the ''Hairy Ainu'') mesocephalic (C. I. 76.5); head mesorrhine. (N. I. 77) to platyrrhine, short nose; nasal root slightly depressed nasal profile straight to convex, face short and of medium breadth, mesoprosophic and orthognathic; jaw and chin well-developed; lips thin, eye colour medium to dark brown; eyes horizontal with wide openings and epicanthic fold usually absent. The Ainus have thick set body and medium or short stature with average height of 158 cm. or 5' 2".

They are distributed in Northern Japan, Yezo and South Sakhalin.

IV. AUSTRALOID OR ARCHAIC CAUCASOID

As the Austaloids closely resembles the Caucasoids in respect of many characters, they are considered as a sub-division of the Caucasoid. They include two main groups — the Australian aborigines and the pre-Dravidian or Australoid or Veddoid. These have been further sub-divided into several types.

1. Australian Aborigines. They live in Australia. These peoples suggest an admixture of an archaic Caucasoid type with some Negroids. Some degree of Oceanic admixture is also noticed. Their characteristics are : medium to dark chocolate brown skin colour, sometimes wavy, rarely straight hair form; hair colour varying from medium brown to black; usually abundant face and body hair, head usually narrow, dolichocephalic (C.I. 73.0), vault gable shaped; brow ridges extremely large; glabellar region very prominent; forehead receding, broad very platyrrhine; nasal root markedly depressed; bridge of medium height; tip very thick, face short, showing medium to pronounced prognathism; chin usually receding, lips full, eye colour medium to dark brown, stature variable and of average height being 165 cm. or 5' 5".

Several morphological types are distinguished, *e.g.*, (i) Murrian of South Eastern Australia (most nearly Caucasoid); (ii) Carpentarian of the Gulf of Carpentaria (Melanesian-Papuan); (iii) Tasmenoid (Negrito-like), etc.

2. Pre-Dravidian (or Australoid or Veddoid). Their general physical characteristics are of Pre-Dravidian; skin colour dark brown to nearly black, hair black and wavy or curly in form, head dolichocephalic (C. I. 73-75) with sloping forehead and prominent brow ridges; nose very broad — platyrrhine and depressed at the root, face short and narrow; prognathism moderate; chin somewhat receding; lips very often thick, stature short, average height being 157 cm. or 5' 2" and body of delicate build.

Pre-Dravidian live in South and Central India. Some of their typical representatives are Indian tribes named Kadar, Kurumba, Panyan, Irula, Bhil, Gond, Khond, Oraon, etc.

(i) *The Veddas of Ceylon.* These also form a typical member of this group. Their physical characters are : skin colour dark brown, hair form wavy or slightly curly; hair colour is black, sometimes with reddish tinge; head dolichocephalic (C. I. 70.5), smallest of all the living human groups forehead slightly receding, brow ridges often pronounced, face short and broad and usually orthognathous; lips thin to medium; chin usually somewhat receding; nose broad — platyrrhine, nasal root depressed, the stature is short (152 cm. or 5') and thick body is of small size.

(ii) *The Sakai or Senoi of southern portion of Malay Peninsula.* This is another representative of the Australoid sub-division. Their physical characteristics include: skin colour varying from yellowish brown to dark brown, hair wavy or curly; hair colour black with reddish tinge, head mesocephalic (C. I. 78), nose of medium breadth and flat — mesorrhine, approaching platyrrhine, face usually arthognathous; lips of medium thickness; chin somewhat weak, stature short (152 cm. or 5').

SOME IMPORTANT TYPES OF CAUCASOID

1. Prospectators. Their distribution may be found in South Italy, Sicily, Spain, west coast of Britain, east coast of Ireland, etc. They appear to be the result of admixture of Mediterranean and Anatolians. Their name 'Prospectator' was given by Fleure. Elliot Smit calls them, ''Maritime Armenoids''. These are characterized by yellow skin, dark hair, brachycephalic head; orthognathus face; strong jaw square in shape; dark eyes; tall stature, etc.

2. Eurasiatic. They are the European brachycephals, most of whom are included under the term Alpines. Two main types may be distinguished among them.

(i) *Alpo-Carparthian.* They are characterized by sallow skin; dark or chocklate brown hair, brachycephalic head; narrow nose with concave profile; broad face; dark brown or hazel grey eyes, medium stature, etc. They are distributed in Russia, Balkan States, Czechoslovakia, France and other parts of western Europe. Among them are found two types : the eastern commonly known as the *Slavs*; and the western known as the *Cevenoles.*

(ii) *Pamiri.* Their characteristic features are : white-rosy skin, colour variable; hair colours — dark to brown, wavy or even curly hair, abundant facial and body hair; brachycephalic head; prominent leptorrhine nose with straight to convex profile; long oval face; straight eyes of light medium colour, rarely blue; medium stature, etc.

They are distributed in Persia, Pamir region etc., typical represented Wakhi, Tajik, Gaicha, etc.

(iii) *Illyrio-Anatolian.* (a) Anatolian (Armenian); (b) Illyrian (Adriatic or Dinaric).

3. Pyrenian. Their physical characteristics are : skin colour dusky pink or ruddy, hair colour chestnut brown, usually wavy form, head mesocephalic, nose narrow and very prominent, face long and orthognathic triangular in form, chin narrow, moderately developed brown ridges, malar region slightly prominent, eye colour chestnut-brown, often greenish and stature medium (166 cm. or 5' 5").

Their concentration is seen in the north of Spain typically represented the Spanish Basque.

4. Semite. The Semitic people are characterized by fine, narrow nose with straight or convex profile, long elliptical face and jet black hair. They are distributed throughout South-West Asia, East and North Africa, etc. Among them two types are distinguished:

(i) *Bedouin.* They are medium to tall-statured people with dolichocephalic head concentrated in Northern Arabia.

(ii) *Himyarite.* They are mesocephalic people of medium stature living in Southern Arabia.

5. Hamite. This type is represented by the Galla, Beja, Hadendoa Abyssinian, etc., who live in Abyssinia, North-Eastern Africa, Arabia, etc. Their physical characters are : skin colour varying from reddish brown to blackish brown, hair form curly to wavy, colour black to dark brown, head dolichocephalic (C. I. 75), nose leptorrhine to mesorrhine, face long oval with thin lips and pointed chin, prognathism usually absent, stature medium (165 cm. or 5' 5") and body of slender build.

6. Half-Hamite. These grouped under the Negroid division, they are the result of mixture of Hamite with Nilotic Negro. Their typical representatives are the Masai, Suk, Nandi, Ba Hima, etc. and tribes of Topotha, Leso, etc. They live in East Central Africa and North-East Africa. Their physical characters are : skin colour variable from light chocolate brown to very dark chocolate brown, hair woolly, head form variable and dolichocephalic (C. I. 73-74) among the Masai, Nandi, etc. and mesocephalic among the Suk (C. I. 77); nose nat; moderately broad to broad, face showing slight prognathism, lips not everted, cheek bones large and high stature variable, average height being about 170 or 5' 7". The Ba Hima of Uganda are very tall people.

SOME IMPORTANT TYPES OF MONGOLOID

1. Sinicus (Chinese). This type is found in the Chinese. Its physical characteristics are : skin colour yellowish brown, hair form straight; texture coarse; colour black, head mesocephalic with a tendency towards hypsicephaly, nose mesorrhine; its root very low; no nasal depression; nasal profile variable, usually straight or concave, place short and broad; cheek bones prominent; eye colour medium to dark brown; eyes oblique; slit narrow; total Mongoloid or internal epicanthic fold, medium stature.

2. Paracoean (Southern Mongoloid). Their skin colour is variable yellowish in the north and olive brown to coppery brown in the south. Other characteristics are : hair coarse and lank; facial and body hair scanty, head brachycephalic (C.I. 80-85), nose short and flat, face broad with laterally prominent malar regions and often with slightly prognathism, eyes narrow; oblique with epicanthic fold, stature variable but usually short; thick set body.

Their purest variety is represented by the Chinese of Hoang Ho. Most of the Pareoeans have mixed with local non-Mongoloid races. Some of the mixed varieties are Southern Chinese, Tibetans, Himalayans, some populations of Japan, Indo-China and Further India.

3. Centralize, Tungus (Mongol). Their physical characteristics are : skin colour varying from yellowish to yellowish-brown, hair form straight texture coarse; colour black; body and facial hair sparse, head brachycephalic, cephalic index ranges from 84 to 87, nose mesorrhine; nostrils flared up; bridge low, face broad and flat with prominent cheek-bones, eyes very often straight; eye colour dark brown and Mongolian fold is present.

Some of the important representatives of this type are Manchus of Manchuria, Tungus of Transbaikalia, Buriat of the neighbouring area of Lake Baikal, Taranchi of East Turkestan, Telangat of Altai, Hazava of Afghanistan, Kalmuk, etc.

4. Turki. The Turkis originally came from Eastern Central Asia. At present their three main geographic divisions may be made : (1) Western groups comprising Turksmand, Ughuz, Uigur Bulgar, Magyar, etc. (2) Central group containing Kirghiz, Kazak, Uzbek, etc. and (3) Eastern group constituted by Yakut and Tatars. Thier physical characteristics are as follows : skin colour yellowish white to brownish, hair colour dark, head highly brachycepahlic, cephalic index ranging from 85 to 87, nose straight and prominent, face oval; cheekbones prominent and laterally enlarged; lips thicker, eyes dark, external epicanthic fold frequently present, stature varying from medium to tall.

11

Races of Asia

From the point of view of Racial Classification

Asia may be divided into three major portions, *viz.*, the northern lowland, the central plateau and the southern and eastern borderlands.

1. The northern lowland. It extends from the northern margin of the central plateau to the Arctic, and from Caspian Sea to Bering Straits. It consists of the steppe region, the Tundra and the Arctic shore.

2. The central plateau. It comprises of two great series of plateaux, the eastern and the western. The eastern plateau includes Tibet, Eastern Turkestan, Northern Mongolia, etc., while the eastern one consists of Armenia, Anatolia and Iran. The third major portion includes India, South-east Asia and some parts of China.

Various peoples of Mongoloid origin occupy most of the northern lowland especially the eastern portion of it. The western steppe is supposed to be the original homeland of the Proto-Nordics. They were dolichocephalic people and they had fair skin. The western plateau is considered to be the area of characterization of the white skinned brachycephals. The region lying south of this which is now dominated by the Semites, was at one time occupied by the Mediterranean and the allied peoples and the Hamites.

3. The eastern plateau. It is considered to be the area of specialization and differentiation of the yellow-skinned Mongoloids. South-east Asia is at present dominated by the Mongoloid peoples. Racial history of India is completely different from that of the other parts of Asia.

Thus, in Asia live both the yellow-skinned Mongoloids and the white-skinned Caucasoid. The former is concentrated in the east and the south-east, while the latter is mainly seen in the west and the south-west.

Haddon has made a general classification of the people of Asia in the following manner:

A. ASIATIC LEUCODERMS

1. Dolicho-Mesocephals

(i) *Indo-Afghanus.* They are characterized by dolichocephalic head, leptorrhine nose and medium to tall stature located in the region lying between the Hindukush and the Sulaiman. From this region they migrated to Northern India. This group is represented by the Rajput, Punjabi, Kashmiri, Afghan, Kafir, etc.

(ii) *Irano-Mediterraneus.* The Persian Caucasus, Hajemi of Persia, Samaritan, etc., are the chief members of this group. They have mesocephalic head, lepto to mesorrhine nose and medium to tall stature.

(iii) *Indo-Iranus.* This group is formed by the Brahui, Baluchi, etc. They are on the border-line between mesocephaly and brachycephaly. The nose is lepto to mesorrhine and the stature is medium to tall.

2. Brachycephals

(i) *Georgianus.* The Imeri and Svani are some of the members of this group. They have brachycephalic head, strong leptorrhine nose and medium stature.

(ii) *Armeno-Pamiriensis.* The chief members of this group are the Tajik, Galcha, Kurds Pamiri, etc. This group is characterized by strong brachycephaly, leptorrhine nose and medium to tall stature.

B. ASIATIC XANTHODERMS

1. Mesocephals

(i) *Protomorphus.* This group is represented by the Khasi, Bodo, Mikir, Formosan, etc., and confined to Assam and South-east Asia. They have mesocephalic head, broad nose and short to below medium stature.

(ii) *Palaearcticus.* Their head is mesocephalic, stature is short and nose is meso to platyrrhine. Platycephaly is their distinguishing characteristics. Some of the members are Kamchadale, Koryak and Tungus. This group is mostly seen in Siberia and Kamchatka.

(iii) *Tibetanus.* The true representatives are the Murmi and Gurrung of Nepal, the Lepcha of Darjeeling, the Eastern Tibetans, etc. They are medium-statured people. Their nose is lepto to mesorrhine. The head form varies between mesocephaly and brachycephaly.

(iv) *Sinicus.* This type is represented by the Chinese. Their stature is medium. Their head is mesocephalic and the nose is mesorrhine.

2. Brachy-Mesocephals

(v) *Altaicus.* Some of the members of this group are the Sagai, Yakut, Lebedin of central Siberia. They are characterized by meso to brachycephalic head, mesorrhien nose and short stature.

(vi) *Nearcticus.* The Chukchi are best example of this group. Their head is broad, nose is mesorrhine and stature is below medium.

3. Brachycephals

(vii) *Meridionalis.* The Siamese, Chakma and Annamites are some of the members of this group confined to south-east Asia. They are medium-statured people. Their head is brachycephalic and the nose is mesorrhine.

(viii) *Palaearcticus brachymorphus.* This group is confined to central and western Siberia represented by the Tuba, Western Tungus, Samoyed, etc. They are short-statured people with brachycephalic head and mesorrhine nose.

(ix) *Tibetanus brachymorphus.* The Limbu of Nepal and the Changpa of Tibet are the true representatives of this group. They are of below medium stature. Their head is brachycephalic and the nose is mesorrhine.

(x) *Centralize.* This group is formed by the Hazara Southern Tungus, Manchu, etc. The Centralize have medium stature, brachycephalic and mesorrhine nose.

SOUTH-EAST ASIA

South-east Asia includes Burma, Siam, Indo-China and Malay peninsula, the population is mostly formed by the Mongoloids. According to Haddon all the Burmese belong to the Pareoean or Southern Mongol group. This type is also found in other parts of South-east Asia. A specialized type represented by the Cambodian or Siamese is recognizable amongst the Mongoloids. They are usually smaller in size and their skin colour is brown. In these respects they differ from the Chinese and the people of Tibet and Siberia.

Amidst the Mongoloids of Malay peninsula, two non-Mongoloid types are also met with. One represented by the Semang and the other by the Sakai or Senoi. The Semang and Negrito people are akin to the Andamanese. They live in the jungles of southern Malay. The Sakai are a Veddid or Australoid people.

The Moi represent another type, where Negrito characteristics are seen in Mongoloid elements. They inhabit the mountains of Annam in Indo-China.

CHINA

The existence of Palaeolithic man in China is evidenced by Sinanthropus and the associated finds. Certain implements provide the archaeological evidence of that period. Neolithic implements have been discovered not only in China proper but also in Mongolia and Manchuria. Remains of chalcolithic culture have also been found in different centres in north-east, north-west and central China.

Origin of Chinese Culture

There are two different views about the origin and development of Chinese culture and racial types. Some believe that the present inhabitants of China are the direct descendants of the aborigines who entered Hongo Ho valley during the early stone age. Their culture has developed from that primitive stage independently and was not influenced by any foreign culture. Others are of the opinion that the present-day entered China from South-west Asia with a highly developed culture and the neolithic Chinese civilization is nothing but the eastern expression of the culture of South-west Asia. During neolithic period the Chinese were in contact with the people of South-west Asia. With the beginning of the Bronze age her culture began to develop in its own way. But no definite racial type can be assigned with certainty to the builders of that neolithic civilization.

Variable Physical types

Physical types are variable in China. The modern Chinese population includes people of tall to short stature and of broad to long head. The northern Chinese are taller. Their heads tend to become mesocephalic. In the south, a Pareoean element is observed. Their stature is short, skin colour is darker, nose is short and head is broad. A shan element has entered into the ethnic make-up of the Cantonese. Persons with longer face and lighter skin colour are also found among the Chinese.

JAPAN

The Ainus

The Ainus at one time, occupied most of Japan. They are at present confined to the northern islands of Hokkaido and Sakhalin. They led a very primitive life and until not long before the Christian era. They had a simple type of neolithic culture. They represent an early stock of the Caucasoid. The basic Japanese came later from Korea with an Iron Age culture. They founded their kingdom and drove away the Ainus to the north, where they live now. In some places, there appears to have been some Ainu blood among certain sections of the Japanese.

The Koshito

Archaeological remains reveal the existence of another group of people in Japan. They are called Korpokguru, 'earth-settlers' who are described as a dwarf people and hence they are also termed as Koshito or 'dwarfs'. It is said that they were exterminated by the Ainus.

Two Physical types

Physically, the Japanese present two main types :

1. It is characterized by broad face with prominent cheek bones, oblique eyes with epicanthic fold and short concave nose, short-statured and thick-set body. Most conspicuous in the Japanese islands and this type forms the actual Japanese population. It is the typical Mongoloid type of Japan resembling the Chinese.

2. The second type, though Mongoloid, shows some Caucasoid-like elements, *e.g.*, wavy hair, growth of beard, etc. It is of Korean origin. It is termed as the Okayama type or Dainiyo type. They have tall stature slenderly built body, long face, prominent nose and straight or oblique eyes. In them epicanthic fold is not very frequent. These characteristics are frequently found among the members of the upper classes of Japan.

3. Besides these two there appears to be another type, the Malay type. It differs from the mainland types like the Chinese but has some resemblance with the Malayans. The Malay type has short stature with broad well developed chest, round face slightly prognathous and short nose. This type which is derived from a Malay sources, came to Japan from the south.

ARABIA

Two Social Groups

In general the Arabs are tall people with long head and face, jet black hair, fine narrow nose and black hair. In the Arabian peninsula they constitute two social groups. One group is formed by the cultivators who lead settled life, while the other group is represented by the nomads. The latter group has preserved the characteristic features of the primitive Arabs.

The Semites

The present-day population of Arabia is mainly formed by the Semites. The Semitic people are characterized by fine narrow nose with straight or convex profile, long elliptical face and jet black hair. They are distributed throughout South-west Asia, East and North Africa. The Semites of Arabia comprise two sections, the Bedawin and the Himyarite. Concentration of the former is seen in Northern Arabia. They are medium to tall-statured people with dolichocephalic head. The Himyarite live in Southern Arabia. They are mesocephalic people and are of medium stature.

Other elements

Besides these, traces of an ancient Hamitic population are also found in some parts of Southern Arabia. Again among the Arabs of South-east region, an European element is observed. A brachycephalic element is also present in Southern Arabia. This element was most probably introduced either by the Pamirians or by the Armenoids.

PERSIA

Two Groups

The modern population of Persia may be sub-divided into two principal groups :

1. The settled Tajik. They represent the old type of Persia. The Parsis of India are still preserving the characteristics of this type.

2. The Persians. Two groups of the Persians are distinguishable — the Farsi and the Lori.

(i) *The Farsis.* These appear to represent a Proto-Nordic type. They are slender people characterized by dolichocephalic head. Their fair skin and abundant growth of hair and beard.

(ii) *The Loris.* They resemble some member or the other of the Mediterranean. They are taller than the Farsis. Their skin colour is also darker. The head is also longer.

Other Ethnic Strains

Apart from these, the Kurds, the Armenians, and the Arabs have also contributed ethnic strains to the population of Persia.

12

Races in India

In different times different anthropologists attempted to analyse the ethnic elements present in Indian population. Of these who have made noteworthy contribution on this aspect, mention may be made of Risley, Ruggeri, Eickstedt, Guha, Hutton, Sarkar and Majumdar.

Classification By Giufrida-Ruggeri (1921)

Ruggeri found the following ethnic stratification in India :

(1) Negrito.

(2) Pre-Dravidians (Australoid Veddaic) — Santal, Ho, Munda, etc.

(3) Dravidians (having affinity with Homo Indo-Africans Aethiopicus), — Tamil and Telegu speaking people.

(4) Tall dolichocephalic (Mesocephalic?) elements — Todo.

(5) Dolichocephalic Aryan (Homo Indo-Europeanus dolichomorphus).

(6) Brachycephalic leucoderm (Homo Indo-Europeanus brachymorphus).

Classification By A.C. Haddon (1924)

Haddon has divided India into three main geographical regions, *viz.*, the Deccan Southern plateau, the Northern plains and the Himalayas of Hindustan and Haddon has dealt with the racial elements in each of these regions separately.

1. Deccan. Haddon has observed the following racial elements in this region:

(i) *Negrito.* A Negrito element is suspected among some populations like the Kadirs.

(ii) *Pre-Dravidian.* They form the oldest population. They are dolichocephalic, short statured, platyrrhine people. Their skin colour is dark brown to nearly black. Some of their representatives are : Bhil, Gond, Oraon, Santal, etc.

(iii) *Dravidian.* Their head is dolichocephalic, nose is mesorrhine, stature is medium. Their skin colour is brownish black. They are Tamil, Malayalam, Telugu, Canarese, etc., speaking people.

(iv) *Southern Brachycephals.* They have mesocephalic to brachycephalic head and medium nose represented by the Panyan in the Tamil district and the Pavara fishermen of the Tinnevelly coast.

(v) *Western Brachycephals.* They are occupying the regions extending from Gujarat to Coorg along the western coast, called the Scytho-Dravidians by Risely. They have brachycephalic head, almost leptorrhine nose, light brown complexion and tall stature. Their examples are : the Nagar Brahmins of Gujarat; the Prabhu, etc.

2. Hindustan. The Indo-Afghan appears to be the predominating type in this region. They are characterized by dolichocephalic head; finely cut, straight or convex, prominent nose; long face; regular feature; medium to tall stature; dark eyes; light brown complexion and black wavy hair. The typical representatives are the Jats, the Rajputs, etc.

In some places, the members of the Indo-Afghan type have mixed with the aboriginal people. This intermixture is more apparent in the lower caste people.

3. The Himalayas. Haddon observed the following racial elements in the region :

(i) *Indo-Afghans.* These are represented by the balti.

(ii) *Indo-Aryan, e.g.,the Kanets.* The Kanets of Kulu Valley exhibit a trace of Tibetan blood among them while the Kants of Lahoul also have some Mongoloid traits.

(iii) *Mongoloid.* This is the dominating element in Nepal, Bhutan, Sikkim, etc.

Assam has been dealt with separately by Haddon. The Assam tribes are mostly Mongoloid. In his Protomorphus division of the Mesocephalic Asiatic Xanthoderms. Haddon has included the Khasi, Bodo, Mishimi, Arlend, etc.

In Assam Haddon observes the following racial elements:

(i) *Dolichocephalic Platyrrhine type (Pre-Dravidian).* This element is strong among the Khasi, Kuki, Manipuri, Kachari, etc. It occurs in weaker form among the Naga Tirbes.

(ii) *Dolichocephalic — Mesorrhine* (Nesiot element). It is noticed among the Naga tribes.

(iii) *Mesocephalic Platyrrhine.* It is seen among the Khasis.

(iv) *Mesocephalic Mesorrhine.*

(v) *Brachycephalic Leptorrhine.* It came from the north and is related to the Eurasiatic group.

(vi) *Brachycephalic Platyrrhine.* It is a variety of the Pareoean.

(vii) *Dolichocephalic Leptorrhine.* It was from India.

Classification by Eickstedt (1934)

Eickstedt's classification is based on both physical characteristics and culture of the peoples. Eickstedt classified the peoples of India into four main divisions, namely:

1. Weddid or Ancient Indians. They are primitive people and they live in jungles. They are again divided into two sub-classes :

(i) *Gondid.* Their skin colour is dark brown and hair curly. Matriarchal influence is seen among them. They use mattock. Among them Toemistic belief is noteworthy. Their examples are : Juangs, Bhils, Oraons, Gonds, etc.

(ii) *Malid.* Their skin colour is dark brown and hair curly; they are peoples with ancient culture; though a foreign influence is observed their examples are : Kurumber, Weddah, etc.

2. Melanid or Black Indians. Racially, they form a mixed group. They are divided into the following classes :

(i) *Southern Melanid.* They live in the southern most plains of India. Matriarchal infleunce is marked among them. Their skin colour is black. An example is Yanadi, etc.

(ii) *Kolid.* They are found in the North Deccan forests. They have strong totemistic beliefs. Matriarchal influence is observed among them. Their skin colour is black brown. Their examples are : Munda, Ho, Santhal, etc.

3. Indid or New Indians. They are culturally advanced peoples, having finer physical characteristics. Their divisions are the following :

(i) *Gracile Indid.* Their skin colour is brown. They have gracile appearance. They are patriarchal people. Their example is the Bengalis.

(ii) *North Indid.* Their skin colour is light brown, these are patriarchal people. Their example are : The Rajputs, Todas, etc.

4. Place-Mongoloid. For example Palayan from Wyanad.

Though, Eickstedt's attempt as a pioneer to classify the Indian people is quite appreciable, his classification is not at all convincing. It is open to severe criticism.

Classification By H.H. Risley (1915)

He excluded the Negritos of Andaman Islands, as they had, according to him, little to do with the peoples of India. Risley divided the peoples of India into the following types:

1. The Turko-Iranian. They have broad heads and fine to medium nose, which is long and prominent. They are fairly tall, the average stature varying from 162 cm to 172 cm. They have plentiful hair on the face. Their eyes are generally dark though grey eyes are not uncommon. Their complexion is fair. These people live in the Baluchistan Agency and Frontier Province, which are now in Pakistan. They are represented by the Balochis, the Afghans, etc. Risley suggests that this type was formed as a result of a mixture of Turki and Persian.

2. The Indo-Aryan. They have long head and in this character they markedly differ from the Turko-Iranians. Their nose is long, narrow and prominent. Their complexion is fair, their eyes have a dark colour. They have plentiful facil hair. They are tall-statured people. They are found to predominate in Rajputana, the Punjab, and the valley of Kashmir. The Jats, the Khatris are some of the examples of this type.

3. The Scythio-Dravidian. This type has medium to broad head, medium nose, fair complexion and scanty hair on face and body. They are medium-statured. They differ from the Turko-Iranians in having larger heads, flatter faces, higher noses and shorter stature. This type is the result of an intermixture of two distinct racial elements, the Scythians and the Dravidians. They are distributed in the region extending from Gujarat to Coorg. While the Dravidian element is more prominent in the socially lower groups of these regions, the Scythian elements predominate among the higher groups of people.

4. The Aryo-Dravidian or Hindustan Type. As the name implies, this type is a result of an intermixture of two distinct racial types — the Aryans in the male and the Dravidians in the female line. Their heads are long with tendency towards medium. Their nose is generally medium but broad noses are also not unknown. Their skin colour is also variable, from light brown to dark. Their stature ranges from 159 cm. to 166 cm. Thus, they are differentiated from the Indo-Aryans in shorter and broader nose. This type is found in the Uttar Pradesh, Rajputana and Bihar.

5. The Mongolo-Dravidian or Bengali Type. Some of the representatives of this type are Bengali Brahmins, Bengali Kayasthas, etc. They differ from the Aryo-Dravidians and the Indo-Aryans in having broader heads. Risely suggests an intermixture of the Mongolians and the Dravidians in this type, to which some Indo-Aryan strains also added. The members of this type have broad head with a tendency to medium, and medium nose which tends towards broad in some cases. Their skin colour is dark with plentiful facial hair. Their stature is generally medium, but short stature also occurs quite frequently. They inhabit Bengal and Orissa.

6. The Mongoloid Type. Their head is generally broad, their nose shows a wide range of variation being fine to broad. Their stature is short or below medium. They have characteristically broad Mongolion face with oblique eyes showing epicanthic fold. Their skin colour is dark with yellowish tinge. Hair on their face and the body are scanty. This type is found in Assam, Nepal and Burma.

7. The Dravidian. According to Risely they are the true aborigines of India and now they have been modified by an infiltration of Aryan, Scythian and Mongoloid elements. They are short-statured people. Their head is long, nose is very broad and sometimes a depression is seen at the root of the nose. Their skin colour is very dark and eyes also have a dark colour. Their hair is also dark, hair is plentiful and occasionally tends to curl. Dravidians are found in the region extending from Ceylon to the Ganges covering the whole of South-Eastern India, Madras, Hyderabad, Central Province and Chota Nagpur. The Paniyans of South India, the Santhals of Chota Nagpur, etc., are some of the best examples of this type.

Risely's classification had to face considerable criticism from different authorities, specially in respect of the Dravidians, the Scythio-Dravidians and the Mongolo-Dravidians.

Classification By B.S. Guha (1937)

B.S. Guha has found the following racial elements, in the population of India :

1. The Negrito. This type is represented by the Kadars, Pulayans (Cochin and Travancore), Irurar and primitive tribes of the Wyanad. They are considered to be the first comers and the true authochtones of India. Their physical characteristics include small, round, medium or long head, nose is straight, flat and broad; they have very short of pygmy stature. Their skin colour is dark brown to dark; hair is woolly, forehead is bulbous; supraorbital ridges are smooth.

The Indian Negritos are more close to the Melanesion Pygmies than to the Andamanese, in respect of the head form and hair structure.

2. The Proto-Australoid. This element is found in the Pulayan women (Travancore), Urali (Travancore), Baiga (Rewa), etc. The tribes like the Male Chenchu, Kannikar, Kondh, Bhil, Santhal, Oraon, belong to this group. These are characterized by dolichocephalic head; markedly platyrrhine nose, depressed at the root; short stature; dark brown skin colour; wavy or even curly hair. Their limbs are delicate. Their forehead is less developed and slightly retreating. Supraorbital ridges are often prominent. They are closely akin to the Australian tribes. They markedly differ from the Negritos in having wavy hair instead of the frizzly or woolly of the latter.

3. The Mongoloid. The Mongoloids are distinguished by scanty growth of hair on body and face : obliquely set eyes showing epicanthic fold, flat face with prominent cheek bones and straight hair. The Mongoloid peoples entered India through the north-eastern routes in successive waves of migration.

The Mongoloid group comprises two types namely, the Palaeo-Mongoloid and the Tibeto-Mongoloid. The Palae-Mongoloids have again been sub-divided into long-headed type and broad-headed type.

(i) *The long-headed type*. It possesses long head, medium nose and medium stature. Their cheek bones are prominent; skin colour is dark to light brown; face is short and flat; supraorbital regions are faintly developed. They inhabit the sub-Himalayan region. This type is found in the tribes of Assam and Burma Frontier. The Same Nagas of Assam and the Limbus of Nepal are said to be true representatives of this type.

(ii) *The broad-headed type*. The other sub-division of the Palae-Mongoloid, the broad-headed, is represented by the Lepchas of Kalimpong. This type is found in the hill tribes of Chittagong, like the Chakmas, the Maghs, etc. Their characteristic features are : broad head, round face, dark skin colour, medium nose, obliquely set eyes which show marked epicanthic fold.

Among the Tibeto-Mongoloids, the head is broad and massive; face is long and flat; stature is tall; nose is long or medium; eyes are oblique having marked epicanthic fold; body hair and facial hair are markedly absent; skin colour is light brown. The Tibetans of Bhutan and Sikkim have these characteristics.

4. The Mediterranean. They comprise the following three distinct racial types:

(i) *The Palaeo-Mediterranean*. The human skeletal remains found at Adittanallur show this type of characteristics. These people probably introduced Megalithic culture to India. At present the Dravidian-speaking people of South India show the preponderance of this type. The Tamil Brahmins of Madura, Nairs of Cochin and Telugu Brahmins form the best example. These are the most ancient people. In many characters they resemble the Proto-Egyptian type. Their distinctive characters are : long and narrow head with bulbous forehead; projecting occiput and high vault; small and broad nose; medium stature; narrow dark face; pointed chin; slightly built body; skin colour scanty hair on face and body.

(ii) *The Mediterranean*. They are found in Uttar Pradesh, Bombay, Bengal, Malabar, etc. Their true representatives are the Numbudiri Brahmins of Cochin, Brahmins of Allahabad, and Maratha ladies of Indore. The Bengali Brahmins also show this type of characteristics. They are characterized by long head with arched forehead; long face; narrow and prominent nose; tall to medium stature; light skin colour, well-developed chin dark hair; brownish to dark colour eyes; plentiful facial and body hair and slender-built body.

Probably this type was responsible for the building up of Indus Valley Civilization.

(iii) *The Oriental* (of Fischer). They very closely resemble the Mediterranean in almost all the characters except the nose which is long and convex in the former. This type is found in the Punjab,

Sind, Rajputana, etc. Its typical representatives are the Punjabi Chettris and the Pathans.

5. The Western Brachycephals. They have been divided into following three types:

(i) *The Alpenoid.* They are characterized by broad head with rounded occiput; prominent nose; medium stature; round face light, skin colour abundant hair on face and body, thickly set body, etc. This type is found among the Bania of Gujarat, the Kathi of Kathiawar and the Kayasthas of Bengal, etc.

(ii) *The Dinaric.* The Alpino-Dinaric people entered India through Baluchistan, Sindh, Gujarat, Maharashtra into Kannada, thence to Ceylon. The presence of this type is found in the Indus Valley site, Tinnevelly, Hyderabad. These people are characterised by the broad head with rounded occiput and high vault; very long and often convex nose, tall stature, long face, receding forehead, darker skin colour, dark eyes and hair. This type is found in Bengal, Orissa and Coorg, represented the Brahmins of Bengal and the Kanarese Brahmins of Mysore.

(iii) *The Armenoid.* The Armenoids show resemblance with the Dinarics in most of the characters. In the former the shape of occiput is more marked and nose is more prominent, narrow and acquiline. The Parsis of Bombay show typical Armenoid characteristics.

6. The Nordics. The Nordics came from the north, probably from South-east Russia and South-west Siberia, through Central Asia to India. Their head is long with protruding occiput and arched forehead. They are tall statured people with long face, strong jaw powerfully built body, narrow and straight nose, fair, complexion eyes often with bluish tinge.

This element is found sporadically in different parts of Northern India specially in the Punjab and Rajputana. The Kho of Chitral, the Red Kaffirs, the Khatash are some of the representatives of this type.

Classification by S.S. Sarkar (1961)

According to S.S. Sarkar following six ethnic elements constitute the main types of the population of India :

1. Australoids. They are known by different names, like Proto-Australoid, Pre-Dravidian, Nisada, Veddid, etc. Certain tribes of South India, *e.g.*, Urali, Kannikar, Malapantaran, Paniyan, Kadar, *etc.*, have to some extent preserved the original form of the Australoids. According to Sarkar, at one time the Australoids were widely distributed throughout India. They form earliest substratum of the population of India. The Australoid make-up is present among all castes of India though its greatest concentration is found among the lower castes.

The physical characteristics of the Australoids are short stature, dark complexion, dolichocephalic head, platyrrhine nose and wavy hair.

2. Indo-Aryan. The Indo-Aryan are frequently met with in the Indus and the Gangetic valley in Western India extending upto Western Bihar. Beyond that region towards east the Indo-Aryan type is sporadic in distribution in eastern Bihar, Bengal and Assam where this type is mostly confined among the higher castes only.

The physical type of the Indo-Arya is quite distinct from that of the Australoid. The Indo-Aryans are tall in stature, lighter in skin colour and eye colour. Their head hair is not so dark as that of the Australoid. Their head is long but massive. Their cranial capacity is higher than that of the Australoid. They are more robustly built than the Australoid. The Baltis of the Hindukush mountains are the best representatives of the Indo-Aryan.

3. Irano-Scythian. After entering India the Irano-Scythians moved southward along the valley of the Indus to arrive at Gujarat, Bombay and Maharashtra extending upto northern Mysore, Deccan, etc. Therefore, this element is frequently observed in the population of these regions. From the western littoral the Irano-Scythians migrated to eastern India following the river valleys of the Narbada and the Sone. The Irano-Scythians are medium statured, with mesocephalic head different from the dolichocephalic Indo-Aryan. In eastern Bihar, Bengal and Assam the long headed Indo-Aryan element is replaced by the medium headed Irano-Scythian. Among the Indo-Aryan the cephalic index vary round 73, while among the Irano-Scythian it ranges between 77 and 79. The Irano-Scythians appears to be more variable in physical features than the Indo-Aryans.

4. Mundari-Speakers. These people are confined to the river valleys and plateaus of eastern Central India, *i.e.*, Chota Nagpur, Orissa hills and Madhya Pradesh. They migrated from east and have some sort of affinities with the Mongoloid.

According to Sarkar, "The Mundari-speakers are a stocky, thickest people with short stature and robust constitution, long head and skin colour somewhat lighter than the Australoid. Their head hair is not the usual thin curly or wavy hair of the Australoid rather their thick straight lank hair is nearly similar to those of the Mongolians."

5. Far-Eastern. From the ancient times India had cultural relationship with the islands of South-east Asia which continued till historical times. Therefore, some amount of Malaya Polynesian elements is observed in certain populations of eastern littoral, more particularly along the Tuticorin-Tinnevalley coast at the extreme south and along the coast of Chittagong hill tracts. According to Sarkar, "The Malayan racial strain is distinct from the ethnic elements, mentioned before in having a darker skin colour, broad to very broad head, short stature with tendency to obesity in general."

6. Mongolian. They are distributed in the North-eastern borders of India and the foothills of the Himalayas. Their skin colour is yellowish. Hair is sparsely distributed in their face and body. They exhibit Mongolian eyefold. By these criteria they are easily distinguishable from the other populations of India.

RACIAL ELEMENTS IN PRE-HISTORIC INDIA

Skeletal remains are few in comparison to the cultural materials unearthed from various prehistoric sites of India. Geographical condition of the country is one of the principal reasons for such a situation. On the basis of the collected skeletal materials one can make an attempt to analyse the ethnic elements that were present in the prehistoric population of India. While discussing racial elements in prehistoric India, one may look at the neighbouring countries on the North-western frontier also as several migrations of people took place from that direction.

Chanhudaro of Sindh

In Chanhundaro of Sind was found a skull of an adult female of about 22-25 years of age. It was studied by Korgman and Sassaman. According to them the skull is dolicho-cranial, the cranial index being 71.07, small and smooth, with small teeth, short, broad palate and small mastoid process. The supraorbital ridges are very slightly developed, but the glabells is relatively quite prominent. The occiput is smoothly rounded. The cranial capacity is 1222 c.c. Others are opinion that the Chanhudaro skull represents a Proto-Mediterranean the type in which ancestral Negroid traits have manifested themselves.

Harappa and Mohenjodaro

Skeletal remains of several individuals were unearthed in the Punjab, west Pakistan and Harappa-Mohenjodaro in Sindh. From Mohenjodaro itself skeletal remains of as many as forty one individuals were collected of which twenty-six skeletons were yielded during the first excavation under the direction of Marshall and fifteen during the second excavation under Mackay.

Examination By Sewell and Guha

Sewell and Guha examined fourteen skulls found at Mohenjodaro. They defined three skulls as Proto-Australoid, six as Mediterranean, one as Mongoloid branch of Apline stock and four possibly as Apline.

View of Sarkar

In his book *Ancient Races of Baluchistan, Punjab and Sind,* Sarkar has given a detailed description of the skeletal remains of Mohenjodaro and Harrapa along with those of other finds. Sarker has drawn similarities between the skulls of the Indus Valley and of Tape Hissar of Iran by analyzing the physical features of the skeletal materials and the methods of disposal of the head. He has summed up that, "The dolichocephals of the Indus Valley, showing a cranial index of 71, are an extension of the Tape Hissar people represented during periods I and II at the latter side. During the III period of Tape Hissar mesocephals, probably of ancient Scythian origin, arrived from Ukarine and Central Russia. They probably entered India almost contemporaneoulsy or afterwards. It is probable that the mesocephals migrated in different waves. The last wave shows weak traces of brachycephaly, which is rare in the Indus Valley. An autocthonous hyperdolichocranial element represented by the Veddid or Australoid ethnic strain appears to be at the base of the Indus Valley people."

Skulls from Bayana and Sialkot

From Bayana, a place near Agra in Uttar Pradesh one skull was collected. Another skull was found in Sialkot in the Punjab. These two skulls were examined by Keith. According to Keith, these are male skulls though they are quite small. They show similarities with that of modern man of the Punjab in shape and size. They are dolichocranial. According to Keith, the Bayana skull is of Aryan type because of the narrow nasal bone. Others think it to be of Mediterranean type with possibility of admixture. As no associated finds like tools or mammalian bones were found along with the skulls, it is difficult to determine their time. Skulls of Bayana and Sialkot show similarity with the skull found at Nal in Baluchistan. Comparative study is possible on that ground only.

Skeleton at Bishwanath

One skeleton was unearthed from a Late Paleolithic site near Bishwanath railway station situated at a distance of about 36 kilometer north of Allahabad in Uttar Pradesh. The skull is mesco-cranial, the index being 76.04. The face is broad and low. The nose is broad and the nasal root is deep. By radio carbon dating method its age has been estimated to be 10,500 years.

Skeletal remains in North Gujarat

Sankalia unearthed several skeletal remains from the microlithic beds in North Gujarat. The skulls suggest that the microlithic men of that area were dolichocephalic. They were proto-Egyptian because they show Hemitic Negroid characteristics.

Remains from Brahmagiri

Several prehistoric cultural materials and skeletal remains have been discovered from Brahmagiri in Mysore. Wheeler has identified the following three cultural sequences in Brahmagiri.

I. Earlier Stone Age cultural and later crude chalcolithic culture.

II. Megalithic culture, an Iron Age culture.

III. Andhra culture.

Sarkar examined the skeletal remains of Brahmagiri. Though remains of about twenty individuals were collected, only eleven were made available to Sarkar for study. Sarkar has identified two racial types. Australoid type and Irano-Scythian. The second type is of medium stature and is mesocephalic. A skull of a child of about twelve years was also found from Stone Age culture of Brahmagiri, which suggests the presence of Australoid type during that period.

Adittanallur Material

From Iron Age site at Adittanallur in Tinnevalley district of Tamilnadu several skulls and skeletal materials were discovered. Zuckermann observed Australoid element in one skull. In other he found presence of Mediterrranean characteristics. Eliot Smith also observed definite Australoid features in Adittanallur skull. In one he identified Armenoid characteristics also.

Prehistoric Finds at Maski

On the basis of the prehistoric finds at Maski in Mysore and other sites in Peninsular India, the cultural history of the Deccan may be traced back to the last 3,000 years or more. The Maski finds suggest three cultural layers. According to Yazdani some of the cultural materials date back to 1,000 B.C. or more. Others are of the period during 700—500 B.C. while others date from 500—300 B.C.

The skeletal materials of the chalcolithic site of Maski present two racial types — one Mediterranean and the other Armenoid branch of Western Alpine. Predominance of these two types are noticeable among the present day inhabitants of Maski. One type is characterized by dolichocephalic head and leptorrhine nose, while the other is brachycephalic and leptorrhine. Along with these two a third type is also observed which is dolichocephalic and platyrrhine. The presence of this third type, in the skeletal materials also which may be considered as Australoid cannot be totally ignored.

Neolithic Remains at Pickhai

From Neolithic remains at Pickhai two skulls were recovered. Iyer described these as long headed. He regarded them as the possibly ancestors on the present day Dravidian of the Decan. Guha considered this type to be Palaeo-Mediterranean.

Skeletal Remains at Nevasa

Ehrhardt studied the skeletal remains of Nevasa in Maharastra and assigned them to be more akin to the primitive people of the Deccan. Others identified them as to be Mediterranean and Proto-Australoid.

Other Skeletal Remains

Besides the above mentioned finds, there are some more sites from where fragments of several human skeletal remains were collected. One can mention a few sites like Rajgir in Hyderabad state, Nilgiri hills of Coimbatore, Nandangarh in Bihar, Burzahom near Srinagar in Kashmir, Nagarjunkonda, Ujjain. Detailed reports on the skeletal materials from many of these sites are not available.

Analysis of the human skeletal remains collected from different parts of India suggest that in Prehistoric India not one but at least three racial types were present in different proportions. Majumdar and others have identified these three ethnic types as Proto-Australoid, Mediterranean and Alpine Armenoid. To these some add Proto Nordic.

NEGRITO ELEMENT IN INDIA

Opinion of De Quatrefages

Opinions differ about the presence of Negrito element in the Mainland of India. This controversy started as early as in the nineteenth century, when in 1877 De Quatrefages expressed the view that Negrito made remarkable contribution towards basic ethnic substratum of the Dravidian and some tribes of India. Slight trace of woolly hair in any population was assigned to the Negrito. In 1895, Ball strongly criticized the view of De Quatrefages and said that De Quatrefage's findings were baseless. Other scholars like Callamand, Jagor and Koerbin were also not prepared to accept the view of De Quatrefages.

View of Keane

On the other hand, in 1896, while discussing the Negrito problem Keane supported De Quatrefages. According to him Negrito traits are present in some South Indian tribes like Kadar, Irula, Kurumba, Malachar, Pali, Vallal as well as among the Beda of Sri Lanka. However, in 1909, he himself expressed doubt about it. How he admitted that the same type of woolly hair as seen among African and Oceanic Negrito was perhaps lacking in the populations of India.

Opinion of Lapicque

After examining the Kadar in 1905 Lapicque said that Negrito element was present in them. However, he revised his view and said that Negrito traits as seen among the Andamanese were lacking among the Kadar, though the latter show a Negrito admixture.

Studies on Vedda

Studying the Vedda in 1893, Sarasin brother did not find any trace of woolly hair among them. In 1905, Turner also arrived at the same conclusion on the basis of analysis of craniometric data. According to Thurston woolly hair is not present in the population of South India. Risley also did not find woolly in any population of India. Inclined to accept this view Haddon did not accept the list of Negrito populations prepared by Keane. Though he listed the Kadar as a Negrito people, yet he expressed his doubt about it. Buxton also did not support the view that Negrito element is present in the tribes of Central and South India.

Opinion of Eickstedt

In his classification of Indian people made in 1933 Eickstedt did not include the Negrito. His Malid group is not Negrito. He clearly stated that Negroid hair was never present in any population of South India. This confusion was due to the fact that most of the investigators failed to distinguish between woolly and frizzly or spiral hair.

Studies of Andamanese

The Andamanese are Negrito according to Risley. "They have had no share in the making of the Indian population." Analysing the anthropometric data, Molesworth formed the opinion that the Andamanese were different from the aboriginal tribes of India. Flower and Turner came to the same conclusion on the strength of cranio metric evidence. The Andamanese are brachycephalic and platyrrhine people. Their cranial capacity is low. They are different from the Australoid in many characteristics. The Andamanese were confined to a particular area. There is no evidence to support that at one time the Negritos were distributed in different parts of the mainland of India. The skeletal materials collected from different prehistoric sites do not indicate the presence of Negrito element in ancient India. Negrito traits are not found in the population of modern India to suggest that at one time it was fairly distributed in India.

Iyer's View

Iyer observed frizzly hair among certain tribes of South India like Kadar, Pullayan, Urali and Kannikar which he considered as Negrito element. But Majumdar pointed out that, "No specific mention has been made of the incidence of this character and no microscopic examination is available to support Iyer's view." Aiyappan's view was different from that of Iyer. According to him, though the so-called Negrito element can be found among a few people of certain tribes of South India, all other tribes exhibit usual South Indian type *i.e.*, Australoid. In ethnical and racial origins the tribal people should not be considered to be different from the other people.

Opinion of Guha

Guha regarded the Negrito to be the original inhabitants of India. His observation was based on sporadic occurrence of woolly hair in certain populations of India, more particularly among the Kadar among whom he found 16 individuals having woolly or frizzly hair. Hair form is one of the racial criteria though Guha put much more emphasis on this single criterion only. In describing this character he used the terms woolly and frizzly indiscriminately. Hauschild pointed out that there is difference between the genetic feature of frizzly hair of the Negroes and ordinary frizzly hair. Ehrenfels made the same mistake. He wanted to prove the existence of Negrito hair in the Kadar. He published some photographs also. While describing the hair form he used different terms like woolly, frizzly, spiral. Sarkar strongly criticized Guha's view. He is not prepared to accept that the Negritos contributed ethnic strains to the basic substratum of the Indian population. The sporadic occurrence of so-called Negrito hair cannot be taken so seriously in the light of modern development of the science of genetics. As has been pointed out by Fischer woolly hair developed from wavy hair as a result of mutation.

Sarkar's Study of Kadar

In 1959, Sarkar along with his colleagues made a detailed study of various aspects of the physical features, *e.g.*, anthropometry, somatoscopy. ABO blood group, dermatoglyphics traits and hair of the Kadar. He arrived at a conclusion that no Negrito element is found among them. The Kadars are very similar to the Australoid tribes of South India. They may be listed as one of the Australoid tribes along with the Paniyan, Kannikar etc. After this study there is no reason to talk about the Kadar as having Negrito traits. So the earlier observation on Negrito element based on the Kadar are no longer tenable.

Haddon Description

Haddon gave a general description of the Negritos. They are very short statured, woolly haired and medium to low brachycephalic. The Andamanese are brachycephalic. De Quatrefeges also described the Negrito as brachycephalic. But according to Guha the Kadars are dolichocephalic. Majumdar does not think that sporadic occurrence of brachycephalic head proves the existence of Negrito element. If the mean cephalic index of a population is 75 or 76, there may be a few individuals with brachycephalic head.

Hutton's View

Another supporter of Negrito elements in India is Hutton. He observed sporadic occurrence of Negrito hair among the Angami Nagas. But Oliver did not find any Negrito element in any of the Naga tribes. Besides woolly and frizzly hair among the Angami Nagas, Hutton has put forward several cultural evidences in support of his hypothesis. However, he had been severely criticized by Sarkar and Majumdar. They have very clearly shown with strong valid arguments that Hutton's suggestions are not acceptable.

Support by Guha and Basu

To support Hutton's view on the existence of Negrito element among the Nagas, Guha has demonstrated the cranial materials collected by him and Basu from the Naga hills. They have classified the skulls into two groups. One group is Mongoloid, while the other is Proto-Australoid or Australoid. The skulls of the second group are similar to those Australoid skulls of Mohenjodaro. Though the authors call them Australoid, they have not cared to compare these skulls with the skulls of Australoid. On the other hand, comparison of those skulls has been made with that of Tasmanian and Melanesian. Perhaps, the reason is that they believe in the cultural similarities between the Naga people and Melanesians. On the basis of comparison they have arrived at a conclusion that the skulls of the second group are similar to that of Tasmanian and Melanesian with regard to low forehead and deep nasal root. These are undoubtedly Australian features. The Negrito elements found in the Papuan and Tasmanian skull were at one time distributed from north-east to south-west frontiers of India. Under the pressure of later migrations these people were driven to Ocenia leaving sporadic evidence of their presence here and there. Thus, Guha and Basu are not very clear to what do they intend to say but to prove somehow or other that the Negritos were distributed over a fairly larger part of India at one time.

The second representatives of the Negritos exhibited by Guha comes from Jewurgi skull described by Taylor as having Negrito features. But neither Taylor nor Guha have mentioned any Negroid feature. As the Jewugri skulls appear to be disfigured, nothing definite can be said on the strength of such evidence.

Concluding Remarks

While dealing with the racial elements in prehistoric India it has already been noted that there is no evidence to indicate presence of Negrito element at that time in the skeletal remains unearthed from different sites belonging to different periods ranging from Neolithic Piklihal and Chalcolithic Mohenjodaro to Iron Age site at Adittanallur. To quote Majumdar, ''Had there been an assimilation of the Negrito race by the Indian population, the characteristic Negrito traits, such as woolly hair and broad head associated with flat nose and dark complexion, would have been met frequently in northern India as well.''

However, one cannot completely rule out the possibility of penetrance of Negrito traits into certain population of India, more particularly a few coastal groups. There are reasons to believe that the Negroid populations established their colonies in some coastal regions like Gujarat, where they came in contact with the local people. As a result, Negro traits were penetrated into the local populations by admixture. But these events which occurred comparatively in recent times were local phenomenon. As such these Negroids did not get chance to contribute their share in a considerable manner to the ethnic make up of the Indian population.

Australoid Element in India

On different occasions different anthropologists had expressed their respective views about the original inhabitants of India. Anthropologists like Guha held the opinion that the Negritos were the earliest settlers of India, while according to Risley the Dravidians were the first to come to India. On the other hand, Sarkar, Majumdar and others consider the Australoids to be the autochthones of India.

Sarkar's View

In ancient Sanskriti literature we come across a certain people referred to as the Dasas, Dasyus and Nishadas. According to Sarkar they appear to be the original inhabitants of India. They were short-statured people. Their complexion was dark and head was long. They had dark wavy hair. A fairly correct description of the physical features of the Nisadas is found in the *Bhagavata Purana* as follows: "black like crow very low statured, short-armed, having high cheek bones, lowtipped nose, red eyes and copper coloured hair."

Various Names

Ethnically these are the Australoids, who are referred to by various names by different scholars. Ruggeri called them Australoids Veddaic. Eickstedt preferred to call them by the term Veddid because of their similarities in physical features with the Veddas of Sri Lanka. On the other hand, Chanda wanted to preserve the earlier term Nishada. The term Pre-Dravidian was perhaps first used by Lapicquo. Haddon also used this term. Sewell and Guha preferred to call them by the term Proto-Australoid, the term was, however, first coined by Dixon. Sarkar first accepted the term Veddid, but later on preferred to use the term Australoid. As the Australoids form a primary human race and the proto type of the race is not known, therefore, they should be called by the term Australoid itself.

The Veddas

The Veddas of Sri Lanka and the tribes of South India show resemblance in their physical features. The Veddas are considered to be ideal representatives of the Australoid. That, however, does not necessarily mean that the Australoid involved in Sri Lanka. Rather they migrated from South India to Sri Lanka. According to Osman Hill the Veddas are the original inhabitants of Sri Lanka.

Australoid in South India

There are a number of Australoid tribes in South India of which mention may be made : Urali, Kannikar and Muthuvan of Travancore; Panyan of Malabar; Irula, Kurumba and Chalaga of Nilgiri area; Chenchu of Hyderabad; Malachar and Kadar of Cochin. The Australoid tribes were not confined to South India only, though their main concentration is seen in that part of the country. Australoid origin, are met with towards north Males of Rajmahal Hill and Pahira of Manbhum. Many Central Indian tribes like Oraon, Gond and Khond are also Australoid. From their present day geographical distribution it appears that the Australoid are jungle dwellers.

Australoid outside India

Australoids are found outside India towards west in South Arabia and Persia. Towards east are seen to live several Australoid populations such as Male of Great Nicobar; Sakai of Malay; Luba and Ulu of Sumatra; Toala of Celebes and Moi in Indo-China. Birdsell observed Australoid traits in North

Australia and called Carpenterian. Thus, the present day geographical distribution of the Australoid suggests that they were distributed far and wide towards west and east with India as the centre.

Who were the original Indians?

To justify that the Australoids and not the Negritos are the original inhabitants of India, Sarkar analyzed the status of these two races from the evolutionary point of view. There are differences of opinion on the question which one was the first to acquire its distinctive physical features — Australoid or Negroid, most of the anthropologists are in favour of the Australoid.

Neanderthal man appeared towards the end of the early palaeolithic period. If we follow Sollas and Von Luschen, we are to accept that Neanderthals are the ancestors of the Australoid. Huxley also regarded that the living representatives of the Neanderthal were the Australoids. Keith, however, did not consider the Australoid as the descendants of the Neanderthals. He was of the opinion that they formed a type of very early man. According to Howells the Australoids form a primary race, the earliest of the living races of the present time. Gates looked at the Pithecanthropus to find out the ancestors of the Australoid. The Negroid traits were first observed in the Grimaldi man. There is no doubt that the Grimaldi type appeared after Neanderthal. Thus, it could be concluded that the Australoid came first then the Negroid.

Woolly hair is one of the most salient features of the Negro. Fisher demonstrated that woolly hair was a later development from wavy hair. This also suggests that the wavy haired Austaloid evolved first and then the woolly haired Negroid. Howells supports this view. According to him, the possible physical characters of the early man are still preserved by the Australoids.

Australoid element in prehistoric India

The Mohenjodaro civilization has been dated between 3250 and 2750 B.C. Sewell and Guha have informed that three skulls of Mohenjodaro are of Australoid type, which suggests presence of this element during that period. The two burial series of Harappa indicate the presence of the different racial types. The people of the lower series were similar to the Australoid. They resemble the same type found in Mohenjodaro. Analyzing the racial elements of ancient Baluchistan, Sindh and the Punjab, Sarkar has noticed a hyperdolichocephalic type, which is Australoid. He is of the opinion, that the Australoid strain appears to be at the base of the Indus Valley people.

The Iron Age site of Addittanallur of South Indian yielded several skulls. According to Guha these are of Proto-Australoid type. Zuckermann and Smith examined two skulls which according to them are quite akin to the Australoid type. Again the skeletal remains recovered from Megalithic and Neolithic sites at Brahmagiri in Mysore indicate the presence of Australoid type. Thus, an analysis of the early skeletal remains unearthed from different parts of India clearly demonstrate the presence of Australoid element in prehistoric India from the very early period.

Sewell is of opinion that the Australoids are related to the Australian aborigines on the one hand and Rhodesian man on the other. Palaeonthropus Palestinus appears to be the connecting link among these early varieties of man. According to others Rhodesian man, Peking man and Homo Soloensis belong to the same racial group. Sewell thinks that there is genetic relationships between Homo Soloensis and the Australian aborigines. All these suggest the antiquity of the Australoid type.

Following Sarkar and Majumdar one can say that there are more reasons than one to regard the Australoids as the original inhabitants of India.

PART C — CULTURAL ANTHROPOLOGY

13

Cultural Anthropology

Culture and civilization have been particularly studied by anthropologists and sociologists. The methods used by the scientists in the study of culture and civilization are empirical. P. A. Sorokin has criticized the students of culture who are inclined to arrange the phenomenon of cultural growth in terms of only one set of factors with possible neglect of the rest.[1] Culture displays a large complexity, multidimensional activity and polymorphous relations. Therefore, it cannot be explained by only functional factors. Pointing out this difficulty, A. J. Toynbee has said. "The riddle of the relation between God's law and human soul's freedom is the last, the most difficult and the most crucial of all questions on our agenda."[2] However, in order to understand culture, it is necessary to be definite about its meaning and components. Toynbee has made a successful attempt to show that one may observe some regularity in cultural processes.

MEANING OF CULTURE

In common parlance the word 'culture' is understood to mean beautiful, refined or interesting but this interpretation does not constitute its adequate definition. Some of the more popular definitions of culture are as follows:

1. "Culture is that complex whole which includes knowledge, belief, art, morals, law, custom and any other capabilities and habits acquired by man as a member of society."[3]

2. "Culture is the organised body of conventional understanding manifest in art and artifact which persisting through tradition, characterizes human group."[4]

3. "Culture is the quintessence of all natural goods of the world, and of

---

1. Sorokin, P. A., *Social and Cultural Dynamics*, Vol. I., Introduction, p. 45, 51, 53.
2. Toynbee, A. J., *A Study of History*, Vol. IX, p. 219.
3. Tylor, E.B., *Primitive Culture*, p. 1
4. Redfield, "Unpublished Lectures", *Social Science*, University of Chicago.

those gifts and qualities which, while belonging to man, lie beyond the immediate sphere of his needs and wants."[5]

4. "Culture is a symbolic, continuous, cumulative and progressive process."[6]

5. "Culture includes all that man has acquired in the mental and intellectual sphere of his individual and social life." In the words of MacIver and Page, "This is the realm of styles, of values, of emotional attachments, of intellectual adventures. Culture, then, is the antithesis of civilization. It is the expression of our nature, in our modes of living and thinking, in our everyday intercourse, in art, literature, in recreation and enjoyment."[7]

6. "Culture refers to those ways of thinking, feeling and behaving that are socially transmitted from one generation to the next."[8]

7. "The system of values and meanings shared by a group or society, including the embodiment of those values and meanings and the material objects."[9]

8. "It is the product of a variety of more or less harmonious activities each pursued for its own sake, the artist must concentrate upon his canvas, the poet upon his typewriter, the civil servant upon the just settlement of particular problems as they present themselves upon his desk, each according to the situation in which he finds himself."[10]

The above-mentioned definitions, except the last one, are those advanced by anthropologists and sociologists. These are functional in nature. According to functional view, "culture is an external combination of independent activities."[11]

Characteristics of Culture

The essential characteristics depicting the nature of culture may be summed up as follows :

1. Culture is inclusive of those elements which man has created and in which he can make improvements.

2. The introduction of novel elements increases the complexity and qualities of culture.

3. It is communicated from one generation to another generation in a psychic form.

4. Culture is found only in human society.

---

5. Joseph Pieper, *Leisure, the Basis of Culture* (1920), p. 20.
6. White, L.A., *American Sociological Review* (Dec. 1947).
7. MacIver, R. M. and Page, C.H., *Society: An Introductory Analysis*, p. 499.
8. Hobbs, D. A. and Blank, S.J., *Sociology and the Human Experience*, John Wiley, New York, 1978, p. 447.
9. David, P., *Sociology*, Prentice-Hall, New Jersey, 1977, p. 566.
10. Eliot, T. S., *Notes Towards the Definition of Culture*, p. 19.
11. See Malinowski: *Scientific Concept of Culture* and Ruth Benedict, *Patterns of Culture*.

Nature of Culture

The above-mentioned characteristic of culture throw light upon its nature. Important facts concerning the nature of culture are as follows :

1. Culture is an acquired quality. Culture is not innate. Traits learned through socialization, habits and thoughts are what is called culture. Man exhibits cultural behaviour because he has capacity of symbolic communication.

2. Culture is communicative. In this way, culture is communicated from one generation to the next. As a result of this, culture is constantly accumulating. The new generation benefits by the experience of the earlier generation through the communicability of culture. In this way, culture becomes semi-temporary and remains unaffected by the extinction of a group or an individual.

3. Culture is social not individual. Every individual takes some part in the transmission and communication of culture, but culture is social rather than individual. It is inclusive of the expectations of the members of groups. Man cannot create culture while existing apart from the groups.

4. Culture is idealistic. In culture are included those ideal patterns and norms of behaviour according to which the members of society attempt to conduct themselves. Society accepts these ideals, norms and patterns.

5. Culture fulfils some needs. Culture fulfils those ethical and social needs which are ends in themselves. Social habits are included in culture. Habits can be formed of those activities only which tend to fulfil some needs. Without fulfilling these needs, culture cannot exist.

6. Culture has the characteristic of adaptation. Culture is constantly undergoing change in concurring to the environment and due to this transformation it is constantly being adapted to external forces but once it is developed the influence of the natural environment begins to decrease. Besides, the various aspects of culture are also undergoing development and some internal adaptation among them consequently is being necessitated.

7. Culture has the quality of becoming integrated. Culture possesses an order and a system. Its various parts are integrated with each other and any new element which is introduced is also integrated. Those cultures which are more open to external influence are comparatively more heterogeneous but nevertheless some degree of integration is evident in all cultures.

In this way, culture is social, idealistic and acquired and fulfils many of man's needs. It possesses the characteristics of communication, adaptation and integration. It is a special quality of man. It is the evidence of his social heritage

COMPONENTS OF CULTURE

According to Clark Wissler the universal components of culture include (1) language, (2) concrete apparatuses like food, house, means of conveyance dress, weapons, utensils, arms, industries and occupations, (3) arts, (4) legendary and scientific knowledge, (5) rituals and blind beliefs, (6) family and marriage, social control, games and other social institutions of the kind, (7) property value, exchange and trade, (8) government and law, (9) war.

These universal components are found in all cultures but their forms are different. Thus, the components of culture are what is known as non-material culture in sociological studies which include abstract things, such as different customs, conventions, methods, arts, knowledge, religion of a society, etc.

Some Terms Connected with the Concept of Culture[12]

1. Cultural Diffusion. The process by which culture traits spread from one group or society to another.

2. Cultural integration. The fitting together of cultural units into a cohesive whole.

3. Cultural lag. A theory which holds that most changes occur first in the material aspects of culture, and that non-material cultural change lags behind material change.

4. Cultural pluralism. The pattern of partial assimilation in which the dominant society allows minorities to achieve full participation, yet at the same time permits them to maintain many of their cultural and social differences.

5. Cultural relativity. The principle that a culture must be understood and judged on its own terms without reference to the values of another culture.

6. Cultural survival. A culture trait that has survived after its original function has disappeared.

7. Cultural complexes. Clusters of inter-related culture traits that function as distinct and separable units in a society.

8. Culture shock. The psychological stress caused when a person faces rapid cultural change.[13]

The bewilderment, frustration and disorientation that immersion in a different culture has upon the unprepared visitor. Culture shock is evidence of the uniqueness of human groupings.[14]

9. Cultural assimilation. A sub-process of assimilation that refers to the extent to which an ethnic or minority group adopts and internalizes the cultural patterns of the larger society.[15]

10. Cultural trait. The simplest unit or element of a culture.[16]

---

12. Popenoe David, *Sociology*, Prentice-Hall, New Jersey, 1977, p. 566.
13. *Ibid.*
14. Hobbs, D.A. and Blank, S. J., *Sociology and the Human Experience*, John Wiley, New York, 1978, p. 447.
15. *Ibid.*
16. Popenoe, David, *Sociology*, Prentice-Hall, New Jersey, 1977, p. 566.

NATURE OF CIVILIZATION

In contrast to the non-material nature of culture, civilization is material. It includes material or concrete things used by man, such as house, household commodities, different kinds of apparatus, instruments, weapons, pots and means of conveyance etc. According to J.L. Gillin, and J P. Gillin civilization is a more complex, and evolved form of culture. A.W. Green has written, 'A culture becomes a civilization only when it possesses written language, science, philosophy, a specialized division of labour and a complex technology and political system." Ancient cultures did not possess all these elements and would consequently be considered as having no civilization. Franz Boas, Ogburn and Nimkoff also treat civilization as a state which follows culture. Ogburn has written that "Civilization may be defined as the later phase of super organic culture." According to Weber, civilization includes useful material objects and the methods of producing and using them whereas culture consists of the ideals, values and the mental and emotional aspects of a group. Merton, Richard Thurnwald and many other sociologists have subscribed to this opinion. P A. Sorokin has opposed it. But this is the opinion most widely prevalent among the sociologists today.

Components of Civilization

Thus, the components of civilization are generally physical, biological and technological. Technique is a part of civilization. Civilization attempts at attaining physical adjustment with the environment. It represents the external structure. It involves techniques of human adjustment with nature. It is the result of processes of natural selection and social selection. The components of civilization are thus external and objective. The study of a civilization includes the study of housing, means of communication, dress, industries, weapons, etc.

Relation of Culture and Civilization

White studying a group, modern anthropologists and sociologists study both the material civilization and non-material culture, since the two are closely related. Both have been developed by the same human processes. Both are complimentary to each other. Culture needs civilization for further growth, civilization needs a culture even for its vital force and survival. The two are therefore interdependent. Life is the most severe and most necessary test of the superiority of a culture. Existence is the first law of human life. A civilization cannot survive without strong stimulus and motive, however high may be its achievements in science. Man is still a struggling unsuccessful hero in this world. A culture which claims any greatness should help man in this upward effort. It should inspire the terrestrial endeavours of man.

DIFFERENCE BETWEEN CULTURE AND CIVILIZATION

In spite of the above close relationship between culture and civilization, the two are very much different. This difference has been particularly pointed out in the field of literature and philosophy. The definition of culture given by T.S. Eliots at the beginning of this chapter, shows those characteristics of it which are not found in civilizations. Culture, as Sorokin aptly calls it, is a "Causal Meaningful System."[17] Civilization, on the other hand, involves techniques. Techniques are differentiations of instinctive behaviour utilized to answer the challenge of Nature. Most of the scientific growth is the growth of technology aimed at achieving man's adjustment with the environment. However, as A.L. Kroeber has pointed out, "Culture is different from mere physical equilibrium, it is a higher unity which should not be subjected to the categories of the inconscient."[18] Thus, civilization implies animal adjustment while culture has much more higher orientation. Thus, while technology may be a condition of the advancement of culture it is not its fulfilment. Civilization is concerned with the physical and external equipment of a community to ensure physical requirements. Culture, on the other hand, is concerned with internal growth. While civilization is external and objective, culture is internal and subjective. It is not mere stimulus-response. It is an expression of creativity of an individual or a group. This distinction between culture and civilization can be summed up in the explanation of culture richness given by Toynbee : "In other words, the process which we are examining involves not merely a simplification of appratus but a consequent transfer of energy or shift or emphasis, from some lower sphere of being or sphere of action to a higher sphere. Perhaps we shall be describing it in a more illuminating way if we call it not simplification but etherealization."[19] Thus, cultures are born by spiritual necessities, the challenges of circumstances. Therefore, culture is particularly spiritual in nature. Civilization on the other hand, is particularly physical, based upon science and technology. While civilization involves the efforts of the masses, cultural advance is the function of a creative minority of artists, poets, philosophers, etc. In the words of MacIver and Page, civilization includes all those things by means of which some other objective is attained, such as typewriter, press, lathes, motor, etc. In civilization are included both basic technology which means the authority of man over natural phenomena as well as special technology or modes which control man's behaviour. On the other hand, culture comprehends such elements as religion, art, philosophy, literature, music, etc. which bring satisfaction and pleasure to man.

Thus culture and civilization differ in the following respects :

1. Civilization has a precise standard of measurement but not culture. The universal standard of civilization is utility because civilization is a means. Culture has no similar qualitative or quantitative standard of measurement because culture is an end in itself. The elements, ideals, values and thoughts, etc., of culture change in accordance with the time and place.

---

17. Sorokin, P.A., *Social Philosophies in an Age of Crisis*, p. 277.
18. Kroeber, A. L., *Nature of Culture*, pp. 112-114.
19. Toynbee, *A Study of History*, Vol. 3, p. 183.

2. Civilization is always advancing, but not culture. The various constituents of civilization, *e.g.* machines, means of transportation and communication, etc., are constantly progressing. But concerning culture, it cannot be asserted that art, literature, thoughts or ideals of today are superior to those of the past.

3. Civilization is transmitted without efforts, but not culture. Objects comprehended by civilization have utility and are connected with the external life of man. Hence, they can be easily adapted from one generation to another or from one country to another but culture is not communicated and adapted with equal facility because it is related to an inner tendency and can be adapted only after the appropriate inner development. It is communicated only to the like-minded. One cannot appreciate art without the quality of an artist nor can any one enjoy music without the sensitivity of a musician. In contrast to culture, civilization does not make any such demand. One may enjoy the products of civilization without sharing the capacity which creates them. Civilization may be adopted without efforts. The adoption of culture depends upon personality and nature.

4. Civilization is borrowed without change or loss, but not culture. When civilization is borrowed by a country or a generation other than its originator, it does not suffer any deterioration, loss or change. Railway, motor cars, aeroplanes, machines, etc., are borrowed as they are but the elements of culture such as religion, art, literature, thought, ideals etc., can never be borrowed in their original character. For example, the Indian Christians are found to possess many elements, borrowed from the Hindu and Muslim religions, which are not to be found in their Western counterparts.

5. Culture is internal and an end while civilization is external and a means. Civilization is inclusive of external things, culture is related to internal thoughts, feelings, ideals, values, etc. Civilization is the means for the expression and manifestation of culture. It is the body while culture is the soul.

CULTURAL GROWTH

The development of culture is a continuous process. In this process while the experiences of the proponents of one culture are accumulated and handed down from one generation to another on the one hand, new elements from other cultures are introduced through accommodation, cross fertilization and diffusion, on the other, and culture progresses as a result of their unification. The existing developed culture of any country is a result of these processes carried out over a period of hundreds and thousands of years. In this development the rate of progress is not uniform. At times it is slow while at other times it is relatively fast, sometimes it is moving towards progress, at others towards deterioration.

In order to understand cultural growth properly, it is necessary to understand those processes of cultural growth which were mentioned above. Briefly, these progresses are the following :

1. Accumulation. To begin with, an individual experiments with an object about which he knows virtually nothing. Of the various experiments he makes, he discards those which have proved fruitless and adopts for subsequent application those which have been successful. In this way, the experience gained in this experimentation is accumulated and passed on by one generation to its successor as social heritage. The development of language has been of tremendous value in this accumulation. New experiments continue to be made, in addition to these experiences. Inventions increase along with the increase in needs. It has been said that necessity is the mother of invention. In this way, both the material and non-material aspects of culture progress through such accumulation. The accumulation continues uninterrupted.

2. Diffusion. Cultural growth results not merely from accumulation but also by the adoption of novel concepts from other cultures. Accordingly diffusion applies to the adoption of new ideas by one individual or society from another individual or society. Almost all the cultures of the world are adopting innumerable new ideas and things from the modern Western culture through diffusion.

3. Accommodation. The new ideas which have been acquired through diffusion have to be accommodated with the other features of the culture. It is only through having accommodated themselves with Indian culture that the numerous objects and various elements of Western culture which have been acquired and adopted in India have become a part of its life and have added to the progress.

4. Cross fertilization. The conjunction of two cultures is beneficial to both since it does not happen that one should borrow the other exclusively. This process of mutual give and take is called cross-fertilization. Due to this, culture retains its vitality and life.

5. Acculturation. When such a conjunction of two cultures occurs, causing cultural growth, and they are intimately related rather than identified, the process is called acculturation. Sometimes a process, called the process of contraculturation, also sets in. It is the opposite of the process of acculturation. For example, many English things were adopted in India but the Swadeshi movement and the development of nationalism abolished and condemned many things of Western origin.

6. Assimilation. In this process of cultural conjunction, when one culture becomes so intimate with another as to lose its individuality, it is called assimilation.

It would have become apparent from the preceding description that the process of cultural growth is not simple, but complex. Many processes are involved in it. In the process of such interaction many cultures have become completely extinct and are only mentioned in history. Great cultures are invariably progressive. This is the secret of their life force. Indian culture is one such example.

THEORIES OF CULTURAL GROWTH

The growth of culture has been a significant subject of research for anthropologists. In this connection the following questions have been particularly raised :

1. How are cultures born?

2. Why the cultural traits and cultural complexes in different cultures are generally similar? This is sometimes known as the theory of cultural parallels. The question is raised about the reason of the formation of cultural parallels. This question has been answered by the anthropologists by means of the following theories.

1. Evolutionism.
2. Diffusionism.
3. Acculturation.

EVOLUTIONISM

Evolutionism in the field of culture was born when Darwin's theory of evolution was most popular. Therefore, this theory has been immensely influenced by Darwin's theory. Some thinkers have, however, pointed out that cultural evolutionism has not been influenced by biological evolution. Of these, the name of Taggart is the most important. He has tried to point out that books on evolutionism in cultural growth were published side-by-side with the publication of Darwin's famous book *The Origin of Species* in 1859. Most of the books on evolutionism in cultural growth were published between 1859 and 1865. Of these the important works were presented by Bachofen, Bastian, Maine, Mclennan and Tylor. According to Taggart in the 19th century no significant influence of Darwin's theory upon evolutionism in cultural growth can be observed. It is generally believed that while Darwin was conducting the researches and propounding theories, the anthropologists were independently working upon evolutionary theory of culture. However, it must be conceded that Darwin's theory definitely influenced evolutionary theory of culture. According to Dr. S.C. Dubey, the theories of evolution in culture were clearly influenced by Darwinism though it will not be proper to say that these theories are Darwinian theories. In 1877 Louis H. Morgan, in his book *Primitive Society* pointed out evolution in human institutions. At the same time Tylor presented his work *Primitive Culture*. These two works are the foundation stones of the evolutionary theory of culture.

Salient Points of Evolutionism

According to evolutionary theory, cultural growth follows Unilinear Sequence. It passes through definite stages which were studied by comparative method. All the societies passed through these cultural stages. In its higher stage of a culture some residues of the primitive stage can be observed. These are known as survivals. They remind us about the earlier stages of the culture. The most important points in the evolutionary theory of culture are as follows :

1. Human culture, particularly social institutions and social thought evolve in unilinear sequence.
2. By the study of cultural elements in different societies through comparative method the above fact has been proved.
3. More developed and higher traditions stay longer in society.

Unilinear Evolution

Morgan, in his book *Primitive Society*, has considered social evolution as unilinear. According to him, societies have passed through the following cultural stages:

1. Savagery,
2. Barbarism,
3. Civilization.

According to Morgan's scheme, the lower status of savagery was the infancy of human evolution. In middle savagery human beings knew about the use of fire and generally depended upon fishing. In upper savagery bow and arrows were generally used. In the first stage earthenwares were invented. In middle stage animal husbandry was developed. In the stage known as upper barbarism iron was used for making different types of implements. Civilization started with the development of alphabet. This theory advanced by Morgan has been supported by Tylor. According to Tylor, ''Simply placing civilized nations at one end of the social series and savage tribes at the other, arranging the rest of mankind between these limits... ethnographers are able to set up at least a rough scale of civilization ... a transition from the savage state to our own.[20]

Morgan has maintained unilinear evolution in the institution of marriage as well. According to him, the first stage in the evolution of marriage was known as promiscuity or sex communism. Marriage institution further passed through the stages of group marriage, Polyandry, Polygamy and Monogamy. This theory has been also supported by other anthropologists through their studies of other human institutions. For example, Tylor studied the evolution of religion in which the first stage was termed as Animistic Polytheism, the second stage as higher polytheistic ideology and the next stage as Monotheism. Similarly, Haddon studied evolution in the field of art. Levy Bruhl studied evolution in the field of Logic. Thus, propounders of evolutionary theory tried to find out the origin of different cultural elements. For example, *The Golden Bough*, published in 13 volumes by Sir James Frazer traces the nature and evolution of religion.

Unilinear theory of evolution has been widely criticized, some important

20. Tylor, *Primitive Culture* (1871), pp. 26-27.

modifications have been made in it, ultimately, leading to some sort of multilinear theory of evolution.

Multilinear Evolution

This theory was supported by Julian Steward. According to it the various stages in the evolution of different cultures were not uniform throughout the world. However, some stages can be identified in cultural evolution. Steward made a comparative study of parallel cultural evolution of cultures of Peru, Mesopotamia, U.S.A. and China and pointed out different stages of evolution. Thus, he not only carried the evolutionary theory forward but also gave it a new direction.

Parabolic Curve

According to some anthropologists, social institutions developed in parabolic curves. First of all, a social institution is born in a specific form, then it develops an entirely different form and evolves it. For example, the institution of property born in the form of communal ownership is again evolving in the form of communism. Same can be said about the human dresses. In the beginning there was a shortage of cloth, therefore not many men used much cloth. In the middle ages dressing of the whole body was considered as a necessary sign of civilization. In modern times the physical culture movement is again leading to nudism. Similar evolution can be traced in the field of sex-behaviour. Sex-behaviour almost everywhere started in the form of sex-communism or promiscuity. Gradually this developed to polygamy and polyandry, etc. Finally with the further growth of cultural values in the field of male-female relationships monogamy was evolved. Most recently the bonds of monogamy are breaking and sex-mores are again becoming more and more loose and permissive. This is particularly true to the Western countries. But societies in the East will also follow suit. However, the sex mores will again harden and the cycle will go on.

In 1945, the famous American anthropologist Leslie White again raised the discussion of evolution in culture. He maintained that culture grows according to the growth of human capacities. The theory of evolution has been rightly discussed and criticized. It cannot be rejected as absolutely imaginary. The proper viewpoint is perhaps in between these two extremes.

DIFFUSIONISM

Evolution of culture is a gradual process. In this process, whereas on one side the experiences of the followers of single culture accumulate and are handed down from one generation to the other, on the other side new elements keep coming into the culture from other cultures through organization, acculturation and diffusion, etc. and the culture grows through their assimilation. The present evolution of culture of any country is the result of these processes carried on through hundreds and thousands of years. The speed of growth in this evolution is not always the same. Sometimes it is fast and at other times it is slow, sometimes towards improvement and sometimes towards a decline.

What is Diffusion?

Cultural diffusion is one of the processes of cultural evolution. Adoption of new things by one individual or society from another individual or society is called diffusion. Almost all the cultures of the world are adopting new things every day through the diffusion, *e.g.*, the influence of the culture evolving at the banks of Nile river reached India; Indian modes of thought reached China and played an important part in the growth of Western culture. It was again due to diffusion that the cultures of Mycene, Crete and Egypt influenced the Greek culture. In the same way, modern cultures also keep on influencing other cultures through diffusion. Ogburn and Nimkoff, while defining diffusion, have written that a transmission of culture traits from one area to another and from one culture to another is called diffusion. Railway trains, motor cars, aeroplanes, cinemas, tanks, telephone, telegraph and television, etc., and thousands of other things seen in the modern world today are examples of such a transmission. Not only instruments and machines but even ideas keep moving from one country to another. Religion of Buddha spread from India to China, Japan, Burma and other countries. Communism from Russia went to other countries. Indian decimal system crossed to Arabia and Europe. The following factors help in diffusion:

(a) Contact and communication, (b) the desire and needs of new traits, (c) competition with old traits and their opposition, (d) respect for those who invent or bring in new traits.

Diffusion is possible among different societies and even in one and the same society; unprecedented development of the means of conveyance and communication have been the cause of high speed of diffusion in the present century. The German scholars, Graebner, Ankerman and Schmidt have done important work in the establishment and spread of diffusion theory. Their ideology is called *Culture Historiche Schule*. According to this ideology, similarity in two cultures cannot be regarded as a result of diffusion so long as historical evidences affecting their mutual contacts are not given.

R. Linton, in his book *The Study of Man* has given in detail the influence of diffusion in American life. For example, the bed which an American leaves in the morning was invented in the Near East and was reformed in Europe, the curtains which he removes are made of the cotton which was first grown in India. If the curtains are made of silk, they were invented in the Near East. If they are made of linen, they were discovered in China. The soft leather moccasin shoes, which he puts on after leaving his bed were made by Red Indians of North America. The bath room which he enters after this, is the result of modern European and American inventions. The trousers which he puts on were first made in India. The soap which he uses in cleaning his hands was first made by the people of ancient Gal. After this, the razor which he uses in shaving was made in Sumer of Egypt. In the same way, among so many other things of his use, necktie is the residual of the shawl used by Croatian people on their shoulders in the 17th century. The felt of his cap is the invention of

Asian Steppes. The umbrella used in rains is a discovery of South-east Asia, and the rubber of the shoes he puts on is the invention of the primitive inhabitants of America. Among his utensils, plate is an invention of China, his knife is made of steel invented in South India, his fork is the invention of Italy in the middle period and his spoon is the invention of ancient Rome. Among the articles of food, orange is the discovery of Mediterranean countries, coffee of Abyssinia, tea of China and sugar of India. The pipe, which he smokes, has been taken from the natives of Virginia and the cigarette that he smokes has come from Mexico. The tobacco used in both these things was first grown in Brazil. If he uses cigar, it is the origin of Antelese of Western Indian archipelago. If he reads a newspaper, it is the product of the printing system invented in Germany. It appears from this long statement of R. Linton that the modern American culture is the result of diffusion from so many other cultures. It shows the importance of diffusion in the evolution of culture.

Diffusional anthropologists disapprove the claim of evolutionists that the similarities found in different cultures of the world are evolved not because of diffusion, but because of separate evolution of similar traits in different cultures, not because of free reciprocal adapatability but because of free evolution. But the fact, that many other different traits of culture change places only through diffusion, cannot be ignored. The claim of evolutionists that evolution is the only cause of cultural similarities is therefore altogether unscientific. On the other hand, their statement that cultures, in their order of evolution, have passed through similar situations everywhere in the world, is also incorrect. That people's culture of one place is undoubtedly influenced by the other reaching there from a superior is a matter of common experience. A mutual exchange of culture does take place among the people living close to one another. For example, people who live close to one another, cannot remain without speaking to one another and speaking can be possible only when they understand and adopt some words from the language of one another. Then, when they begin to speak, a change in their wearing apparel, ornaments, utensils and even in outside life through mutual cultural influence can be observed. Diffusion in cultures coming in close contact with one another is thus unavoidable. Migrating individuals carry culture traits from one place to another and diffuse them into people of the place where they reach. Thus, diffusion is one of the causes of finding similar cultural traits among different culture groups.

German Diffusionists

Among the modern diffusionists who have laid stress on the importance of diffusion in the growth of culture, there are two classes in Europe — German diffusionists and British diffusionists. In the beginning of the 20th century, Graebner, Ankermann and Schmidt presented in Germany the theory of diffusion in culture and since then their disciples have been regularly advocating the theory. These diffusionists believed that a diffusion of different cultural traits took place in the world in different places and periods and these cultural traits later spread to other parts of the world through diffusion. The cultural traits which thus spread through diffusion can be clearly identified in culture. This class of German diffusionists is known as *Culture Historiche Schule*, because it has shown the contribution of diffusion in particular culture by sketching its historical evolution. These scholars exemplify diffusion mostly through material culture and do not give evidence from diffusion of social institutions. But Graebner's contribution to the study of culture, in establishing criteria of quantity and form of diffusion, was very important. He stressed the point that in the absence of historical evidence, it cannot be said on the basis of outward similarity alone that similar traits appear in two cultures due to cultural diffusions. The evidence of diffusion will be accepted only when, along with similarity of form, there appears similarity of number and the arrangement of constituent elements of cultural traits.

Culture area approach. German diffusionists presented the view of culture area in order to define diffusion. When Graebner and other thinkers were engaged in search of facts to prove the example of diffusion, Franz Boas raised the question why diffusion, after all, took place? Boas classified the study of diffusion into different stages. According to him, facts about different situations should be described first. After that, proceeding from particular to general, analytic study should be done wherein, before talking about continents and the world, a factual distribution of special culture traits need be given. According to Boas the root causes of diffusion lie in the psychic make up of an individual.

What Boas meant by restricted area was called cultural area by Clark Wissler ? Wissler pointed out that narrowing down the diffusion area was necessary. He showed how no culture trait, specially if it is non-material, can migrate to distant areas without undergoing a change in transit. It loses some of its specialities in the process of diffusion and picks up from other cultures some such traits which it did not possess in the beginning. According to Wissler, there is a central point of diffusion in every culture area and the limits of diffusion are fixed. The forms of culture traits continuously keep changing in proceeding from central point to their limits and their traits become indistinct. Material obstacles in the diffusion of culture provide the cause of the change. Mountains, oceans, deserts and distances cause obstacles in the process of diffusion. Besides this, the areas, through which the traits of any culture are diffused, break its adjustment and it is not diffused as it is. To prove his theory, Wissler sketched many different American cultures and described the technological, artistic and institutional traits of every area. He showed that many particular human societies can be found in one and the same cultural area. Some people live in the boundary limits of two cultural areas and are found to possess traits of both these cultures. These areas can be called boundary areas.

British Diffusionists

As has been said before, besides the *Culture Historiche Schule*, the names of British diffusionists are included among the scholars who examined cultural diffusion. In fact, British scholar, Tylor, talked about cultural diffusion much earlier than German and American diffusionists. He had written that culture was like a plant which is diffused from one place to an other much more rapidly than its free growth. He had drawn a map of the diffusion of many culture traits which can be known, not from the name of British diffusionist, Tylor, but from the name of E.W. Smith, W.J. Perry and their disciples. They came among the diffusionists first, but were also the first in losing their names. They are also called Egyptologists because they have regarded Egypt as a centre of world culture. E. Smith and Perry stressed the point that evolution of culture everywhere in the world originated through diffusion from Egypt, but their theory has not been proved in figures. They have given a strange argument to prove their viewpoint. They said that people greatly lacked in their imaginative and inventive capacities. They said that people invented only through excitements created by very favourable environment and that a favourable environment of the kind was available only in ancient Egypt. Thus, they maintained that human culture originated first among Egyptians whom Perry has called the Progeny of the Sun and that it was from there that cultural institutions were diffused everywhere in the world.

There were many such errors in the theory of British diffusionists because of which it was greatly criticized. Hutton pointed out that many culture traits originated generally in different areas due to different causes. Hutton gave many examples to prove it, such as fire piston, he said, was invented independently in Asia and France. Magic, medicine and many other technological apparatuses were similarly invented separately in different areas of the world. Perry tried to give a counter reply to this criticism of Hutton. It is true that just as the evolution of similar culture traits in different places alone is not enough to declare the diffusion theory to be incorrect, in the same way, it would not on the other hand appear correct to say that culture traits have been diffused from one place to everywhere on earth. The truth is that there cannot be only one reason of sameness of culture traits. If one culture trait is the outcome of free evolution in cultures existing separately, the other culture trait reaches other places through diffusion from the place of its origin. It is not correct to say that human being is quite unimaginative and uninventive, and to say that evolution of culture has passed through similar situations everywhere in the world would be equally incorrect. No cultural evolution can be shown in one straight line. The fact is that the very question whether a particular culture came into existence through evolution or diffusion is wrong, because, as a matter of fact, both of these processes are responsible for the growth of culture. A particular or a similar culture trait can be caused by evolution or diffusion, and which of these is the real cause cannot be ascertained by any pre-established theory. It can be decided only after studying actual facts related to it.

ACCULTURATION

Whenever culture traits or culture complexes spread from one culture to another, it is called diffusion. When the whole system of life in a culture begins to change under the influence of any other culture, it is the process of acculturation or contra-culturation. Linton, Redfield, Herskovits, Hoizer and Beals have given many examples to define the process of contra-culturation. According to Herskovits, when a child learns to obey its cultural traditions in the process of development, it is called acculturation. When there is an exchange of culture traits and culture complexes between two cultures, it is transculturation, but when in place of one system of life in any culture, another system is established, it is contra-culturation. An assimilation may take place in this, but often it does not happen.

What happens is that the afflicted culture first disintegrates and next, when improvement in it begins anew, its individuality is lost and it takes a new form. Such a process can be called contra-culturation. For example, among the tribals of Chota Nagpur in India, individuality had ended at first under the exploitation and poverty in which they lived for centuries, but, when the country became free, their insistence on cultural, social, economic and political freedom developed in them in the shape of Jharkhand movement under various political influences, but it was not their previous original form. Scholars, who illustrated this process of contra-culturation, say that no culture of the world today possesses its unadulterated form, which means that every culture has taken a lot from other cultures. They also insist that it is not enough to say, as diffusionists do, that different cultures have taken a lot from one another through diffusion. It is also necessary to say what and how they took from it.

CULTURAL INTEGRATION

Various theories have been presented to define integration of culture in the modern age. The main theories among them are given below :

1. Functionalist Theory
2. Theory of Patterns of Culture
3. Theory of Themes
4. Theory of Style of Life.

A detailed description of these theories is given below:

1. Functionalist Theory. Great emphasis has been laid on the functional view in anthropology. According to this view, every culture trait and culture complex in culture has some special work to do and it exists for its aim to do it. When its work is done, it ends. Thus, no cultural trait has any importance without work. Nothing is unnecessary in culture. Whatever and whenever it becomes unnecessary, it ceases to exist. In this way, every culture is found to be internally complete; its every part is closely related to the other and no part can be known by separating it from other parts. Every culture trait can be defined with reference to other traits. In other words, functionalists lay stress on completeness of culture. These culture traits, which appear to be unimportant and useless when examined separately, begin to appear important when referred to other culture traits.

Functionalists define the internal structure of culture. Various kinds of social, mental and material factors are included in culture. What is the relation among these factors which makes them meaningful ? Functionalists answer this very question. They maintain that there is an internal co-ordination among the factors. This co-ordination makes every culture an integrated whole. The question, why is it so, has not been answered by functionalists in one and the same manner. According to Malinowski, culture is the means of keeping man's bio-psychic identity intact. It helps man in keeping his mental and literary existence high. In this way,, every aspect of culture, may it be economic organization or social organizations, may it be religion or language, depends on human needs. Now, since these needs are related among them, the various aspects of culture are also related among them. No culture trait is separate from this integrated whole. In this way functionalists reject the view of evolutionists that there are some functionless traits also in culture. Functionalists say that these traits are called functionless because evolutionists are not capable of defining them. According to Malinowski, all culture traits are related among them and every trait can be defined with reference to the whole.

Malinowski defines cultural diffusion in a new way. According to him, culture trait can retain its original form even after diffusion, but it will do only that work in a new culture which it can possibly do. It is only due to a close relation among the various factors of culture that, whenever there is a change in some new factor, some change can be perceived in the whole culture.

According to Malinowski, every culture is born to supply the bio-psychic needs of the local people and it should therefore be defined in that form. In this way, all the cultures of the world cannot be learnt by similar original causes. Culture does not depend on any impartial or full values. It supplies the local wants. In this way, Malinowski establishes cultural pluralism. But where Malinowski regards the various factors of culture as part of one integrated whole, there he fails to show the relations among human inspirations which are satisfied by these factors. In his concept of a human being, man is only a collection of various wants and tendencies.

Besides Malinowski, Radcliffe-Brown also has accepted the functional theory of culture. According to him, the purpose of integration of culture is not only to maintain the existence of an individual but is also to maintain the existence of the society as well. Integration of culture is both idealistic and factual. If integration is lost, the society too will come to an end. Every institution of culture helps in this work of culture. Its aim is not to supply a particular need. It is to maintain the existence of the whole human society in total culture.

Malinowski and Radcliffe-Brown have both viewed cultural integration in the form of culture content. According to D.N. Majumdar, both these viewpoints are partial. The claim of Malinowski that form depends on function is wrong. According to Majumdar, the form has its own independent existence and integration depends on it.

2. Theory of Patterns of Culture. This theory of cultural integration was presented by Ruth Benedict. Ruth Benedict took inspiration from the field of art and aesthetics. According to her, integration in any culture is due to the arrangement of its content in a temporary or a permanent style. This arrangement is called pattern by Benedict. There is a particular style in every part of a culture and these separate styles combine together and present a grand design of the culture as a whole. This is the configuration of culture. The production of this re-union in culture is due to the common tendency seen in all the aspects of culture. This main tendency is called a special genius of culture by Ruth Benedict. It is this genius of a culture that brings about its integration. This alone is the basis of the integration of form. According to Benedict, there are two kinds of this genius found in human society — one is Apollonian and the other is Dionysian. The word "Apollonian" is made by a Greek word 'Apollo' which means peaceful sun deity. Apollonian genius is found in those cultures which have peace and tranquility as their main qualities: and this same is the cause of their integration, an example of which can be found in the Pueblos of New Mexico. The word 'Dionysian' is derived from the name of a Greek god Dionysius who appears to be connected with drinking and a luxurious life. In this way, dionysian genius is found in a culture in which great deal of storms and changes are experienced, an example of which can be found in Dobu and Kwakiutl cultures on the north-west coast of America. According to Dr. D.N. Majumdar an integration of the theories advocated by Malinowski, Radcliffe-Brown and Ruth Benedict is necessary to reach a better theory of cultural integration.

3. Theory of Themes. M. E. Opler presented the theory of themes in order to define cultural integration. Themes mean those common inspirations which create various types of behaviours in a culture. According to Opler, Benedict's theory limits the genius of the people's attempt of self-fulfilment in a culture. On the other hand, in Opler s theory of themes, integration is not tied down to any special kind of behaviour. Opler leaves an investigator free in every field to discover the basis of integration. His theory of cultural integration is thus far more elastic than that of Benedict. Specific expressions of cultural integration in each individual case can be found out through any theme. Opler has applied the theory of themes in describing the culture of a race known by the name of Apache'. Like the theory of Ruth Benedict, Opler's theory is also a key to the specific structure of the mode of life of any kind.

4. Theory of Style of Life. The latest theory to define cultural integration is the theory of style of life. Style of life does not include only culture but it includes the most fundamental and permanent elements. It includes the means of livelihood only to the extent to which they can be helpful in giving a practical shape to the conception of good life. Style of life includes explicit and implicit judgements about right conduct. It also includes comparatively less important elements which explain the individual character of some group. Redfield, who presented the theory of the style of life, regards the style of life like the concept of manners. Lionel Trilling includes explicit and implicit expressions of values in manners. But as D.N. Majumdar has stated, Redfield only tells where the principle of integration can be found located, but he himself does not present any principle of integration.

From the above description of various theories of cultural integration, it is clear that none of these theories is sufficient in this respect. The best thing here would be to make use of the universal viewpoint which will include specifications of all the theories.

CULTURAL LAG

The word lag connotes crippled movement. Hence, cultural lag means the faltering of one aspect of culture behind another. For example, if either the material or the non-material aspect of culture were to stay behind the other, it would be a case of cultural lag. It is generally observed that material culture progresses faster in comparison with non-material culture.

OGBURN'S THEORY

The term cultural lag originated in a famous sociologist W. F. Ogburn's treatise entitled *Social Change*. The term was coined by Ogburn. According to him, culture has two aspects, one material and the other non-material. The material aspect, as compared with the non-material, tends to progress rapidly. Thus, the non-material part lags behind. It is this faltering action which is termed cultural lag. Defining cultural lag in their work, *Handbook of Sociology*, Ogburn and Nimkoff have written that "the strain that exists between two corelated parts of culture that change at unequal rates of speed may be interpreted as a lag in the part that is changing at the slower rate for the one lags behind the other." Citing an example of cultural lag in his *Social Characteristics of Cities*, Ogburn has stated that the number of policemen per 10,000 residents is less in towns in which the population is increasing than the towns in which it is decreasing. This situation Ogburn has represented diagrammatically, thus :

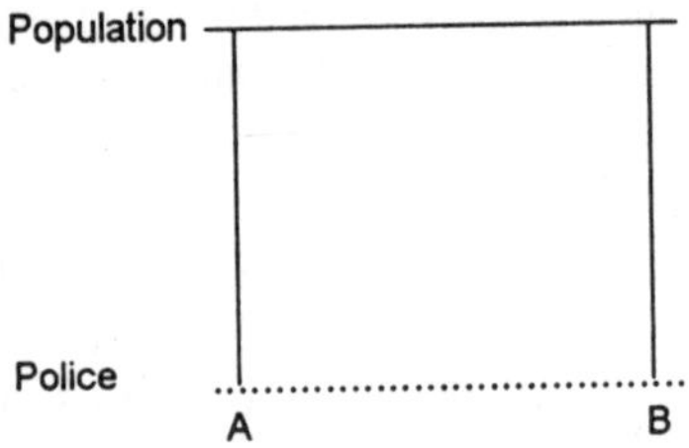

In this diagram, the line above represents the increase in population while the one below shows the increase in the police force. It has been assumed that at the point A the police force was adequate for a town. The population of the town increased rapidly but the police force did not expand till population had reached the point B. In this way, the difference between 'A' and 'B' indicates that while the population increased continually, expansion in the police force lagged behind. Similarly, presenting another example of cultural lag Ogburn has stated that the advent of the motor car was disastrous for railway companies as many became bankrupt as a result of their inability to compete with motor trucks for hauling material over short distances.

Some Examples from Indian Conditions

In Indian conditions one comes across many forms of cultural lag. During the last two hundred years much has been borrowed from the West in India's material culture and such towns as Delhi, Calcutta and Bombay are in no way inferior to the Western towns in respect of superficial gaudiness. But in spite of having borrowed so much from the West in its material culture, Indian culture has undergone very limited changes in the sphere of non-material culture. In this way, so far as the question of borrowing from the West in education is concerned, a tremendous lagging behind from material culture is evident in India's non-material culture. Another example of cultural lag can be found in the condition of Indian women. In India women share equal rights with men in receiving education, casting votes, taking equal part in the social, political and religious life, and they are progressing in this direction. And yet how different is an Indian woman from her Western counterpart in her sentiments, feelings, thoughts and ideals ! The fact of the matter is that whereas the Indian woman owes much to the Western in one direction, she is still much the same as she was in another. It is not true that there has been no transformation or change in this direction but rather it is a fact that the change is very little compared with the change that has occurred in the other directions.

Culture is changing very rapidly in the sphere of fashion dress, artificial beautification, art, recreation etc., but the change in the sphere of religious notions is comparatively very slow. The present age is called the age of science and rationalism and the West is considered the most advanced in this respect but how scientific and rational is the Christian outlook, both medieval and modern, concerning beliefs, rituals etc.? Actually, we are seeing newer and newer superstitions in the age of science. In this way, in the modern age, cultural lag in the various elements of culture is evident in all cultures, be it Indian, Japanese, English or any other. Lumley has written correctly that it seems as if many pedestrian soldiers or a complete army are marching out of step or as if some of the performers of an orchestra are playing this year's music on their instruments while others are playing last year's music and still others last century's music or even more ancient music at the same time. Such music would not be particularly musical or melodious. But this is the picture of every culture.

Causes of Cultural Lag

What is the cause of this cultural lag ? The main cause is that the various elements of culture possess varying degrees of changeability. As has been said before, changes in religious opinions are slow and few. It is doubtful whether the major religions, Christianity, Islam, Buddhism and Hinduism have undergone any change in the last few hundred years although major changes in the dress, standard of living, methods and even the values of life, of their respective followers are only too apparent. The same slow speed of change is true not only of the major religions but also of the religions of ancient people. For example, in America, the Red Indians have changed enormously in their methods of obtaining food, of fighting and of using the gun and the horse, but their religion is still more or less intact. Similar to religion the speed of the change in law is also slow though not quite as slow as the changes in religion. A major cause contributing to the slow speed of change in law is that traditions are deeply respected in law. In many countries, particularly in England, traditions are valued very much. The judges dispense justice on the basis of precedents. New laws are enacted only when extreme difficulty is experienced in some spheres due to their absence. It is evident that laws change after other changes have taken place. For example, in the earliest days of the Industrial Revolution the number of factories increased rapidly and they employed women and children in addition to the men. There was no law pertaining to the hours of work of these labourers, their wages and working conditions, hence the capitalists, taking advantage of their helpless conditions, exploited the labourers causing widespread dissatisfaction. Only then did the government wake to this predicament, and the labour laws came into existence. Even now many examples can be cited of cases where changing conditions have necessitated newer and more adequate legislation which has not been enacted or implemented. In India, the question of coloration of hydrogenated vegetable oil is a case in point. Like the labourers, the women had to launch movements for a long period before they could manage to have laws concerning their rights. Technology progresses at a faster rate than does non-material culture. But even in technology, the rate of change is not uniform everywhere. For example, at present the speed of change in chemistry and electrical science is faster than the speed of change in power production.

Similarly, cultural lag is responsible, in the main, for the existing international tension. Science has made the world a small one. The discovery of atomic power has precipitated a stage in which there should be a solid organization of the human race on an international scale so that a conflagration destructive of the entire world may be avoided. But the hearts of men are as yet unprepared for such a change. Narrow nationalism has not yet vanished, but is assuming aggressive forms in some spheres. In addition to the difference in the rate of change of the various elements of culture, one major cause of cultural lag is man's psychological dogmatism. Man commonly respects old concepts and dogmas or mores. He finds it convenient to follow the path of his ancestors. In such spheres as religion, novelty is not only objected to but is also regarded a sign of depravity.

Criticism

Many sociologists have indulged in bitter criticism of Ogburn's theory of cultural lag. According to Mueller, cultural lag is artificial and imaginary. Some other scholars regard it as a very simple background to the understanding of social change. James W. Woodard and R. M. MacIver has put forward the following objections to Ogburn's theory of cultural lag :

1. Ogburn's distinction between material and non-material culture is not clear. Again, it is not necessary that non-material culture should invariably lag behind material culture.

2. A major defect of Ogburn's theory lies in the fact that the same term cultural lag has been employed for all disequilibriums occurring in the process of social change. MacIver has in this connection, suggested the use of many terms for the various types of disequilibriums and conflicts, such as technological lag, technological restraint, cultural clash, cultural ambivalence, etc.

3. According to cultural lag, one thing progresses forward while another lags or restricts. Hence, this word should not be used in the context of those objects in whose case the encouraging as well as the restraining objects are similar and possess a common standard of evaluation.

CULTURAL COMPLEX

The simple unit of culture is the cultural trait. These cultural traits develop concurrently and collect together like a bunch of flowers and gain in their importance in terms of the degree of significance they have for the behaviour of human beings. This bunch of collected traits is called a cultural complex. These cultural complexes are formed according to the various needs of life. In this way cultural complexes concerning food habits, the different occupations, etc., can be seen in different cultures. Examples of cultural complexes found in Indian culture are in the form of the caste system, joint family system, the principle of karma, etc. Metallic utensils are indicative of the cultural complex concerning food habits in Indian culture. Among these cultural complexes some develop more than the others and become more influential and effective. But in any one culture, these cultural complexes exhibit a high degree of concurrence among themselves. Cultural patterns, which are representative of the unique nature of any culture are formed by them.

TECHNOLOGICAL LAG

The word lag connotes a tendency to hesitate or falter behind. Hence, the term technological lag is indicative of a condition of technological progress in which the various interdependent elements lose their state of balanced progress and cease to exist in a state of equilibrium. As a result of this imbalance, the entire process of production is slowed and sometimes even completely stopped. Ogburn has given a beautiful example in this context. The importance of forests in preventing soil erosion through rain and in preventing the spread of deserts is a matter of common knowledge. In order to get the benefit of these functions, both protection of forests and afforestation are essential, and all countries make efforts in this direction. On the other hand, many forests are destroyed because wood is needed for fuel, furniture and many industries. In this situation it is essential to strike an adequate balance between the growth and destruction of forests. An equilibrium can be maintained only when the number of trees cut and the number planted afresh is equal. If the number of trees cut exceed the corresponding number of those planted afresh, the balance is disturbed and in consequence, the rainfall is decreased, the desert encroaches upon cultivable land and agriculture suffers. This imbalance is an example of technological lag. If no consideration is directed to a state of technological lag, the organization of industries is disturbed and can result in loss.

CULTURE AND PERSONALITY

In the modern age, many anthropological studies of personality in primitive cultures have shown intimate relation of personality and culture. These studies have shown that man is a far more cultural being than imagined by the psychologists. In this connection, the discoveries by Ralph Linton and Abram Kardiner are notable. These anthropologists found that in every culture there is a basic personality type which is an outcome of cultural influences on the individual. As these cultural influences change so also change the basic personality types. About the Alorese of Indonesia, Kardiner has written that in their society the basic personality type is a doubtful, quarrelling, cowardly and parasitic person, whereas in our society, such a person will be considered as psychopathic and abnormal. According to Ralph Linton, in certain islands of the pacific the same anxiety, rituals, customs and taboos are found about food as about sexual behaviour in our society. These studies prove that every society has a particular culture which profoundly influences the personality of its members.

The British anthropologist Malinowski has presented functional approach to culture. According to him, culture should be studied with a view to find out what it does for him. Ruth Benedict has presented important discoveries regarding national character. She studied Zuni Indians of New Mexico, Dobu tribe of Malanesia and the Kwakiutl tribe of Vancouver Island. These studies showed many such motives to be acquired which were formerly considered to be hereditary.

The members of Zuni tribe use rituals and magic to fulfil their aims and purposes. Their religious practices show complex traits. Ritualistic activities take a major part of their time. They have a keen memory regarding the details of rituals. Ruth Benedict found imitative magic among them. For example, they rolled big stones down the slopes in order to bring rains on the faith that the thunderous sound made by the stones will make the clouds thunder and rain. Thus, among them religion was mixed with magic. Competition and conflict is comparatively rarer. They are non-violent and do not like change in daily routines. Their example shows that man is not aggressive by nature. Competitions, conflict and aggression are results of cultural influences.

The Dobu tribe of Malanesia are exactly a contrast to Zuni in temperament and personality. In them one finds abundance of conflict, competition, combat and violence. In Dobus also religions mixed with magic but this magic is used to bring harm to others or to defend oneself against others. Most of the individuals in this tribe are deceivers. They scarcely care for promises and compromises. In their society, the promises are normally broken. They do not think it to be wrong as it is in other cultures. This difference in the personality traits of Dobu and Zuni individuals is due to the difference in their cultures.

The Kwakiutl tribe, as against Zunis, does not believe in religious practices. They are materialist. In their society, wealth determines status and social prestige. Hence, everyone is seen busy in earning money by hook or by crook. Those who have less money feel ashamed on account of it. The tendency of self-assertion is fairly clear, self-assertion is exhibited in a strange custom known as potlatch. In this the rich person destroys his wealth before others to show that he can destroy even more than they have.

All the above mentioned studies of personality type in primitive cultures show how personality traits differ in different cultures. Culture determines methods of child rearing, form of social control, mores, customs, rituals, myths, legends, and ways of thinking and living. All these influence personality. Culture determines the standard of normality in a society. Thus, what appears normal personality in a culture, may appear abnormal in another. Thus, culture determines personality.

PRIMITIVE AND MODERN SOCIAL GROUPS

Differentiation between primitive and civilized society has been made in various ways. According to Durkheim and some other thinkers, there is a great difference between a primitive and a civilized society in that there is greater division of labour in a civilized society than in a primitive society. Division of labour in human society goes on increasing along with increase in the evolution of civilization. There is very little division of labour in a primitive society. The necessary things for the family members are produced in the family itself. Every work, from cutting wood, weaving of cloth and building of houses to the task of cultivation is done by every family separately. On the other hand, in a civilized society, the work of weaving cloth is done by weavers or in a cloth factory; the work of building houses is done by masons and labourers; the work of cutting the wood is done by wood-cutters or in a mill raised for that purpose. Not only this, but in modern and huge factories, one labourer makes only one part of an article and, in this way thousands of labourers are engaged in making separate parts of one and the same thing. In a civilized society there is a marked specialization in social, economic, political and business matters; in matters concerning health and medicine and, in brief, in every aspect of life.

Relation between Useful and Cultural Activities

According to MacIver, a great difference between primitive and civilized society lies in the fact that there is no difference between the cultural and the useful in a primitive society. In the words of MacIver, in a primitive society, "the means of living are not, as so often with us, detached from the end of living." In the civilized society of today one person is found turning files for eight hours in the office, the other is engaged in making a motor car; one waves a green flag to the railway engine and the other is busy in performing a juggler's show. Do all these bring them food or do they satisfy their need ? Do these roles satisfy the physical, mental and spiritual needs of the clerk ? The answer is 'no'. Why then does he go on turning them the whole day ? The reason is quite plain. He does all that because he gets money out of it to help him in buying things which will ultimately satisfy his needs. In this way, these efforts of the clerk, bus driver, railway guard and the juggler are only the means but not the ends. They do not satisfy the needs of their lives. They are only useful for the satisfaction of their wants. In the same way, the importance of factories, shops, cloth mills and the like consists in their being useful. People do not get pleasure from them and nor do they live for them. Life is not in them, and nor is it for them, but they are all for life. The individual of a civilized society does not keep an eye on life nor on pleasure but on the usefulness or the gain. They try to do their work with steadiness, laboriousness and cleverness, so that they may have maximum benefit from them. They do it all like a machine. It has no cultural importance. On the other hand, every work of an individual in a primitive society, may it be fishing, hunting, cultivating or building a house, has a cultural importance. They have traditions, festivals and fables connected to them. They dance, sing and make merriment after a hunting expedition. The work, instead of being the means, becomes an end in itself. They take joy in it and it is their life.

But it does not mean that every work in a primitive society has purely a cultural importance. Along with its being cultural every work is useful as well. As a matter of fact, a primitive man makes no difference between cultural and useful. For him, art for art and art for life are not two opposite views. Their art is both useful and cultural. Baskets, mats, lances, bows and arrows and such other things have their cultural values along with their being useful as well. In a primitive society, useful and cultural are similar things. Malinowski has written, "The meagre furniture, the hearth, the sleeping links, the mats and pegs of a native hut, show a simplicity, even poverty of form, which, however, become immensely significant through the depth and range of sociological and spiritual association". In this way, speed of a change, in primitive society, is not so fast that the means of production may be separated from their cultural background. There is not too much and varied specialization in works. Sentiments are connected even with the things of daily use. In this way, there appears a mixture of the useful and cultural in every aspect of life in a primitive society. MacIver has written that "Ritual is as important as craftsmanship in the making of a canoe or in the cultivation of the soil. Prayers are as important as arms in the conduct of war. Religion is compounded with magic and cannot be divorced from the business of living. The dance is as much a means of warding off evil spirits or of inducing fertility as it is a mode of social recreation. The success of a fishing expedition is as much endangered by a woman's touching a fishing tackle as by unfavourable weather, sickness comes from spells and the breaking of taboos. The people are bound in spirit to the soil, the home of their ancestors and their gods. Everything in nature is instinct with social meaning and enshrined in social ceremony. Culture, technique, authority, people and land are subjectively unified."

Importance of Basic Personality Type

It reveals one more distinction between primitive and civilized societies. Because of this mixture of the useful and cultural, some individual qualities of the people of every primitive society are also common. Kardiner has called it basic personality structure. This basic structure is commonly found in all the individuals of a primitive society, although there are individual dissimilarities also in them besides this basic structure. In this way, the inhabitants of Samoa Island take pleasure in life and are jovial. The inhabitants of Admiralty Island are suspicious and comparatively serious. This similarity of viewpoints and attitudes is not visible in any group of civilized societies. Civilization and culture are found more mixed in primitive societies than in civilized societies. This does not mean that there is no similarity and unity of any kind among the people of civilized societies. The difference is only this, that unity and organization in primitive societies is all inclusive; whereas in civilized societies, it is visible only in some aspects of life. The personality of a person in a primitive society is formed by social rules, traditions, methods, festivals and religion etc. Environments in a civilized society are more complicated and a person is more free. In this way, there are more varieties in a civilized society than a primitive society.

Relation of Culture with Soil and Consanguinity

Another difference between primitive and civilized societies is this that in primitive societies culture is bound to soil and consanguinity or blood groups, whereas in civilized societies, various cultures are seen on one and the same ground and one and the same culture is seen in many countries. For example, one and the same culture is found in different countries of Europe, whereas in India there are many cultures in one and the same country. The reason of this difference is that philosophy, art, literature and science are so much improved today that they cannot be fastened to the boundaries of any one country. In the same way, religion in a primitive society is tied to the local boundaries. Deities in tribes are their own deities just as their festivals are their own festivals. The religious importance of a particular thing in a tribe increases with the increase of its usefulness. In this way, the people of a tribe, living in a bamboo forest, make their houses, weapons and utensils of bamboos and even make cloth from bamboos. Not only this, they also regard the bamboo to be something sacred and their deities live in bamboos. Thus the local mountains, rivers, trees and the like are given religious importance. In civilized societies, where religion, on the one hand is their own, it is not, on the other hand, so much limited by the boundaries of the country.

The difference between primitive and civilized society, as given above, is a relative difference, because primitive and civilized societies are two stages of one and the same form of evolution. Evolution is an upward process from a relative, uncertain and a matchless homogeneity to a relatively certain and a synthesized non-homogeneity. Religion, culture and economic organization of a primitive society are the starting steps in the cultural evolution of man.

14

Pre-Historic Cultures

1. The first stage in pre-historic cultural evolution was that of *Stone Age.* In the stone age, as is clear from its name, people used things made of stone. Stone age itself is divided into the following four parts :

(a) Eolithic period

(b) Paleolithic period

(c) Mesolithic period

(d) Neolithic period.

2. Copper age

3. Bronze age

4. Iron age.

Classification of the Cultures of paleolithic Period

Cultures of Paleolithic period are classified as under :

1. Early or Lower Paleolithic Period. This includes the following three cultures:

(i) Pre-chellean culture

(ii) Chellean or Abbevillian culture

(iii) Acheulian culture.

2. Middle Paleolithic Period. It includes the following cultures :

(i) Levalloisian culture

(ii) Mousterian culture.

3. Late or Upper Paleolithic Period. It includes the following cultures :

(i) Aurignacian culture

(ii) Solutrean culture

(iii) Megdalenian culture

(iv) Azilian culture.

A brief description of the above cultures will explain the special features of the old or the paleolithic period.

1. Pre-chellean Culture. All those apparatuses are counted in pre-chellean culture which were found before the chellean culture. The period of 5,40,000 to 4,80,000 years hence is regarded as the period of pre-chellean or chellean culture. In this period such flakes in stones are found as were formed on breakage.

2. Chellean Culture. Chellean culture is traced from the apparatus found at a place called Chelles at a distance of eight miles from Paris in France. Some scholars call it by the name of Abbevillion. Pre-chellean and chellean cultures existed for 60,000 years. Hand-axe was invented in chellean culture and the flakes were removed from stones. The remains of pre-chellean and chellean cultures have been found in almost all the places in the world. In this period, hunting and collecting of fruits were the means of man's livelihood. Chellean man put on clothes made of hides. The climate was not so cold in the period. Men lived in the open in Europe.

3. Acheulian Culture. This culture flourished for about 3,00,000 years from 4,30,000 to 1,30,000 years. Hand-axe in this culture had evolved to the extent that it could be used for pealing, slicing, cutting, scratching and boring and for all other works of the similar kind. In this culture, flakes were made by cutting stones. In this culture men put on clothes made of animal hides, fire had already been invented, women caught fish, men gathered fruit and went hunting. When no food was found, man was sometimes killed and eaten. Ropes and baskets were made.

4-5. Levalloisian and Mousterian Cultures. Very few apparatuses of levalloisian culture are available. Only mousterian culture, therefore, has been described in the middle paleolithic period. In this culture men had begun to live in caves. In this culture, stone flakes were made through percussion method. The apparatuses of this culture are small and can generally be used on one side. The main apparatuses are — stone leveller, saw, knife, lance and spear points, slicing instruments and sculptural instrument, etc. Some ornaments also are found. There are proofs of both the system of laying the dead and of binding it with creeper trunks. Along with the dead his apparatuses were also buried with it. Dead bodies are found buried so carefully that it appears that they believed in the after world. They were hunters and wanderers. They worshipped almost everything and believed in witchcraft.

6. Aurignacian Culture. The period of this culture is 1,00,000 to 50,000 years back from today. The work of making flakes went on during this period. Apparatuses of bones were made along with those of stone. Beads, necklaces, hair-clips and many other ornaments had come into vogue. People lived in caves, on the walls of which pictures of bulls, deer and horses, etc., have been found painted, sculpture was also in vogue along with painting. The chief apparatuses of this period are — flake knife, flakes leveller, core leveller, boring instruments, piercing instruments, pointed flakes, double sided fish hooks, bone needles, bone lancets, hair pins, horn spoons, beads of bone shells, stone beads, horn beads, stone axes, lances, earthen lamps, flecklaces head of female statue and painting of wild goats.

7. Salutrean Culture. Among the remains of this culture, beautifully cut apparatuses are found. Main examples of the same are — heads of elephant tusks, bone-needles, horn lances, beads with holes, saw, engraving instrument, piercing instruments, lancepoints, arrow-points, willow leaf-like lance or, knife, plural leaf-like knife.

8. Megdalenian Culture. The period of this culture is 50,000 to 20,000 years back from today. Most of its apparatuses were made of bone and horns. Elephant tusk was extensively used. Painting was much improved in this culture. Among the remaining big lances with different kinds of paintings are found. Paintings of hunting and dancing are also found in caves. These people were skilful sculptors as is clear from animal-models engraved on stones. They used to bind and bury dead bodies. Among the main instruments of this period, pointed lances made of bone and horns, single and double sided forked lances made of horns, pointed sticks of horns and elephant tusks and edgeless sticks of bones have been found. Besides these, are other instruments, such as those made of bone, shell with a hole, beads with holes and made of stone, mortars made of stones and lamps, etc.

9. Azilian Culture. Many painting on stones have been found in Azilian culture. Men and the use of bows and arrows while hunting have been shown in paintings on the walls of caves. Strange pebbles have been found. Pointed lance with a hole, lance made of bones, loops used in catching fish, arrow point made of stone and many other things are found among the weapons. In other apparatuses, a stone leveller, many kinds of piercing tools and stones used in grinding, rubbing and polishing, etc., have been found. A grinding mill used in this period has also been found at a palace called Caspigni in France. In a French cave known by the name of 'Masde Ajil' the name which was later given to this culture heaps of burnt corn was found. This made people to believe that cultivation was one of the occupations in this culture.

Neolithic Culture

This period from 11,000 to 12,000 years back from now is regarded as the period of neolithic age. This age is divided into two main cultures. The first part of this age is called the period of Campignian culture. The later part is known as the period of Robenhausean culture. Two revolutionary changes in the human culture took place during neolithic age — one was the introduction of agriculture and the other was that of animal husbandry. Plough was therefore invented. Potter's wheel is also a gift of this age. Cutting instruments of hard stone were also made. A great revolution took place in pottery. Earthen pots began to be baked, polished and painted. Before this age, there were pots only of stone. In this age, earth was used in making pots and pot making was much improved. The art of cloth making was also invented and the people therefore began to grow cotton.

Campignian Culture Apparatuses

In compignian culture, which was the first part of Ncolithic age, earthen pots have been found. Among the weapons, big and small axes, of horn, axe of core, spear made of deer bones, fishing hooks of bones, etc., have been found. Besides these, there are other apparatuses such as grinding stone, various kind of levellers, big needles of the bones of deer and birds, combs and beads of bones.

In later part of neolithic age known as the period of Robenhausean culture, many wooden apparatuses have been found, such as boat, bow, club, spoon, hammer, etc. Earthen apparatuses have also been found, such as a jar and other pots.

B.C.	Pre-History (Important Dates)
4,60,00,00,000	Age of Earth.
3,30,00,00,000	Earliest known rocks (found in Greenland).
2,00,00,00,000	Life appears.
60,00,00,000	First large scale occurrence of fossils.
3,00,00,000	First old world monkeys' fossils (Oligocene period Fayum, Egypt).
2,00,00,000	Early ape fossils Dryopithecinae (Miocene period — E. Africa, India; parts of Europe).
1,70,00,000	Earliest known hominids (Lower Pleistocene — Australopithecus, and Homo habilis S. Africa, E. Africa.) Oldowan culture — first stage of Paleolithic or Old Stone Age (hunting and food-gathering) which persisted until end of Ice Age, c. 8,000 B.C.
4,00,000	Homo erectus stage (Java, China, Africa) in which were found crude chopping tools and early hand-axes. Heidelberg jaw Vertezollos remains (Europe).
1,80,000	Ancestors of Neanderthalers and Homo sapiens, with advanced hand-axes (Europe : Steinhem and Swan scombe).
70,000	Neanderthalers (Europe, Asia, N. Africa). Rhodesian Man (S. Africa). Solo Man (Java). Fake tools.
40,000	First cold phase ends. Neanderthal race becoming extinct. Second cold phase. Homo sapiens (Modern man). Implements show significant advances; small knife-blades, engraving tools, Paintings and sculpture; magic rites and ceremonies. Cro-Magnons with Aurignacial culture.

18,000	Final culmination of last ice age. Aurignacian culture dying out to be replaced by solutrean and then by the Magdalenian cultures. Great flowering of Paleolithic art.
15,000	First immigrants from Asia to cross Behring Straits.
15,000	Last glaciers in Britain disappeared. Proto-Neolithic in Middle East. Agricultural settlements (*e.g.*, Jericho). Settled way of life leading eventually to such skills as weaving, metallurgy; inventions as ox-drawn plough wheeled cart.

CULTURAL STAGES IN INDIA

Various races have been coming to India from times immemorial. The civilizations of these races differed a great deal from one another. On entering India, they had conflicts with the earlier inhabitants of this country. These conflicts affected their respective culture, and through the process of assimilation and synthesis, Indian culture grew all the more richer.

Effect of Negrito Race

According to J.H. Hutton, the oldest race reaching India was Negrito. They were not very high from the point of view of civilization. They did not know how to make use of the instruments made of stones and bones, how to cultivate the land, how to make earthen wares or how to build houses. They are now found in Andaman Island only. They could not affect the Indian culture very much. Still, as Suniti Kumar Chatterji says, Indian Hindus learnt to worship the banyan tree for begetting children and for the peace of soul of their dead from the Negrito race.

Arrival of Proto-Australoid Race

The race which arrived in India after the Negrito race was Proto-Australoid or the primitive Australian race. They are specially found in central India or in south-east India in the present age. They are also called 'Austric' in English and 'Agneya' in Hindi. Santhal, Munda, Birhor, Asur, Korba, Coorg, Juang and such other tribes are related to the Proto-Australoid race.

The people of Australoid race were more civilized than the people of Negrito race. They greatly influenced the material and religious life in India. Suniti Kumar Chatterji says that the Indians learnt, in the material field, how to cultivate the land with the help of pick-axe and to grow rice, bananas, coconuts, brinjals, betel leaves, lemons, jamboo fruit and cotton from them. The use of vermilion, betel leaf and nut in their marriage and other ceremonies have been taken from them. It was from them that the words like 'ban', 'lakut', 'shalmali', 'krikuwaku', 'matang', 'gaj', etc. were added to Sanskrit language. In the religious field, they brought to India many things like the belief in rebirth, various fabulous stories about the origin of creation, a myth about incarnation of God in a tortoise, belief about the existence of gods in stones, the worship of various creatures like snakes, crocodiles, monkeys, etc., the idea about eatables and non-eatables, about touchables and non-touchables and prohibitions, throwing of the ashes of the dead bodies into the Ganges and the other so-called sacred rivers and river-worship, etc. The interesting stories in Mahabharat and Ramayan about Vasuki, the ruler in 'Patal lok', the origin of the creation from snakes and eggs, interesting stories about Ganesh, etc. have been taken from the mythical stories of this race. Perhaps this very race taught the Indians how to count, the dates according to moon-phases and fixation of sacred festivals, etc.

Arrival of Dravidians and their Influence

The people of Dravidian or Mediterranean race came to India after the Proto-Australoid race. They were more civilized than the people of both the races which came to India earlier. Their influence on Indian culture was still greater. Under their influence, new gods and new methods of worship came to the Indian religious field. In fact, the word 'pooja' (worship). which means offering of flowers, belong to Dravidian language. The acceptance of an idol as representative of some god, to offer it flowers and tree leaves, to offer it vermilion and sandal paste, to burn incense before it; to ring bells, to sing, to dance before it, to offer and accept sweets and such other ways of worship were given to Indians by the Dravidian race. The chief new gods, who began to be worshipped under the influence of the Dravidians, were Shiva, Uma, Kartikeya, Hanuman, Shitala and Ganesh, etc. The Aryans, who came to India after Dravidians, married Dravidian women because of scarcity of Aryan women, and then the worship of Shiva-linga among the Aryans began. By reading *Padma, Skandha, Shiva, Vaman,* and other *Puranas,* it was learnt that saints and other great men among the Aryans tried their utmost to keep away the worship of Shiva-linga from their Aryan religion but their Dravidian wives brought it into the Aryan society. Under the Dravidian influence, the number of gods increased. Gods and goddesses, village god, family god and other gods of Hindu relgion, supposed to be 330 million in number, are all the result of their influence. There is no reference to the sacred places of worship and river worship in the Vedas. There was prime importance of *Yajna* in Vedic culture. The importance of the sacred places of worship increased under the influence of the Dravidians. In the same way, they also preached the worship of the trees like those of tulsi, banyan-pipal, bel and many others. In *Padma Puran* Bhakti says to Narad, "I was born in a Dravidian country, was brought up in Karnatak, lived in Maharashtra for some period and I grew old in Gujarat." Thus, this system of devolution is also given by Dravidians. It was Dravidians who gave Indians the festivals of Holi and Basant.

Arrival of Aryans and their Influence

Aryans made the greatest contribution towards the development of the Indian culture. They came to India after the Dravidians. It is their tongue which is in use today in the major parts of India. Their Vedas are the main roots of the Indian culture. The contribution of the Aryans towards the Indian culture has been thus described by Dr. Jadunath Sarkar : (1) A feeling of sympathy and adjustment. (2) Wonderful evolution of science and philosophy. (3) Aryans' fixation of adjustment among different castes through their principle of *varna* system. (4) Spread of civilization among the demons and wild tribes through "Tapovan" system.

Muslim Influence

Muslims came to India after the Aryans. In his book entitled *Influence of Islam on Indian Culture*, Dr. Tarachand has written that the influence of Muslims on the various parts of Indian life has been very great and this influence has been seen specially on Hindu customs, on the very minute things of their family, on music, dress, cooking methods, marriage traditions, festivals, fairs and on the institutions and manners of the Maratha, Rajput and Sikh courts.

Influence of the British

After the Muslims, the British deeply influenced all aspects of Indian culture. The spread of English language brought hundreds of English words into the Indian languages. The influence of Western culture on the prose, novels, one act plays and poetry, etc. in Indian literature can be clearly seen. Western education created a wave of reformation in the whole country. Under influence of Western ideology, Brahmo Samaj, Arya Samaj, Theosophy, Rama Krishna Mission and many more names among the social reformation movements in India are specially mentioned. Western ideas inspired argumentation and reasoning, broad-mindedness and freedom of thought. Whereas on the one side, the ideas of equality, freedom and nationality helped in uprooting the social evils like *Sati* custom, killing of female children, child marriage and prohibition of widow-marriage, on the other hand, they created a political awakening in the country. The present form of administration in India is the outcome of the great influence of the British ideology. The present economic organization joint stock companies, managing agencies, big factories, production through machines, railways, telegraph, telephone, aeroplanes and other means of conveyance and communication were brought to India from the West. As a matter of fact it requires a full volume to describe the influence of Western culture on India. This influence has regularly been on the increase and it is also needed for the country's progress, although its assimilation is equally necessary.

The above examples prove the validity of the statement that India has been, from times immemorial, the meeting place of conflicting races and civilizations marked by a process of assimilation and synthesis.

CULTURAL STAGES IN INDIA

Pre-historic culture can generally be classified into three period : (1) Stone age, (2) Bronze age, and (3) Indus Valley culture. Stone age can again be classified into Paleolithic period and Neolithic period.

Paleolithic Period

The first people to control the peninsular part of India probably belonged to paleolithic period. Paleolithic period is taken to include fossils and instruments of that age in India; it is discovered from the fossils of those people who made instruments of stone, that they lived at the end of the Glacial period or in the beginning of the inter-glacial period. Their big instruments of flakes are found in north India, Rawalpindi and in the valley of the Narmada, etc.

Neolithic Period

The cultural chains of the Neolithic period in India are found in the valley of the river Sone which is a tributary of the Ganga. It can be classified into three parts : (1) Beginning, (2) Middle, and (3) End. It belongs approximately to the second inter-glacial period. Evolution of stone instruments had begun before the end of the Sone period. Types of industries are found in the last Sone period : (a) Construction of instruments from round stone, and (b) Method of making core tools without removing the flakes.

Madras industry is a contemporary of the Sone industry. Its instruments have the shape of a pear or an egg. They have sharp edges on both sides. These are called hand-axes. Many small and beautiful instruments were the products of this industry. In this industry, stone hammers were used for rough work and the horn or wooden points were used for making small and beautiful things. Microlithic industry has been widely spreading in India. Traces of the industry are found in Mahadev hills of Madhya Pradesh, some parts of Andhra Pradesh and Karnatak, Central India. Gujarat and in some places upto Sindh and Punjab.

Muski Culture

Many cultural stages are found in a place called Muski in Raichur District of Karnatak. According to Yazdani, the tomb pots, polished stones and flakes found at the place belong to a period of about 1000 years before Christ or still earlier. The period of bead forms, decorated utensils and the clay models found here, seem to be somewhere between 500 to 700 B.C. There are certain things which belong to the period even between 300 to 500 B.C. Gold articles are also found here.

Kashmir Culture

Some traces of Neolithic culture period have been found at a place called Berjahm lying between Srinagar and Gunderbal. The period of the places of black pots and the samples of the engraving found here appear to belong to the second or the fifth century before Christ. The period of polished axes, bone needles and pots is the period of Neolithic culture of the fifth millennium B.C.

Rohri Culture

Various marks of hard stone industry have been found at Rohri, Sakkhar and Karachi in the Sindh province of Pakistan. Some long and thin flakes found here, can be compared with the flakes of the Harappa culture. The double-sided hand-axe found here, seems to belong to an earlier period.

Mysore Culture

According to Wheeler, the marks of the Stone Age and Iron Culture are found in the culture of Brahmagiri, a place in Karnatak. Besides stone axes, some other articles and slightly coloured handmade pots belonging to Microlithic industry are found here and there. This period is calculated to be the beginning of first millennium B.C. Cartwheels, utensils and the use of iron in the building of tombs are the marks of Iron Age.

The cultural marks found in Andhra, appear to belong to a period from first to the third century B.C. The cultural marks of the Bronze Age are found in Baluchistan, Makran, Khurram, Jhalwan and Sindh.

Buffware Culture

These are three classes of Buffware culture in India on the basis of pot painting. They are as follows :

1. Quetta Culture. All the pots of this place are black. There are well measured designs on them. Among these, there are beakers, cups and saucers.

2. Amri-Nal Culture. It has been found at a place called Amri in Sindh and Nal in south Baluchistan. Small towns with houses made of stone or clay bricks and printed pots like those of Kulli culture are found here. Black paintings on red pots and a lance or a saw painting on the instruments are like those of Harappa culture.

3. Kulli Culture. Because of their system of funeral rites and clay idols of women and animals, Kulli culture is separated from Amri-Nal culture. Remains of very beautiful art are found here. Use of stone in building construction; glass, beaker, dishes and other pots of like shapes, pots as tomb articles, clay idols, things made of brass and bronze and even the models of fish and birds, besides those of cows and bullocks, are certain specialities of this culture. It appears to be a contemporary of Harappa culture.

Jhob Valley Culture

Jhob culture is found on north-west mountains and in Bolan and Quetta passes. Black designs on permanent red backgrounds in the art of pottery are found here. Small glasses and bottles generally have solid thick bottoms. Even the paintings of women along with those of deer, bullocks and fish, etc. have also been found. Their women models have ornaments on their hands and feet and round their necks. The period of this culture seems to be upto the fourth millennium B.C.

Indus Valley Culture

About 250 or 270 years before Christ is said to be the period of this culture. Its distinctive marks are mainly found from the excavations of Mohanjodaro and Harappa. Harappa is in the district of Montgomery and Mohanjodaro is situated at a distance of about 25 miles from Larkana in Sindh. Things found in both these places are very similar.

From the description of these various stages of Indian culture it is clear that Indian culture is very ancient. The Indus valley culture, specially found in Harappa and Mohanjodaro, has proved beyond doubt that the people in India had reached a very high standard of culture about a thousand years before the evolution of a comprehensive human culture in the West took place. New discoveries in future may prove the Indian culture to be all the more dignified.

15

Growth of Civilisations

What is Pre-historic Age ?

Man appeared on earth lacs of years ago. The story of development and evolution of man is known as History. The history of man is based on the recorded, documentary evidence. Obviously, the documentary record of man dates from the time man had mastered the art of writing and this is fairly recent. But man roamed on the earth for millions of years when he lacked the wherewithals to reduce his ideas and feelings into history. This long period of unrecorded history is known as pre-historic age.

Proto-History

Between the pre-historic age of which no record of any kind is available and the recorded history there is a linking period of which archaeologists have tried to build some kind of system through a painstaking effort of analyzing and synthesizing of fossils and artefacts of pre-historic age. This linking period is known as Proto-History.

Characteristics of Proto-History

This link or chain shares the characteristics of both pre-historic and historic periods. Like pre-historic period it lacks all documentary evidence; but the remains, artefacts and fossils available enable scholars to build up a fairly scientific record of the day-to-day activities as well as progressive sophistication in the life style of pre-historic man.

This brief but highly articulate story of man's evolution provides the basis of modern man and is therefore a vital link in the story of mankind. The Indus Valley Civilisation is a characteristic example of this.

THE IMPORTANCE OF ARCHAEOLOGY

Scope of Archaeology

The proto-history is a long tale of man's evolution. This important knowledge has become available through the excavations of various sites on the earth. This has lead to the discovery of the tools and implements used. The earthenwares as well as fossils of men and animals have been discovered. This is the province of archaeology. The scholars known as archeologists try most painstakingly by the use of modern scientific means to build up a coherent system of the life of pre-historic man.

Importance of Archaeology

Without the knowledge of the origin, evolution and development of pre-historic man it is not possible to tell the full and comprehensive story of man. Indeed, without this knowledge, even the recorded history is like a castle built upon sand which has no firm foundation and is upset by the slightest draught of air. This is the reason that scholars have undertaken excavation work at various sites to collect the remains of stone implements, pottery and paintings etc. to study these minutely with a great skill lest these crumble. The modern hi-technology has enabled scholars known as archeologists to piece up the story of man from as early a date as possible. The rapid advancement in science has provided us tools and instruments by which we can fix up the period of fossils and other remains. One day, therefore, we may be able to tell a coherent tale of man ever since his appearance on Earth.

THE EVOLUTION OF MAN ON EARTH

Appearance of Man

We cannot fix the date and time of man's appearance on Earth. But, according to scientists the Earth is as old as 4.5 billions years, and from this we can infer with fair amount of certainty that man appeared on this earth few lacs of year ago.

Evolution of Living Beings

When Earth came into existence it was too hot for life of any kind to survive. Earth did not cool enough for supporting life for 1.5 to 2 hundred crores of years. The nascent form of life first to appear was that of jelly like creatures which lived in shallow sea water. Later on reptiles with an outer covering to protect them from the heat of sun appeared. These included reptiles like various insects. Along with these the vegetable life appeared in marshy land. The first to appear were creatures that could survive only in water but gradually amphibians which could survive in water as well as land appeared. The characteristic example is that of frog.

Ovarians and Egg Laying Creatures

In the course of time, climate of earth so changed that all types of life and vegetation perished. But now ovarian or egg-laying creatures appeared on earth. These included snakes and crocodiles. This period lasted for crores of years.

Changes due to Struggle to Survive

In the course of evolution only those species of animal and vegetable kingdom could survive which were able to adjust themselves to the changing natural clime. As a result of the struggle to survive suitable changes in the shape and size of animals took place. The green pastures came into existence all around the land. Thus, began a new and more sophisticated period in the evolution.

A number of vertebrate species, birds and mammals came into existence. The animals which suckled their offspring came into existence. Now reproduction diversified and the young ones were born from eggs as well as uterius. There are a number of species of mammals.

The Primates

The primates are most advanced in this order. Among the primates are the monkeys, langur and chimpanzees. The scientists hypothesize that Man is more advanced form of these species. In the course of time the primates came to live on earth from their arboreal abode. Some primates tried to stand and walk on two feet. This gave strength to their four feet and gradually they started grasping and holding things in their fore-feet.

Homo Erectus

Thus homo-erectus (who stands erect) was born. Besides, they possessed superior intellectual capacity. It was this capacity which sets man apart from other fellow creatures. The intellectual capacity helped man to use and dominate his surroundings to his advantage. However, this is still not quite explained logically or demonstrated scientifically how some primates developed into men and, in Aristotle's word became rational animals while others still remain primates and do not reach the mark of man. There is obviously either some missing link or man and primates are qualitatively apart.

Fig. 15.1. Homo Erectus.

Fossils of Man

The fossils of man dating back to more than one lac years have been found buried deep under the rocks which have been found at various sites in the world. The first fossil of homo-erectus who used stone implements was found in Central Africa. Later, similar kind of fossils were found in Java (Indonesia), Peking and Heidelberg (Germany).

Rational Criterion of Man

The criterion setting man apart from other creatures is not the physical features but his intellectual capacity which is certified by the fact that he made tools and used them to control in a way his environs.

STONE AGE

The Ancient Man

The ancient man was not much different from animals; he was, like animals, totally dependent upon nature and roamed the earth like them. However, he had a gift not to be found in animals. That is he had a superior mind and a capacity to relate and discriminate. He lived in caves which were surrounded by big rocks and stones. He cut and ground them into sharp edged implements by which he hunted animals to feed himself. He also used wood and bones to make implements, but by and large his implements were made of stones. This is why that this period is known as Stone Age. For convenience it has been divided into three parts (1) Paleolithic, (2) Mesolithic, and (3) Neolithic.

PALEOLITHIC AGE

Paleolithic period is the second period of Stone Age characterized by rough or chipped stone implements. In the absence of any documentary evidence it is difficult to determine the date and period of stone age man. However, it can be surmized that this is very ancient and relates to appearance of man on earth. This is certain that this period lasted lacs of years.

Characteristics of Paleolithic Age

1. Tools and Implements. The tools and implements of this age are rough and ugly but they are useful in hunting animals. Among these the axe, the

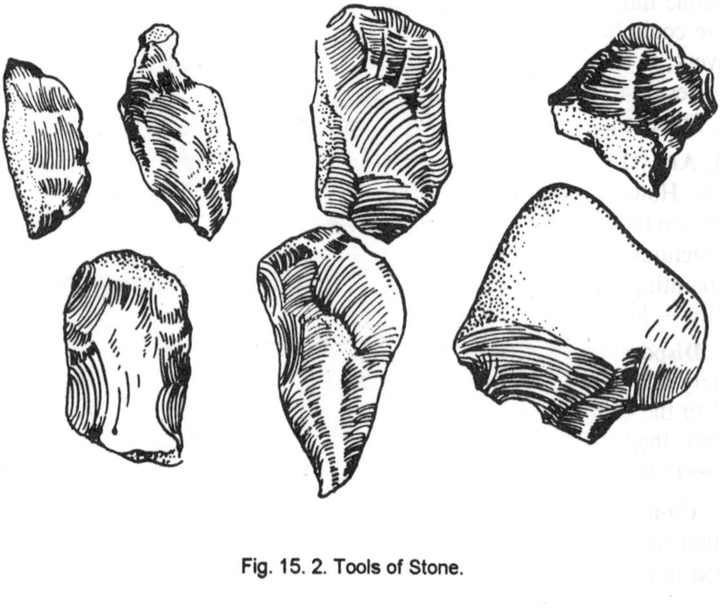

Fig. 15. 2. Tools of Stone.

cutter and the shield were prominent. With the increase in the mental powers of man the implements became more and more sophisticated. Besides stones, the stone age man made use of wood, bones and ivory to transform these into weapons of hunt and self-defence. In the last period of this age man could make bows and arrows. He also developed spear and lance to hunt animals from a distance. Even needle was developed by this time.

2. Food. For food the stone age man was entirely dependent upon nature. He collected edible roots and branches of trees, hunted animals and also captured fish. As far as food was concerned, he had no choice but to eat whatever was available. He was both a herbivore and carnivore. His life was full of struggle and to capture Hobbes' phrase brutish, nasty and short.

3. Clothing. As regards clothing man lived more or less like animals. In winter, however, he covered himself with animal skins and barks of trees. The discovery of needles of bone and ivory in excavation suggest that he stitched the animal skins with the help of rope made of skins.

4. Housing. The paleolithic man lived under the open sky or shades of the trees. He preferred to live near the banks of rivers. Initially he did not know if the caves could be used for the purpose of shelter. But gradually he learnt to make use of caves to protect himself from rain and extreme wintry conditions. Where the caves were unavailable he made tents using the skins of animals and stitching these with needles made of bones.

5. Discovery of Fire. It is difficult to say with any amount of certainty how man came upon the discovery of fire. But the most plausible hypothesis is that man perceived a little flame which results from friction of two stones. Thus, an idea came into the mind of man that by striking two stones against each other the fire could be kindled. Indeed the discovery of fire was man's most fruitful discovery; it revolutionized his life. Now instead of eating raw meat he could fry it. Beside it came handy to ward off ferocious beasts. Now he could outwit them. The fire made his life relatively secure.

6. Art. The major portion of man's life was consumed providing food for himself. However, whatever little time he could spare he spent drawing some pictures on the walls of caves. The pictures are mostly of animals. Prominently, these pictures are drawing of deer, bear and stag. In Europe many caves having such paintings have been found. This is the clear indication of man's mental capacity — his innate love of art.

7. Disposal of Dead. The stone age men used to bury some stone implements, jewellery and food etc. along with the dead man in the belief that these may be useful to the dead. Before burying the dead they used to paint the corpse red. Probably, they did so in the belief that red colour may revive man who has died. They seem to have some kind of belief in the world hereafter.

8. Communal Life. In all probability the wisdom had dawned upon the man that he could accomplish more by uniting. It was easier to hunt animals for food in groups rather than alone. He had also realized that he could protect

Fig. 15.3. Figures of Game on Cave Wall.

himself better from the attack of wild beasts by some sort of cooperative activity. This grouping together led to formation of communes and gradually each commune worked under the leadership and control of one man. This person was the chief of the commune. Thus, there were as many chiefs as the number of communes. It is quite probable that women played the role of rearing children and looking after other household activities and men went out in fields away from their women and children in order to hunt and gather food. This period of man's evolution lasted as late as 10,000 B.C.

MESOLITHIC PERIOD

Mesolithic period of stone age is the transitional period between paleolithic and neolithic stone ages. In the paleolithic age man was primarily a hunter and depended totally on nature. In the neolithic age he mastered the art of agriculture. In between these two periods was a linking period or middle stone age. In the mesolithic period the ice age was substituted by forests and greenery.

1. Habitat. Now man formed groups and lived together in big caves in mountains. However, he did not live permanently at one place but kept moving about and settling at different places according to the demands of climate.

2. Food. Like paleolithic man, the mesolithic man was primarily a hunter but, in due course, he started domesticating dog and using it to enable him to hunt wild animals more efficiently. Gradually, he domesticated a number of animals like cows, buffaloes and goats. Thus, from a hunter he became a shephered, too.

3. Tools. The mesolithic man, like paleolithic, used rocks, bones and wood to make his tools and weapons. But now these were more sophisticated. These

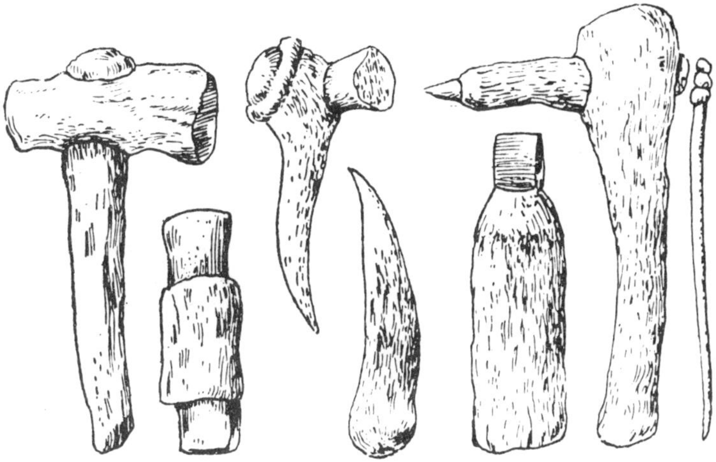

Fig. 15.4. Hunting Weapons.

were relatively small but more sharp-edged. Men also used them as arrows. However, hunting remained the sole source of food.

NEOLITHIC AGE

Neolithic period is the last period of stone age characterized by polished stone implements. By the time man reached the neolithic age, he was no longer exclusively dependent upon natural forces. Now he began to use and control natural forces. In place of a mere hunter he became an agriculturist and shepherd. The life of neolithic man was more organized. He lived in clans and made tools and implements which were sophisticated and polished. As soon as man discovered the art of tilling the land, sowing seeds and harvesting them a sea-change came in the life of man. The scholars have dated this period between 10 to 5 thousands B.C.

Characteristics of Neolithic Age

1. Discovery of Agriculture. The West Asia, Persia and North Africa were once vast pastures suitable for keeping animals. But with the climatic changes, the greenary was wiped and in place of green pastures, desert emerged. Now man became much worried about procurement of food. He had seen seeds becoming plants, some of which were edible. But he had not so far mastered the art of agriculture. Necessity is the mother of invention. Some bright genius tried planting seeds in wet land and see it develop into crop. From this the mastery of agriculture was a natural corollary.

2. Habitat. With the development of agriculture the man ceased to be a wanderer, his nomadic life ended. He made shelters and stayed there permanently. His shelters were made of mud and wood. The roofs were thatched. The evidence of initial mastery of agriculture are found in Persia, Syria, Egypt and Thailand.

3. Cattle-breading. Consequent upon the changes of climate, the cattle-breading came into existence. As pastures became deserts, man became the provider of food to animals. Gradually, man learnt to procure milk from the milch cattles. The bull was pressed into service to till the land. Man manufactured the implements needed for tilling the land, that is, plough.

4. Food. Unlike the paleolithic man, the neolithic man was no longer dependent upon animals for food and therefore did not have to run hither and thither all day for his food. Now he could grow wheat, barley and maize as well as vegetables to feed himself. However, man did not become herbivorous but continued to eat fish and animal meats.

5. Pottery. As the man learnt to grow crops he felt the need to cook it. He could not roast or fry vegetables, and for this purpose he needed utensils. As said earlier, the necessity is the mother of invention. The first pot and pans man used to cook his food were made of clay. Not only did man made pots, he even drew some ornamental figures on these utensils. This suggests that an artistic streak is inbred in man. In the recent past Prophet Mohammed told people that if you have only two coins — with one buy bread and with the other a flower. The use of pots for cooking and keeping the food made the life of neolithic man become relatively comfortable.

6. The Discovery of weaving. In the neolithic age man made two vital discoveries : weaving and knitting. Now, besides leather, man used cotton and jute for weaving clothes. The excavations in Egypt and West Asia disclose the discovery of spinning wheel. Man by now had learnt making yarn and weaving clothes with it.

7. Tools. The neolithic man made a vast advance on making tools and implements. These were now more utilitarian besides being good looking and well polished. Man now made very good hammers, lances, sickle and hunting weapons. He also acquired the skill of carpentry.

8. Discovery of potter's wheel. The discovery of the wheel was a brilliant achievement. Now man could with its help become a skilled potter, and made pots of various shapes and sizes and by applying fire to dry pots he made very useful and durable pots which did not melt by water or heat.

9. Religious beliefs. The early man realized the presence of some extra-ordinary powers beyond his ken in the natural forces. The fire, the storm and trees were mysterious to him and he projected some exceptional powers to them and began worshipping these. The discovery of idols of women made of clay suggest that man worshipped mother goddess. The fertility, that is to give birth to humans probably impressed his mind and therefore he put women on a higher pedestal.

Fig. 15.5. Potter's wheel.

10. Eschatology. The neolithic man buried his dead, and alongwith the dead he also buried food and weaponery in an apparent belief that it may be useful to him in his future life. Alongwith the burial, man also started cremating the dead. The ashes and bones of dead man were collected and put in big pots which were buried underground.

BEGINNING OF COMMUNAL LIFE

As man became agriculturist his life became systematic and organized. Bcsides agriculture, some people took to breeding and rearing animals useful to them. Thus there came into existence a certain division of labour. Some people took to agriculture while others became shepherds and still some others specialized in the making of tools and implements. The remaining few became carpenters. Now man began to live in families. However, the excavations done at various sites do not suggest the existence of king etc. But there must have been some elders to guide the men. They must have set up a code of conduct for man. Such codes are even today found in some primitive societies. Earlier, the land may have been held in common but gradually there was a division of land. The neolithic man also made discoveries of bronze and copper. The neolithic age provided a stepping stone to the development of modern civilizations. The study of Mesopotamian, Egyptian and other civilizations will follow :

THE NEOLITHIC MAN

The transition of neolithic man from his paleolithic kin was a tremendous step formed. The neolithic man hunted animals, but this was more of a hobby and thrill than a dire necessity. The paleolithic man had no option but to hunt either by engaging in direct confrontation or with the help of his rugged stone weaponry. The idea of rearing milch animals for alternative source of food had not struck him. He was totally at the mercy of natural elements. However, the clever neolithic man was not only a shepherd but understood how to procure food from the mother Earth. The agriculture compelled man to forsake his life as a wanderer, a nomad but to set up permanent shelters of mud and wood. This led to stone age civilizations.

Agriculturist Civilization

The post-stone age civilizations were primarily agriculturist. And for the growth of agriculture, some necessary conditions must be met. First and foremost, the land should be fertile and there must be a dependable source of irrigation, last but not least, there should be green pastures for animals to feed. These conditions could be met only on the banks of rivers. Thus, naturally, mankind's ancient civilization developed and thrived at places which were near the banks of rivers and where climate was temperate. Excessive heat or cold is not conducive to agriculture.

RIPARIAN CIVILIZATION

Thus, the four places where ancient civilization developed and thrived were riparian. These are Indus valley in Pakistan, Mesopotamian civilization on the bank's of rivers Tigris and Euphrates; Egyptian civilization or the banks of great rivers Nile and the Chinese civilization on the banks of rivers Hwang-ho and Yangtze-kiang. As the geographic features of these four ancient civilizations were similar, naturally these shared common fundamental features. But however, these were not the replicas of each other, each had its distinguishing features. There was however give and take among them. They not only affected each other but were source of inspiration to modern Civilization.

INDUS VALLEY CIVILIZATION

Like the other riparian civilizations of the world, there developed an advanced rural civilization on the banks of river Indus. The span of this civilization extended all over the banks of river Indus and its tributaries.

Discovery

In the year 1922-23, the Archaeological Department of India undertook excavation of big mound in the province of Sind and District Larkana now in Pakistan. As a result of excavation of this mound by the bank of Indus, Indus valley civilization was discovered.

Buried under this mound were the remains of a highly advanced urban civilization. This place, is known as Mohenjodaro, *i.e.*, the Mound of Dead.

Likewise excavation at the site of Harappa in the District of Montgomery on the banks of Ravi, the relics of a highly advanced civilization have been found. The civilization found as a result of excavation in Larkana and Montgomery are interlinked, both come under the caption Indus Valley Civilization. The discovery of relics of an urban civilization in Mohenjodaro and Harappa is the conclusive proof of the fact that a highly advanced urban civilization existed prior to the inflow of Aryans in this sub-continent.

Span of Indus Valley Civilization

In the beginning it was believed that the span of Indus Valley Civilization was confined to Harappa, but the latest research shows that its span extended over a vary large part of India-Baluchistan in West, Ropar in Punjab, Kalibanga in Rajasthan, Lothal in Gujarat and Kausambi in the Ganges Valley.

The Architects of Indus Valley Civilization

It cannot be said with any amount of certainty as to who were the architects of this civilization. Some scholars are of the opinion that the Dravidian natives of India were its creators, but others are of the opinion that Aryans also contributed to it. In the absence of any conclusive evidence, the above is not generally acceptable. In as much as this civilization is highly advanced urban civilization, it is presumed that people of different races contributed to it. The relics found here lend substance to this viewpoint.

Its Chronology

All scholars are agreed that Indus Valley civilization is one of the most ancient civilizations, but there can be no definite dating of it. Marshal fixes the time of this civilization anywhere been 3250 B.C. to 2750 B.C. But now the majority of scholars accept the viewpoint of Wheeler that Indus Valley civilization lasted between 2500 B.C. to 1700 B.C.

Characteristics of Indus Valley Civilization

By all standards, Indus Valley civilization was an advanced urban civilization. Its inhabitants were capable of reading. This is shown by written clay plates and seals. Unfortunately, this script remains undeciphered till date. The idea of the nature of this civilization can be had from seals, pottery, toys, idols and jewellery. In the absence of our ability to read the Indus script we know very little about it definitely. Yet it can be asserted without the fear of contradiction that it was an advanced highly organized civilization.

1. Layout of Cities : (i) *Planning*. The relics found in Mohenjodaro reveal a well-planned out city. The main roads of the city were East to West and North to South. These divided each other at a right angle. This divided the town in many sectors. In each sector there were blocks of houses which were built in a planned manner.

(ii) *Roads*. The relics of roads found in Mohenjodaro show that the roads were 80 m. long and 10 m wide. Though, these were mud roads, these were kept meticulously clean. The roads were fit for the bullock cart travel. At measured places big dustbins were kept to prevent blocking of roads by refuse. People must have travelled on these roads day and night as we find lamp posts on the road side at measured paces.

(iii) *Drainage System*. Mohenjodaro had an excellent drainage system. All roads and blocks had brick-built covered drains. The drains in the houses were connected to block drains which were further connected to drains on the roads. There were pit holes at measured paces to collect and dispose of the refuse. Even, the contemporary European civilization did not have a drainage system as efficient as that of Mohenjodaro.

(iv) *Supervisory Body*. Looking at the road and drainage systems in Mohenjodaro one cannot help concluding that there must have been some supervisory body like municipality; otherwise it would not have been possible to maintain clean roads and an efficient drainage system.

(v) *The Houses*. In Mohenjodaro, on the sides of roads and alleys, there are ruins of buildings which were built with bricks. Some houses are double-storeyed and these had staircases. The roofs were built of wood. All the houses had a courtyard on whose sides were rooms built. Each house had a bathroom, a toilet and a kitchen. The rooms had windows which opened on the side of alley and not road. This was probably done to prevent pollution of the road.

(vi) *The Great Bath and Granary*. The ruins of Mohenjodaro bear witness to public halls and community buildings. This clearly suggests that people lived in families in residential blocks but there were buildings where a large number of people could gather on special occasions. Of particular interest is the ruins which clearly show that people of Indus civilization lived a rich and diversified life, a life that was not a monotony. There was a Great Bath which was used for communal bathing. The swimming pool was erected on a raised platform and was made 12 m. long, 7 m. wide and 3 m. deep. In order to go into the pool there were brick stains on two sides. It has also a provision of drainage. On a raised platform there were small cubicles on three sides which were probably used for changing clothes. Near the bath there are two big wells which were used to supply water to the pool. The ruins of a room for hot water bath have also been found. The Great Bath is a building of architectural excellence and this suggests that the citizens of Indus valley were highly civilized and sophisticated. The mains of granaries to store wheat etc. have been found at various sites.

2. Social Life : (i) *Food*. The staple food of Indus Valley people was wheat, barley and peas etc. The ruins of objects used for grinding and pounding wheat and barley have been found. The Indus valley man had a mixed diet of milk, butter, eggs and meat.

(ii) *Clothing*. The Indus Valley man used mostly cotton for cloth but was not unfamiliar with wool as well. The remains of needles found attest that he could stitch. From the idols found we can infer that men and women had a variety of clothing. Both coarse and fine clothes have been found.

(iii) *Jewellery*. The use of jewellery was widespread and common to both men and women. The men used chains and rings and women used bracelets, bangles etc. The use of coral and ivory was widespread.

(iv) *Cosmetics*. The Indus valley man was fond of good appearance. Men sported long hair and women were particular about the hair-do. The relics found suggest that the combs made of ivory were in common use.

(v) *Entertainment*. The excavation at Indus valley site have unravelled a variety of means to while away time and enjoy the thrill. The Indus valley man was fond of chaupar, a game played with three dice or kauris. He also loved to watch cock-fight and also sung and danced. The excavation has revealed whistles, banjos and icons of birds and animals.

3. Economic Life. (i) *Agriculture*. The Indus valley soil was very fertile and agriculture was the primary occupation. The main crops grown were wheat, barley and peas. The dates were also grown at some places. The remains of cotton clothes suggest that cotton was also grown.

(ii) *Animal husbandry*. The Indus valley man reared cattles. He kept cows, bulls, sheep and goats. The toys found suggest that people of Indus valley domesticated small animals and birds like cats, dogs, monkeys, rabbits, cocks, peacocks and parrots.

(iii) *Art and Craft*. The Indus valley man was a skilled craftsman :

(a) *Weaving*. He was a weaver as attested by the discovery of clothes and spindle. He was skilled at knitting designs of flowers and other patterns. There appears to have been a full-fledged cottage industry in textiles.

(b) *Pottery*. The Indus man was a skilled potter. He made beautiful pots and other utensils.

(c) *Sculpture*. The artists of Indus valley sculpted statues using clay and stone.

(d) *Drawing*. The pots and utensils were decorated by drawing circles, triangles and other patterns. The excavations have thrown up many a seal having drawing of women and birds. All this shows that Indus man was an artist of very high category. The fine examples of jewellery have also been found.

(e) *Metal Work*. From Mohenjodaro a figure of dancing woman has been found which is very impressive. The statues of bronze have also been found. Besides bronze, other metals were also used and swords and spears have been found.

(iv) *Trade*. The Indus valley man was interested in trade and commerce. The discovery of granaries shows that grain was brought from villages and stored. The trade was not only via land-routes but also via waterways. The small ships were used for this purpose. The Indus valley man had trade relations with Afghanistan, Persia and Egypt; this is borne out from the ruins found here. The discovery of different sizes of weights show the advanced stage of trade and commerce.

4. Religious Life. No direct evidence of the religious beliefs of Indus man is available. But one is able to decipher their religious beliefs from the idols and drawings on seals and coins. The Indus man believed in gods and goddesses as well as in natural forces. The Mother goddess was the single most widespread object of worship. In Indus ruins we have found a statue of an ascetic which is most probably that of Pashupati Shiva. The Sun, Fire and Water were the natural forces worshipped. The Bull was also revered.

5. Disposal of Dead. The corpses were disposed of both by cremation, *i.e.*, putting them on fire and also burying them underground. The corpses were also exposed in open to be devoured by vultures, the bones were gathered and buried underground. While burying their dead, Indus valley people used to keep food and other necessities of daily life. This was probably done in the belief that this may be useful to dead in their life hereafter.

6. The Indus Script. Like Mesopotamian and Egyptian civilizations, Indus man had also developed a pictorial script. However, this is still to be deciphered.

Importance of Indus Valley Civilization

Before the discovery of Indus valley civilization it was commonly believed that Indian civilization began with Aryan civilization. Now it is established that there was an advanced level of civilization even before the Aryan civilization and now it is proved that the most ancient civilization emerged in India. The lay-out of Indus valley was unique and one cannot help marvelling at the skills mastered by them. There is a clear-cut influence of the religious beliefs of Indus valley on the later Indian civilization. This is why Indus valley civilization is so important.

MESOPOTAMIAN CIVILIZATION

Location

Mesopotamian civilization is one of the eminent ancient civilizations. This civilization flourished in south-west Asia between Tigris and Euphrates rivers extending from the mountains of Asia Minor to the Persian Gulf. In Greek, the space between two rivers is called Mesopotamia and since this civilization flourished between two rivers, it is called Mesopotamian.

In the ancient time the southern part of Mesopotamia was Sumer and it was the pivot of this civilization. The northern region of Mesopotamia is known as Babylon or Akkad. The mountain regions of north are known as Assyria. In this valley a number of civilizations flourished known as Sumerian, Babylonian, Assyrian and Chaldean. These civilizations belong to Mesopotamian civilization.

On the whole there were tremendous strides in social, religious, economic, cultural and architectural fields in Mesopotamia and their influence extended to other civilizations of the world.

Political History

(i) *Sumerian Civilization*. The cities of Mesopotamia made first and foremost advance in irrigation. Some of these centres emerged as places of trade and commerce. The history of Sumer or Akkad goes back to 3,200 B.C. In the history of south-west Asia, Sumerian civilization is most ancient. The people of Sumer turned the marshes of Tigris and Euphrates into a fertile land and developed a sophisticated plan of irrigation. The idea of urban settlement also originated here. Some scholars consider it to be the oldest civilization. However, it is difficult to tell the people who were Sumerians as people of Akkad, a province in the north-east of Sumer were of different clans, but, however they had adopted the culture and tradition of Sumerians. In 2500 B.C. a powerful king had succeeded in creating a new state by merging Sumer and Akkad. However, as this new state has had no natural barriers, it was a prey to frequent external incursions. In 100 years this state disintegrated.

(ii) *Hammurabi*. In the history of Mesopotamia, the remarkable event is that of emergence of a new dynasty. In 1792 B.C. the most renowned and powerful ruler was Hammurabi. He was an astute ruler and his code of conduct occupies a pre-eminent place in the world history. Hammurabi gradually extended the frontiers of his state and its boundaries included present day Iraq. He extended the boundaries of his state to include Babylon, Akkad and Sumer. The culture promoted by him is now known as Babylonian civilization.

(iii) *Hittite*. In 1600 B.C., Babylon was run over by a nomad tribe Hittite. A town 'Asur' on the banks of river Euphrates was the focal point from where Assyrian Empire spread. However, the Assyrian empire was run over by the tribals known as Berbers.

Characteristics

1. The Rise of City States. Among the various cities of Mesopotamia, the city of URA occupied a pivotal place. The excavations carried out in this city have revealed that it was a side area divided into three distinct parts. The one part was called sacred and it had many temples. It was made on mound with bricks. For safety there was a brick wall around this mound. The temples were dedicated to city gods and priests used to pray and meditate here.

2. The Statecraft. The seat of power in Babylonia was the people. They had an assembly. It had two chambers; one of these was open to all adults and there was a higher assembly which was represented by elders and enlightened persons. The king had to take counsel from both in matters of state policy. But as this was a long-winding process it was not useful when quick decisions were needed to combat external threats. This led to abolition of Assembly and its replacement by a central authority known as Pitesi. As the empire spread, more and more Pitesis were appointed. These Pitesis looked after religious as well as secular affairs. Gradually, things changed and all authority came to be vested in the king, and king was considered to be the representative of God on earth.

3. Social Life. (i) *Social Stratification.* The society was class based and there was distinction of high and low, and the low castes had no rights. They were slaves.

The first order citizen included king, who was considered God on earth, and members of his household, priests and high state officials. The second order was made by traders, artists, landlords and shopkeepers. While second order citizens had rights, though less than those of first, the third order was made up of slaves who obviously had no rights. Their duty was to serve the first and second orders.

(ii) *Housing.* The houses were made of clay bricks which were dried in the sun. There was courtyard around which rooms were built. Though good in structure these were no match to the housing plan of Indus valley.

(iii) *Food.* The staple food of Babylonians consisted of wheat and barley. They also used milk and butter as well as meat and fish.

(iv) *Clothes and Jewellery.* The Babylonians used to wear clothes of cotton, wool and sheep skin. However, aristocratic ladies lived in great luxury. They used a variety of cosmetics and sported ornaments made of gold and silver. The main jewels were necklace, bangles, ear-rings and finger rings. The poor used copper for making jewels.

(v) *Status of Women.* The women occupied a place of honour in Babylonian society. Monogamy was prevalent. The use of purdah was confined to aristocratic ladies. The dowry was prevalent but it remained the property of the bride and she could dispose it of if her husband died.

4. Law code of Hammurabi. Hammurabi was a renowned ruler of Babylon who introduced a common law code for all the tribes. He nullified the mutually opposite customs and traditions of tribes. The edicts of Hammurabi were carved on stones. His law code comprised of 242 rules. These were carved on a 44 metre tall stone slate. These rules pertained to property, trade, agriculture and family.

Hummurabi law code covered every aspect of life. An offence by any one against his fellow citizen was deemed to be an offence against the king and the king was duty bound to punish the offender. However, the degree of punishment was not the same for every class. Indeed, the crimes of higher class against the lower carried light punishment which was heavy if the same crime was committed by a lower caste against the higher class.

5. Religious Beliefs. Mesopotamians believed in gods and goddesses. The more important ones were Shamas (sun god), Anus (sky god), Enil (wind god) and Nannar (moon god). There was a main most revered, temple in every city. The presiding deity of the temple was the god of the city and rulers ruled under

Deity's name. Every temple had vast land gifted to it. The people also gifted many a valuables to the temple. Thus, priests came to wield over whelming influence in secular matters as well.

Jigurat. The guiding and protecting Deity of each city was held in great awe. A large and beautiful temple was built in its name either on a mountain or on a raised platform. The temple besides being a place of worship, had in it a granary and an administrative office. Thus, it was the focus of power. These temples were multistoried and the Deity was supposed to reside in the uppermost storey. From these roof tops astrologers used to study stars and planets. Mesopotamian people did not worship gods from a sense of sin and punishment and with a desire of getting relief from gods. They worshipped out of a sense of reverence. They believed that though gods may get angry with man, they did not punish him. It was not thought proper for gods to punish or reward.

6. Disposal of Dead. Mesopotamians used to bury their dead in one of the rooms of the house and used to keep with the corpse things of day-to-day needs. They worshipped their elders.

7. Art and Sculpture. The artists and sculptors of Mesopotamia were highly skilled in their fields. Due to paucity of stones, the houses were made of clay bricks. The walls of the houses were decorated by drawing on them colourful patterns. The structure of temples is indicative of their skill. The inside walls of the temples were ornamentally decorated in multicolour. The pieces of china clay were pasted on walls to create beautiful patterns. The seals founded in excavation are beautifully painted, witness to their high skill and refined taste.

8. Occupation: (i) *Agriculture*. The agriculture was the primary occupation of Mesopotamians. The land was fertile and the irrigation system good. They grew wheat, barley and dates.

(ii) *Animal Husbandry*. The animal husbandry was the secondary occupation of Mesopotamians. They domesticated and reared cows, sheep and goats. There were vast pastures hedged on sides and royal shepherds looked after the animals. Besides keeping animals and growing corns, they developed big orchards of grapes and olives.

(iii) *Industry*. The state of industry was quite advanced. The artists were laborious and made fine goods of wood, ivory, gold and copper. The first discovery of potter's wheel is attributed to Mesopotamia. The cotton and woollen clothes were quite common. Mesopotamians were skilled in making weapons of bronze and copper. However, the goods made by Mesopotamians were inferior to Indus Valley products.

9. Trade and Commerce. Trade and commerce flourished in Mesopotamia. The traders had links with other countries. Babylon was the hub of international trade. The gold, silver and high quality wood were imported from other countries. Instead, the ornaments made of gold and silver were exported. The trade was done by land as well as waterways.

10. Cuneiform Alphabets. The Mesopotamian script was wedge-shaped. The cuneiform script is the rare achievement of Babylonians. The characters were inscribed on moist clay plates with the help of a sharp edged pen. The ideas could be conveyed pictorially or audio-visually. The Cuneiform scipt was audio-visual.

11. Science and Astrology. Mesopotamia had made remarkable advances in science. The priests here were skilled in the art of astrological predictions and mapping the sky. They had divided the calendar in twelve months and had discovered many planets to which they gave names. They used to prepare astrological tables (Ephimeris) which were linked to the movement of the moon. As we use decimal system of counting Mesopotamians counted in the scales of sixty. This is the reason that an hour is divided into sixty minutes and a minute in sixty seconds. The circle was, for this very reason, divided into three hundred and sixty parts.

Importance

The Mesopotamian civilization was very much advanced in administrative set-up, scientific discovery, the artistic creations and industry. The law code and the collection of books in libraries is indicative of Mesopotamian mastery over the art of writing.

EGYPTIAN CIVILIZATION

1. Location

Egypt is situated in the North-East sector of the continent of Africa; it is a small but highly advanced country. Egypt is aptly called the gift of river Nile because agriculture and transportation were possible only because of the perrenial nature of the river Nile. On the green banks of Nile was born a highly developed civilization. The land neighbouring Nile is very fertile and the superior most cotton in the world is grown here. But for Nile Egypt would be a desert.

2. Political History

The Egyptian civilization is one of the most ancient. In the beginning Egypt was comprised of small city states. But around 4000 B.C. Egypt was divided into two segments — the Northern Egypt and the Southern Egypt. The history of Egypt has three epochs — the ancient, the middle and the modern epochs. In 3400 B.C. a renowned and able king Menes integrated the Northern and Southern spheres into a united kingdom with the capital Memphis near the modern Cairo. In this period world famous pyramids were constructed. On account of the excellence and architectural perfection of these constructions, this period is also known as the Age of Pyramids. The span of this period is approximately between 2980 to 2475 B.C. The architectural skills made a great advance during this period. Egypt could not sustain its integrity very long. The social and political upheavals lead to its disintegration and the emergence of feudal lords.

After a reign by feudal lords, the middle epoch of Egyptian history begins. The span of middle age was approximately between 2160 to 1788 B.C. In the middle of 18th century B.C., the alien race of Hyksos trounced Egypt and established their hegemony over it. Hyksos were nomads but their civilization was quite advanced. Soon Egyptians reoccupied their land. This emergence of Egyptians as victors ushered in a new period known as modern period of Egyptian history. The span of this period is between 1580 to 1090 B.C. During this period a great emphasis on armed preparedness was laid and as a result the Egyptians conquered many new territories. The major strides were made in science during this period. By 1000 B.C. Egyptian's power disintegrated and gave way to foreign occupation.

3. Administration

In Egypt the political set-up was religion-based. The king emperor, called Pharaoh was the fountain power. He was a supreme authority in the state. As the country was too big to be ruled centrally by one person, it was divided into small administrative units which were put under the control of, what we call in modern times, governors.

The king emperor was not only an administrative head but was supreme commander, head priest and chief justice as well. To make peace or war was the sole prerogative of the king. He also made rounds of his kingdom to see for himself the efficiency of administration and proper execution of welfare works. The appointment of governers was made by the Pharaoh himself. Apparently, Pharaohs considered themselves secure and well protected and did not therefore keep a permanent army. But in time of needs he fell upon the backing of the armies kept by temples and by provinces. The main central authority was located in his palace. In order to help the central administration he appointed Ministers and priests to aid and assist in the administration.

4. Social set-up

(i) *Social Stratification.* In the social hierarchy, the king and members of his family enjoyed the supreme status. After them in importance, were feudal lords, priests and royal officials. The middle order class was comprised of scribes, artists, artisans and non-slave agriculturists. The lowest order consisted of slaves who had been taken prisoners during wars. Barring the members of royal class all other persons were free to pursue any profession or occupation.

(ii) *Living Conditions.* The society was based on class distinctions. The aristocrats lived in houses made of pucca bricks. These houses were well ventilated and there was provision of adequate sunshine. Surrounding the houses were parks and gardens. Both men and women sported costly jewellery. Women of Egypt were fond of cosmetics and ornamentation. The poor and slaves used to live in thatched huts, they had to work hard to earn a livelihood. The clothes were made of cotton. As noted earlier, the best quality cotton is grown in the Nile delta.

(iii) *Entertainment.* The wrestling, the boxing and watching bull fight were the main sources of entertainment.

(iv) *Food.* As regards food there was plenty, they ate wheat and barley bread, fish, mutton, milk, cheese and dates. The aristocrats also drank wine made of grapes.

(v) *Status of Women.* In Egypt women were treated with honour and enjoyed equal rights with menfolk. The paintings of this period indicate that women used to participate in fetes and festivals. The monogamy was the dominant system of marriage. The property belonged to women and on death of their husbands the property was inherited by wives and daughters.

5. The Religious Beliefs

They worshipped various gods and goddesses by making icons and statues of them. The Egyptians worshipped various natural forces, they believed that behind all natural forces there was a presiding deity. As such they worshipped sun for sustaining life and existence, moon for dispelling darkness and Nile for providing fertile land and promoting growth for various corns and cotton. Besides these gods, Egyptians worshipped mountains, springs and various animals and birds.

In temples the worship was conducted by priests. Besides worship and prayer, the priests also used to oversee and control the temple properties. In wars the priests used to lend support to the king by offering themselves alongwith their armies. This lead to rise in their status.

6. Burial

The Egyptians were staunch believers of reincarnation of soul. In order to dispose of their dead, Egyptians used to mummify them. That is, they used to embalm corpses with an ointment which prevented rigor mortis and putrefaction, placed them in beautiful wooden boxes and used to bury them in rooms, inside pyramids.

7. Art and Architecture

(i) *Cave painting.* Millenia passed after our ancestors painted their magical images on cave walls. Gradually men tamed animals, and finally some men started to raise crops. They did not give up hunting but settled down. Now they had an efficient way of controlling their food supply. This is the reason that ancient civilizations are riparian.

(ii) *Pyramids.* More then 5000 years ago, the people of the Nile valley developed a highly refined civilization that flourished for about 3000 years. It contributed an architecture, art and literature of outstanding quality. It is known for Pyramids which were temples and mysterious ancient massive structures found in Egypt having typically a square ground plan, outside walls in the form of four triangles that meet in a point at the top and inner sepulchral chambers enclosed tombs abounding with sculpture, murals and craft work.

(iii) *Wall painting.* As early as about 3000 B.C. the oldest Egyptian wall painting we know was made in a tomb in Hieraconpolis, and during these early centuries that powerful form of art known as the Egyptian Style developed a tradition which persisted for age and fascinates mankind even today.

8. Religion

Egyptian art is rooted in religion. The Greek historian, Herodotus later wrote that the Egyptians were the most religious of all people. Highly intelligent, with a scientific bent they invented the first known calender. They had an attitude of awe and reverence regarding nature and assumed that nature was animated by powerful spirits, by gods when they depicted as human figures, often with animal heads. Ra (Sun god) rode his boat through the waters of heaven during the day and travelled in his night vehicle through the underworld, the country of the dead, at night. Osiris the ruler of the underworld had a son Horus who is depicted with animal head (Falcon). The kings or Pharaohs were also considered gods, sons of Almighty Ra. The royal Pyramids were gigantic stairways to aid the deceased kings return to heaven. The shape of Pyramids may have been a sun symbol, representing the rays coming down to earth. The Egyptians believed in eternal life. This belief influenced Egyptian art. Art was the key to mysterious power, catching the very essence of beings and things in representations that gave them eternal life. Wall paintings depicted all the pleasures to which the deceased was entitled. We see paintings depicting scenes of hunting, fishing and harvesting, craftsmen are working and servants are bringing offerings. The tombs were built to last for ever, as sculpture provided an eternal body lest mummified corpse perish.

9. Hieroglyphic Script

Egyptians learned the art of writing from Sumerians, but then script was different. It was pictorial and Greeks later called it hieroglyphic, the sacred sign.

10. Science

(i) *Mathematics.* In the construction of Pyramids Egyptians display deep knowledge of mathematics. They could count upto lacs, but they were innocent about zero. They knew the use of it with the help of which they could calculate areas of geometrical figures.

(ii) *Calender.* As referred above they invented the solar calendar under which the year was divided into twelve months and the months into 30 days. Five days were added to each year. Thus, their year was of 365 days, very close to modern calculation.

(iii) *Paper.* Egyptians had probably discovered paper. The word paper is derived from papyrus. For writing they used sharp-edged bamboo pens.

(iv) *Medical Science.* The Egyptians were far ahead of others in their knowledge of anatomy. The use of frequent laxatives was considered to be panacea of all ills. The material used to mummify corpses which have surived thousands of years of ravages of time bear testimony to their advanced knowledge of science.

11. Occupations and Industry

(i) *Agriculture*. The major occupation of Egyptians was agriculture. The fertile valley of Nile was fit for growing multicrops in a year. The wheat, the barley, the peas and cotton were grown in abundance. They also knew horticulture and grew grapes, dates and olives.

(ii) *Cattle-breeding*. The Egyptians had tamed bull, cow and goats. They also fished and hunted wild pigs.

(iii) *Industry*. The industry was fairly developed. In particular the carpentry was of a very high order. Beautiful furniture was made and it was studded with ivory and other precious jewels. The high class furniture was patronized by feudal lords and pharaohs. The utensils of clay and stone were made. The jewellers were skilled in making beautiful ornaments. The women were skilled in weaving yarn and making beautiful clothes. The animal skin was also used in making garments. The paper was made from the tree bark.

12. Trade and Commerce

The corn was stored in granaries and trade was done through waterways. The money was not yet invented, therefore the value of goods was measured by the weight of golden rings. The jewels, ornaments and cloth were exported.

The Gift of Egyptian Civilization

Undoubtedly Egypt had reached a very advanced level of civilization 5000 years ago. The political and social life was well structured and there was harmony and peace. This suggests good harmony between various classes. In architecture and science Egyptian civilization had reached a high pinnacle of glory. Thus, Egypt left indelible impression upon later civilizations.

THE CIVILIZATION OF CHINA

1. Cradle of two rivers

Like other ancient civilisations, the Chinese civilisation emerged and flourished in the cradle of its two rivers Hwang-ho and Yangtse Kiang. Though Hwang-ho used to engulf large areas of land during floods and it was known as river of sorrow, but, as a matter of fact, when the floods receded, the land under floods would become highly fertile so much so that this land is ranked among world's most fertile tracts.

2. Political History

The story of Chinese civilization is based on legends and folklore and not on any hard evidence. As lacs of years old fossil of man has been found near Beijing it is correctly supposed that the advent of man in northern China goes back in hoary past. However, the factually substantiated period of Chinese civilisation begins with Sang dynasty.

(i) *Sang Dynasty.* The Sang dynasty flourished over a period between 1765 to 1122 B.C. This dynasty gave China a very advanced level of civilization. The Emperor of Sang dynasty was first and foremost a head priest like Roman Pope. Under him there were many priests. The people here had their peculiar script. They were knowledgeable about metals and in all probability they were the inventors of chariot.

(ii) *Chao Dynasty.* The period of Chao dynasty starts from 1122 B.C. They organized the small states into a big federal structure, but the Chao kings could not prevent an internecine battle among various small states. The neighbouring tribes found the soil fertile for occupation and the hegemony of Chao dynasty ended in 250 B.C.

(iii) *Zhin Dynasty.* The power now shifted in the hands of Zhin dynasty. The emperor Hwang T. Shih belonged to Zhin. He suppressed the revolt of opponents with iron hand and established his empire. It was after his name that the country came to be known as China. In order to ward off incursions of Barbars from north, he constructed the big wall of China. In year 202 B.C. the reigns of powers shifted to the hands of Hunan dynasty. This dynasty flourished for 400 years and made substantial contribution to Chinese civilization. Ultimately Huns acceded to power.

3. Statecraft

(i) *Monarchy.* The king was all-in-all. He was temporal as well as spiritual head of the state. He was also the Chief Justice of his country. Though an autocrat with unbridled powers, he took counsel from his advisors and ministers.

(ii) *Administrative departments.* The main administrative departments of the state were Army, Religion, Justice and Education.

(iii) *Feudal lords.* There were feudal lords under king who administered their respective territories. The lords had their own armies which included Cavalary as well as Infantry.

(iv) *Competitive examinations.* The administrators were chosen by written test in literary matters and once chosen they were rigorously trained. The scholarly officials incharge of preparing administrators were known as mandarins. In the matter of choice of officials China was first in world history to introduce competitive tests.

4. Social Life

(i) *Social stratification.* The Chinese society, like the Mesopotamian and Egyptian, was stratified and classified. The uppermost strata included king and his relatives. The next in order of rank and status were literatures and intelligent. Below them were craftsmen and artisans. The lowest order comprised of slaves.

(ii) *Family.* The smallest unit of society was family and, likewise India, the joint families were in vogue.

(iii) *Patriarchal society*. Primarily, the society was patriarchal and the eldest male of the family enjoyed supreme status. There were however few examples of matriarchal societies. The tradition played a very significant role in this society.

5. Economic life

(i) *Agriculture*. The chief occupation of Chinese was agriculture and prosperity of nation rested upon it. The land was fertile and various corns were grown on it.

(ii) *Sericulture*. China was world famous for its sericulture.

(iii) *Crafts*. Besides agriculture, there were skilled craftsmen. There carpenter and potter were the main craftsmen. There were master jewellers also.

(iv) *Trade and Commerce*. The trade of China was very prosperous. It imported and exported goods by land routes as well as waterways.

6. Religion

Under the Sang and Chao dynasties the religion of people was polytheistic. The natural forces were considered gods. Like Indians, Chinese worshipped Mother Earth, sky, wind and other natural forces as gods. They also worshipped their elders inside the temples. They believed that souls of the dead gain infinite power. Like Egyptians they used to bury alongwith the dead his favourite articles. They used to offer food, meat and wine to their gods. The usual ceremonies were conducted by priests but the major ceremonies were conducted by the king himself.

7. Philosophy

In the 6th century B.C. two great philosopher saints were born in China, namely Lao-tse and Confucius. They condemned orthodoxy. Lao-tse introduced Taoism which has the following features — numerous gods, Lao, the ultimate and unconditioned being could be attained by virtue if thrift, humility and compassion were practised. Confucius (551–479 B.C.) was mainly a social reformer who emphasized the respect of elders and adherence to tradition.

8. Script

Chinese script is very old. It is pictorial. All objects and ideas are represented by appropriate pictorial symbols. The Chinese script has no alphabets. Calligraphy plays a vital role in it.

9. Arts and Crafts

(i) *Paintings*. The Chinese were art lovers. Their paintings are extremely lively and beautiful. The most notable branches are water-colour, paintings on paper or silk, chiefly delicate landscapes, and pottery produced at high temperature with great skill, often with wonderful colours and glazes. Painting dates back to Han Dynasty at least 206 B.C. — A.D. 220.

(ii) *Pottery*. Pottery was made in China in pre-history times.

(iii) *Architecture:*

(a) *The Great Wall*. The famous great wall of China is the epitome of Chinese skill in architecture. The wall is 2400 k.m. long and 5 meter high. Its width is such that a railway train can run on it. It is dotted with minarets used as check posts.

(b) *Pagodas*. The pagodas (towers of many storeys) of China are another example of very high architectural skill. The pagoda had tall statues of Buddha and its walls were ornamentally decorated.

(iv) *Sculpture*. Under the influence of Buddhism, Chinese carved many a statues, most of these were those of Buddha and Bodhisatvas. There were sculptures of animals and birds too.

10. Science

The scientific progress made by Chinese is marvellous :

(i) *Calender*. Like Egyptians, the Chinese also produced a solar calender. Though they did not have Ephemeris, they knew that a year was comprised of 365 ¼ days.

(ii) *Meteorology*. The Chinese were expert meteorologists and could predict weather. They knew calculation of π.

(iii) *Medicine*. The Chinese made remarkable progress in the field of medicine. They used herbs as well as needles to cure diseases. Acupuncture is a typical example of their medical skill.

(iv) *Science of Earthquakes*. They also invented an instrument to measure and forecast earthquakes. They had also mastered the decimal system of calculation.

(v) *Geography*. They sent their messengers to different parts of the world and these travellers wrote travelogues which exhibits their geographic knowledge.

(vi) *Inventions*. The Chinese invented magnetic compass, motor propelled by weather and also a solar dial to register time. The most remarkable gift of the Chinese is their invention of paper and printing press.

Contribution to World Civilization

In the development of modern civilization, the Chinese civilization has made remarkable contribution. The Chinese discoveries in science and mathematics have proved very crucial. The system of recruitment of government servants through competitive examinations, now in vogue in the world, was the unique contribution of the Chinese. They were also the first inventors of paper and printing press. They also taught the world sericulture and art of pottery. The magnetic needle which transformed the sea-faring is a Chinese contribution to world. The spread of Buddhism in China brought it into relation with other Asian civilizations.

PART D — SOCIAL ANTHROPOLOGY

16

Introduction to Social Anthropology

Social anthropology, as is clear by the nomenclature, studies social organization and social institutions. In the words of Charles Winick, "Social anthropology is the study of social behaviour especially from the point of view of the systematic comparative study of social forms and institutions."[1] According to R. Firth, "One of the broadest way of defining social anthropology is to say that it studies human social processes comparatively."[2]

According to Radcliffe Brown, field work in a society does not give a direct experience of culture but of social relationships. Of these, only those relationships are important which are repeated everywhere, since they alone provide the essentials of social organization. Raymond Firth and Radcliffe Brown have also insisted upon the distinction between social organization and social structure. In the words of Majumdar and Madan, "Social organization stands for how social structure works in time."[3] In his book *Foundations of Social Anthropology*, Nadel has pointed out some criteria of anthropological studies. Such studies are primarily studies of modes of communication.

To conclude in the words of Majumdar and Madan, "Thus studies of human societies may be studied not in terms of culture but in terms of structures which embody culture."[4]

Social anthropology is an important branch of anthropology. Anthropology, as is clear from its name, is a scientific study of the science of man. From this definition of anthropology, it is clear that social anthropology studies the man at least. But this alone does not clear the difference between social anthropology and other branches of anthropology. The difference will be clear by giving the

1. Winick, C., *Dictionary of Anthropology*, p. 21.
2. Firth, R., *Elements of Social Organization* (1951), p. 2.
3. Majumdar, D. N. and T. N. Madan, *An Introduction to Social Anthropology*, Bombay, Asia, 1957, p. 33.
4. *Ibid.*

meaning of the word social". Social Anthropology is social. The meaning of the word "social" is enough to show how the field and viewpoint of social anthropology is different from other branches of anthropology. Piddington has said, "Social anthropologists study the cultures of contemporary primitive communities."[5] But this definition of social anthropology is a little narrow because social anthropology does not only study primitive cultures but studies contemporary cultures also. From this point of view, the definition of social anthropology, given by Dr. S. C. Dube is more appropriate. According to Dr. Dube, "Social anthropology is that part of cultural anthropology which devotes its primary attention to the study of social structure and religion rather than material aspects of culture."[6] It is thus clear that social anthropology studies the different aspects of social structure such as social institutions, social relations etc. "The part of cultural anthropology which treats of social phenomena is called social anthropology."[7] In this connection Dr. Srinivas has given a sufficiently detailed definition of social anthropology. He writes: "It is a comparative study of human societies. Ideally, it includes all societies primitive, civilised and historic."[8] Charles Winick has also called social anthropology a comparative study. According to him, "Social anthropology is the study of social behaviour, especially from the point of view of the systematic comparative study of social forms, and institutions."[9] In brief, social anthropology is a comparative study of social behaviour and social phenomena of men of all countries and ages.

SCOPE OF SOCIAL ANTHROPOLOGY

While defining social anthropology, Beals and Hoizer write, "It is concerned with culture *per se*, whether it belongs to the primitive men of the stone age or the European City-dwellers of today."[10] Although it is more properly a definition of cultural anthropology, yet it surely and clearly shows that the field of social anthropology is very wide. It includes a study of different parts of culture, social institutions, economic institutions and political administration. The main branches of social anthropology are given below:

1. Ethnography
2. Familial anthropology
3. Economic anthropology
4. Political anthropology

---

5. Piddington, R., *An Introduction to Social Anthropology*, Oliver & Boyd, London (1952), p. 2.

6. Dube, S. C., *Anthropology*, p. 2.

7. Penniman, T. K., *A Hundred Years of Anthropology*, Gerald Duckworth & Co. Ltd., London (1952), pp. 13-14.

8. Srinivas, M. N., *Social Anthropology and Sociology*, p. 28.

9. Winick, C., *Dictionary of Anthropology*, p. 21.

10. Beals and Hoizer, *Introduction to Anthropology* (1956), p. 8.

5. Symbiology and linguistics
6. Thought and art.

1. Ethnography. Ethnography is the main field of social anthropology. As is clear from its name, it studies the human races. Its scope also includes the study of cultures of different races.

2. Familial Anthropology. Family is the basic institution of society. Social anthropology, therefore, studies the family also. This branch of social anthropology is known as familial anthropology. It takes up a comparative study of the families of different cultures and societies. It studies the different forms of family along with its progress. A family is based on marriage. Familial anthropology, therefore, includes a study of different forms of marriage. It also includes other blood relations along with marriage.

3. Economic Anthropology. Economic rules play an important part in social organization. Some radical changes take place in social structure along with a change in economic administration. Social anthropology, therefore, minutely studies economic administration of primitive and civilized human societies and of different levels of evolution in them.

4. Political Anthropology. Political administration also has an important place in social structure along with economic administration. Social anthropology, therefore, studies all types of political administration, laws, governments and rules of punishment, etc. This branch of social anthropology is known as political anthropology.

5. Symbiology and Linguistics. The study of different symbols of human behaviour, which are current in languages of different societies, supplies many important facts for the study of society. Social anthropology, therefore, studies all these also. The whole linguistics field falls within this branch of social anthropology. The main branches of linguistics are given below:

(i) *Descriptive linguisitics.* It studies the individual and regional languages. (ii) *Historical linguistics.* It is a historical study of languages; (iii) *Comparative linguistics.* It studies the contemporary facts about language; (iv) *Common linguistics.* It studies the difference between the minimum and maximum roots of some languages.

6. Thought and Art. The study of thoughts in theoretical study is very important. Thought includes religion, magic, science, even legends. Social anthropology is a comparative study of all these things in ancient human societies. Art is an important part of culture and culture depicts the interior of a society. Social anthropology studies sculpture, metallurgy, and even dancing and instrumental and vocal music.

SOCIAL ANTHROPOLOGY AND CULTURAL ANTHROPOLOGY

Dr. D.N. Majumdar and other contemporary anthropologists have regarded social anthropology as a part of cultural anthropology. Cultural anthropology studies the mode of life of the contemporary primitive man. Cultural anthropology has four branches, *e.g.*, linguistics and symbiology, thought and art, economic anthropology and social anthropology. Social anthropology studies the different kinds of social life and its evolution. In this way, according to Dr. Majumdar, linguistics, symbiology, economic anthropology and thought and art are outside the scope of social anthropology. According to this point of view, familial anthropology and political anthropology only form the part of social anthropology. This is clear from the foregoing discussion about the scope of social anthropology. But familial anthropology and political anthropology are closely related to the other branches. American anthropologist Morgan, was the founder of social anthropology. Social anthropology and cultural anthropology differ more in their subject matter than in their modes and concepts. While cultural anthropology studies culture, social anthropology is a study of social structure, social organization and social relations. Morgan studied anthropology through the study of society. Durkheim showed that social relations are different from psychological relations and that both the relations should be given their sociological definitions. In this way social anthropology studies anthropology in the terms of society. According to contemporary American anthropologists, social anthropology is only a branch of cultural anthropology because culture is a wide concept than society and includes far greater scope than what is included in the study of social life.

Study of Recurrent Social Relations

It is clear from the above explanation that in the subject of the field of social anthropology there are different ideologies. But there is no doubt that social anthropology has its own special place in anthropological studies. Radcliffe Brown is of the opinion that we come across social relations everywhere but culture nowhere, while working in the field of society. Some of these social relations are important and are often repeated. It is these repeated social relations which form the social structure. Social structure is formed by the mutual relations among individuals. Thus, the repeated facts of social life can be known through the study of social structure. Individuals face alternatives within the framework of social structure. A selection has to be made among these alternatives and its results are important. This selection helps in forming social organization and gives rise to social changes. Social structure can be compared to anatomy and social organization can be compared to physiology. In brief, social organization is the practical form of social structure. Social anthropologists of Britain have made comparative studies of the classical forms of human behaviour through an application of the concepts of structure and organization, etc. Claude Levi Strauss has called social anthropology a study of communication. There is mutual communication in society among individuals and groups. This communication is carried on through words and symbols which have special meaning. In this way, the study of linguistics, thought and art is included in the field of social anthropology. Institutions of marriage and family have to be studied for a study of communication between man and woman. In the same way, social organization is made and material culture develops on the basis of an exchange of commodities and services among different individuals and groups. According to Strauss, therefore, human societies should be studied in terms of social structure and communication and not in terms of culture.

It is clear from the above discussion that cultural anthropology and social anthropology study almost the same subject matter through different concepts. It is true that the scope of cultural anthropology is a little wider but it is difficult to draw a line of demarcation between the two on the basis of scope. The real difference lies in the fact that while cultural anthropology studies culture, social anthropology studies social relations, social structures and social organizations. This difference between cultural anthropology and social anthropology helps in describing the nature of social anthropology.

NATURE OF SOCIAL ANTHROPOLOGY

An examination of social anthropology reveals that social anthropology possesses the essential elements of a science.

1. Social anthropology makes use of scientific method. All methods of social anthropology are scientific. They make use of scientific techniques, like schedule, participant observation, historical method and case history, etc. First of all, they gather facts through observation. Then they are recorded in an orderly form. Afterwards, this matter is classified and in the end, common principles are made on the basis of accepted facts. The validity of these principles are examined.

2. Social anthropology is factual. Social anthropology is a comparative study of the facts about social relations and actions. Participant observation is its main method. In this method, an anthropologist goes to live among people whom he has to study. Thus, his study is in accordance with facts.

3. The principles of social anthropology are universal. The rules of social anthropology are proved in all countries; so long as the circumstances are the same, there is no chance of an exception in them.

4. The principles of social anthropology are veridical. Thus, the principles of social anthropology always prove true on verification and even on re-verification. Their validity can be verified by anybody and at any time.

5. Social anthropology defines cause-effect relations. Social anthropology discovers cause-effect relations in social facts, events and actions, etc. For example, an anthropologist, after his comparative study of various cultures tells us about life style to be found in a particular culture and the extent to which the life styles undergo a change with cultural changes. Thus, social anthropology answers "what" along with "how".

6. Social anthropology can predict. On the basis of cause-effect relationship, a social anthropologist can guess the future and can predict social actions and events, etc. He can decide "what will be" on the basis of "what is'' after knowing the cause-effect relations. For example, by observing cultural change, he can predict a change of life pattern.

It is clear from the foregoing discussion of the nature of social anthropology that social anthropology is a science. It contains abstract forms of thought. Scientific study is possible only through abstract forms. The rules of these abstract forms decide the behaviour of concrete things. In this way, the rules of social anthropology are universal and veredical in practical shape. Social anthropology has brought revolutionary change in the notions of psychologists, sociologists, politicians and social reformers. It has given a hope for organization of human society in future and has presented useful suggestions to decide the patterns of its organization.

AIMS OF SOCIAL ANTHROPOLOGY

Pointing out the aim of scientific study Ralph Piddington has proclaimed: ''The aim of any science is to study a specified part of the real world and from a study of facts to formulate theories which shall serve as recipes for human conduct, whether that conduct be the carrying out of further research or the taking of practical steps for the promotion of human welfare.''[11] Based upon this criterion, Piddington has admitted two aims of social anthropology. The primary aim of social anthropology is to gather nformation about human nature. Human nature is a controversial subject. Different scholars have laid emphasis upon different aspects of human nature. The primitive man and society present human nature in its most rudimentary and raw form. Therefore, their study is useful for the understanding of the basic essentials of human nature without much influence of culture upon them.

Another aim of social anthropology is the study of the processes and result of cultural contacts. Most of the primitive societies are gradually coming in contact of more developed cultures. This contact is gradually creating social, religious, economic and political problems and disorganization. Administrators and the social planners require the help of social anthropologists in the understanding of processes and consequences of cultural contacts. According to the Royal Anthropological Society of Great Britain and Ireland, the most important aims of social anthropology are the following:

1. The study of primitive culture in its present form.
2. The study of cultural contact and specific processes.

   This includes exploration of the influences of outer groups creating cultural changes.

3. Reconstruction of social history.
4. Search for universally valid social laws.

Thus, the chief aim of social anthropology is to study human society, social institutions, culture and kinship bonds in their most elementary form. Besides

11. Ralph Piddington, *An Introduction to Social Anthropology*, p. 7.

being useful for the understanding of present day human societies, it adds to our knowledge of human history as well as the nature of social institutions. That is why social anthropology is closely related to history and archaeology.

The above aims of social anthropology are particularly evident in the utilization of functional method in its study. According to Malinowski, in the functional method we try to discover those human needs which maintain his bio-psychic existence and finally his higher intellectual survival. The functional method also helps us in finding out ways and means for the fulfilment of these needs. As Radcliffe Brown has aptly pointed out, culture is an integrated system. It serves certain functions with reference to human societies. The functional method aims at the discovery of the general principles required for the explanation of cultural phenomena. It is clear that the discovery of the functions of social institutions, needs and culture, etc., in primitive societies provide a solid foundation for the understanding of developed societies and culture. For example, it has been discovered that culture is a means or tool to simplify fulfilment of human needs to give us a knowledge of ends and means, to develop social institutions, etc. It has been discovered that components of culture act separately as well as together. All this has been useful in the understanding of present day societies.

UTILITY OF THE STUDY OF PRIMITIVE SOCIETIES

According to S. F. Nadel, "The primary object of social anthropology is to understand primitive people, the cultures they have created and the social systems in which they live and act."[12] Thus, social anthropology primarily concentrates on the study of primitive societies. Explaining the meaning of the term primitive society, Evans Pritchard says, "When anthropologists use it (the word primitive society) they do so in reference to those societies which are small in a scale with regard to numbers, territory and range of social contacts, and which have by comparison with more advanced societies a simple technology and economy and little specialization of social function."[13] Ralph Piddington points out the following (traits), characteristic of primitive societies:[14]

1. The primary trait of primitive societies is illiteracy and the absence of writing or literature.
2. The primitive societies have social organization based upon small groups such as clans, tribes or totems, etc.
3. The technological level of development is very low.
4. The social relationships based upon locality and blood relationships are the most important.

---

12. Nadel, S. F., *Understanding Primitive People, Oceania*, Vol. XXVI (1956), p. 159.

13. Evans Pritchard, *Social Anthropology*, The Free Press, Glencoe, Illinois, 1954, p. 8.

14. Ralph Piddington, *An Introduction to Social Anthropology*, Oliver and Boyd, London, 1952, p. 5.

5. There is generally an absence of economic specialization and too much division of labour.

Thus, the primitive societies are little communities. Robert Redfield has called it, "the folk society".[15] According to him the absence of systematic art, science and theology is also characteristic of primitive societies.

The above mentioned traits of the primitive societies are rather relative and not absolute. For example, in some primitive societies in West Africa, members of some of them are literate. Again, some societies have a fairly organized political organization in spite of lower technological level. Therefore, the above traits are not necessary characteristics of every primitive society.

As to the question why social anthropologists have concentrated upon the study of primitive societies, Ralph Piddington calls it only a historical accident.[16] In the 18th century during the period of industrial revolution the Europeans travelled far and wide in search of new markets. They were closely followed by Christian missionaries. They discovered several interesting primitive societies. This interest gradually took the form of anthropological studies.

In 1859, a new chapter in the study of primitive societies was opened with the advent of Darwin's *Origin of Species*. Herbert Spencer presented his theory of social evolution on the basis of the biological evolution theory of Charles Darwin. According to him human societies have passed through different stages of evolution before arriving at the primitive stage. This theory led to the study of primitive societies in order to have a deeper understanding of the process of social evolution.

Another reason why scientists were drawn to the study of primitive societies was their challenge and strangeness. Pointing out to the difficulty in the understanding of primitive law Sir Henry Maine has said, ". . .the phenomena which early society presents us with are not easy at first to understand....It is a difficulty arising from their strangeness.... One does not readily get over the surprise which they occasion when looked at from a modern point of view."[17] Similar difficulty was felt by Lewis Morgan in his study of primitive religion. To quote his words, "It may never receive a perfectly satisfactory explanation since all primitive religions are grotesque and to some extent unintelligible."[18] Other notable anthropologists were equally influenced by the strangeness of primitive societies. Kroeber admitted, "The institutions were strange in flavour" to which anthropology "turned its attention".[19] This strangeness was a challenge to the social anthropologists. Therefore most of them were encouraged to study different aspects of primitive societies. The studies of primitive societies however

---

15. Redfield, Robert, "The Folk Society", *The American Journal of Sociology*, 1947.

16. Ralph Piddington, *op. cit.*, p. 6.

17. Maine, H., *Ancient Law*, 1888, pp. 119-120.

18. Lewis Morgan, *Ancient Society*, 1877, p. 5.

19. Kroeber, *Anthropology*, Harcourt Brace and Co., New York, 1923, p. 2.

gradually demonstrated that they were not strange but akin to civilized societies. In the words of S. F. Nadel, "Today the tendency is to empasize not the strangeness of primitive society, but its akinness to our own. Often, indeed, observers seem animated by the desire to demonstrate how, after all, man is the same everywhere.[20]

Another important reason for the study of primitive societies is their utility in the understanding of more civilized societies. Firstly, this is due to the primary nature of primitive societies and secondly, due to the simple and small units of human societies. Naturally, the knowledge of primary, simple and small human societies led to the understanding of the fundamentals of modern complex big societies. Therefore, Kluckhohn maintained that the study of primitive societies facilitates the understanding of more complex societies.

According to Evans Pritchard, however, primitive societies are also studied because of their intrinsic value. They are interesting and exhibit ways and means of existence with minimum facilities. Being the basic and fundamental units of human society, they reflect the natural state of human society.

It is a matter of normal experience that otherness attracts our attention and arouses our curiosity, the otherness also excludes the possibility of partiality. Therefore, the primitive societies can be studied more scientifically.

The primitive societies are fast changing in the present day world, due to culture contact. Their originality is disappearing rapidly. Therefore, the scientist is even more interested in studying these primitive forms before they are finally extinct. The data gathered by such studies are useful for comparative studies and the study of cultural processes. In the words of Evans Pritchard, "These vanishing social systems are unique structural variations, a study of which aids us very considerably in understanding the nature of human society, because in a comparative study of institutions the number of societies is less significant than their range of variation."[21]

But the most important reason for the attention of social anthropologists to the study of primitive societies, is methodological. It is a scientific principle that in a scientific investigation, one should start with the most simple and elementary phenomena, gradually stepping towards more complex ones. Therefore, the study of primitive societies is a necessary prelude to the understanding of more complex human societies. For example, the study of social institutions like family and marriage in primitive societies, gives us a better insight into their complex form in civilized societies.

20. Nadel, S. F., *The Foundation of Social Anthropology*, 1953, p. 5.

21. Pritchard, Evans, *Social Anthropology*, p. 9.

17

Basic Concepts of Social Anthropology

SOCIAL STRUCTURE

Social structure is a concept which is now being widely used in sociology as well as in anthropology. Structure has been defined as a property of empirical data. It is a property of objects, events and series of events. It is known through observation or analysis. The constituent of an object or event exhibits the properties of the structure. Thus, structure is articulation or arrangement. It includes formal characteristic, it may be contrasted with function and with contents, material or qualitative character.

In spite of so much currency of the term structure in sociological and anthropological circles, some scholars, including Linton and Lowie, have shown their displeasure at its use. A prominent anthropologist Kroeber has openly questioned its usefulness. According to him, "Structure appears to be just yielding to a word that has a perfectly good meaning but suddenly becomes fashionably attractive for a decade or so — like 'streamlining' — and during its vogue tends to be applied indiscriminately because of the pleasurable connotation of its sound."[1] Raymond Firth has pointed out to the fluid and vague character of the concept of structure by saying that, "Any science must have a budget of terms of general application, not too closely defined, and...structure may be one of them."[2] In spite of these criticisms, the concept of structure has come to stay.

Meaning of the Concept

It has been rightly pointed out by Meyer Fortes that, "Notable advances have been made in the theory of social structure of homogeneous societies...."[3] According to S.F. Nadel, however, the term is still on trial and discussions about it tend to be polemical. This concept was widely used by Herbert Spencer

1. Kroeber, *Anthropology*, 1948, p. 325.
2. Firth, R., *Elements of Social Organization*, 1951, p. 29.
3. Meyer Fortes, *Social Anthropology at Cambridge Since 1900*, 1953, p. 39.

and Emile Durkheim. They have used it in a wide and blanket fashion. It has become a synonym for system, organization, complex pattern and type. The following are some important definitions of social structure:

1. "Social structure is the web of interacting social forces from which have arisen the various modes of observing and thinking."[4]

2. "The orderly or patterned way that individuals and groups of people relate to each other."[5]

3. "It is useful to distinguish three levels of social structure: (1) the interpersonal relations, or social relationships level, (2) the group, or organization level, and (3) the community, or society level (the social environment of groups and organizations)."[6]

4. "The study of social structure is concerned with the principal forms of social organization, *i.e.*, types of groups, associations and institutions and the complex of these which constitute societies.... A full account of social structure would involve a review of the whole field of comparative institutions."[7]

5. "Group structures represent the kind of reality into which we are born and within which we find work and recreation, rewards and penalties, struggle and mutual aid.... All the various modes of grouping...together comprise the complex pattern of social structure .... In the analysis of the social structure the role of the diverse attitudes and interests of social beings is revealed."[8]

6. Structure of culture means, "The progressive combination of trades, in complexes, areas and patterns."[9]

7. "The components of social structure are human beings, the structure itself being an arrangement of persons in relationships institutionally defined and regulated."[10]

8. Social structure is made up of, "Human beings considered not as organisms but as occupying positions in social structure."[11]

9. The units of social structure are the inter-personal relations which, "become part of the social structure in the form of status positions occupied by individuals."[12]

---

4. K. Mannheim, *Ideology and Utopia*, 1936, pp. 45-6.

5. Popenoe, D., *Sociology*, Prentice Hall, 1977, New Jersey, p. 571.

6. *Ibid.*, p. 44.

7. M. Ginsberg, *Reason and Unreason in Society*, 1947, pp. 1, 8.

8. R. M. MacIver and C H. Page, *Society*, 1950, pp. 209, 212.

9. Melville J. Herskovits, *Man and His Works*, 1948, p. 169.

10. Daryll Forde and A.R. Radcliffe Brown, *African Systems of Kinship and Marriage*, 1950, p. 82.

11. A.R. Radcliffe Brown, *Structure and Function in Primitive Society*, 1952, pp. 9-10.

12. Eggan, *Social Organization of the Western Pueblos*, 1950, p. 5.

10. Social structure is, "the interrelations of groups, explicitly excluding inter-personal relations."[13]

11. Social structure contains, "parts and relations of diverse nature and variability," and pertains to "social events and organizations as their 'variable' aspects."[14]

12. Social structure, "consists of a set of ideas about the distribution of power between persons or groups of persons."[15]

13. Social structure is the, "whole network of social relations in which are involved the members of a given community at a particular time."[16]

14. "Structure indicates an ordered arrangement of parts, which can be treated as transposable, being relatively invariant, while the parts themselves are variable."[17]

15. "We arrive at the structure of a society through abstracting from the concrete population and its behaviour the pattern or network (or 'system') of relationships obtaining between actors in their capacity of playing roles relative to one another."[18]

Components of Social Structure

Thus, social structure includes the interpersonal relations or social relationships or patterns of interaction and secondly the inter-group relationships or social system and organization and thirdly the social environment of groups and organization. Microsociology studies the interpersonal relations. Macro-sociology studies the communities and societies. In this connection Nadel has pointed out to the following reservations which must be remembered in analyzing the term social structure :

1. The phrase "playing roles relative to one another" does not merely mean "playing roles *vis-a-vis* one another". Relationships other than face-to-face relationships are also included in social structure.

2. Social structure should include not only the role-playing actors but also the structure of sub-groups and other divisions of society.

3. The terms network and pattern are not synonymous but indicate two different levels of social structure. Nadel calls them network interactions and pattern distributions. In his own words, "Thus, I shall mean by 'pattern' any orderly distribution of relationship exclusively on the grounds of their similarity

---

13. Evans Pritchard, *The Nuer*, 1940, p. 262.

14. Fortes, *The Web of Kinship Among the Tallensi*, 1949, p. 340.

15. *Notes and Queries on Anthropology.*

16. Leach, *Political Systems of Highland Burma*, 1954, p. 4.

17. Nadel, S. F., *The Theory of Social Structure*, Cohen & West Ltd., London, 1969, p. 8.

18. Talcott Parsons, *Essays in Sociological Theory*, 1949, p. 34.

and dissimilarity."[19] "By network, on the other hand, I mean the interlocking of relationships whereby the interactions implicit in one determine those occurring in others."[20]

4. When a society is constituted by distributive patterns, it contains a fixed number of sub-divisions characterizing the patterns. Similar fixed patterns may be observed in the interaction of actors expected to play particular roles.

SOCIAL FUNCTION

The functional approach in sociology has been caught in a terminological confusion. Too often a single term has been used to symbolize different concepts, just as the same concept has been symbolized by different terms.

Meaning of Function

The term function has been interpreted as follows :

1. Function refers to some public gathering or occasion
2. The term function is equivalent to the term occupation.
3. Function refers to the activities assigned to the incumbent of a social status, and more particularly, to the occupant of an office or political position.
4. In mathematics it refers to a variable considered in relation to one or more other variables in terms of which it may be expressed.
5. In the biological sciences the term function is understood to refer to the vital or organic processes considered in the respects in which they contribute to the maintenance of the organism.

According to Radcliffe Brown, "The function of a recurrent physiological process is thus a correspondence between it and the needs of the organism." And in social sphere these individual human beings, "the essential units," are connected by networks of social relations into an integrated whole. The function of any recurrent activity, such as the punishment of a crime, or a funeral ceremony, is the part it plays in the social life as a whole and therefore the contribution it makes to the maintenance of the structural continuity.

According to Malinowski, things are known "by their function, by the part which they play within the integral system of culture, by the manner in which they are related to each other within the system."

Therefore, function is the part which a unit plays in conformity with the needs of society. Merton says, "Function involves the standpoint of the observer, not necessarily, that of the participant. Social function refers to observable objective consequences, and not to subjective dispositions (aims, motives, purposes)."

---

19. Nadel, S. F., *The Theory of Social Structure*, Cohen & West Ltd., London, 1969, p. 15.

20. *Ibid.*, p. 16.

Single Concept, Diverse Terms

Terms referring to the concept of function are purpose, motive and aim. But these terms clearly refer to the explicit ends-in-view of the representatives of the state, or refer to the subjective anticipation of the results. But the concept of function involves the objective dispositions and not the subjective dispositions.

Manifest and Latent Functions

"*Manifest functions* are those objective consequences, contribution to the adjustment or adaptation of the system which are intended and recognized by participants in the system."

Therefore, this type of function is known to the society. Society knows the consequence. Consequence is observable and is sanctioned by the society, *e.g.* an educational institution educates the members of the society or rather socializes the members. So this part which an educational institution is playing is known to the society and that is why society has recognized the educational institution for this. So this is the manifest function of the educational institution.

Another example may be the family institution. Family first of all produces the members of the society and then socializes them. Family teaches a Member what the society expects from him. So this function of family institution is known or recognized by the society and therefore the function which a family does is a manifest function.

Latent Functions : These are correlatively those which are neither intended nor recognized.

The relations between the, "unanticipated consequences" of action and "latent functions" can be clearly defined. The unintended consequences of action are of three types :

(a) Those which are functional for a system, and these comprise the latent function.

(b) Those which are dysfunctional for designated system, and these comprise the latent dysfunction.

(c) Those which are irrelevant to the system which they affect neither functionally nor dysfunctionally.

Distinction between Manifest and Latent Functions

This distinction removes the confusions which often take place between conscious motivation for social behaviour and its objective consequences. Emile Durkheim's analysis of the social function of punishment in his book *Division of Labour in Society* is focused on its latent functions (consequences for the community) rather than confined to manifest functions (consequences for the criminal).

R.M. MacIver in his book, *Community*, says : "In addition to the direct effects of institutions, there are further effects by way of controls which lie outside the direct purpose of men.... This type of reactive form of control ... may though unintended, be of profound service to society."[21] MacIver here indicates the latent functions of social control which are not known to society.

W. I. Thomas and F. Znaniecki in, *Sociological Classics*, "The Polish Peasant in Europe and America" say, "Although all the new institutions are thus formed with the definite purpose of satisfying certain specific needs, this explicit and conscious purpose... every one of these institutions is not merely a mechanism for the management of certain values but also an association of people each member of which is supposed to participate in the common activities as a living concrete individual."[22]

Thus, these and other numerous sociologists, have distinguished between manifest and latent functions. This distinction has been used in the analysis of racial intermarriage by Merton, in social stratification by Kingsley Davis, in propaganda as a means of social control by T. Parsons, in anthropological theories by B. Malinowski, in problems in the sociology of knowledge by Merton and by so many other sociologists.

Purposes of the Distinction

The following are the purposes of distinction between Manifest and Latent functions :

1. The distinction aids the sociological interpretation of many social practices which persist even though their manifest purpose is clearly not achieved.

2. The concept of latent function directs attention towards another range of consequences.

3. Ceremonials may fulfil the latent function of reinforcing the group identity by providing a periodic occasion on which the scattered members of a group assemble to engage in a common activity.

4. The distinction directs the attention of the sociologist to precisely those realms of behaviour, attitude and belief where he can apply his special skills.

5. Armed with the concept of latent function, the sociologist extends his inquiry in those very directions which promise most for the theoretic development of the discipline.

6. The latent functions are unintended and generally unrecognized. Social and psychological latent functions increase the knowledge.

7. Latent functions represent greater departures from "commonsense" knowledge about social life.

8. The pattern of conspicuous consumption, the manifest function of buying consumption goods are explicitly designed. People buy expensive goods because the manifest equation "costliness is the mark of superiority of goods" is linked to the latent equation "costliness is the mark of higher social status."

21. *Op. cit.*, p. 15.

22. *Op. cit.*, p. 7.

9. The concepts of manifest and latent functions are indispensable elements in the theoretic repertoire of the social engineer. In this sense both of these concepts are practical as well as theoretical.

Structure and Function

The social functions of an organization help to determine the structure including the recruitment of personnel involved, just as the structure helps determine the effectiveness with which the functions are fulfilled.

Three Postulates

Many of the major sociological practitioners of functional analysis have been devoted to theoretic formulations and to the cleaning up of concepts. Some of these sociologists have steeped themselves in data directly relevant to a functional frame of reference. But few sociologists have cleared the prevailing confusion regarding how one goes about the business of functional analysis. The plenty and variety of functional analyses, however, lead us to the conclusion that some methods have been employed. It awakenes the hope that much may be learned from these methods.

Although methods may be profitably examined without reference to theory or substantive data, methodology or the logic of procedure, of course, has precisely laid that as its assignment. Empirically oriented disciplines are more fully served by inquiry into procedures if this takes due account of their theoretic problems and substantive findings. For the use of "method" involves not only logic but, also the practical problems of aligning data with the requirements of theory. It is mainly but not solely in anthropology that functional analysts have commonly adopted three interconnected postulates. These postulates have proved to be debatable and unnecessary to functional orientation.

According to Radcliffe Brown, substantially, these postulates hold the following principles :

1. **Functional.** Standardized social activities or cultural items are functional for the entire social or cultural system.

2. **Sociological.** All such social and cultural items fulfil sociological function.

3. **Indispensability.** These items are consequently indispensable.

Merton's Observations

R.K. Merton has reviewed the first two postulates as follows : "In scrutinizing, first, the postulate of functional unity, we find that one cannot assume full integration of all societies, but that this is an empirical question of fact in which we should be prepared to find a range of degrees of integration. And in examining the special case of functional interpretation of religion, we are alerted to the possibility that, though human nature may be of a piece, it does not follow that the structure of non-literate societies, like that of highly differentiated 'literate societies', a difference in degree between the two, say, the existence of several disparate religions in the one and not in the other may make hazardous the passage between them." From critical scrutiny of this postulate, it developed that a theory of functional analysis must call for *specification* of the social units subserved by the given social functions, and that items of culture must be recognized to have multiple consequences, some of them functional and others, perhaps, dysfunctional.

Merton's review of the second *postulate of universal functionalism*, which holds that all persisting forms of culture are inevitably functional, resulted in other considerations which must be met by codified approach to functional interpretation. He said, "It appeared not only that we must be prepared to find dysfunctional as well as functional consequences of these forms but that the theorist will ultimately be confronted with the difficult problem of developing an organ for assessing the net balance of consequences if his research is to have bearing on social technology." Clearly, expert advice based only on the appraisal of a limited, and perhaps arbitrarily selected, range of consequences to be expected as a result of contemplated action, will be subject to frequent error and will be properly judged as having small merit.

The third *postulate of indispensability* according to Merton, entails two distinct propositions: (1) Alleging the indispensability of certain functions and this gives rise to the *concept of functional necessity or functional prerequisites.* (2) Alleging the indispensability of existing social institutions, culture forms, or the like, and this when suitably questioned, gives rise to the concept of *functional alternative equivalents or substitutes.*

Wide Field of Functional Approach

The functional orientation is of course neither new nor confined to the social sciences. The central orientation of functionalism is expressed in the practice of interpreting data by establishing their consequences for larger structures in which they are implicated. It has been found in virtually all the human sciences such as biology, physiology, psychology, economics, law, anthropology and sociology. The prevalence of the functional outlook in itself is no warrant for its scientific value. However, it does suggest that cumulative experience has forced this orientation upon the disciplined observers of man as biological organism, psychological actor, member of society and bearer of culture.

Functional Method in Sociology

More immediately relevant is the possibility that experience in other disciplines may provide useful methodological models for functional analysis in sociology. To learn the canons of analytical procedure in these often more exacting disciplines is not, however, to adopt their specific conceptions and techniques, lock, stock and barrel. To examine the *Methodological* framework of biological researches is not to adopt their substantive concepts.

The logical structure of experiment, for example, does not differ in physics, chemistry or psychology, although the substantive hypothesis, the technical tools, the basic concepts and the practical difficulties may differ enormously. Nor do the near-substitutes for experiment controlled observation, comparative study and the method of "discerning" differ in their logical structure in anthropology, sociology or biology.

PREVAILING POSTULATES IN FUNCTIONAL ANALYSIS

Functional analysts have adopted three interconnected postulates. These are as follows :

1. Postulate of the Functional Unity of Society. Radcliffe Brown characteristically puts this postulate in explicit terms on the concept of function as follows :

"The function of a particular social usage is the contribution it makes to the total social life as the functioning of the total social system. Such a view implies that a social system has a certain kind of unity, which we may speak of a functional unity. We may define it as a condition in which all part of the social system work together with a sufficient degree of internal consistency, *i.e.*, without producing persistent conflicts which can neither be resolved nor regulated."

But social usages or sentiments may be functional for some groups and dysfunctional for others in the same society. For example, the functional interpretation of religion deriving from the Durkheim's orientation which was based largely upon the study of non-literate societies, these authors tend to single out only the apparently integrative consequences of religion and neglect its possibly disintegrative consequences in certain types of social structure. Some facts are as given below :

(i) When different religions co-exist in the same society, there is often deep conflict between the several religious groups. In what sense then, does religion make for integration of "the" society in the numerous multi-religion societies?

(ii) Human society achieves its unity primarily through the possession by its members of certain ultimate values and ends in common. But what is the evidence indicating that "non-religious" people, say, in our own society less often subscribe to certain common "values and ends" than those devoted to religious doctrines?

(iii) In what sense does religion make for integration of the larger society, if the content of its doctrine and values is at odds with the content of other, non-religious values held by many people in the same society?

Such functional analyses show that religions provide integration of those who believe in same religious values, but it is unlikely that this is meant, since it would merely assert that integration is provided by a consensus on any set of values.

In non-literate societies, there is but one prevailing religious system so that apart from individual deviants, the membership of the total society and the membership of the religious community are virtually co-extensive. In this type of social structure a common set of religious values may have as one of its consequences the reinforcement of common sentiments and of social integration. But this generalization cannot be applied to other types of society.

2. Postulate of Universal Functionalism. The items of culture must be recognized to have multiple consequences, some of them functional and others perhaps dysfunctional. This postulate holds that all standardized social or cultural forms have positive functions. Malinowski advances this in *Anthropology* in its most extreme form when he says, "The functional view of culture insist therefore upon the principle that in every type of civilization every custom, material object, idea and belief fulfils some vital function."

The postulate of universal functionalism is of course the historical product of the fierce, barren and protracted controversy over survivals which raged among the anthropologists over the question that a custom cannot be explained by its present utility but only becomes intelligible through its past history. But the evolutionary theory of culture made rethinking on it necessary.

This postulate also faced criticism from a range of non-functional consequences of existing cultural forms. Present cultural forms have a net balance of functional consequences either for the society considered as a unit or for sub-groups sufficiently powerful. This formulation at once avoids the tendency of functional analysis to concentrate on positive functions and directs the attention to other types of consequences as well.

3. Postulate of Indispensability. This postulate shows that every cultural item satisfies some vital need of society, and cannot be substituted by any other item. Malinowski advances this in *Anthropology* in this form : "In every type of civilization, every custom, material object idea and belief fulfils some vital function, has some task to accomplish, represents an indispensable part within a working whole."[23] Again, he points out, "Thus magic fulfils an indispensable function with culture. It satisfies a definite need which cannot be satisfied by any other factors of primitive civilization."[24]

The account of the role of religion by Davis and Moore seems at first to maintain that it is the institution which is indispensable. "The reason why religion is necessary ... religion plays a unique and indispensable part in society." It is the function of religion but not the institution of religion, which is regarded as indispensable.

The postulate of indispensability contains the following assertions :

(a) It is assumed that there are certain functions which are indispensable in the sense that, unless they are performed, the society will not persist. This

23. *Op. cit.*, p. 132.

24. *Ibid.*, p. 138.

then, sets forth a concept of functional prerequisites, or preconditions functionally necessary for a society.

(b) It is assumed that certain cultural and social forms are indispensable for fulfilling each of these functions. This involves a concept of specialized and irreplaceable structures.

In contrast to this concept of indispensability of cultural forms, there is then the concept of functional alternatives or functional equivalents, or functional substitutes. Just as the same items may have multiple functions so may the same functions be diversely fulfilled by alternative items.

So in this postulate the indispensability of functions gives rise to the concept of functional necessity, and the indispensability of institutions gives rise to the concept of functional alternatives.

THE CONCEPT OF ROLE

Historically speaking, the concept of role was first introduced by Pareto in 1916. It was he who first recognized sociological significance of the labels such as lawyers, physicians, engineers, artists, etc., which indicate their roles. For Pareto the recognition of labels was a step in the special analysis of social elites. In 1920, Max Weber more generally and explicitly analyzed the methodological issues involved in the classification of human beings. He pointed out that the understanding of the origin of a society must be preceded by a functionally oriented investigation. It is necessary to know as to what kind of typical action leads to such classification. From 1925 onwards the term role was more and more used by the American sociologists such as W. I. Thomas, E. W. Burgess and others. The first explicit formulation of the term role was advanced by George Mead in his book *Mind, Self and Society*, published in 1934. Ralph Linton formulated the concept in anthropology in his book, *The Study of Man*, in 1936. Since then the term role is being widely used by anthropologists, sociologists and psychologists. A most systematic treatment of this concept has been presented by Talcott Parsons, Shils and Balesand in their work, *Working Paper in the Theory of Action*, published in 1953. Though, some psychologists have demanded the invention of a better term in place of the concept of role, it has not been actually done so far. According to T.M. Newcomb, "the concept of role is not very suitable because of its dramatic and literary connotation and the figure-of-speech use it encourages."[25] S.F. Nadel shares Newcomb's misgiving about the loose and confused use of the term role. He, therefore, devotes himself to the analysis of the problems of role analysis.

Definitions of Role

1. "Social roles are part and parcel of an individual's behaviour when

---

25. R. H. Roher and Muzafer Sherif (Eds.), *Social Psychology at the Crossroads*, 1951, Article by T. M. Newcomb, p. 39.

interacting with other people in various situations. Every social situation has a role expectancy for us to fulfil."[26]

2. "A set of expectations and behaviours associated with a specific position in a social system."[27]

3. "A role represents the dynamic aspect of a status .... When he puts the rights and duties which constitute the status into effect, he is performing a role. Role and status are quite inseparable, and the distinction between them is of only academic interest."[28]

4. "As already indicated, the role concept is basically a type of class concept. Like the class concept of Logic it labels and brings together numbers of individuals, human beings in our case in virtue of certain properties they have in common."[29]

5. "*Ex-definitionis* the role concept has to do with behaviour or differential behaviour, and the characteristics constituted by it."[30]

6. "There are no roles without statuses or statuses without roles, role representating 'the dynamic aspect of a status'."[31]

7. "The role is status translated into action, the role being the processal aspect of status, as status is the positional aspect of the role."[32]

Problems of Role Analysis

Explaining the importance of the concept of role, S. F. Nadel has pointed out : "Its usefulness, in simplest terms, lies in the fact that it provides a concept intermediary between 'society' and 'individual'. It operates in that strategic area where individual behaviour becomes social conduct, and where the qualities and inclinations distributed over a population are translated into differential attributes required by or exemplifying the obtaining social norms."[33] Thus role provides a strategic area, an intermediary concept. Societies rest on rules or norms. Thus they depend upon what Nadel calls, "constancies of behaviour". These constancies of behaviour are known as institutions and groupings. These again, can be further analyzed into constituents such as castes, goals, expectations, rights and duties, etc. The concept of role bridges the gap between

---

26. Donald A. Hobbs and Stuart J. Blank, *Sociology and the Human Experience*, New York, John Wiley, 1978, p. 58.

27. Popenoe, D., *Sociology*, Prentice Hall, 1977, New Jersey, p. 570.

28. Ralph Linton in Marcellow Truzzi (Ed.), *Sociology : The Classic Statement*, New York, Random House, 1971, p. 92.

29. Nadel S. F., *The Theory of Social Structure*, Cohen & West Ltd., London, 1969, p. 22.

30. *Ibid.*, p. 23.

31. Ralph Linton, *The Study of Man*, p. 114.

32. Talcott Parsons, *The Social System*, p. 25.

33. Nadel, S. F., *The Theory of Social Structure*, Cohen and West Ltd., London, 1969, p. 20.

society and individuals. It refers to individuals seen as bundles of qualities. The bundle corresponds to a class or type concept. Although the concept of role has been criticized by some scholars, no better substitute has been provided.

According to Nadel the role concept is basically a type of class concept. It labels and brings together a number of individuals. It always refers to existing real human beings. These human beings are classified broadly according to two types of properties : (1) Contingent properties which include physiological characteristics over which the individual has no control, such as sex, age, physiological characteristics, etc. (2) Achievement properties which the individual is free to assume and aim at, such as interests, attitudes, proficiencies, etc.

The Role *versus* the Class

S.F. Nadel has pointed out the following distinctions between the concept of role and the concept of class :

1. The role concept has to do with differential behaviour and the characteristics constituted by it. The classification in various classes depends upon contingent properties.

2. Roles materialize only in an interaction schedule. Their behavioural characteristics appear both in the active and passive voice. The class characteristics, on the other hand, are generally passive.

3. Role is purposive, repetitive and constant. This condition does not apply to classes. In the words of Nadel, "But while the class concept refers merely to accidental just so likenesses which however constant, could be quite otherwise, the role concept refers essentially to a lawful or normative conformity, in the sense that the shared attributes exhibited by individuals are understood to follow from the rules of the society or to involve them in some manner."[34]

4. The class concept requires the respective individuals to share only one property which serves as the differentia. The role concept requires the presence of a series of interconnected characteristics.

Methods of Defining the Roles[35]

According to Nadel there are three interconnected methods being used for defining the rules or norms underlying a particular role. These methods are used by anthropologists and sociologists, in the investigation of social norms:

1. The first method, then, is concerned with establishing the frequency and regularity with which the attributes assumed to make up the role appear together in fact, the result being the statistical 'normality' of the role series.

2. The second method is concerned with the explicit statements and assertions of the people (made with a given degree of consensus and authoritativeness) as to the conduct appropriate to given roles, these are all

34. *Ibid.*, p. 24.

35. *Ibid.*, p. 25.

value judgements, indicating the believed-in or desired 'normality', and hence the normality codified.

3. Thirdly, the existing role norms are also demonstrated by what we may call the maintenance machineries of the society, that is, by the sanctions of whatever kind, which forestall or follow deviant behaviour.

Pointing out the interconnection between these three methods, Nadel remarks, "Let us note that the first and third methods involve the piecing together of the role, while the second may furnish us with the total picture.[36] Thus, these three methods do not always give the same results.

While the class concept has the implication of further characteristics, the role concept refers to whole series of characteristics and never to one only. This series may be determined by the norms of the society. This is, however, conventional and arbitrary. The separation of entitlement and conduct which is possible in role, is not possible in class. Thus, class concepts are broader and looser than role concepts. This, of course, is a matter of degree. Exceptions might be available here and there.

Role and Status

A role must have a halo effect, without it, it is reduced to a label or category. An example of this halo effect in a role is the concept of bureaucrat. This is true about a role in the full sense of the term. However, certain terms bearing the label of roles might be in fact what Nadel calls, "Non-roles or near-roles or quasi-roles." These have been further defined by him. As he points out, quasi-roles may be named as status. Thus, status can be elaborated into roles and roles have a foundation in status. Most of the writers have accepted that roles and status are interdependent. Role behaviour is something translated into action. This translation, however, is not all at one, or in a piece. Rather, roles are enacted face by face, occasion by occasion, in a process extending over time. It is translated attribute by attribute. Role behaviour is materialized in interaction settings or situations. Thus, explaining the relationship of role and situations, Nadel concludes : "Thus, the relation between role attributes and situations may be of a 'one-in-all' or of a 'one-to-one' kind. But the same role may include both kinds of attributes : nor does this distinction seem to be relevant in any other respect apart from its bearing on role perception."[37]

Attributes Concerning Role

The attributes describe the internal structure of roles. Different attributes are not equivalent. The attributes concerning roles, according to Nadel, may be classified into the following three main grades :

1. Peripheral attributes. These are the attributes whose variation or absence

---

36. *Ibid.*

37. *Ibid.* p. 31.

does not affect the perception or effectiveness of the role. Thus, they are optional and admit alternatives.

2. Sufficiently relevant. These attributes are firmly entailed in the roles. Their variation or absence makes difference to the perception or effectiveness of the role by making it imperfect or incomplete.

3. Basic or pivotal attributes. The absence or variation of these attributes changes the whole identity of the role and the interaction it would normally provoke. Thus, "The basic or pivotal attribute is simply the attribute aspected to entail the rest of the series." In its absence other attributes appear as illegitimate, unexplained or different in meaning.

Role Name

The analysis of attributes in a role explains the difference between a true role and a quasi-role or mere status. In the latter, one finds a disproportionate number of optional attributes reducing the relevant attributes to a few. The ordering of the attributes in a given role creates the problems of scaling or ranking. Nadel points out to the necessity of a criteria for identifying pivotal characteristics of a role. His own method of doing it is to refer to the semantic content of the conventional role name. The semantic approach is based upon the fact that role names are shorthand symbols for the array of properties which the entity name is presumed to possess. Thus, the role name is prescribed. However, this approach is workable only when the linguistic usages are unambiguous, agreed and consistent with the social practice. In certain cases the semantic structure of the role name itself seems to indicate the basic attribute. Secondly, in the analysis of attributes one should look for the governing properties.

Occupational Roles

Some social psychologists, however, define roles as 'patterns of behaviour' (or of relationships or 'expectancies') applying to persons 'occupying specific positions' or 'fulfilling definable functions' in the society.[38] According to Nadel this viewpoint is legitimate in social psychology but not for the anthropologists and sociologists. To quote his own words, "Since, as an anthropologist, I view roles as modes of acting 'allotted individuals' by the norms of the society, I am concerned also with this very allocation and the principles on which it is based, which means that my definition and analysis of roles must include their 'basis', the conditions entailing the 'further characteristics', as much as these characteristics themselves."

---

38. E. L. and R. E. Hartley, *Fundamentals of Social Psychology*, 1952, p. 486; T. M. Newcomb, in *For a Science of Social Man*, ed. John Gillin, 1954, p. 252; Muzafer Sherif, in *Social Psychology at the Crossroads*, 1951, p. 25.

Recruitment *vs.* Achievement Roles

This entailment can be of two kinds.[39]

1. Recruitment role. In the first type of role, then, the governing property is an inevitable or fortuitous state in which individuals find themselves; it then entails the further characteristics — all the other attributes in the series — as consequences or concomitants (as when mature age carries with it such-and-such privileges or responsibilities).

2. Achievement role. In the second type of role, where the governing property is a behavioural attribute, active or passive, which individuals are free to choose as a goal or objective, the 'further characteristics' are entailed either as necessary preconditions or again as consequences and concomitants (as when priesthood requires celibacy and a decorous life, and promises an elevated status).

Thus, the recruitment role is identified by a governing property which indicates the method of recruitment. The achievement role, on the other hand, is based upon the precondition. The preconditions, however, belong to the prehistory of the role and not to its actual performance. The prehistory of the role however is important in the phases of role performance. Roles having relevant prehistory have two instead of one basic attribute, of which while one refers to the conditions of recruitment, the other is crucial in the role. In a recruitment role, the individual is forced or compelled into the given role with restricted choice. In achievement roles he embraces the role for its desirability, voluntarily committing himself, to its various implications. According to Nadel, "Achievement roles mean much the same as achieved status ignoring the looser meaning of 'status'."[40] The recruitment roles, on the other hand, are connected with what is known as ascribed status. The concept of ascription, however, does not cover all the recruitment roles. The principle of allocation in recruitment roles depends upon the process of accommodation in society. In achievement roles the principle of allocation is the desirability. To think of roles in terms of allocation is to think of them in economic terms. This economic aspect of role systems was first expressed by Pareto in his book *Mind and Society*. Nadel, however, calls it one-sided and points out that desirability must be supplemented by the principle of accommodation. Some roles however may not fit in any category on the grounds of allocation. Then, some roles may be viewed both as recruited or achieved such as kinship roles of father, mother, husband, but then the element of compulsion enters into the desirable role. The element of compulsion again, varies in different cultures. The ascriptive role ascribed statuses are concealed and attenuated recruitment roles. Their names identify them with achievement roles but they include compulsive characteristics of recruitment roles. The achievement itself has a wide and flexible meaning in different cultures and in the same culture in different situations.

39. Nadel, S. F., *The Theory of Social Structure*, Cohen and West Ltd., London, 1969, p. 36.

40. *Ibid.*, p. 37.

Role *vs.* Game

Thus, according to Nadel, role assumptions may be compared with a set of rules or rules of game. The role behaviour exhibits the following features like the rules of a game.[41]

1. The rules of the game have a given latitude, allowing certain options and disallowing others, with varying degrees of strictness; some moves are altogether excluded since they would simply change or deny the identity of the game which is the exact counterpart of our 'hierarchy of relevance'.

2. The overall firmness with which the whole set of rules applies corresponds to the institutionalization of the roles in the social system; and as in all institutionalizations, the respective expectations are diffused through the society.

3. Finally, as in many games played according to rules, the moves open to the players, that is, the attributes they are expected to acquire or display will follow a more or less rigorous sequence, so that a particular attribute must not appear or will not be effective unless some other specified attribute is already present.

Asymmetrical Roles

Besides recruitment roles and achievement roles Nadel admits a third type of roles which "have no precise hierarchy, there being no definite focus or pivot in the series."[42] Examples of such roles are : friend, enemy, lover, patriot. These role names have no reference to any governing attribute. They indicate the role character by generalizing in a summary fashion.

Conformity and Deviance of Roles

W. J. H. Sprott has rightly pointed out that, "one of the features of our own time is the indeterminacy and rapid changing of roles."[43] Thus, one finds in modern society, so many changes and disintegrating roles. While observation of the rules of the game of role may be called conformity, the non-observance is known as deviance. In the words of Nadel, "The deviancy role, we might say, is a role with a negative coefficient."[44] Every role performance has a built-in element of self-regulation. This is governed by the system of rewards and punishments in society. While conformity is rewarded, deviance is punished. Thus, one notices positive and negative feedback in roles of performance as conformity and deviance. This dyadic model governs the role performance in society. The mutual steering built-in to processes of interaction in a society functions only in as much as the persons involved in it acknowledge each other's role and have congruent assumptions about them. This steering process

41. *Ibid.*, p. 42.

42. *Ibid.*, p. 42.

43. W. J. H. Sprott, *Social Psychology*, 1952, p. 156.

44. Nadel, S. F., *The Theory of Social Structure*, p. 50.

is not necessarily held up until the sanctions are actually encountered. Secondly, the role behaviour is not corrected only by this mutual steering in the course of normal role interpretation. Thus, according to Nadel, "the roles linked in the mutual steering process posit or implicate one another."[45]

This mutual implication may be of the following two types :

1. Interactive types. When roles are designed to meet in direct interplay, each role having a given efficiency (or responsiveness) *vis-a-vis* another.

2. Distributive type. This is only indirectly interactive, representing the corollary of the basic fact about all roles, that they are differential modes of behaviour.

The above mutual implication of roles signifies division of labour in a society. It is what Talcott Parsons calls the role inventory of any society as a role system.

THE COHERENCE OF ROLE SYSTEM

Most of the roles in a society are heterogenous, without a common logical locus, incapable of interrelation and thus incapable of yielding a coherent embarrassing structure. The following roles are, however, an exception :

1. Leadership or authority role. These always imply, as part of the influence vested in them, the supervision of all or numerous other roles in society, disparity and mutual inclusiveness notwithstanding.

2. Expressive roles. The name is meant to indicate that there the actors' task is the communication of ideas and emotional experiences through manipulating, applying and perhaps creatively adding to the expressive symbols current in the society.

3. Service roles or occupational roles. Roles which imply the rendering of services to others and involve that kind of contractual relationship.

Dependent *vs.* Independent Roles

Among the logically related roles, Nadel distinguishes between dependent and independent roles. As he puts it, "To turn to logically related roles, we shall see that they form a continuum between two extremes. One is constituted by roles in the case of which the logical relation also implies, with logical compulsion, a relationship between the respective actors. In other words, a given role is so conceived that, by its character, it requires to be enacted *vis-a-vis* another counterpart or correlative role. The second extreme is constituted by roles in the case of which the logical relation merely means that actual relationships between the actors are possible, not in any logical sense necessary. For reasons which will become clear presently I will call the first type of roles dependent, and the second, independent roles. It seems convenient to start with the latter."[46]

45. *Ibid.*, p. 57.

46. *Ibid.*, pp. 79-80.

TABLE 1

Role Chart by S. F. Nadel[47]

Recruitment roles		Achievement roles				
Independently defined	Dependently defined	Independently defined ... ... Dependently defined				
	Relational roles	Proprietory roles	Expressive roles	Service roles	Relational roles	
1	2	3	4	5	6	7
On the basis of somatic features, age, sex, personality extraction, origin, descent, kinship, etc.	Kinship roles	Roles indicating possession of skills, resources, learning, etc.	Belief roles creative roles (*e.g.* 'artist') communication roles (*e.g.* 'orator')	So-called occupational roles	Symmetrical : membership roles, partnership roles, rivalry roles	Asymetrical : Managerial roles authority, leader ship roles, hierarchical (status) roles, patronage roles, etc.

47. *Ibid.*, p. 85.

While the dependent and independent roles represent only extremes, there are roles in between these extremes. In this connection Nadel has pointed out the following three types of roles :

1. Service and expressive roles. These require a 'public' more or less specified in role terms, with counterpart roles such as 'patients', 'customers', an 'audience', a 'congregation'.

2. Authority or leadership roles. These roles have a weaker counterpart. Their counterpart roles may be synonymous with that widest public, the 'rest of society' (the 'subjects' of a ruler, the 'followers' of a leader).

3. Distributive roles. In these roles the correlative aspect is the weakest and independence of the role the strongest. In the words of Nadel, 'This category includes roles named on the basis of belief, ethnic origin, age, residence, personality or somatic characteristics and similar autonomous differentia...''[48]

Some Terms Connected with Role

In the analysis of the concept of social role, it is necessary to define certain other terms applicable to the explanations of actual functioning of roles in society. These terms include role conflict, role set, role exception, role strain and role performance. The following are some of the more popular definitions of these terms :

1. Role conflict. (i) Incompatibility between two or more roles that an individual is expected to play.[49]

(ii) Incompatibility between two or more roles that an individual is expected to perform simultaneously. The existence of mutually exclusive expectations for behaviour.[50]

2. Role expectation. All the expectations that specify proper and improper behaviour for an individual occupying a given position. What one is expected to do while playing a specific role.[51]

3. Role performance. The degree to which an individual acts in accordance with the expectation of a given role. Role performance is our behaviour that more or less fulfils role expectations.[52]

4. Role set. The set of roles associated with a single status.[53]

---

48. *Ibid.*, p. 86.

49. Popenoe, David, *Sociology*, Prentice-Hall, New Jersey, 1977, p. 570.

50. Hobbs, D. A. and Blank, S. J., *Sociology and the Human Experiences*, Johan Wiley, New York, 1978, p. 461.

51. *Ibid.*

52. *Ibid.*

53. Popenoe, David, *Sociology*, Prentice-Hall, New Jersey, 1977, p. 560.

5. Role strain. Conflict or stress caused by the incompatible demands of a single role.[54]

Analytical Aspects of Relationship Structure

A relationship structure means any social structure that defines the action ideally and/or actually. It interrelates two or more individuals such as the doctor-patient relationship. Analysis in terms of relationship structure focuses attention on the individual actor components of a relation. It analyzes the various aspects of a particular relation.

There are six analytical aspects of a relationship structure which include two extreme categories :

1. Cognitive aspect. This deals with the recognition of the aspects of relationship, *i.e.*, its members and purpose. This is divided into logical and non-logical action. A logical action is one where the intended consequences and motives coincide with each other, for example, doctor-patient relationship wherein the purpose is to cure the patient. In a non-logical action the subjective motive predominates over objective consequences as in the case of religious action.

2. Membership criteria aspects. This examines the characteristics of members of a particular relation or the choice of members. Thus in a *universalistic* relationship like that of the doctor-patient there are common categories which define membership. Any doctor can treat any patient. On the other hand, in a father-son relationship only particular persons are eligible to be members. Such relations are *particularistic*.

3. The substantive definition aspect. This defines the content of the relationship or the activities and rights and obligations of a relationship. Thus, in a *functionally specific* relationship the rights and obligations and activities of the relationship are well-defined as in the case of doctor-patient relationship. On the other hand, in a functionally diffused relationship, the rights, obligations and activities are vague and open as in the case of father-son relationship.

4. The affective aspect. This deals with the emotional components of pleasurable or painful significance to the actor. Thus, in an intimate relationship the members have emotional attachments and are affected by the relationship, such as in father-son relationship. On the other hand, an *avoidant* relationship is formal and places restraint over affective displays as in the case of doctor-patient relationship.

5. The goal orientation aspect. This deals with the aims or purposes of the relationship. Thus, in an *individualistic* relationship the members lay strees upon their own gains irrespective of consideration of the motives of the other party such as businessman-customer relation. In a responsible relationship the

54. *Ibid.*

members care for other's goals also while looking after their interests as in the case of doctor-patient relationship.

6. The stratification aspect. This deals with the hierarchical order in a relationship. Thus, in a hierarchical relationship the members are differentiated into higher and lower ranks as in father-son relationship. In a non-hierarchical relationship the members are ranked equally as in the case of doctor-patient relationship.

These analytical aspects serve as tools for the comparative analysis of social structure in several senses. In the first place, they are such concepts that in terms of them some empirical statements may be conceivably made about any relationship. Thus, one may say that nationality, functional specificity and universalistic criteria are the three functional requisites of relations in an industrial society. As larger and larger number of more or less well-confirmed statements of this sort accumulate we can make increasingly fruitful predictions about the possible range of variations in structural patterns of a society.

More specifically, however, this set of concepts is useful because it provides a framework in terms of which one may compare the following different sets of relationships : (1) different types of relationships in a single society, (2) similar types of relationships in different societies, and (3) different types of relationships in different societies. Further, by arranging the wide array of relationships in a society in definite categories these concepts provide a clear picture of the relationship structure of a society. Some examples are as follows :

The doctor-patient relationship in U.S.A. is said to be rational, universalistic, functionally specific, avoidant, responsible and non-heirarchical whereas the businessman-customer relationship is rational, universalistic, functionally specific, avoidant, individualistic and non-hierarchical. In traditional China, it was non-rational, particularistic, functionally diffuse, intimate, responsible and non-hierarchical.

Finally, while the businessman-customer relationship in modern U.S.A. is rational, universalistic, functionally specific, avoidant, individualistic and non-hierarchical, the father-son relationship in traditional China is non-rational, particularistic, functionally diffuse, avoidant, responsible and hierarchical.

TYPES OF ROLE DIFFERENTIATION

Role refers to the part played by an actor in a particular context. In drama we speak of the role of a king, servant, etc. In life also we have to play different parts in our relations to society. Thus, we are fathers, mothers, sons, teachers, employers, etc. A person may have to play several roles at the same time in his day-to-day dealings in society such as of a father, son, employer, buyer, etc.

The structure of role differentiation in any society is concerned with the structure of distribution of the members of the system among the various positions and activities in the system. A minimum number of role differentiation is a prerequisite for any society's survival because there are activities in a society which must be performed by certain designated members at a time.

There are seven types of role differentiation in any society. They are :

1. Role differentiation on the basis of age. Differences in age are relevant to differences in biological capabilities of persons. This refers to the biological life spans of an individual. On the basis of absolute age, individuals are classified into infants, children, adults and old people. While infants and old people are totally dependant upon other members of the society, children may partially support themselves while adults may support the other age groups. Relative age refers to the relative differences in years between two individuals. For example, brothers have role differentiation on the basis of their comparative age. Roles are differentiated on the basis of relative age because of the different capabilities of individuals according to their age.

2. Role differentiation on the basis of generation. By generation we mean an individual's position relative to other individuals in order of birth in his direct biological line of descent. Role differentiation on this basis refers to the role of father-son, grand-children, grand-parents, etc. The functional explanation for this type of role differentiation lies in the requisite of sexual recruitment and its implications and general differentiation on this basis rests on the recognition of a kinship structure.

3. Role differentiation on the basis of sex. This distinction is between males and females. In physiological terms the sexes are differentiated in terms of the roles which members of each of these two types are capable of performing in the production of new members of the species.

4. Role differentiation on the basis of economic allocation. Economic allocation refers to the distribution of goods and services among the various members of a society. The structure of production includes all structures from whose operation goods and services accrue to the society. The structure of consumption includes all structures from which operation of goods and services are allocated to the various members. The functional requisite for role differentiations of this type lies in the functional necessity of providing for the physiological adjustment of members of a unit. This includes the provision of food, clothing and shelter. The economic role differentiation is vast and varied. Mainly, it consists of the roles of producer, distributor and consumer.

5. Role differentiation on the basis of political allocation. Political allocation refers to the distribution of power over and responsibility for the actions of the various members of the society involving on the one hand the use of coercive sanctions including force. Power is the ability to exercise authority and control over the actions of others. Responsibility is the accountability of an individual for his own acts and acts of others. The functional requisite for political allocation is to effectively control disruptive behaviour. It is possible for a relationship to have mutually equal power and responsibility.

Roles on the basis of political allocation refer to that of the governors and the governed, ruler and citizens, etc. or power holders and responsibility bearers.

6. Role differentiation on the basis of religion. Religion refers to the aspects of action directly oriented to ultimate ends. The functional requisite rests on a discussion of a shared and articulated set of goals. Religious roles refer to those of initiators, the initiated, priest and worshipper, preacher and disciple, etc.

7. Role differentiation on the basis of cognition. Cognition refers to the knowledge or understanding of a situation or phenomenon. The functional requisite of cognition rests on the requisite basis for cognitive structures. Role differentiation on this basis rests on several bases.

18

Researches of Radcliffe-Brown

In his book *Novum Organon Renovatum*, Whewell has rightly said, "The fundamental principle and supreme rule of all scientific terminology is that terms must be constructed and appropriated so as to be fitted to enunciate simply and clearly true general proposition.[1] Agreeing with this principle Radcliffe-Brown, in his book, *Method in Social Anthropology*, starts with giving clear definitions of various methods and concepts in social anthropology. As he himself says about the necessity of conceptual clarification, "One of the difficulties that the reader of the literature of anthropology has to face is the fact that the same word is used in different meanings by different writers, and many anthropological terms are sometimes used ambiguously or without precise definition."[2] Therefore, while defining social structure, Radcliffe-Brown has taken recourse to social organization and other related concepts.

FALLACY OF MISPLACED CONCRETENESS

According to Radcliffe-Brown, "The empirical reality with which Social Anthropology has to deal, by description, by analysis and in comparative studies, is the process of social life of a certain limited region during a certain period of time."[3] He sounds a warning here by pointing out to the "fallacy of misplaced concreteness" "which results from treating abstractions as though they were concrete realities."[4] Societies should not be taken as separate discrete entities. According to him in order to describe social life, one should describe its general features which provide data for the science. He defines the subject matter of Social Anthropology by social life. Defining this subject matter further he says, "The social life as a phenomenal reality is a process consisting of a multitude of actions of human beings, more particularly their interactions and joint actions."[5] Social life, again, can be divided into Synchronic and Diachronic

1. *Op. cit.*, 3rd edn., 1858.
2. *Op. cit.*, p. 38.
3. *Ibid.*, p. 139.
4. *Ibid.*, p. 138.
5. *Ibid.*, p. 139.

aspects. Synchronic description takes social life as it is at a certain time without reference to changes in its general features. Diachronic description gives an account of such changes. A social anthropologist has to provide both the descriptions.

SOCIAL STRUCTURE AND SOCIAL ORGANIZATION

Before defining the elements of social structure, Radcliffe-Brown has clarified the distinction between social structure and social organization. According to him, social structure refers to an arrangement of persons. On the other hand, "Social organization is the arrangement of activities of two or more persons which are adjusted to give united combined activity."[6] Social organization can be explained by the example of modern army or tribal groups, industrial groups, sports groups, etc. Social structure, on the other hand, can be explained by the example of modern army or tribal groups, etc. The distinction between social organization and social structure will be further clear from the definition and explanation of the term "Social Structure" which now follows :

MEANING OF SOCIAL STRUCTURE

In the words of Radcliffe-Brown, "Social structure, therefore, is to be defined as the continuing arrangement of persons in relationships defined or controlled by institutions, *i.e.*, socially established norms or patterns of behaviour."[7] In this definition of social structure, two phrases require further clarification, the continuing arrangement of persons and socially established norms or patterns of behaviour.

Continuing Arrangement of Persons

According to Radcliffe-Brown, social structure is a continuing arrangement of persons in relation to each other. This arrangement of persons is different in a village, a city or a primitive tribe. The characteristics of this arrangement are in fact the characteristics of social structure. In other words, the characteristics of social structure are the characteristics of social groups which constitute it.

Structural Features of Social Life

According to Radcliffe-Brown, the most important structural features of social life are as follows:

1. Existence of social groups. Social structure consists of all kinds of social groups within it.

2. Internal structure of groups. These groups, again, have a specific internal structure. For example, the family group consists of the relations of father, mother and children to each other.

6. *Ibid.*, p. 140

7. *Ibid.*, p. 147.

3. Arrangement into social classes. These groups, again, are arranged into social classes and categories such as the castes in Indian society and the economic classes in western societies.

4. Social distinctions. There is again a system of social distinctions between different classes based upon sex, authority, economic distinctions, caste distinctions, etc. One finds a system of social distance between them as can be seen between Brahmins and Sudras in India.

5. Arrangement of persons in dyadic relationship. Dyadic relationships are person to person relationships such as those found between master and servant. In social structure one finds arrangement of persons in dyadic relationships.

6. Interactions between groups and persons. Finally, the most important feature of social structure is the interaction between groups and the interactions between persons. An example of interactions between groups is seen when one nation goes to war with another. Interactions between persons can be seen in social processes involving cooperation, conflict, accommodation, etc.

Constituents of Social Structure

As has been already pointed out, social structure is constituted by continuing arrangement of persons in relationships. These arrangements of persons are generally in the form of social groups. According to Radcliffe-Brown, "By social group we mean a body of persons having certain cohesion."[8] The social groups are named differently according to their different forms such as a family, a horde, a clan, a kinship, a tribe, etc. Radcliffe-Brown has defined each of these types of social groups clearly.

1. The Family. According to Radcliffe-Brown, "The family as a group was formed by marriage and the birth of children and came to an end as a separate group on the death of the husband, thus having continuous existence for only a limited number of years."[9] Thus, family is composed of a man with his wife or wives and their young children. It is a domestic group. It has its own hearth, shelter and food supply. Several families constitute a horde.

2. The Horde. Thus, the internal structure of the horde consists of family. According to Radcliffe-Brown, "A horde may be described as being politically autonomous, under the authority of the old men, and as being very largely self-sufficient economically."[10] The hordes constitute a clan. They occupy the territory of the clan. On an average each horde consists of not more than 50 persons.

3. The Clan. Several hordes together constitute the social structure of the clan. Men connected with a particular territory form a distinct social group known as clan. According to Radcliffe-Brown, "The clan was a continuing

8. *Ibid.*, p. 143.

9. *Ibid.*, p. 142.

10. *Ibid.*

group which the natives themselves thought of as having come into existence at the beginning of the world and as being eternal; as members were lost by death they were replaced by the birth of new members.''[11] The clan is a unit of fundamental importance in the primitive social structure. A woman belonged to a clan of her father. Marriage between persons of one clan was forbidden. The country was usually divided into clans. The male members of the clan constituted the continuing nucleus of the horde. The female members moved out after marriage and other female members moved in as wives of the men. The clans constituted a wider system of structure known as a tribe.

4. The Tribe. In the words of Radcliffe-Brown, ''A number of clans had the same language, and had similar customs; they therefore formed a linguistic community, which is referred to as a Tribe.''[12] A tribe is not a politically united group, its members do not unite in any combined action. It is the hordes of some tribe or different tribes which engage in fighting.

5. The kinship system. Persons of different hordes and of different tribes are linked by means of a kinship system. Explaining the nature of the kinship system, Radcliffe-Brown has said, ''The basis of the reckoning consisted of actual geneaological relationships, including therein the relations between fellow-members of one clan.''[13] Thus, the kinship system cuts across the tribal relationships. Kinship relationships were classified into a number of categories. Each category was denoted by one kinship term distinguished as being nearer or more distant to other kinship relationships. The arrangement of relationships was dyadic, *i.e.*, person to person relationship. Persons used to visit kinship members in other clans and tribes. Thus, kinship cuts across clans. Each person had his own particular position in the total kinship of structure due to his status in descent, marriage, etc.

6. The moieties. Sometimes a primitive social structure is divided into two moieties. Each moiety includes a number of tribes. Each clan belongs to one of the moieties. Thus, a moiety is wider than a tribe. In the words of Radcliffe-Brown, 'Essentially the system is a classification or grouping of class which cuts across the classification into tribes or linguistic communities.''[14]

7. Social sections. According to Radcliffe-Brown, the primitive society may have a further dichotomy into two alternating generation divisions. Each clan contains at all times the adults and the children, male and female, thus, there is a four-fold division of society into sections which have particular names. These sections determine marriage and kinship relationships.

8. Totemic group. Each clan is a distinct totemic group having its own sacred totem centres, its own myths, its own rites. Each clan has its own

---

11. *Ibid.*

12. *Ibid.*

13. *Ibid.*

14. *Ibid.*, p. 143.

totemic solidarity and continuity which differentiates it from other clans. There are totemic ceremonies. Thus, totemic group maintains solidarity of primitive society. They provide the religious structure of society.

9. Social classes. According to Radcliffe-Brown, in some primitive societies one may find division of social structure into social classes. An example of such a division is the division between chiefs and commoners in Polynesia. Social classes, however, are not found in all the primitive societies.

Principles of Description of Social Structure

From the above mentioned description of the structural system in a primitive people, Radcliffe-Brown formulates the important principles concerning the description of social structure :

1. The description of social structure should include not only the social groups and social classes but the whole set of socially fixed relationships of person to person as in kinship system.

2. Thus, the social structure at a particular place and time consists of the whole set of social relationships among members.

3. Social relationships should be defined in terms of social institutions.

Importance of Social Institutions

As has been already pointed out in the definition of social structure given by Radcliffe-Brown, it is a continuing arrangement of persons defined or controlled by institutions. The institutions, as has been pointed out by Radcliffe-Brown in the same definition, are socially established norms or patterns of behaviour. Radcliffe-Brown has defined an institution as, "...an established or socially recognized system of norms or patterns of conduct referring to some aspect of social life."[15] An example of institution is the family which sets the patterns of behaviour of the members in relation to one another. Thus, social institutions provide the measure to proper conduct of a person in a certain relationship. They define for a person how he is expected to behave and also how he may expect others to behave. Deviance from the norms of institutions is derogated. Each institution carried a system of sanctions behind it. Institutional relationships determine the structural features of social life. In the words of Radcliffe-Brown, "Social structure therefore has to be described by the institutions which define the proper or expected conduct of persons in their various relationships."[16]

Structural Continuity

Thus, social structure is an arrangement of persons in institutionalized roles and relationships. The continuity of this arrangement is known as structural continuity. Since the individuals and groups constituting social structure

15. *Ibid.*, p. 145.

16. *Ibid.*

constantly change, one group or person being substituted by another group or person, the structural continuity is dynamic. In this continuity, while the matter changes, the form remains the same. The matters of social structure are the individual human beings who are born and who die. The form of social structure is supplied by social institutions. Thus, social institutions are responsible for the dynamic formal structural continuity. In the ultimate analysis, social structure, according to Radcliffe-Brown, involves two important constituents, one, the human individuals and groups and the other, their arrangement through social institutions. In other words, it is the continuing arrangement of persons in relationships defined by social institutions which is known as social structure.

It may be noted here that Radcliffe-Brown has been known as a structuralist in Social Anthropology. He stresses the importance of the comparative method in Social Anthropology. His approach to social structure is anthropological. This is amply clear by his above mentioned explanation of social structure with reference to primitive social structure. His Social Anthropology, however, is Comparative Sociology. Therefore, his observations on the concept of social structure are equally useful in social anthropology as well as in sociology.

KINSHIP SYSTEMS

What is Kinship System ?

Radcliffe-Brown, the famous social anthropologist has presented his concept of kinship system in his book, *Structure and Function in Primitive Society* (Glencoe, Illinois: Free Press, 1952, Chapter III, pp. 49-89). Defining the term kinship system he says, "By a kinship system then, I mean a network of social relations of the kind just defined, which thus constitutes part of that total network of social relations that I call social structure."[17] Thus kinship system is a part of social structure. It includes definite social groups of which the most important is the domestic family. The domestic family may be of different forms and size, and observing different manners of life. Besides the domestic family the kinship systems include unilinear groups of kindred — lineage groups, clans and moieties. The most fundamental characteristic of kinship system is the dyadic relations between person and person in a community. In the words of Racliffe-Brown, "Thus a kinship system, as I am using the term, or a system of kinship and affinity if you prefer so to call it, is in the first place a system of dyadic relations between person and person in a community, the behaviour of any two persons in any of these relations being regulated in some way, and to a greater or lesser extent, by social usage."[18] Thus, kinship system in essence, is a network of social relations of dyadic type. In this network the rights and duties of relatives to one another are defined by social usages. An important part of kinship system is the ancestor worship. It affects the relations of living persons to one another. Kinship system includes the terms used in the

17. U. Parsons, E. Shils and others (Ed.), *Theories of Society*, The Free Press, New York, 1965, p. 280.
18. Radcliffe-Brown, A. R., *Structure and Function in Primitive Society*, p. 280.

society in addressing or referring to relatives. It also includes the ideas of the people about kinship system.

Constituents of Kinship System

From the above discussion of the definition of kinship system it is clear that its constituents are as follows :

1. Elementary family. In the words of Radcliffe-Brown, "The unit of structure from which a kinship system is built up is the group which I call an 'elementary family', consisting of a man and his wife and their child or children whether they are living together or not."[19] Thus, there can be no elementary family without a child. Children, however, may be adopted. The elementary family creates three kinds of relationships : (1) Relationship between parents and child. (2) Relationship between children of the same parents. (3) Relationship between husband and wife. Of these the second are known as sibling relationships. After marriage the man belongs to a second elementary family in which he is husband and father.

2. Elementary family relations. In a social system there are so many elementary families which constitute what Radcliffe-Brown calls different orders of relationship. These orders are as follows :

(i) *First order relationships.* These are constituted by the above mentioned three types of relationships existing within an elementary family.

(ii) *Second order relationships.* These are the relationships which depend upon the connection of two elementary families through a common member, and are such as father's, mother's, brother's, wife's, sister's, etc.

(iii) *Third order relationships.* These include relationships such as father's brother's son and mother's brother's wife. According to Radcliffe-Brown besides the above mentioned three orders of relationship there may be fourth, fifth or eighth order. In any given society a certain number of relationships are recognized for social purposes. These relationships have attached to them certain rights and duties. They are known for certain distinctive modes of behaviour. It is these relationships which Radcliffe-Brown calls kinship system. In his own words, "It is the relations that are recognized in this way that constitute what I am calling a kinship system, or, in full, a system of kinship and affinity."[20]

3. Compound family. In the words of Radcliffe-Brown, "Compound families can be regarded as formed of elementary families with a common member."[21] In a polygynous family there is only one husband with two or more wives and their respective children. Another form of compound family is monogamous, formed by a second marriage, giving rise to what we call step-relationships and such relationships as that of half-brothers.

---

19. *Ibid.*, p. 279.

20. *Ibid.*

21. *Ibid.*

4. Genealogical relations. Genealogical relations are those which are the result of interlocking of elementary families. This may be of various ranges, narrow, wider or very wide. This range is an important character of kinship system.

5. Rights and duties. As has been already pointed out, kinship system includes the rights and duties of the members towards each other, defined by kinship terminology.

6. Kinship usages. Relations are described by social usages which are observed in the social contacts of the members of a society.

Kinship usages are patterns of collective behaviour which exhibit a regularity of structure. Some usages are such as Ancestor worship, Avoidance, Joking relations, etc.

(i) *Avoidance*. In all societies some sort of avoidance is found in kinship relations as is observed in the relations between daughter-in-law and her parents-in-law. Radcliffe-Brown explains it as whenever people come in contact with each other the possibilities of cooperation as well as of conflict are always equally present, and hence the kinship usage of avoidance.

(ii) *Ancestor worship*. According to Radcliffe-Brown, ancestor worship is a part of kinship system. It is constituted by their relations of the living persons to their deceased kindred. Ancestor worship affects the relations of living persons to one another.

7. Definite social groups. The kinship system includes the existence of definite social groups of which the most important are domestic families which may be of various forms and sizes. A domestic family may consist of a single elementary family or it may be a group including a hundred or more persons. Besides domestic families, kinship systems may include unilinear groups of kindred-lineage groups, clans and moieties.

Clan. As has been already pointed out, clan is an important constituent of kinship system.

8. Terminology. Finally, kinship systems include terminologies, which denote relationships among different persons. Terminology is also known as nomenclature. It is an intrinsic part of kinship system as much as an intrinsic part of language. According to Radcliffe-Brown, "In the actual study of a kinship system the nomenclature is of the utmost importance."[22] It affords the best possible approach to the investigation and analysis of the kinship system as a whole. The relations between the nomenclature and the rest of the system are relations within an ordered whole. Radcliffe-Brown's main concern, in his comparative studies, has been the discovery of the nature of these relations. A common feature of kinship system is the recognition of certain categories or kinds into which the various relatives of a single person can be grouped. The nomenclature of kinship is commonly used as a means of establishing and

22. *Ibid.*, p. 248.

recognizing these categories. A single term may be used to refer to a category of relatives and different categories will be distinguished by different terms.

Choctow and Omaha American Examples

Radcliffe-Brown has explained the importance of genealogy and kinship terminology by referring to Morgan's studies of two North American Tribes known as Choctow and Omaha. In his studies of the Choctow tribe, Morgan found that a man calls his father's sister's son by the same term of relationship that he applies to his own father and his father's father. Reciprocally a man calls his mother's brother's son by the term for "son". Consistently with this he applies one term of relationship to his father's sister and her daughter, and speaks of his mother's brother's "daughter". This is an example of matrilineal organization. Another type of terminology was found by Morgan in the Omaha Tribe. He found that a man calls his mother's brother's son "uncle", *i.e.* mother's brother, and calls his mother's brother's daughter "mother" so that reciprocally he speaks of his father's sister's son by the term that he uses for his sister's son, and a woman uses a single term for her own son, her sister's son and her father's sister's son. According to Radcliffe-Brown, it is not necessary that each tribe must be either patrilineal or matrilineal type, it may be a mixture of both.

The Diffusionist Viewpoint

For more than a century the subject of kinship has occupied a special and important position in Social Anthropology. The diffusionists used the method of conjectural history to study kinship systems. Thus, in an essay on primitive marriage, McLennan suggested the origin of the custom of exogamy from marriage by capture and the proposition that the most ancient system in which the idea of blood relationship was embodied was a system of kinship through females only. In his book on ancient society Lewis Morgan offered a conjectural outline in the history of the whole course of social development. This method, however, hinders the development of a scientific theory of human society as it depends much upon conjectures about past and future.

By a "kinship system" Radcliffe-Brown means a system of kinship and marriage or kinship and affinity. According to him the unit of structure from which a kinship system is built is the elementary family, consisting of a man, his wife and children. He uses the investigation method of observing the actual operations of kinship relations in primitive societies. The existence of the elementary family creates three special kinds of social relationships — that between parents and child, between children and between husband and wife. These are the relationships of the *first order.* Relationships of the *second order* are those which depend on the connections of two elementary families through common members, for example, father's father, mother's brother, etc. In the third order are such relations as father's brother's, mother's brother's wife, etc.

In any given society a certain number of these relationships are recognized for social purposes. They have attached to them certain rights and duties and certain distinctive models of behaviour. These relations constitute a kinship system. A most important characteristic of a kinship system is its range. In wide-ranging relations of non-European countries a man may recognize hundreds of relatives towards each of whom his behaviour is defined.

Thus, a kinship system is, in the first place, a system of dyadic relations between person and person in a community. The behaviour of any two persons in any of these relations is regulated in some way by social usage. A kinship system also includes the existence of definite social groups. The first of these is the domestic family. In many kinship systems unilinear groups of kindred play an important part. The network of social relations of a kinship system constitutes part of the total network of social relations or social structure. Ancestor worship is a part of the kinship system as it constitutes a relation between living persons and their deceased kindred. Kinship terminologies are a part of the kinship system. Between the various features of a particular kinship system there is a complex relation of interdependence.

The diffusionists tried to explain the Omaha and Choctow customs of calling a father's sister's son by the same term he uses to his father and also the same nomenclature used to one's mother's relatives by conjecturing that they resulted from the custom of marrying one's mother's brother's wife. According to Radcliffe-Brown, however, all over the world there are important relations between kinship nomenclature and social practices. Kinship nomenclature affords the best possible approach to the investigation and analysis of kinship systems.

One common feature of kinship systems is the recognition of certain categories or kinds into which the various relatives of a single person can be grouped. The actual social relations between a person and his relatives is fixed by the category to which the relative belongs. Kinship nomenclature is used as a means of establishing and recognizing these categories. A single term may be used to refer to a category of relatives and different categories will be distinguished by different terms. Thus, for example, we call the father's brother and mother's brother as uncle.

The kinship systems thus employ certain forms of Morgan's classificatory terminology. In these systems the distinction between lineal and collateral relatives is clearly recognized and is of great importance in social life. Sometimes this is subordinated to the principle of solidarity of the sibling group. Thus, for instance, the mother's sisters are treated as relatives of the same 'kind' as the mother, both in terminology and in certain principles of behaviour and attitude. In a number of systems the mother's brother is also treated as a relative of the same kind as the mother. He may be called male mother as in the Bantu tribes of Africa. This treatment is given to even the relatives of a third or fourth generation. Thus, the classificatory terminology is a method of providing a wide range of kinship organization by establishing a few categories of relationship under which a large number of near and distant relatives can be included. The distinction of generations forms another aspect of kinship system. In some societies there is a generalizing tendency in the behaviour of relatives of different generations. Lineage plays an important role in the distinction of generations and in fixing kinship obligations.

Thus, while the method of conjectural history studies single problems of kinship in isolation and speculates upon their origin, the method of structural analysis aims at a general theory of kinship by a systematic classification of observable kinship systems by observing particular features and by analyzing their similarities and social implications.

Method of the Study of Kinship System

Radcliffe-Brown's work *Structure and Function in Primitive Society*, as is clear by the title, is a structural study. His is a structural-functional approach. He employs structural method for the study of person-to-person relationship in a kinship system. He studies the role of kinship terms through the functional method. His query is as to "how one part of the system is related with the other part of the system or with the total system shall be known through structural method."

He has no quarrel with the use of historical method in Social Anthropology but he is vehemently against the use of conjectural history in Social Anthropology. He emphasizes that anthropological interpretation must be based upon sound data. Conjectures should not be made to fill the gaps of data information. He defines his own method by saying, "How one part of the system is related with the other part of the system or with the total system shall be known through structural method." This method is based upon the hypothesis that between the features of a particular kinship system there is a complex relation of interdependence. This hypothesis leads to the method of sociological analysis. It requires a systematic comparison of a sufficient number of sufficiently diverse systems. These should be compared as wholes or as systems. According to Radcliffe-Brown, "Our purpose is to arrive at valid abstractions or general ideas in terms of which the phenomena can be described and classified."[23] He has criticized the hypothesis as those of Kohler, Rivers and Morgan, etc. as *a priori*, lacking evidence and conjectural. In this controversy between Rivers and Kroeber, concerning the relationship of terminology and features of social organization, Radcliffe-Brown holds almost a middle position. In opposition to Kroeber and in a certain sense in agreement with Rivers, Radcliffe-Brown holds that all over the world there are important correspondences between kinship nomenclature and social practices. On the other hand, he disagrees with Rivers' contention that terminology may be taken as causal explanation.

Types of Kinship Terms

In different social systems different types of kinship terminology may be observed. Of these the most important types of kinship terminology are as follows :

---

23. *Ibid.*, p. 23.

1. Classificatory terminology. According to Radcliffe-Brown, "A nomenclature is classificatory when it uses terms which primarily apply to lineal relatives, such as 'father', to refer also to collateral relatives.[24] The word classificatory has long been in use. Therefore, though it is not an ideal word, it may be accepted.

2. Terminology denoting solidarity of the sibling group. According to Radcliffe-Brown, "A group of siblings is constituted by the sons and daughters of man and his wife in monogamous societies, or of a man and his wives where there is polygamy, or of a woman and her husbands in polyandrous communities."[25] The solidarity of the sibling group is shown in the social relationships between its members.

Characteristics of Kinship Structure

By his structural study of the kinship system, Radcliffe-Brown has arrived upon the following characteristics of kinship social structure:

1. Changing system. According to Radcliffe-Brown, kinship systems are made and remade by man through social processes.

2. Solidarity of the sibling group. Another characteristic of the kinship system is the solidarity of sibling group.

3. Unity of the sibling group. This refers to the unity of the group in relations to a person outside it and connected with it by a specific relation to one of its members.

4. Sex as the principle of differentiation. In many kinship systems sex is an important basis for differentiation between different members.

5. Seniority as the principle of differentiation. Where seniority is strongly emphasized, a man may distinguish between the senior brother and the junior brother either in behaviour alone or both in behaviour and terminology, but there still remains a common element in the pattern of behaviour towards all fathers.

6. Division into generation. The distinction of generation has its basis in the elementary family, in the relation of parents and children. A certain generalizing tendency is discoverable in many kinship systems in the behaviour of relatives of different generations. There is in fact a generalized relation of ascendancy and subordination between the two generations.

7. Combination of alternate generations. This means that relatives of the grandfather's generation are thought of as combined with those of one's generation over against the relatives of the parent's generation.

8. Terminology for generations. By a comparative study Radcliffe-Brown arrives at the following four types of relationships between terminology and generations denoted by them :

24. *Ibid.*, p. 285.

25. *Ibid.*

(i) The term of relationship does not carry a connotation referring to any particular generation and is used to mark off a sort of marginal region between non-relatives and those close relatives towards whom specific duties and over whom specific rights are recognized.

(ii) Terms in which there is a conflict or inconsistency between the required attitude towards a particular relative and the required general attitude towards the generation to which he belongs.

(iii) Those resulting from the structural principle, whereby alternate generations are combined.

(iv) This includes the systems of Choctow and Omaha type and also certain others, and in these the distinction between generation is set aside in favour of another principle, that of the unity of lineage group. According to Radcliffe-Brown, "A lineage group consists of all the members of a class who are alive at a particular time." Lineage may patrilineal or matrilineal. A partilineal or agnatic lineage consists of a man and all his descendants through males for a determinate number of generations. A matrilineal lineage consists of a woman and all her descendants through females for a determinate number of generations. The lineage group is important for the solidarity of society. According to Radcliffe-Brown, "By the principle of the unity of the lineage group I mean that for a person who does not belong to the lineage but is connected with it through some important bond of kinship or by marriage, its members constitute a single category, with a distinction within the category between males and females, and possibly other distinctions also."

Functions of Kinship Terms

1. Kinship terms help to maintain kinship system of person to person relationship in kinship systems.

2. Kinship terms perform the function of dividing persons into generations. This is clear by the above-mentioned discussion.

3. There are four uses of kinship terms as have been shown in the above-mentioned four classes of kinship terminology.

Value of Sociological Analysis

According to Radcliffe-Brown the use of structural-functional analysis of kinship system gives the following valuable results :

1. Systematic classification of kinship systems.

2. Understanding of particular features of particular systems firstly by revealing the particular features as a part of an organized whole; and secondly by showing that it is a special example of a class of recognized phenomena.

3. Valid generalization about the nature of human society, *i.e.*, about the universal characteristics of all societies, present and future, leading to sociological laws.

After his discussion of the study of kinship systems and his criticism of the method of conjectural history and support of the structural-functional method in this area of research, Radcliffe-Brown concludes, "We cannot reach agreement as to the validity or the value of results unless we first reach some agreement as to objectives and the proper methods of attaining them."

THE RITUALS

In his book *The Andaman Islanders*, A. R. Radcliffe-Brown has investigated the physical characteristics, language, culture and technology of this primitive society. This book is a major contribution to the development of modern anthropological techniques. Radcliffe-Brown maintains that there can be no demonstrable certainty of conclusions through historical method in anthropology. As he said. "During the course of my work a systematic examination of the methods available for such reconstructions of the unknown past convinced me that it is only in extremely rare instances that we can never approach demonstrable conclusions and that speculative history cannot give us results of any real importance for the understanding of human life and culture. The work of the historical ethnologists of the last twenty-two years has only served to confirm me in that opinion."[26]

Meaning of Ritual

According to Radcliffe-Brown, communication among men is not only through words but also through gestures and signs, etc. Rituals, in a culture, are meaningful activities that are considered valuable and which are collective expression of sentiments. As Radcliffe-Brown has said. "Just in the sense that words have meanings, so do some other things in culture — customary gestures, ritual actions and abstentions, symbolic objects, myths, they are expressive signs. The meaning of a word, a gesture, a rite, lies in what it expresses, and this is determined by its associations within a system of ideas, sentiments and mental attitudes."[27]

Characteristics of Ritual

Thus ritual, according to Radcliffe-Brown, posseses the following characteristics :

1. Certain social values are attached to rituals.

2. Rituals have force behind themselves, sometimes of fear, of terror of unknown forces and evil spirits and sometimes of the goodwill and sanction of the society.

3. Rituals have the characteristic of stability. They are observed in the same way generation after generation.

---

26. *Op. cit.*, p. vii.

27. *Ibid.*, p. viii.

4. Rituals have the trait of being repeated on particular occasions. This can be seen among tribals on different occasions.

5. Rituals express group behaviour which includes beliefs and customs of the group concerning life and nature.

6. Rituals are the collective expressions of sentiment. This can be seen in rituals connected with weeping.

Structural-Functional Approach

According to Radcliffe-Brown, "Ethnology is faced with the dilemma that it must either give up for ever all hope of understanding such things as myth or ritual, or it must develop methods for determining as accurately as can be what meanings they have for the people to whose culture they belong."[28] Thus, he has tried to develop proper methods for determining the meaning of different elements of culture in his anthropological studies. In his study *The Andaman Islanders*, he puts the problem in these words, "We have to explain why is it that the Andamanese think and act in certain ways. The explanation of each single custom is provided by showing what is its relation to the other customs of the Andamanese and to their general system of ideas and sentiments."[29] Radcliffe-Brown's approach in this study can be called structural-functional. He conducted empirical research in Andaman. He tried to show the relevance of ritual in their social life. The relevance of rituals is shown by pointing out their function in the collective life. According to Radcliffe-Brown, "The discovery of the integrative function of an institution, usage, or belief is to be made through the observation of its effects, and these are obviously in the first place effects on individuals, on their life, their thoughts, their emotions. Not all such effects are significant, or at least equally so. Nor is it the immediate effects with which we are finally concerned, but the more remote effects upon the social cohesion and continuity."[30] Thus, according to Radcliffe-Brown, the meaning and function are two different but related terms. He points out that the social functions of mythology on ritual cannot be discussed without an understanding of particular myths and ritual actions.

The Meaning of Function

Explaining the meaning of function in ethnology, Radcliffe-Brown has pointed out, "The notion of function in ethnology rests on the conception of culture as an adaptive mechanism by which a certain number of human beings are enabled to live a social life as an ordered community in a given environment."[31] This adaptation, according to Radcliffe-Brown, has two aspects, external and internal. The external aspect can be found in the relation of the

---

28. *Ibid.*, p. ix.

29. *Ibid.*, p. 230.

30. *Ibid.*, p. 10.

31. *Ibid.*, p. ix.

society to its geographical environment. The internal aspect can be seen in the controlled relations of individuals within the social unity. Radcliffe-Brown has used the term, "social integration" to cover all the phenomena of internal adaptation.

The True Comparative Method

Radcliffe-Brown is against comparison of one item in a culture to the corresponding item in another culture. According to him in a true comparative method, we have not to compare one isolated custom of a society with a similar custom of another. We have rather to compare the whole system of institutions, customs and beliefs of one society with those of another. To put it in his own words, "In a word, what we need to compare is not institutions but social systems or types."[32]

Hypothesis of Study

In a scientific study, according to Radcliffe-Brown, elaboration of hypotheses and the observation and classification of facts should be carried on independently. The theorists and the observers should work with systematic cooperation. Thus, he starts his study of the Andaman Islanders by making certain workable hypotheses. In his own words, "Stated as briefly as possible the working hypotheses here adopted is as follows : (1) A society depends for its existence on the presence in the minds of its members of a certain system of sentiments by which the conduct of the individuals is regulated in conformity with the needs of the society. (2) Every feature of the social system itself and every event or object that in any way affects the well-being or the cohesion of the society becomes an object of this system of sentiments. (3) In human society the sentiments in question are not innate but are developed in the individual by the action of the society upon him. (4) The ceremonial customs of a society are a means by which the sentiments in question are given collective expression on appropriate occasions. (5) The ceremonial (*i.e.*, collective) expression of any sentiment serves both to maintain it at the requisite degree of intensity in the mind of the individual and to transmit it from one generation to another."[33]

Radcliffe-Brown, in this study, has used the term social function "to denote the effects of an institution (custom or belief) in so far as they concern the society and its solidarity or cohesion."[34] Thus, the social function of ritual in the life of Andaman Islanders is to maintain and transmit from one generation to another the emotional disposition on which the society depends for its existence. Radcliffe-Brown has shown that there is a correspondence between the customs and beliefs and systems of social sentiments. He has also pointed out that there is a correspondence between the sentiments and social structure.

---

32. *Ibid.*, p. 230.

33. *Ibid.*, p. 234.

34. *Ibid.*

Thus he has pointed out relationship between social structure and social function. He has, however, not tried to discover the historical origin of these customs.

Rules of Method

In his study of Andaman Islanders, Radcliffe-Brown has laid down the following rules to be observed :

(1) In explaining any given custom it is necessary to take into account the explanation given by the natives themselves. Radcliffe-Brown depends upon the explanation of a ritual given by the natives themselves, as against his own explanation of it. He has criticized the attempts of those anthropologists who tried to discover their own subjective meaning in primitive rituals. He points out that the savage also seeks to rationalize his behaviour. He seeks to formulate reason for his conduct. This reason is not identical with the psychological cause of the action. However, it is intimately connected with the action itself. The anthropologists have not only to explain the ritual but also the reason that natives give for following it.

(2) The assumption is made that when the same or a similar custom is practised on different occasions it has the same or a similar meaning in all of them. For examples on some occasions in a culture, personal names are not used. Here, it should be taken for granted that there is something common to all these occasions and hence the avoidance.

(3) It is assumed that when different customs are practised together on one and the same occasion there is a common element in the customs. This rule is the inverse of the preceding rule. To illustrate, if different rituals are observed by mourners on a single occasion, it shows that there is some common element in all these rituals.

(4) Comparisons of customs of different races should be avoided. Radcliffe-Brown has explained all the above mentioned rules with reference to different forms of rituals such as those practised in marriage ceremony, peace-making ceremony, initiation ceremonies, etc.

Functions of Rituals

As has been already pointed out, the function of a ritual, according to Radcliffe-Brown, is a social function. This social function, again, means its effects upon social solidarity. Thus, the social function of a ritual, in maintaining or expressing social solidarity or social cohesion, is precisely speaking. its function. In chapter five of his book *The Andaman Islanders*, Radcliffe-Brown has discussed the following ceremonies and explained the meanings of rituals in them : the marriage ceremony, the peace-making ceremony, the initiation ceremony, the ceremonies connected with economic activities, and the ceremonies connected with death, etc. By the study of these ceremonies he draws the following conclusions concerning their social functions :

(1) Expression of affective states of mind. Every ceremony is an expression of affective states of the mind of two or more persons. Thus, the weeping rituals express feelings of social solidarity.

(2) Consciousness of duty. The ceremonies are however not spontaneous expressions. A sentiment of obligation is attached to them. It is the duty of everyone in a community to participate in a ceremony. Thus, again a ritual expresses the feeling of social solidarity.

(3) Connected with laws regulating the affective life. Each ceremony may be explained by reference to fundamental laws regulating the affective life of the community. For example, weeping or embracing are the psychological expressions of the affective life of human beings.

(4) Renewal of social sentiments. Social solidarity requires a constant renewal of social sentiments. This function is performed by the ceremonies towards those taking part in it. For example, the peace-making ceremony is a method by which feelings of enmity are substituted by feelings of friendship. Similarly, the different rituals performed in a marriage ceremony renew the bonds of attachment.

(5) Fulfilment of social needs. It is clear from the above discussion that the ceremonies and rituals are the means to fulfilment of social needs. These social needs and their fulfilment is as follows :

(i) For its existence, a society depends on the presence in the minds of its members, of a certain system of sentiments by which the conduct of the individual is regulated in conformity with the needs of society. This is done by means of ceremonies and rituals.

(ii) Sentiments affect social cohesion. Ceremonies and rituals renew social sentiments.

(iii) Though the sentiments are innate but they are developed by the action of society. This development of sentiment is necessary for transition into adulthood. This function is performed by ceremonies.

(iv) Ceremonial customs of society are the means by which sentiments are given collective expression on appropriate occasions. This helps in maintaining collective consciousness and keeping social solidarity intact.

(v) The ceremonial expression of any sentiment serves to maintain it in the minds of individuals and also transfer it from one generation to another.

WEEPING RITUALS

Among the most important rituals practised by the Andaman Islanders on the occasion of different ceremonies are the weeping rituals. As has been already pointed out as a rule, when the same ritual is observed on the occasion of many different ceremonies, its function in all these ceremonies should be interpreted as identical. In the words of Radcliffe-Brown, "The weeping and exchange of presents when friends come together is a means of renewing their feelings of attachment to one another. The weeping at marriage, at initiation, and on the occasion of death is a reaction of difference or compassion when feelings of solidarity are attacked by a partial breaking of the social ties that bind persons to one another."[35] The weeping ritual in the life of Andaman Islanders, may be observed on the following occasions :

(1) Meeting of friends or relatives after a long time. In Andaman sometimes people have to go outside the island for a long time. They are away from their friends, family and relatives for some time. Now when they return to the island and meet their friends and relatives they embrace them and weep with uncontrolled joy.

(2) Peace-making ceremony. Sometimes two individuals or two groups come in conflict due to some powerful emotions. Now after some time, when any one of the party realizes its mistakes, they meet each other, embrace and weep on their mistakes. This weeping, undoubtedly releases tension and increases mutual friendship and attachment.

(3) At the end of the mourning period. Mourning period is a period of some duration beginning from the death of a member of kinship relation. It is supposed that during this period the soul of the dead person lives with the family. Therefore, all the other relatives live away from them. The family also does not take part in social activities. At the end of the mourning period the bereaved family meets the other members of the community and weep together. This renews their social attachment.

(4) On the dead body of the family members or relatives. People weep on the dead body of the family members due to emotional attachment. As he is no more with them, they express their affection by weeping over the corpse. This weeping is obligatory. It is an expression of relationship with the dead person as the body represents the person.

(5) Recovery of the bones of the dead person. Bones represent the dead person. When they are recovered from the grave they are wept over. By this ritual the affection that was once felt towards the dead person is revived and is now directed to the skeletal relics of the man or woman.

(6) On the occasion of marriage. On the occasion of marriage there is a lot of weeping. It makes feelings real in those who take part in it. By it social ties are modified. When the mother of the bride or the bridegroom weeps at the marriage she feels her son or daughter is being taken away from her care. Thus, she feels the sorrow of partial separation. She consoles herself by weeping and expressing her tenderness towards her child. This ritual makes her feel that the child is still an object of her affection and still bound to her in spite of the fact that he or she is being taken away from her.

(7) Initiation ceremonies. At various stages of the initiation ceremonies the female relatives of a youth or girl weep over him or her. The above mentioned explanation of weeping in marriage also holds true at the initiation

35. *Ibid.*, p. 246.

ceremonies. At every stage of this cermony the social ties that unite the initiate to these relatives are modified or weakened. Weeping is the means by which the significance of this change is impressed upon those taking part in it. For the mother it expresses her resignation at her necessary loss. It acts as a consolation by making her feel that her son is still hers though now being drawn from her care.

Importance of Weeping Rituals

The above mentioned different types of occasions for weeping have different value. According to Radcliffe-Brown, "In the first three instances enumerated above the rite is reciprocal, *i.e.*, two persons or two distinct groups of persons weep together and embrace each other, both parties to the rite being active. In the other four instances it is one-sided; a person or group of persons weep over another person (or the relics of a person) who has only a passive part in the ceremony. Any explanation, to be satisfactory, must take account of the difference between these two varieties."[36] Mourning expresses attachment which is very important in the domestic life of Andaman Islanders. The purpose of weeping rituals is to affirm the existence of a social bond between two or more persons. The weeping rite is the affirmation of social bond. This is expressed in the embrace and weeping of the persons meeting each other after a long time. Weeping is an expression of tender emotion. The embrace awakens the feeling of affection or friendship. In peace-making ceremony weeping follows renewal of the friendship. It is an affirmation of social solidarity. Radcliffe-Brown has summed up the explanation of weeping rituals in these words, "I regard it as being the affirmation of a bond of social solidarity between those taking part in it, and as producing in them a realization of that bond by arousing the sentiment of attachment. In some instances the rite therefore serves to renew social relations when they have been interrupted, and in such instances the rite is reciprocal. In others it serves to show the continued existence of the social bond when it is being weakened or modified, as by marriage, initiation or death. In all instances we may say that the purpose of the rite is to bring about a new state of the affective dispositions that regulate the conduct of persons to one another, either by reviving sentiments that have lain dormant, or producing a recognition of a change in the condition of personal relations."[37]

THE DANCING RITUAL

Beside the ritual of weeping, the most important ritual in the life of primitive people is dancing. The basic characteristics of dancing are as follows:

1. Means of enjoyment. Dancing is a means of enjoyment. It is frequently a rejoicing. It is a natural expression of pleasure. In it not only the mind but also body takes part in the natural expression of pleasure.

---

36. *Ibid.*, p. 240.

37. *Ibid.*, p. 245.

2. Rhythmical activity. Dance is rhythmic. It enables a number of persons to join in the same actions and perform them as one body. The dancer is in a condition in which all the bodily and mental activities are harmoniously directed to one end.

3. Activity of the total body. The dance involves the activity of as many muscles of the body as possible. It brings into play the whole muscular system.

4. Social solidarity. As every adult able bodied man must take part in dance, it is a means to maintain social solidarity. It gives the pleasure of self surrender. In the words of Radcliffe-Brown, "In this way the dance produces a condition in which the unity, harmony and concord of the community are at a maximum, and in which they are intensely felt by every member."[38] Thus, dancing is a means of uniting individuals into harmonious whole. It makes them actually and intensely experience their relation to that unity of which they are the members.

5. Stimulation of self-regard. Dance stimulates self-regarding sentiment by giving an opportunity to the individual for exhibiting his skill in dance. It affects the sentiment of the dancer towards his fellows. According to Radcliffe-Brown the conscious motive of dance is personal vanity.

6. Gratification of personal vanity. Thus, dance offers an opportunity for the gratification of personal vanity. This is particularly clear from the various types of adornment of body of the dancer.

7. Increase of personal value. Thus, dance increases personal value of the person. He realizes that his personal value depends upon the harmony between himself and his fellows.

Types of Dances

Just as weeping is observed on different occasions similarly dancing is a ceremonial observed on different occasions.

1. Dance before setting out to a fight. Among Andaman Islanders there is a custom always to have a dance before setting out to fight. This dance performs two functions. In the first place, it arouses a sense of group unity in the mind of every individual. Secondly, it intensifies the collective anger against the hostile group. Thirdly, it produces a state of excitement and elation which is important in fighting.

2. Group dances at dance meetings. A normal feature in the social life of the Andamans is the dance meetings. These are regularly held on different occasions. In these meetings two or more local groups meet each other for a few days. For the greater part of the year these groups use to live separately. Dance meetings renew social solidarity, which was weakened by long separation. To quote Radcliffe-Brown, "The function of the dance-meetings was therefore

38. *Ibid.*, p. 252.

to bring the two groups into contact and renew the social relations between them and in that way to maintain the solidarity between them."[39]

3. Ordinary dance. This is the dance of individuals on different occasions. It satisfies vanity of the dancer. It arouses social sentiment. It stimulates self-regard. It increases personal value of the dancer.

Functions of Dances

The characteristics of dance mentioned earlier express its functions. Thus, it is a means of enjoyment. It is a play and an exercise. It increases social solidarity. It stimulates self-regard. It gratifies personal vanity. It increases personal value. To quote Radcliffe-Brown, "Thus, it appears *that not only the ordinary dance but* also the war-dance, and the dance-meetings owe their place in the life of the Andaman Islanders to the fact that dancing is a means of uniting individuals into a harmonious whole and at the same time making them actually and intensely experience their relation to that unity of which they are the members."[40]

RITE OF ADORNMENT

An important feature of primitive life is different types of adornment on different occasions. Such adornments may be seen on the occasion of initiation ceremonies, marriages, dance meetings and other social occasions. Adornment is not only for the living persons but also for the dead body. A corpse is decorated before burial in the same manner as the body of a dancer. The bride and bridegroom are painted with white clay and wear ornaments of shells following the day of their marriage. The following three different substances are used for painting the body :

1. Common clay which may be gray, yellow or pink. This is used in three different ways. Firstly, after the death of a relative, a man or woman smears the corpse all over with common clay. Secondly, common clay is used in initiation ceremonies when it is spattered over the initiate in the turtle eating and pig eating ceremonies. Thirdly, the most common use of common clay is to decorate the bodies of man and woman with various types of patterns.

2. A fine white pipe clay which is rarer and more highly prized.

3. A red pigment made by mixing burnt oxide of iron with animal or vegetable fat or oil.

4. Besides clay various types of shells and beads are used for the purpose of adornment.

Functions of Adornment

1. Increase of the value of the individual. According to Radcliffe-Brown, "We may conclude therefore that the painting of the body with white clay and

39. *Ibid.*, p. 253.

40. *Ibid.*

the wearing of ornaments, of dentalium shell is a rite or ceremony by which the value of the individual to the society is expressed on appropriate occasions."[41] This is particularly the purpose of adornment on the occasion of marriage.

2. Drawing attention. An important purpose of the adornment of bride and bride groom is to draw the attention of their fellows. This is also the purpose of adornment on other social occasions.

3. Increase in social value. The decoration of the body on initiation ceremonies is the expression of the increased social value of the initiate.

4. Regard for the dead. The custom of decorating a corpse before burial, expresses the regard of the surviving relatives and friends for the dead person. It expresses their sense of his value.

5. Attainment of goodwill. According to Radciffe-Brown, "When a man is painted he feels that he has the regard and goodwill of his fellows, and those who see him, at any rate in the instance of a bridegroom or initiate, realize that he has deserved their regard."[42]

6. Protective function. Magical properties have been attributed to so many plants, animals and animal substances in different primitive societies. Similarly, bones of animals as well as human bones have been usually believed to have magical properties. Adornment by means of things having magical properties arouses a sense of security in the person. Sometimes one wears bones to cure himself of certain illness. At other times he wears for protection against evil spirits. The fibres of different trees are considered to have magical value and therefore worn on different occasions.

7. Aids to beauty. As Radcliffe-Brown has pointed out, if an Andaman Islander be asked why he paints himself with white clay, or why he wears a belt or necklace of shells, he replies that he does so in order to look well. Adornments on the occasion of marriage usually adorn the bride and the bridegroom.

Social Protection by Different Objects

As has been already pointed out, some objects are considered as having protective power, such as different types of plants, animals, fibres of some trees, bones and shells, etc. This protective power is based upon the social value of these things. As Radcliffe-Brown has pointed out, the well being of the society and its members is believed to be dependent upon these things. The leaves of different trees used in the ceremony of a girl's first menstruation are said to have protective power. Similar is the case of the leaves used at turtle eating ceremony, pig eating ceremony and the initiation ceremony. Radcliffe-Brown has maintained the following three propositions about the protective power of the objects in Andaman Society, "They are as follows : (1) any object that

41. *Ibid.*, p. 256.

42. *Ibid.*

contributes to the well-being of the society is believed to afford protection against evil; (2) the degree of protective power it is believed to possess depends on the importance of the services it actually renders."[43] These propositions have been proved by giving evidence from the use of different types of materials, plants, trees, animals and animal substance, etc. Not only positive but also negative instances of protective power are available. Protective power is attributed to bones of animals which are made into personal ornaments. High degree of protective power is attributed to human bones. The social value of fire is experienced by every member of the community, though it is not used for adornment. Again, different foods have different social values. The value of a food is both positive and negative. The turtle and the pig are considered to have special values and eaten on ceremonial occasions.

Meaning of the Ceremonial

Explaining the meaning of ceremonial at the end of fifth chapter of his book, *The Andaman Islanders*, Radcliffe-Brown has written, "The chapter has shown that what I have denoted as ceremonial consists of (1) collective actions, (2) required by custom, (3) performed on occasions of changes in the course of social life, and (4) expressing the collective sentiments relating to such social change."[44] Thus, ceremonials do not include the magical practices of the medicine men. Brown admits that the above mentioned definition of ceremonial does not give a very clear distinction between ceremonial on the one hand and art, play and morals on the other. He regards painting of the body with white clay after marriage or initiation as ceremonial. On the other hand, the painting of a new bow canoe with same clay in the pattern should be called art. Besides painting, dancing is a ceremonial. It is a ceremony at the end of mourning but then objection may be raised in calling ordinary dance a ceremonial. Radcliffe-Brown admits that it is difficult to distinguish between ceremonials, art, play and morals. But he points out that though the modern man distinguishes between all these, in primitive societies they were undifferentiated. Therefore, the distinction of ceremonials from art, play and morals is not necessary. In the words of Radcliffe-Brown, "Those elements of culture that we now differentiate and call by different names were, in primitive societies, undifferentiated and not clearly to be distinguished from one another, and a striving after too great a precision of definition in dealing with such a culture as that of the Andamans leads, I think, not to a clearer understanding, but to the opposite."[45]

Functions of Ceremonial

1. Social education. Thus, the function of a ceremonial is primarily social and moral function. It is a means of providing social education. For example, the initiation ceremony constitutes a sort of moral and social education. It is

43. *Ibid.*, pp. 264-65.

44. *Ibid.*, p. 328.

45. *Ibid.*, p. 329.

a recognition of the change of status of the initiate. Similarly, marriage ceremony is the social recognition of the change of status of the bride and bridegroom. Thus, the ceremonials provide social education.

2. Moral education. Besides social education, ceremonials are important means of moral education. Initiation ceremony teaches self-control and self-restraint. It teaches control of hunger. It teaches endurance of pain. Secondly, the ceremonials teach the initiate for the first time in life to view life and its duties and obligations seriously. In the words of Radcliffe-Brown, "It is in the initiation ceremonies that the moral force of the society, acting through foods is chiefly felt, and the same experience is repeated in a less intense form in the rite of painting the body after food." [46] Thus, ceremonial is the means by which the individual is made to feel the moral force of the society acting upon him either directly or in some instances indirectly through those things that have important effects on the social life.

3. Socialization. Thus, ceremonials are important means of socialization. They modify primary instincts. They increase the feeling of social dependence. They make one realize that dangers can only be avoided by the help of the society and by conformity with social customs. In the words of Radcliffe-Brown, "By its action upon the individual the ceremonial develops and maintains in existence in his mind an organized system of dispositions, by which the social life, in the particular form it takes in the Andamans, is made possible, using for the purpose of maintaining the social cohesion of all the instinctive tendencies of human nature, modifying and combining them according to its needs."[47]

4. Social solidarity. The ceremonials increase social solidarity. In the words of Radcliffe-Brown, "An important law of sociology is that the solidarity of a group is increased when the group as a whole finds itself opposed to some other groups, so enmity between two tribes or nations increases the solidarity of each; and so also, the antagonism between the society of the living and the world of the dead increases the solidarity of the former."[48] This clearly applies to the function of ceremonials in the Andamans. Social solidarity also increases by the expression of collective emotions at the time of mourning, war or social ceremonies.

5. Social control. Radcliffe-Brown has maintained, "I have tried to show that the ceremonials and customs are the means by which the society acts upon its individual members and keeps alive in their minds a certain system of sentiments."[49] The ceremonials give birth to the sentiments and keep them alive, social control is exercised through a system of social obligations.

---

46. *Ibid.*, p. 327.

47. *Ibid.*

48. *Ibid.*, p. 328.

49. *Ibid.*, p. 324.

Ceremonials are the means by which the individual experiences the moral force of the society through the feeling of moral obligation. The power of the ceremonials compels him to subordinate his egoistic desires to social demands. Thus, ceremonials are the means by which society maintains important social sentiments necessary to maintain social control. The rules of prohibition concerning the ceremonials also serve this purpose. The above functions of the ceremonials may be observed in the case of collective weeping, dancing, adornment, etc. on the occasion of different ceremonies such as that of initiation, marriage, death ceremony, etc.

CRITICAL EVALUATION

Like every other accomplished scientist A.R. Radcliffe-Brown, in the fifth chapter of his book, *The Andaman Islanders*, discloses his hypothesis in the interpretation of Andamanese customs and beliefs. He rightly maintains that since the origin of primitive ceremonials is lost in the hoary past, the only significant and relevant joy of the anthropologist is to attempt an interpretation of the meanings of ceremonials in the social life of the primitives. However, this interpretation is itself based upon the hypothesis concerning the nature of society. In the second paragraph of this chapter Radcliffe-Brown presents his hypothesis concerning the nature of society. He says, "Every custom and belief of a primitive society plays some determinate part in the social life of the community, just as every organ of a living body plays some part in the general life of the organism."[50] In this statement while nobody will question the first part, that every custom and belief of a primitive society performs some social function, the second part exhibits organic bias in Radcliffe-Brown's concept of society. This organic bias becomes even more explicit when he says, "The mass of institutions, customs and beliefs, forms a single whole or system that determines the life of society, and the life of a society is not less real, or less subject to natural laws, than the life of an organism."[51] The analogy between organism and society, in the statement, has been drawn too far. It has been forgotten that man's life is not subject to natural laws as much as the life of an organism since, while he is influenced by the environment, he also determines it to a considerable extent. Continuing the analogy between society and organism Radcliffe-Brown writes, "To continue the analogy, the study of the meaning of savage customs is a sort of social physiology, and is to be distinguished from the study of origins, or changes of custom in just the same way that animal physiology is distinguished from the biology that deals with the origin of species, the causes of variation, and the general laws of evolution."[52]

50. Radcliffe-Brown, A. R., *The Andaman Islanders*, The Free Press of Glencoe, New York, 1964, p. 229.

51. *Ibid.*, pp. 229-230.

52. *Ibid.*, p. 230.

This reduction of sociology of customs to social physiology and its point to point identification with animal physiology suffers from the fallacy of levelling down. In the hierarchy of human knowledge, the higher explains the lower and not *vice-versa*. Thus, organic structure cannot explain social structure. It is needless to point out here the distinctions between organism and society as accepted even by Herbert Spencer, the pioneer of the Theory of Social Evolution. While the parts of an organism are incapable of independent existence, the individuals in a society are independent and not completely determined by the social structure. The interdependence between the individual and society cannot be explained on the analogy of the interdependence between an organ and the organism. Sociology may borrow certain terms from biology and physiology but their essential limitations in the explanation of social phenomena should never be forgotten. It is due to seeing too much in the analogy between organism and society that Radcliffe-Brown insists that the mass of institutions, customs and beliefs forms a single whole or system. It may be so in an organism but not necessarily in a culture. A culture, on the other hand, is rather formed by congeries of sub-cultures and sub-systems which may not always be homogenous or connected with the central core but rather sometimes, heterogeneous and entirely unconnected with and even sometimes detrimental to the general social life. One may interpret the relation of sociology to social physiology on the pattern of the relation of biology to animal physiology, but the distinction should never be forgotten.

In fact, Radcliffe-Brown is so much sure of his hypothesis concerning the nature of society and the consequent deduction that instead of openly enquiring whether connections or correspondence exist or not, he declares, "An attempt will be made to show that there is a correspondence between the customs and beliefs of the Andamanese and a certain system of social sentiments, and that there is also a correspondence between these sentiments and the manner in which the society is constituted."[53] It is clearly against the norms of scientific inquiry to believe something as established before it is actually discovered. The correspondence mentioned here in fact is the subject of enquiry and not something already confirmed and verified.

Finally, this brief critique of the Organic Bias in Radcliffe-Brown's concept of primitive society may be closed with an advice from the celebrated contemporary logicians, Morris R. Cohen and Ernest Nagel, "The advice is that analogies or resemblances should be noted between the facts we are trying to explain and other facts whose explanation we already know. But which analogies, we are tempted to ask? We can always find some resemblances although not all of them are significant."[54]

---

53. *Ibid.*, p. 234 (*italics* mine).

54. Cohen, M. R. and Ernest Nagel, *An Introduction to Logic and Scientific Method*, Routledge and Kegal Paul, London, 1961, pp. 221-222.

19

Researches of Bronislaw Malinowski

In his book *Argonauts of the Western Pacific*, Bronislaw Malinowski has given "an account of native enterprise and adventure in the Archipelagoes of Melanesian New Guinea".[1] As he has himself pointed out he is mainly concerned with the economic activity of the Trobriand Islanders. This activity centres around the institution known as KULA. Thus this monograph is particularly concerned with one phase of the savage life only. However, as Malinowski has said in the preface of this book, "One of the first conditions of acceptable ethnographic work certainly is that it should deal with the totality of all social, cultural and psychological aspects of the community, for they are so interwoven that not one can be understood without taking into consideration all the others."[2] Therefore, the book deals with the economic theme but repeated reference has been made to social organization, magic, mythology and folklore. As J. G. Frazer has appreciated in the foreword to this book, "It is characteristic of Dr. Malinowski's method that he takes a full account of the complexity of human nature."[3]

DEFINITION OF THE KULA

Before pointing out the essentials of Kula, Malinowski starts with a temporary definition of this institution. He says, "The Kula is a form of exchange, of extensive inter-tribal character; it is carried on by communities inhabiting a wide ring of islands, which form a closed circuit. This form of exchange is carried on under definite rules of transaction and elaborate magical ritual and public ceremonies. Therefore, the Kula is a big complicated institution.[4]

THE CHARACTERISTICS OF KULA

The above mentioned definition of the Kula has been exemplified by an analysis of the characteristics of the Kula ring. According to Malinowski,

1. *Op. cit.*, Routledge and Kegan Paul Ltd., London, 1966.
2. *Ibid.*, p. 16.
3. *Ibid.*, p. 9.
4. *Ibid.*, p. 82.

"Every movement of the Kula articles, every detail of the transactions is fixed and regulated by a set of traditional rules and conventions, and some of the Kula are accompanied by an elaborate magical ritual and public ceremonies."[5] The characteristics of the Kula are as follows :

1. Participation of limited number of men. On every island and in every village a more or less limited number of men lake part in the Kula. They receive the goods, hold them for a short time and then pass them on.

2. The article cannot be retained for long. In the Kula transaction one receives arm shell or necklace of red shell discs and then it has to be handed on to one of his partners. His partner, in his turn, gives him the opposite commodity in exchange. Thus, no one can keep an article for a long time. Those who do not exchange fast are criticized as miserly. In any case no one can keep an article for more than a year.

3. Once in the Kula always in the Kula. This rule shows that one transaction does not finish the Kula relationship. Kula partnership between two men is a permanent and life long affair. The articles are always travelling and changing hands.

4. Ceremonial exchange. According to Malinowski, though Kula appears to be an economic exchange, in fact it is ceremonial. In the words of Malinowski, "The main principle underlying the regulations of actual exchange is that the Kula consists in the bestowing of a ceremonial gift, which has to be repaid by an equivalent counter-gift after a lapse of time, be it a few hours or even minutes though sometimes as much as a year or more may elapse between payments."[6]

5. Secondary activities and features. Side by side with the ritual exchange of arm-shells and necklaces, the natives carry on ordinary trade, bartering commodities of use. Besides, there are other activities such as the building of see-going canoes for the expeditions, certain big forms of mortuary ceremonies and preparatory taboos.

6. An organic whole of several tribes. The Kula is a big and complex institution. According to Malinowski, "It welds together a considerable number of tribes, and it embraces a vast complex of activities, interconnected and playing into one another, so as to form one organic whole."[7] The participants, however, have no knowledge of the total outline of Kula. No one knows how big it is or what sociological function it performs. No one has an integral picture of Kula in his mind. It is the ethnographer who alone has any idea about the total institution. The ethnographer here performs three activities: (1) He has to find out that certain activities which appear meaningless have a meaning; (2) He has to find out what is essential and what is accidental;

5. *Ibid.*, p. 81.

6. *Ibid.*, p. 95.

7. *Ibid.*, p. 83.

(3) Finally, he has to construct the picture of the institution based upon laws and rules of transaction.

7. Economic institution. Kula is essentially an economic institution. It is hence that Malinowski has called it, "a form of trade". Trade, however, in this context has a wide interpretation. It includes almost the total social life. It is rooted in myth-backed traditional law and surrounded by magical rights. It is a life-long transaction. It involves duties and privileges.

8. Spontaneous. Kula is not done under stress of any kind. Its main aim is to exchange articles which are of no practical use. Therefore, it is more a part of culture. It is a means of establishing inter-tribal relationships on a large scale. In the words of Malinowski, "Myth, magic and tradition have built-up around it definite ritual and ceremonial forms, have given it a halo of romance and value in the minds of the natives, have indeed created a passion in their hearts for this simple exchange."[8]

THE MAIN RULES AND ASPECTS OF THE KULA

The exchange of articles in Kula ring is based upon certain rules of transaction. These rules are as follows:

1. Transaction between partners only. The Kula transaction can be done only between partners and not between any two persons.

2. Formal partnership. The manner of partnership is definite and formal. It constitutes a life-long relationship.

3. Variation of partners. The number of partners a man has varies with his rank and importance, a commoner may have few partners whereas a chief would have hundreds of them.

4. Interpersonal relationship. "Two Kula partners have to Kula with one another, and exchange other gifts incidentally; they behave as friends, and have a number of mutual duties and obligations, which vary with the distance between their villages and with their reciprocal status."[9]

The rules of partnership lead to the following cumulative effects :

(i) In the Kula ring there is a network of relationships, interwoven together.

(ii) Objects given by one in time travel some very long distance and reach the direct partner or someone else.

(iii) In the long run, not only objects of material culture but also customs, songs and general cultural influences travel along the Kula route.

5. Definite rules of transaction. Every man has to obey definite rules as to the geographical direction of his transactions. He constantly passes the arm-shells from left to right, and the necklaces from right to left.

---

8. *Ibid.*, p. 86.

9. *Ibid.*, p. 91.

6. Circular exchange. In Kula one finds a circular exchange or a ring or circuit of moving articles. According to Malinowski, "On this ring, all the villages are placed in a definitely fixed position with regard to one another, so that one moves always on either the arm-shell or on the necklace side of the other."[10]

7. No back-trading. According to another rule,. the arm-shells and shell-strings always travel in their own respective directions on the ring and they are never, under any circumstances, traded back in the wrong directions.

8. Non-stop exchange. The exchange of Kula articles never stops. A man who is in the Kula never keeps any article for longer than a year or two.

9. Influence of personal power. Success in Kula is ascribed to special personal power, due mainly to magic, and men are very proud of it.

10. Community consciousness. The whole community glories in a specially fine Kula trophy, obtained by one of its members.

11. Nature of individual transaction in Kula. The individual transaction in Kula is based upon the following regulations and principles :

(i) *Ceremonial gift.* Kula means the bestowing of a ceremonial gift. This gift has to be repaid by an equivalent counter-gift after a lapse of time which may be from few hours to as much as a year. This exchange of gifts is based upon decorum and not upon the principle of barter.

(ii) *No enforcement.* According to Malinowski, "The second very important principle is that the equivalence of the counter-gift is left to the giver, and it cannot be enforced by any kind of coercion."[11] The exchange is governed by social consciousness and social code.

(iii) *Noblesse oblige.* According to the rule known as *noblesse oblige*, the noble members such as chiefs are under obligation to make exchange according to their status. More and more generosity is expected from the members comparable to their high status.

(iv) *No primitive communism.* Malinowski rejects the idea of primitive communism of savages. He is also against the diametrically opposed idea of the acquisitive and ruthlessly tenacious native. According to him the savage is as much normal as the civilized man.

(v) *No actual haggling.* In Kula transactions there is no actual haggling nor a tendency to do a man out of his share. The giver is quite as keen as the receiver that the gift should be generous. A man who is fair and generous in the Kula will attract a larger stream to himself than a mean one.

The above principles, according to Malinowski, can be summarized into two main principles. In his own words, "The two main principles, namely, first that the Kula is a gift repaid after an interval of time by a counter-gift, and not

10. *Ibid.*, p. 93.

11. *Ibid.*, p. 96.

a bartering; and second, that the equivalent rests with the giver, and cannot be enforced, nor can there be any haggling or going back on the exchange — these underlie all the transactions."[12]

ASSOCIATED ACTIVITIES AND SECONDARY ASPECTS

The Kula is associated with preliminary and secondary activities. This precedence is implied in the institution itself. The preliminary activities are intimately associated with the Kula. These include, the building of canoes, preparation of the outfit, the provisioning of the expedition, the fixing of dates and social organization of the enterprise. The secondary activity is trade.

The secondary trade includes the following activities :

1. While some of the things are carried to be given away as presents, a good deal is carried in order to pay for the objects desired at home.

2. Big Kula centres are not efficient in any of the industries of special value. The necessary goods are procured by minor trading expeditions.

PRIMARY NATURE OF KULA

Order of precedence in Kula activities shows its primary nature as follows :

1. The dates are fixed, the preliminaries settled, the expeditions arranged, and the social organization is determined with regard to Kula.

2. The big ceremonial feast held at the start, refers to the Kula.

3. The final ceremony of reckoning and counting the spoils refers to Kula.

4. The magic refers only to the Kula.

5. Where Kula is practised, it governs all the other allied activities.

6. The primary nature of Kula is expressed both by the working of all the arrangements as well as by the behaviour and explicit statement of the natives.

KULA AND MAGIC

The institution of Kula is intimately associated with magic. This is clear by the following facts :

1. Belief in magic. The belief in the efficiency of magic dominates the Kula, as it does in so many other tribal activities of the natives.

2. Magical rites. Magical rites must be performed over the seagoing canoe when it is built, in order to make it swift, steady and safe.

3. Soliciting Luck. Magic is performed over a canoe to make it lucky in the Kula.

4. Averting dangers. Another system of magical rites is performed in order to avert the dangers of sailing.

12. *Ibid.*, p. 98.

5. Overseas expeditions. Kula magic is connected with overseas expeditions. It consists in numerous rites and spells, all of which act directly on the mind of one's partner, and make him soft, unsteady in mind, and eager to give Kula gifts.

Kula Community

According to Malinowski, "A Kula community consists of a village or a number of villages, who go out together on big overseas expeditions, and who act as a body in the Kula transactions, perform their magic in common, have common leaders, and have the same outer and inner social sphere, within which they exchange their valuables."[13] The Kula community consists of the following :

1. It consists of the small, internal transactions within a Kula community or contiguous communities.

2. It consists of the big overseas expeditions in which the exchange of articles takes place between two communities divided by sea.

Thus, the Kula trade involves trade within the district, inter-district trade and overseas expeditions. There is a permanent trickling of articles within the village and from one village to another. But in overseas trade a whole lot of valuables are exchanged.

13. *Ibid.*, p. 103.

20

Primitive Social Organization

In the words of Elliott and Merrill. "Social organization is a state of being, a condition, in which the various institutions, in a society are functioning in accordance with their recognized or implied purposes."[1] According to M.E. Jones, "Social organization is a system by which the parts of society are related to each other and to the whole society in a meaningful way."[2] The essentials of social organization, as mentioned in these two definitions are equally available in primitive as well as civilized societies. According to Ralph Piddington, "The most important bases of social organisation are sex, age, kinship, locality, social status, political power, occupation, religion and magic, totemism and voluntary associations."[3] These factors are particularly observed in primitive social structure. However, distinctions may be observed in different primitive societies about these traits.

M.J. Herskovits[4] has classified the social classes into those based upon kinship and those not connected with kinship system. In the primitive society the family is the unit of social organization. Most of the needs of males and females are fulfilled in the family. These families again, may be of different types such as nuclear family, joint family, matriarchal and patriarchal family, etc. After the family, the next unit of the social organization is the clan. Clan is the group of people considering themselves descending from a common ancestor. Like family, the clan is also based upon kinship organization. Besides the clan, the primitive social organization includes what is known as phratry and dual organization, etc. Again, another important part of primitive social organization is totem groups based upon totemism. Totemism is the belief according to which members of a clan are related to some natural object, tree, plant or animal in some supernatural way. Therefore, the members of the clan express similar faith towards the object of totem. This commonness increases

1. Elliott and Merrill, *Social Disorganization*, Harper & Bros., New York, 1950, p. 4.
2. M.E. Jones, *Basic Sociological Principles*, Ginn and Col, New York, 1949, p. 195.
3. Ralph Piddington, *An Introduction to Social Anthropology*, Oliver and Boyd, London, 1952, pp. 107-108.
4. M.J. Herskovits, *Man and His Works*, New York, 1956, p. 289.

the "we consciousness" among the members of a clan. In social organization the main elements are status and role, class system and other institutions and associations.

STATUS AND ROLE IN PRIMITIVE SOCIETY

A social organization is constituted by human beings having different status and role. The status of an individual is achieved by his sex, age, birth, physical traits, marriage and family, etc. Each status is connected with corresponding role. Every individual has to fulfil roles peculiar to his status in society. In primitive society, particular roles are connected with the status of the chief and the priest, etc. The males and females have different status on the basis of sex distinctions. Some statuses are ascribed while others are achieved. The former are hereditary while the latter are acquired. The following bases of distinctions of the status and role may be observed in primitive societies.

1. Sex distinctions. The sex distinctions found in almost every society can be primarily explained on the basis of biological distinctions. However, These distinctions are also cultural. Biologically, the status of the female is generally lower than that of the male. She is generally always thought to be in need of protection. This is equally true of the developed societies as the Hindus as well as the primitive tribes. Again, in primitive societies the status of women is lower as compared to that of men, in the context of religion and magic. For example in the Toda tribe of Nilgiri the women are not allowed to visit dairies since they ale thought to be impure due to menstruation. On the other hand, it is precisely on the basis of religion and magic that the status of women is higher than that of men. For example, among Khasi tribe the status of women is higher. Some tribes have a status in between these two extremes. For example, among the Andamanese both the males and females have almost equal status in matters concerning religion and magic. The roles of different sexes are particularly evolved on the biological basis. Besides, every society and culture allots separate functions to both the sexes. According to Whiteman, in the Pueblo tribe, while the roles of males are cooperative, the roles of females are competitive. While the males carry on agriculture, hunting, weaving, woodcutting, etc. the women are concerned with house-keeping, cooking, child rearing, etc. According to Powermaker, in the Lasu tribe the division of labour on the basis of sex distinctions is strictly observed. While the male cannot do anything worthy of a female, the same is also true about restrictions on the male roles for the females. The roles of the males are generally connected with gardening, fishing, hunting, tool-making, house-building, etc.; the roles of females are concerned with agriculture and household affairs. Then there are some functions such as basket weaving, child care, magic and medicine etc. which are jointly carried on by members of both the sexes. As a rule one may observe a universal pattern of the role distinctions mentioned above. However, in some societies the women carry on functions peculiar to men in other societies and *vice-versa*.

Among such exceptional societies may be counted the Khasi tribe of Assam in which while the males carry on child rearing, cooking, and housekeeping, etc., the females are busy with the outdoor functions. In Navaho tribe blanket weaving is the function of women while the same has been entrusted to men in Hopi tribe. Among Maricopa Indians pottery is the function of the female while weaving is a male job. In spite of some exceptional societies having a reversal of roles based upon sex, most of the human organizations depict a universal pattern of the roles based upon sex distinctions. Murdock,[5] studied some 224 societies and concluded that while hunting is the male job, the females are entrusted with cooking, gathering fuel, pottery, weaving, etc. While 86 per cent fishing and 85 per cent animal husbandry is entrusted to males, the rest is done by the females. The reason of this universal pattern is the biological fact that hard jobs are more suitable to males while delicate jobs are suitable to females. Within these biological limits, there may be minor distinctions concerning roles due to culture.

2. Age distinctions. In almost every society one may observe distinctions of roles according to age. The children and the old people are almost everywhere given only delicate jobs or kept free. Their status correspondingly, is lower than that of the adolescent, the youth and the middle-aged person. It may be that in some societies children may be particularly cared but this hardly makes any change in their status. According to L. Simmons, generally in all societies the status increases with age. However, it will be wrong to think that this is purely due to physical maturity. Age is respected as experience and knowledge generally increases with age. Therefore, it is not the age but the experience and knowledge which are the cause of higher status of the aged persons. For example, among the Gond tribe the aged people are respected due to their capacity for guidance and advice in different fields. In most of the primitive tribes the government, religion, magic and economic organization is dominated by the aged people since they are concerned with matters which are generally above the understanding of children and youth. Children are nowhere permitted to indulge in matters concerning religion and magic since it may lead to annoyance of the supernatural powers resulting in huge losses to the whole community.

Among the aged people the aged males have a status higher than the aged females. The reason of this distinction is that the roles peculiar to males carry more power. For example, males are generally concerned with outdoor functions involving politics, government, religion, magic and economic organization. Therefore, it is natural that their status should be higher than that of females generally working indoors. In indoor life, however, the status of the aged female may be higher than that of the aged male.

The above pattern of respect connected with age may be observed among those primitive societies where the struggle for existence is not very harsh. On

5. G.P. Murdock, "Comparative Data on the Division of Labour by Sex", *Social Forces*, Vol. 15, 1937, pp. 551-553.

the other hand, if this struggle is harsh, the aged are sometimes considered to be burden. For example, among Eskimo people some persons almost kill their parents since they are not economically useful but burdens to the family. Due to the feeling of unproductivity and helplessness, the aged people in this tribe themselves urge their children that they may be killed. In some other tribes the aged people are kept under such natural circumstances where they die automatically. According to anthropologists this custom does not show lack of respect towards the aged people. Among Indian tribes generally the status of aged people is high. They make significant contributions to administration. Administration is generally conducted in terms of clans, of which each has a clan chief. The clan chief has a council of the elders as an advisory body. In Australia, administration is known as the rule of the elders or gerontocracy.

3. Property distinction. Property and wealth constitute almost a universal status symbol. It is the most important factor ensuring higher status. However, the concept of property and wealth differs in different societies. For example, minerals and petroleum are not as much valuable in a primitive society as in an industrial society. Similarly, while animals may be wealth in a particular society, in a different society they may not be so. In ancient times, the number of slaves was a measurement of wealth. However, this type of wealth is no more witnessed anywhere. Wealth and property provide a higher status not only due to their capacity to afford consumption but also due to the capacity of sacrifice which they make possible. In some tribes, a person may achieve a higher status only when he sacrifices his property. Such custom may be observed among so many Indian tribes. Among American Indians those persons are given higher status who have lots of food and dresses and houses and can also liberally distribute them among others. In primitive societies emphasis is not on collection of wealth but its distribution. In some tribes even the food is eaten after proper distribution. A strange custom known as potlatch is found in Kwakiutl tribe of North-West coast of North America, in which there is a competition for destroying wealth, or exhorbitant spending which correspondingly adds to social prestige. Thus, it is clear that property and wealth are the bases of a higher status in primitive societies. However, this higher status depends upon liberal donation and distribution to others.

PRIMITIVE CLASS SYSTEM

In the words of E. A. Hoebel, "A social class is a group within a society, whose members hold a number of distinctive statuses in common who, through the operation of the roles associated with these statuses, develop an awareness of their like interests as against the unlike traits and interests of other groups."[6] The class system depends upon the stage of culture. The higher the stage of culture and the more complex it is the more class distinctions will be observed in it. This class distinction is not so clearly seen in primitive societies. The

6. Hobel, E.A., *Man in the Primitive World*, New York, 1958, p. 415.

reason for this is that there is not much difference in the economic, social and political matters of the primitive societies. The natural resources are available to everyone and the political power is not very much defined. There is hardly a question of surplus wealth or property. According to Grinnall, one may find a rudimentary form of class system among plains Indians of America. Some distinction based upon economic classes may be observed in western Apache people. In some other tribes one may observe three or four professional classes such as the warriors, the artisans, the priests and the laymen. On the West Coast of America the Indians can be distinguished as free people and slaves. The slaves serve their masters. The free men have all the rights over the slaves. In some Mexico tribes one may find two or more classes. No significant class distinction can be observed among Chenchu and Kamar tribes in India. However, class distinction is clear among Gonds and Bhils. And yet there is hardly much class consciousness among primitive people nor is class the basis of social tensions and rivalries. Like other social factors, the class system is found in its most rudimentary form in primitive societies.

INDIAN TRIBAL SOCIAL STRATIFICATION

The Indian tribes constitute an important part of Indian society, though their social organization and social institutions are very much different from those of the Hindus and Muslims. The Indian tribes have been divided into the following classes :

1. North-eastern aboriginals. These tribes are found in Assam, Tripura and Manipur. Their number totals around 21,00,000. They belong to the Mongol race and their language resembles the languages of Austric family. The important tribes in this class are the Kukis, Nagas, the Mikirs, etc.

2. Central aboriginals. These tribes live in Vindhyachal, Satpura, Kekal and Aravali mountains. The important among these are Gonds of Madhya Pradesh, Bhils of Rajasthan, Santhals of Chota Nagpur, Ho of Singhbhum and Manbhum, Khond and Kharia of Orissa, Sawara of Ganjam and the Mundas. This class of Indian aboriginals is the largest in number. The number of Santhals alone is about 25,00,000. Most of these aboriginals are engaged in shifting cultivation Some are engaged in small scale cottage industries. Some of these live in very dense forests and difficult terrain of mountains. They lead a very primitive type of life away from the civilized world.

3. Southern aboriginals. These are the tribes of South India. The most ancient tribes in India are found in Kerala, of which the maximum number is that of Kadar. Other important tribes in this class are the Todas of Nilgiri, Chenchu of Hyderabad and the Kanikar and Kurovan of Travancore Cochin. In some of these tribes there is matriarchal type of social organization and matrilineal type of family.

Besides the above mentioned main classes of Indian aboriginals, tribes are found in Andaman and Nicobar, Northern Himalayas, the districts of Chamba and Mahasu, Dehra Dun and Darjeeling. About the variety of Indian tribes it has been rightly said, "A geographical survey of India reveals distinct cultural and social regions with marked differences in the type of habitations, social institutions and psychological traits of population." Some of the Indian tribes, such as the Nagas and Santhals, are absolutely isolated from civilization.

Spatial Groups

Tribal social stratification is constituted of spatial groups. Spatial groups are those which are constituted because of spatial contiguity of their members. Such are the clan or sib, tribe and band, etc.

Clan or Sib

The clan or sib is an important part of the tribal organization. It is only an extensive form of lineage constituted of blood relations. A clan is constituted by including all the relatives of either the mother's or the father's lineage and all the offspring of one ancestor, in such a lineage. In this way, many lineages constitute a clan. The clan emanates from some major biblical or imagined ancestor of the family. Being prominent and respected this ancestor is accepted as its founder. All the lineal descendants of the family are introduced by his name. A clan is never constituted by combining the lineages of both the mother and the father. It is invariably unilateral. Its descendants are of either matrilineal or patrilineal lineage. Thus, in brief, a clan is that collection of unilateral families whose members believe themselves to be the common descendants of a real or mythical ancestor. It is that exogamous combination of unilateral families whose members are related by some common ties. The following characteristics of the clan are evident from its foregone definition.

1. Exogamous group. The clan is an exogamous group since all the members of a clan believe themselves to have descended from a common ansestor. Consequently, they do not marry any member of their clan. Marriage is contracted only out of the circle of one's own clan.

2. Common ancestor. As has been already pointed out, the organization of the clan is based on the conception of a common ancestor. This ancestor may be real or mythical.

3. Unilateral. The nature of the clan is unilateral, *viz.*, in one clan there is either the collection of all families on the mother's side or of all the families on the father's side.

Types of Clan

According to its unilateral nature, the clan may be of two types :

1. Matrilineal clan. In this all the offspring of one woman are held to be members of one clan. At the same time the sisters and brothers of the woman are also members of this clan. In this way a matrilineal clan includes a woman, her offspring, her sisters and their children. But it does not include the children of the brothers.

2. Patrilineal clan. In this clan are included a man, his children, his brothers and sisters and the children of the brothers but not of the sisters.

Clans have different names based on different grounds. The main grounds among them are the following :

1. Seers. Clans are named after the names of seers, for example, Shandilya, Bharadwaj, etc.

2. Totem. Clans are named after the names of the totem such as Kunjam, Naagsori, etc.

3. Substitute names. Clans are named on the basis of substitute names such as Kamar, Jagat, etc.

4. Topography. Clans are named on the basis of some topography, for example, Mahanadiya, Jaunpuriya, etc.

Functions of Clan

The main functions of the clan are as follows:

1. Mutual assistance and protection. The members of a clan possess a 'we feeling' because of their belief in descent from a common ancestor. They are prepared not merely to assist one another but even to lay down their lives for each other. When one member of the clan is injured all the members share his pain. Two sayings are prevalent among them. (i) "Strike my clan brother and you strike me", and (ii) "The blood of the clan is my blood."

2. Control over members. Individuals indulging in anti-social acts are extradited from the clan. In this way, the conduct of clan members is controlled. Extradition from the clan proves more effective and disastrous than even a death sentence for the member.

3. Legal function. It is the universal legal function of the clan to punish miscreants and maintain peace and order in this manner.

4. Exogamy. With the help of the law of exogamy the clan arranges marriages from outside the group. This, on the one hand, avoids conflicts between men for a woman within the clan and on the other serves to increase cordiality and friendship with the members of other clans.

5. Governmental Functions. The clan performs all the governmental (administrative) functions for its members. The heads of the various clans meet and form a committee for the tribe which serves to mediate in the conflicts between clan members and takes political decisions in war and peace time.

6. Property. In the villages where agriculture is carried on it is the clan which arranges for agricultural land. The head of the clan distributes the land. When a person is deprived of the membership of the clan he is also deprived of this land. Members can only rent the land.

In addition to the above-mentioned functions, the clan also caters to the religious preferences of its members. Generally, the head of the clan is also its priest. It is he who consummates the religious undertakings of all the members.

Distinctions Between Clan and Caste

Clan and caste differ from each other in the following respects :

1. Clan is a well-organized group based on a mythical ancestor. Caste is a real, actual, organized group.

2. Clan is an exogamous and caste an endogamous group. Members of the clan marry outside the clan. Members of the caste cannot marry outside the caste.

3. In the clan individuals possess the same status. In the caste individuals possess higher and lower social status.

Distinctions between Clan and Tribe

The clan and tribe are different and distinct from each other on the following counts :

1. A clan has no definite topographical area whereas members of a tribe generally live in a definite geographical location.

2. A clan has no definite language while the tribe has a common language.

3. A clan is an exogamous group. A member of a clan cannot wed a member of his own clan. The tribe is commonly an endogamous group, although, with increasing contact among neighbouring tribes consequent upon an increase in the means of transportation, the tribe has now lost much of its endogamous character.

Tribe

According to *The Imperial Gazetteer of India*, "A tribe is a collection of families bearing a common name, speaking a common dialect, occupying or professing to occupy a common territory and is not usually endogamous, though originally it might have been so." Defining the tribe in *The Dictionary of Sociology*, George Peter Murdock has stated that it is a social group in which there are many clans, nomadic bands, villages or other sub-groups which usually have a definite geographical area, a separate language, a singular and distinct culture and either a common political organization or at least a feeling of common determination against strangers. According to Bogardus, "The tribal group was based on the need for protection, on its blood relationships and on the strength of a common religion." According to another view, two essential elements of tribe are a common dialect and a common topography. In short, the tribe is a group of persons having a common definite territory, common dialect, common name, common religion and a common culture, in whom there is a blood relationship and consequently a feeling of unity, who have a peculiar political organization and who generally marry within their own group. To quote D. N. Majumdar, "A tribe is a collection of families or groups of families bearing a common name, members of which occupy the same territory, speak the same language and observe certain taboos regarding marriage, profession or occupation and have developed a well assessed system of reciprocity and mutuality of obligations."

Characteristics of the Tribe

The following characteristics of the tribe are evident from its various definitions :

1. Definite common topography. The tribe inhabits and remains within a definite and common topography. In the absence of a common topography the tribe would also lose its other characteristic features as community sentiments, common language, etc. For this reason a common habitat is essential for a tribe.

2. Consciousness of unity. But a group of people living in a particular geographical area cannot be called a tribe as long as its members do not possess a consciousness of mutual unity. This psychological element is an invariable and essential characteristic of the tribe.

3. Common language. The members of a tribe speak a common language. This also helps to generate and evolve a sense of communal unity among them.

4. Endogamous group. The members of a tribe generally marry into their own group but due to increased contact with other tribes, the consequence of an increase in the means of transportation, the system of marrying within the tribe is also changing.

5. Ties of blood relationships. A major cause of the sense of communal unity in the tribe is the tie of blood relationship between its members. The members of the tribe have faith in their having descended from a common, real or mythical ancestor and hence believe in blood relationship with other members.

6. Experience of need For protection. The members of a tribe very much experience the need for protection. Keeping this need in view, a political organization of the tribe is established and all authority for administration is vested in one person. This leader employs his mental power and skill in protecting the entire tribe. A tribal committee is formed to render assistance in the form of advice to the tribal chief. As a general rule, the tribal chief accedes to the wishes of the committee. The tribe is divided into numerous small groups each of which has its own chief. These chiefs solve the problems of their own groups and act according to the directives of the tribe.

7. Political organization. In this way each tribe has its own political organization which maintains harmony and avoids notes of discord among its members and protects them.

8. Importance of religion. Religion is of great importance in the tribe. The tribal political and social organization is based on religion because social and political laws become inviolable once they are granted religious sanctity and recognition. In the form of ancestor worship, tribal religion has rendered important service in developing the habits of obedience. The authority of a common religion is an important characteristic of the tribe.

9. Common name. The tribe has a common name.

10. Common culture. Resulting from a feeling of unity, common language, common religion, common political organization, etc., a common culture is found to exist in a tribe.

11. Organization of clans. A tribe is constituted of many clans. There exist laws of mutual reciprocity among its members.

Distinctions between Tribe and Horde

A nomadic horde is a group of a small number of people. When the members of the nomadic horde increase to a very sizable figure it is christened a tribe. A very strong community feeling exists in both horde and tribe which differ from each other mainly in respect of size. In both, such economic activities as collection of fruit, animal hunting, animal husbandry, fishing, etc., are carried on. In both, a similarity of blood relationships is to be found. In both, there is a conglomeration of families. The chief of the group is well respected and obeyed in both. In spite of such a great extent of similarity, the horde and the tribe differ from each other in the following respects :

1. In the tribal group the need for protection stands out more prominently, as compared to the horde.

2. The tribe is bigger in size than the nomadic horde.

3. In the tribe, religion is more developed than in the horde because in the former a greater solidarity and strength of political and social laws is to be expected.

4. Being of large and more cumbersome size the tribe possesses a weaker sense of unity than does the horde.

5. Tribe is divided into many smaller groups but the horde has no such sub-divisions.

6. Agricultural occupation is an accepted mode of life in the tribe whereas in the horde agriculture is not indulged into any large extent.

7. The tribe inhabits a definite locality. On the other hand, instead of staying at a definite place the horde wanders over a definite geographical area.

Distinction between Tribe and Caste

Marriage within the clan is forbidden both in the tribe as well as in the caste. Both generally condemn marriage outside the group. The modern development in the means of transport and communications has induced increased contact between members of various tribes and has weakened the laws of endogamy in both. The two do exhibit considerable similarity, yet they also differ in the following respects :

1. According to Risley the convention of endogamy is not rigidly enforced in the tribe whereas such is the case in a caste. But this view of Risley does

not appear to be universally true since the law of endogamy is enforced with extreme rigidity in some tribes.

2. Max Weber writes in *Social Structures* that when an Indian tribe loses its territorial significance it assumes the form of an Indian caste. In this way, the tribe is a local group whereas the caste is a social group.

3. The caste was originated, in ancient Hindu society, with a view to division of labour on the basis of profession and occupations. The tribe came about because of the evolution of community feeling in a group inhabiting a definite geographical area.

4. According to D. N. Majumdar the tribe looks upon Hindu ritualism as foreign and extra-religious even though indulging in it and in the worship of gods and goddesses whereas in the caste these are necessary parts of religion. The tribes of Madhya Bharat which are called Hindu and Kshatriya tribes are better acquainted with their own 'Bonga' than with the Hindu gods.

5. According to Max Weber the status of all people is similar in the caste, whereas there is much difference of status and rank in the tribe. This view of Max Weber does not apply to all castes. Differences of rank and status can be found in many castes also.

6. There is greater consciousness of differences in status and rank in the caste than in the tribe.

7. The caste is never a political association whereas the tribe is a political association.

8. The names of clans in castes are adopted from some saint or mystical savant, such a Vashishtha, Vishvamitra, Bharadwaj, Kashyap, etc. In the tribe the clans are based on totem, for example the clans in the Komti tribe of Mysore are named after all kinds of fruits, vegetables, spices, foodgrains, etc. The list presented by Thurston in *Castes and Tribes of Southern India* seems to indicate that hardly any name in the animal and vegetable world remains to be used as the basis for a totem name.

9. In the caste, individuals generally pursue their own definite occupations because functions are divided under the caste system. In the tribe, individuals can indulge their fancies in whatever profession they please because there is no fixed relation between them and the occupations.

Actually, now the tribes are gradually being converted into castes. Risley has mentioned four processes in this transformation : (1) By changing one's lineage. (2) By accepting the principles of any school of Hindu religion. (3) By joining Hindu religion. (4) By entering into relations with Hindus without changing name.

According to D. N. Majumdar a tribe can enter Hindu society by adopting clan and name of a caste.

As a result of these changes, the differences between tribe and caste are being continually reduced.

21

Kinship

Kinship Terms

In every society and culture, there are certain fixed terms to designate kin of various types. For example, among Hindus, wife's sister is called *sali* and her brother is designated by the term *sala*. Morgan has divided these kinship terms into two categories : (1) Classificatory, and (2) Descriptive.

1. Classificatory kinship terms. Classificatory designations apply to more than one relation or to a kin group. For example, among Kuki clans, the term 'Hepu' is used for father's father, mother's father; mother's brother; wife's father; mother's brother's son; wife's brother and wife's brother's son. In the same way, among Kerdjari clans, father, father's brother and grandfather's brother are all designated by the single term 'Tablu'.

A difficulty arises here. When more than one relation is designated by a single term, will it not cause some difficulty? Some arrangement or the other is therefore made regarding designations of this type, so that a specified person may be separated from the group. For example, in Hindu society, the name of the person is also added for a distinction among relations of different types as Kailash *mama*, Ramu *chacha*, etc. If the person designated is present, mere looking at him serves the purpose. According to Malinowski, the tone of speaking also indicates the specific person of a designated group. Besides these three modes, the name of consanguinity, group or place is sometimes added to create a distinction among different relations of one group, as *chachi* of Meerut, *bua* of Agra, *tau* of Bombay, etc.

2. Descriptive kinship terms. In comparison to classificatory kinship terms, descriptive kinship terms are those which describe the speaker's exact relation with the person addressed. For example, 'uncle' is a classificatory term, whereas 'father' is a descriptive term. Nowhere in the world and in no society, classificatory or descriptive kinship terms are used exclusively. Descriptive kinship terms are more in use in civilized societies, while classificatory kinship terms are more in use in primitive societies. For example, the term '*Aja*' is used for mother, for father's brother's wife and for mother's sister among Naga people of Assam. In the same way, father, father's brothers, sister's husband are all called '*Apa*'. The term '*Ami*' is used for father's sister, wife's mother, husband's mother and husband's brother's wife. Among Kuki clans, father's father, mother's father, mother's brother's wife's father, mother's brother's sons, wife's brothers and the sons of wife's brother are all called by the term '*Hepu*'. Among Angami Nagas, elder brother, elder sister's husband, wife's elder sister, husband's elder brother, elder brother's wife, mother's brother's wife and father's brother's wife are all designated by a single term '*Shi*'.

Significance of Kinship Terms

W.R.H. Rivers has said, while describing the importance of kinship terms, that they refer to those social functions for which they are used. For example, among Indian tribes, the term '*mama*' is significant of the social functions of the person designated by this term. Many other scholars have given other interpretations of the significance of kinship terms besides that of Rivers. According to some anthropologists, classificatory terms are used because of certain similarities found among the group of people who are designated by those terms. According to Kroeber, names of kinship terms are given to people only to distinguish them from one another and there is no deep significance in them. According to D.N. Majumdar, only one term is used for many persons or kins because vocabulary in primitive societies is not much evolved and therefore there are no separate terms to show those persons or kins separately. All the interpretations given above, about kinship terms, may be true to some extent. The use of classificatory terms may be the outcome of one thing or the other. It may be due to an undeveloped language, to a similarity among the group of individuals or to some social functions of the group.

What is Kinship?

While defining kinship, Charles Winick has written in *The Dictionary of Anthropology*, "Kinship system may include socially recognized relationship based on supposed as well as actual geneological ties." In this way, kinship included not only the descendants but also all those persons who are tied together by social relations. Levy Strauss has therefore called it an arbitrary system of ideas. Adopted sons and daughters are also regarded as kin, although they have no blood-relation of any kind.

In defining kinship, D. N. Majumdar has said, "In all societies people are bound together in groups by various kinds of bonds. The most universal and the most basic of these bonds is that which is based on reproduction, an inherent human drive, and is called kinship." The desire to have children gives birth to two kinds of bonds. One is husband and wife and the bond among their kins; the other is father and mother and a bond among their children. The first kind of bond is created by social and legal definition of marriage and is therefore called affinal kinship and the individuals connected to it can be called affinal kins having no blood relation among them. The second kind of bond is that of blood relation found in parents and their children and even among sisters and brothers.

Kinds of Kinship

From the above discussion, it is clear that there are two kinds of kinship which are given below :

1. Affinal kinship. It includes wife and husband and their new relations resulting from that marital relation. The kinship is the result of marriage.

2. Consanguinous kinship. It includes the parents and their children, of a biological origin or adopted. Among primitive societies, if the role of a father in the birth of a child is unknown, the wife's husband is accepted as father of that child.

According to the range of kinship, it can be divided into the following three categories :

1. Primary kinship. It includes wife and husband, parents and their children who are directly related to one another.

2. Secondary kinship. It includes those kins who are related to the primary kin of an individual, such as a step-mother, brother-in-law and sister-in-law.

3. Tertiary kinship. It includes the primary kins of the secondary kinship. The order of kinship established mutual behaviour patterns in a society like the joking relationship between a man and his wife's sisters and brothers.

Hoebel's View

Hoebel has also defined a family group. According to him a family group is a wide and one-sided group comprising a common ancestor and his successors having blood ties and it does not last for more than five or six generations. In this way, a family group is a group of successors of one and the same ancestor. In a modern family, members of both the families, father's family and mother's family, are included in a family group. It has therefore been called a bilateral grouping. But. as has been said before, family groups in primitive societies are one-sided. Their groups may be matrilineal and also patrilineal.

1. Matrilineal kinships. In this, a family group starts from a female ancestress. Children of a brother are excluded from the family but the children of a sister are included in the family group. This family group is found in a matrilineal system.

2. Patrilineal kinship. In our society, we have a family group of this type. In this, the children of a sister are excluded from the family and the children of a brother are included in one and the same family. In counting the lineage of a family unit, father's father and his father are counted. On the other hand, in a materilineal family, mother's mother and her mother alone are counted.

Beside the matrilineal and patrilineal kinships, cognate kinships and collateral kinships are also found. Cognates are those who make a lineage from father to a son in a straight line. When other relations, like uncle and nephew, maternal uncle and his sons, are included in considering the lineage of a family, they are called collaterals as they are not in a straight line.

Parallel Cousins

All the father's brother's children and father's sister's children, mother's brother's children and mother's sister's children are included among parallel cousins. Parallel cousins are of two kinds :

1. Cross cousins. These include the children of father's sisters and the children of mother's brothers. In Gond, Kharia, Kadar, Oraon, Khas and some other primitive tribes of India, marriages among parallel cousins are allowed. But such marriages are allowed in certain circumstances or on certain conditions.

2. Parallel cousins. They include all the cousin sisters and brothers as mentioned above and marriages among them are allowed in certain circumstances.

Mother Sib

Persons of the mother's various generations are known as mother sibs. Among matrilineal societies the idea of mother sib was prominent. The conception of consanguinity prevailed only after the establishment of a patrilineal society. Morgan has regarded the idea of mother sib to be more antique than the idea of consanguinity from the point of view of evolution. Siblings were considered to belong to one and the same blood and matrimony among them was prohibited. Manu has written that only that girl should be selected for marriage who happens to be neither mother sib nor consanguineous. But this prohibition gradually lost its force and marriage began to be arranged between mother sibs.

Avunculate

Among the natives of Trobriand, an archipelago, a boy leaves the house of his father at the age of ten years and begins to live in the maternal uncle's family where he gets education and helps his maternal uncle in his work. The maternal uncle also looks after his nephew. The same custom is prevalent among the primitive tribes known as Heda living in the north-west of America. According to this custom, the boy accepts the religion, magic and property, etc. of his maternal uncle. This system is called Avunculate. Among Hopi and Zuni people, the son lives in the house of his father upto the marriageable age, but it is his maternal uncle who is responsible to arrange his marriage rites. This system of Avunculate is found only among matrilineal societies. But there are some examples of this system among partilineal societies also. The system of Avunculate is also found among Khasi and Toda matrilineal societies in India.

22

Family

What is the family? To know this, it is necessary to know the various definitions given by different sociologists who have defined the family differently, according to their individual viewpoint. Some of the major definitions are :

1. *Biesanz and Biesanz.* "The family may be described as a woman with a child, and a man to look after them." In common parlance people sometimes interpret the word family to mean a wife but it is evident from this definition that in sociology the child is an indispensable part of the family.

2. *MacIver and Page.* "The family is a group defined by a sex-relationship sufficiently precise and enduring to provide for the procreation and upbringing of children." In this way a temporary alliance between a man and woman for sexual gratification cannot be said to constitute a family. In order to constitute a family the sex relationship should necessarily be permanent and definite enough to allow for the procreation of children and to allow for an appropriate arrangement for their upbringing.

3. *Clare.* "By family we mean a system of relationships existing between parents and children." In this way, the family is a system of relationship, as a part of society. The family does not mean a place or location but it is a web of mutual relations between the family members in the same way in which the meaning of society lies not in its being a group of human beings but in being a web of relations between them.

Essential Characteristics of Family

Some idea of the essential characteristics of a family must have been evident by a perusal of these various definitions. The essential characteristics of the family are the following :

1. Permanent relations between husband and wife. The family is constituted of the husband and wife and their children. Thus, a permanent relation of some kind between man and woman is the main characteristic of the family. Marital relations in different countries may be more or less permanent, but the relations between man and woman have some degree of permanence in all cultures. Without this, neither can the children be brought up nor can there be any family. Even in societies where polygamy and polyandry are customary the husband-wife relationship does possess some kind of permanence.

2. Permanent sexual relationship. The family rests on permanent marital relations because one more object of it is the establishment of permanent sexual relationships. Without marriage there can be no family even though there may be several relations. When the marital relations break up, as in case of divorce, the family disintegrates. Proper upbringing of children can be expected only when there are permanent conjugal relations.

3. Attachment of blood relations. Another necessary characteristic of the family is the existence of blood relationships among the members. These blood relationships can be real as well as imaginary. The members of the family are generally the descendants of the same ancestors. The relation between adopted children and their parents is accepted as legal but blood relationships mean no more than that, among the members of family, there should exist an attachment of the degree of blood relationships. It is generally believed to be necessary that there should exist no blood relationship between husband and wife.

4. Financial provisions for the subsistence of the members. In a family there is financial provision for the upkeep of its members, old folk, children, women folk, etc. The earning members of the family arrange for the sustenance of the other members. In this way, the members of the family are enmeshed in the ties of duties and rights. In different cultures the burden of earning may fall on different members. At some places the women go out to work while the men do the domestic chores but the principle that there should be provision in the family for the sustenance of its members is accepted almost everywhere.

5. Common habitation. If the members of a family reside at different places, it would be difficult to call them a family in spite of there being blood and other relationships. It is a different matter for a member to leave temporarily or for the entire family to change its habitat but generally all the members of a family live in one residence be it one room or an entire place rented or the ancestral home of the family. Among the nomadic people also the members of one family stay together at one place.

6. Nomenclature. Among the essential characteristics of the family is a distinct nomenclature which serves to identify the family.

In this way, the family is a group of individuals in which men and women have the permanent sex relations of husband and wife, which is distinguished by a name, in which there is adequate financial provision for the sustenance of its members, in which there is the attachment of blood relations among the members and who live in a common habitat.

IS THE FAMILY REALLY UNIVERSAL ?

Family is the first institution in the history of man. In the ancient age men lived in small families, which lacked any kind of organization or permanence. But they served to fulfil simple biological and psychological needs. Generally, the family consisted of husband and wife and their offspring. The powerful men possessed many wives and thus they lived in big families with their wives and children. When man became oriented to agriculture, many families formed a group and stayed permanently at some place for farming. When these people started partaking of each other's pain and happiness as neighbourly gestures, social relations increased and in this way many families formed a community and the next step was the creation of nation. In this way, family as the primary group slowly evolved into human nations.

Family is a fundamental unit of human society. Its foundations rest upon man's biological and psychological needs. In the modern age, many functions of the family have shifted to other institutions but nevertheless, there are many biological and psychological needs which man cannot satiate without family. Havelock Ellis, in his penetrative essays, has shown that the importance of a mother's milk for the child cannot be obtained in any other manner. Psychologists have proved that the absence of family affection has a serious impact upon the child's development. Sexual passions can be satisfied even outside the family but it can never be the source of emotional fulfilment. That "man is a social animal" implies that man cannot live without a family. Thus, family is a fundamental unit of society.

Family Has a Nuclear Situation

The family has a nuclear situation in human society. In primitive societies the entire organization is based on the family units while the division of labour in society is also based on the family. In the complex structure which is society today, the family has lost some of its importance, but even today the activities of most members are of the family or contiguous to it. It is seen that people work and labour more for the comfort of their wives, children and other members of family than even for personal comforts. Thus, even now the family is the nucleus of a major part of man's activities.

Proper Organization of Society Depends upon Family

Proper social organization depends upon proper organization of families. If the families disintegrate in some society, then the society will never be safe. One major cause of social disorganization is family disorganization. Families develop the characters of the members of society. Freud and other psychologists have proved that a child, when a man, exhibits the same character and mental tendencies which he acquires in the family. In the opinion of Adler, a man's role in the family determines his role in society.

Family Socializes the Individual

In this way a person is socialized in the family. Defining family, Merrill writes, "Family is an enduring association of parent and offspring whose primary functions are the socialization of the child and the satisfaction of the members." According to Dewey and Tufts the family is a social agency for the education and protection of the race. It is in the family that the child acquires such important qualities as sincerity, sympathy, self-submission and realizing responsibility, etc. It is the character developed in the family which helps the child in becoming an important and responsible member of society. Wright was quite correct in stating that in every family, the child gets an opportunity for free expression of thoughts and developing his entire personality. Psychologists have incontestably proved that the proper development of the child is impossible without a good environment in the family. The tendencies and habits which he acquires in the family, he finds impossible to shed later on. According to Freud, the viewpoint of a child towards the senior in the family determines his attitude and viewpoint towards the elders in society. The child's first school is his home and family. According to Prof. R.G. Collingwood, the child's education should be in the hands of the parents in the family. The parents should participate in all the child's activities. A child learns much by imitating his superiors. Mahatma Gandhi and some other thinkers paid personal attention to the development of their children. It is the family which imparts practical education to the child concerning the customs in society, conduct, other important elements of culture, preservation of health, love, sympathy, cooperation, etc.

It is evident from the above account that the family is the primary and fundamental unit. Confucius remarked quite correctly that if you want to improve society improve its families. Society will improve automatically when the families improve.

Family is the Conveyer of Traditions

The family moulds the character and personality of the individual. It is through the family that society imparts its culture to the individual. Thus, the family is very important in the form of a socializing agency. In the essay, *The Family Conveyance of Tradition*, Paul Schreker wrote that a particular function of the family is to sanction children. Like marriage, the institution of family is constituted by different elements of culture. It is due to this reason that it has religious, judicial, political, artistic and linguistic aspects. Whenever a new thought impresses itself upon an age, the family takes a new form from it in order that the upbringing and mental tendencies may be harmonious to that thought. Politics and law were dominant in Rome, so the family organization there was such as to ensure the upbringing of children in harmony with the culture. Today, the economic order is predominating. So the family has changed its form, it makes the mental tendencies concur with the new culture. In this way, the family makes the individual harmonious with the culture of society. In the family. the child acquires knowledge about the current customs, mores, traditions, etc.

Society Controls Individual through the Family

Social life is a web of relationships. In order to maintain these relations properly a system of rights and duties is organized which will avoid any conflict between the members of society and allow them to develop as complements to each other. In order to avoid any breach of this harmony between the individuals in society, the society applies numerous kinds of control on the individual. They are taught to obey the elders, have sympathy for the young and for others. A strict control over sex relationships is necessary for maintaining the social order, otherwise disintegration will spread over the complex social life of today. Relationships between men and women will lose their solidarity. Illegitimate children will be born with no one to look after them. Although the anthropologists Mead and Malinowski have discovered societies where control over sex relations is inordinately lax without disturbing the social order, such an order is completely contradictory to the thinking of today's cultured person. It is the family which does this work of controlling sex passions for society. In all cultures, the families exercise some degree of control over the unmarried members till they attain the matrimonial state. In the same way, the family acts as a preventive to the individual in keeping him from bad habits and crimes like drinking, theft, etc. Not many parents would like their children to embark on careers of crime. Even the worst person tries to prevent his children from adopting similar habits and consequently any objectionable behaviour on the part of children is punished and laudable effort suitably rewarded. They thus drop bad habits and learn good things. In this way, the making of a good citizen in society depends upon the parents.

In every society some values and ideals are regarded as high and signs of culture. Whichever person exhibits these in greater quality is respected in society. For example, Indian society treats religious and spiritual qualities as supreme and a person who is possessed of them is appropriately respected everywhere. Besides, in India, pre-marital and extra-marital sexual relations are controlled as a necessary measure. The responsibility of creating these high social values in the individual lies with the family. It is true that the character of every person is different from any other by nature but the family environment also has a big hand in forming them. Most of the famous religious persons of the world like Gandhi were deeply influenced by someone religious person in their respective families. In the making of great men the mothers have always had a major part to play. The differences in the ideals of people related to different cultures are born in their families.

The Individual Learns his Mother Tongue in the Family

In every society the culture, conduct and values are very strongly related to the language spoken. Literature is the mirror of culture in society and literature is based on language which plays by no means a mean part in man's socialization. The credit for the complex order of human society must go to man's linguistic superiority over other animals and the language one picks up in the family. Human children brought up by animals in the forest are seen to be completely ignorant of matters of language. They communicate their wishes by signs in animal language, walk on all fours, eat raw meat and exhibit the least signs of humanity. A child brought up in a human family grows into a human being. To go even further, a child developing in a cultured family is cultured while one brought up in baser circumstances is coarse. The child is first taught language in the family. This is his mother tongue through the medium of which he exchanges thoughts. If some Indian child is brought up in some English family, English will become its mother tongue. Thus, the major element in the child's socialization in the form of language comes to him in his mother's lap.

Besides the above mentioned elements, an individual receives a number of other things from his family. Not unusually, even the person's occupation in society is decided by his family. Even in the modern age many people carry on the paternal business and occupation for which they are trained in the family from the start. It is no uncommon occurrence that a jeweller's son shows interest in the same business from his infancy and becomes able very soon.

Thus, in brief, the family educates the individual in culture, conduct, behaviour, custom, tradition, religion, laws of thinking, ideals, values, occupations, obedience of duties and proper use of authority, etc. It would be no exaggeration to say that the family is the most important institution in man's moral development.

FUNCTIONS OF THE FAMILY

Classification of the Functions of Family

Different sociologists have classified the functions of family differently. Ogburn and Nimkoff have divided family functions into six categories: (i) Affectional function, (ii) Economic function, (iii) Recreational function, (iv) Protective function, (v) Religious function, and (vi) Educational function.

Groves classified family functions in the following manner :

(i) Protection and care of the young; (ii) Regulation and control of sex impulses; (iii) Conservation and transmission of the social heritage; and (iv) Provision of opportunity for the most intimate contacts.

Reed has attributed the following functions to family : (i) Race perpetuation. (ii) Socialization, (iii) Regulation and satisfaction of sex needs, (iv) Economic functions.

Major Functions of the Family

From the foregoing classifications of family functions it is evident that the main functions of the family are of two types :

(i) Basic and universal, and (ii) Traditional.

Basic and Universal Functions of the Family

The following are the basic and universal functions :

1. Biological functions. The most fundamental biological functions are :

(a) *Reproduction.* According to the Hindu *Shastras* procreation is the main function of the family. Commentators on the Hindu *Shastras* have written that the religious activities of man cannot be consummated unless he has a son and he cannot repay his ancestral debt. He has to suffer in hell if he has no son. In almost all societies of the world barren women are the objects of scorn and derision. And in some societies marriage ability is attributed only to a woman who gives evidence of her fertility by conceiving a child before marriage. Hindu *Shastras* permit a second marriage if there is no issue from the first wife. The woman conceives a child from another man through 'niyoga' if her husband is impotent or otherwise incapable of procreation. In most human societies of the world the child is believed to be the nucleus of the family. Procreation perpetuates the family. It increases the population of the country. Some Hindu thinkers have considered reproduction to be the sole aim of marriage. In the rituals of Hindu marriage the groom says to his bride, "I accept you in order to obtain good offspring."

(b) *Procuring of food, housing and clothing.* Food, housing and clothing are indispensable to the existence of human life. A major biological function of the family is the procuring of these amenities for its members. The earning members of the family provide food and clothing for all the rest. Every family has a house to live in and the food for the family members is generally cooked at home.

2. Psychological function. The second fundamental and universal function of the family is psychological. Ogburn has included affectional functions in the necessary or vital functions of the family. According to Groves, it is the function of the family to provide opportunities for the establishment of intimate relations. Burgess and Locke have written, "Mutual affection is becoming the essential basis of marriage and the family." The individual receives affection, sympathy, love and psychological security in the family. The relations between man and woman in the family are not exclusively physical. Profound conjugal affection for each other is generated in husband and wife by working together in the family and by sharing each other's joys and sorrows. An all-round development of the individual is not possible in the absence of family love. The family has an important part especially in the development of the child's personality. Ralph Linton has written that merely the satisfaction of bodily needs is not sufficient for the proper development of the infant. Children are in greater need of individual attention, love and satisfaction of response.

3. Satisfaction of sexual needs. The fundamental function of the family, according to Reed, is to regulate and gratify sexual needs. Manu accepts sexual satisfaction besides reproduction as the aim of family. Vatsyayan also looks upon sexual satisfaction as the primary objective of the family. In the modern age, the fulfilment of sexual needs is one of the primary functions of the family. When sexual needs remain unsatisfied in the family it starts disintegrating. To quote Havelock Ellis. "With failure of sexual harmony, the marriage structure rests on shifting sands."

4. Protection and care of the young. According to Groves the protection and care of children is one necessary function of the family. The human child is the most helpless and weak being. A family is needed in order to maintain its existence and to ensure its coordinated and balanced development. Its balanced development is achieved with difficulty without the care of the parents and other family members.

Traditional Functions of the Family

The following are the traditional functions of the family :

1. Economic functions. The family performs many economic functions also, some of which are as follows :

(i) *Division of labour.* The work is divided among the members of the family according to their status and role. The male members generally do the work which means out of door movement. The women generally take care of the domestic chores while the children undertake only such work as can assist in their development. While this division of labour prevents putting excessive burden on the shoulders of one individual it ensures the systematic performance of the family activities. All people undertake responsibility and work co-operatively.

(ii) *Arrangement of income.* Money is needed for such of the family requirements as food, clothes, habitation, etc. The family is the centre of economic activities, consumption, etc. The family makes arrangements for an income in an effort to fulfil the needs of the family members.

(iii) *Organization and care of property.* Most families possess some property in the form of a house, farm, jewellery, money, etc. The family looks after this property and in case such a contingency arises it also equitably distributes it among the members. The family is the judge of what property an individual shall receive, and who shall look after the property and how, and other important questions.

2. Social functions. The social functions of the family are important since the family is the fundamental and primary unit of society. The following among many social functions deserve mention :

(i) *To establish status.* An important function of the family is the determination of an individual's status in the society. The modes of earning wealth of an individual are also generally determined by the family.

(ii) *Socialization.* The family imparts learning to the individual on all those subjects whereby he can become an ideal member of society. It carries out the socialization of the individual. It acquaints him with the various modes of conduct in eating, conversing, coexisting, etc.

(iii) *Social control.* Another function of the family is to exercise social control over the individual. The prevalent moral norms are enforced upon the individuals and their conduct and thoughts are controlled so that the order in society may remain intact. In the family, the anti-social tendencies of the individual are watched.

(iv) *The accumulation and transmission of social heritage.* The family keeps the social heritage intact and hands it over to the generations to come. As a result, the social traditions, customs and ideals, etc., are transmitted continuously from one generation to the next.

(v) *Assistance in the choice of a life partner:* The family renders assistance to the individual in his choice of a life partner. Although in the modern age, people have started preferring personal choice of a life partner yet in India even now in most cases the choice of the bride or the groom is still the province of the other family members.

3. Religious functions. In. the Hindu *Shastras* family life has been considered the basis of the fulfilment of religious duties. The *Shastras* prescribe the wife as essential in the fulfilment of duty. The literal meaning of the Hindi equivalent of the word 'wife' means the woman who accompanies the man in the performance of the religious rituals, which were considered incomplete in the absence of the wife. Besides this, the performance of religious activities also demanded the presence of a son. Thus, in the ancient Hindu system the main function of the family was the fulfilment of duty. Living in the family the members fulfilled their religious duties. Now, the religious activities of the family have been materially reduced.

4. Cultural functions. The family keeps the culture of society alive. It moulds its members according to the social culture. The children are educated in the various aspects of culture from their infancy. The family creates such an environment for them that they learn to live and to behave in accordance with their culture. The older members of the family impart education in matters of conduct, thinking, religion and ethics, etc. to the children.

5. Recreational functions. The family provides entertainment for its members. The love between husband and wife, the halting utterances of the children, the scoldings and preaching of the elders and other such occurrences serve to create an atmosphere in which everyone can find an object which can interest him or her.

ORIGIN OF FAMILY

Family, as an institution, is to be found even in the most primitive of human societies in the world. Since the earliest time in human history the family, too, has been constantly known. Thus, the family is perpetual. There can be no question of its having originated. In the words of MacIver and Page, "The family has no origin in this sense that there ever existed a stage of human life from which the family was absent or another stage in which it emerged." Yet there is much controversy and difference of opinion with regard to the question of the origin of the family. Some of the important theories in this connection are as follows :

1. Theory of sex communism. According to some sociologists, in ancient times, any man or woman could establish sexual relations with any other man or woman. There was no restriction whatever on sexual relations. Such a stage is called the stage of sex communism. In order to prove this theory, the support of such customs of ancient tribes is invoked which make it appear that in ancient times control over sexual relationships amounted to nothing. Many customs of this kind have been noticed by anthropologists studying occasions of festivity. Presenting wives and daughters to a guest for sexual gratification as a sign of hospitality, and exchange of women etc., have been found practised in many ancient tribes. In many ancient tribes the father of the offspring is not ascertained. But in spite of extreme variety of restricting customs concerning the establishment of sex relationships, incest has been forbidden in almost all tribes. Hence, the theory of sex communism does not appear to be tenable.

2. Patriarchal theory. In ancient times it was Aristotle and Plato who supported the patriarchal theory, while among its modern proponents, Sir Henry Maine is notable. According to this theory, the family in its most ancient form was patriarchal in which the father was the most powerful and the unquestionable authority. In Rome, he was empowered to the extent of sentencing his sons to death. He was called the patriarch.

This theory is defective in as much that it, too, cannot be applied to human societies because in many societies the mother instead of the father, was the supreme authority.

3. Matriarchal theory. Hence, on the other hand, some people propounded the matriarchal theory of the origin of the family. Briffault had supported this theory in his book *The Mothers*. He has written that in ancient societies people were not aware that the offspring had any relation with paternity. And in societies which practise promiscuity there is no knowledge of who the father is. But the mother is known definitely everywhere. Consequently, it seems more reasonable to believe that the ancient family was matriarchal. The patriarchal family originated in these matriarchal families. The importance of the father increased with the progress of civilization and the development of agriculture.

The matriarchal theory was as much one-sided as the patriarchal theory because in different human societies one finds families of both kinds. MacIver has written that in the tribal societies existing today, it is the patriarchal family which is to be seen. Hence, Briffault's theory of the origination of the patriarchal from the matriarchal family does not find universal application.

4. Theory of monogamy. Westermarck has propounded the theory of monogamy in his book, *History of Human Marriage*. Among its supporters are Darwin, Zuckerman and Malinowski. According to Darwin, the family originated in the male's feeling of ownership and jealousy. In ancient society the powerful male wanted to possess individual ownership of the female and he succeeded in his design by virtue of his physical prowess. Later on, this right of the male was normally accepted in society. Zuckerman and Malinowski with Westermarck, agree to and support the fact that the same custom is found in semi-human societies and also among the apes who are believed to be man's ancestors.

According to MacIver, the monogamic theory does not offer a complete explanation of origin of the family. It cannot be accepted that the family originated in this manner everywhere.

5. Evolutionary theory. The American sociologist Morgan has put forward the evolutionary theory of the family. According to him the family has passed through the following five stages :

(1) Consanguine family. In this stage of the family marriage between blood relations was not forbidden.

(2) Punaluant family. Evolving further, the next stage saw the imposition of restrictions on incestuous marriage and the family group arrived at the stage of the punaluant family. In this stage brothers of one family marry all the sisters of another family. Even in this stage sex relationships among themselves were not definite.

(3) Syndasmian family. In this stage one man married one woman but the sex relationships of the women married into the family were defined and certain.

(4) Patriarchal family. In this stage man's ascendancy and dominance in the family had fully blossomed. He could marry many women and have sexual relationships with them.

(5) Monogamous family. This is the present stage of the family. In this, one man can marry only one woman at one time and one woman, too, can marry only one man at one time.

Evolution in the institution of family can be believed but what cannot be believed is the same sequence of stages in evolution of the family in all societies. Thus, Morgan's theory does not appear to be correct in its practical form. Besides, there is no reason for believing the stage of monogamous family to be the ultimate stage of the family. Actually, historical facts do not bear out Morgan's theory. Morgan's theory is hypothetical.

6. Multiple factor theory. According to many contemporary sociologists, the sequence of the evolution of family has been different in different societies. In the words of Ralph Linton, "Societies have not followed a single consistent line of evolution but a multitude of diverging lines." In this way modern sociologists accept the multiple factor theory of the origin of the family. MacIver and Page have written, "Rather a complex of human desires and conscious needs, finding different expressions in different environments, everywhere gave birth to some kind of family system." In this way, many factors conspired in the origin of the family.

According to MacIver, the various factors in the origin of the family can be divided into three groups :

1. Sex. This is a fundamental or innate tendency in man. The family originated in the need for permanent means of its satisfaction and gratification.

2. Reproduction. The family originated in the strong desire for reproduction and the need for a permanent co-operation between man and woman for the nourishment of the offspring.

3. Economic organization. From the economic viewpoint women and children depend upon the male. Consequently, a permanent institution of family was required.

Actually, it is difficult to make definite assertions with regard to the truth of and the factors in the origin of an institution as complex and as human as the family. The subject must be considered from a more comprehensive and more sympathetic viewpoint.

FORMS OF FAMILY

Many forms of the family have been described, on the basis of different viewpoints in sociology. Many distinctions in family have been based upon nature of residence, name of ancestry, power, dominance or mother or father, etc.

1. Distinctions of family according to the nature of residence. The following distinctions of family are made according to the nature of residence : (i) *Matrilocal residence.* In this kind of a family the husband goes and lives in the home of the wife.

(ii) *Patrilocal residence.* In this kind of a family the wife goes and lives in the home of her husband. Now-a-days most families conform to this type.

(iii) *Changing residence.* At some places it is customary for the husband and wife to alternate continuously between each other's residences. One year the husband lives with the wife and the next year the wife lives with the husband.

2. Distinctions of family on the basis of ancestry. The forms of the family are also classified on the basis of traditional ancestry. The main forms are :

(i) *Matrilineal families.* In these the mother is the basis of ancestry. The woman is believed to be the prime ancestor of the family. Ancestral tradition and inheritance are affected through the mother. The rights of each member of the family depend on his relation to the mother, hence they are also known as the mother right families.

(ii) *Patrilineal families.* In these families the ancestor of the family is the man and traditional ancestry continues through the father. Now-a-days this type of family is the most common.

3. Distinctions of family on the basis of authority : (i) *Matriarchal families.* In these the mother wields the authority. According to MacIver and Page, the actual administrative power is in masculine hands even in societies where the womenfolk are rulers. Hence, in their opinion the word matriarchal is misleading and should be replaced by the word maternal. Matriarchal families are to be found in the Nayar and Thiya castes of Kerala and Khasi and Garo tribes of Assam in India.

(ii) *Patriarchal families.* In these the entire authority is in the hands of the father. In ancient Rome and Greece the patriarch used to be the absolute ruler.

4. Other distinctions of family. The following distinctions of family are based on the dominance of the mother or the father in the family :

(i) *Matronymic.* In these the name of the family or ancestry is in the name of the mother, such as Gautami, Saumitra. etc.

(ii) *Patronymic.* In these the family is named after the father, Warner has accepted the following two distinctions of family :

(a) *Family of orientation.* In which the individual is born.

(b) *Family of procreation.* In which the individual marries and procreates.

Some other distinctions of family are the following :

(i) *Immediate family.* This consists only of the mother, father and their children.

(ii) *Conjugal family.* In it the husband and wife live and sexual relations exist between them.

(iii) *Extended family.* In this, besides the wife and husband other relatives also live.

(iv) *Consanguine family.* In this live only those who are related by blood, such as brother, sister, father, son, etc. In the Nayar families of Malabar, the husband does not conduct his wife to his house after marriage and the daughter, though married, remains in her father's house.

5. Distinctions of family on the basis of marriage. On the basis of marriage also many distinctions of family have been made. The major forms among them are :

(i) *Polygamous or polygynous family.* In this one man marries many women and lives in a family with his wife and children.

(ii) *Polyandrous family.* In this one woman marries many men and lives in a family with all of them or with each of them alternatively.

(iii) *Monogamous family.* In this one man marries only one woman and establishes a family.

ASPECTS OF FAMILY

Religion and Family

In ancient India, a life of domesticity was regarded as the basis for the fulfilment of duty. The name '*patni*' implies that woman who accompanies the man in the performance of his religious duties. According to the Hindu *Shastras* no man can complete religious activities without a wife. Even today it is in the family that the individual is educated regarding religious customs and functions. The important work of imparting elementary religious education to the members of society was everywhere the responsibility of the family. But now the relation of religion to the family has weakened and has been much reduced since now-a-days the interest in religion is declining, and in addition to this religion is looked upon as a private affair in which the family need not interfere.

Family from the Economic Viewpoint

Family is the centre of economic activities. It is the family which utilizes the production of society. Sometimes the entire family jointly pursues an occupation. Agriculture, especially, is an occupation which is pursued jointly by the entire family and in it the men do the work of plantation, irrigation and sowing, the women that of cutting the crop while the children take over light work such as grazing the herds of animals. Inheritance also stems from the family. The family protects property, makes arrangements for an adequate income and endeavours to fulfil the needs of the members. It is the family which provides the support for the old, disabled, unemployed and helpless.

Family from the Government Viewpoint

In the ancient Roman family, the head had all the authority of the absolute ruler vested in him. In the Roman law it was prescribed that the father could put his sons into jail, sell them and execute them. In this way, in ancient times the right of administration was the possession of the *Pater Familia*. Now-a-days the family no longer possesses such unbridled authority to punish the individual. Only the state has authority to sentence a person to imprisonment or death. Nevertheless the family does much to assist the state in running the government machinery. It exercises control over the conduct of the individuals and prevents them from indulging in anti-social activity. The government consequently finds it easier to maintain order. The family inculcates in the child the habit of discipline from the very beginning. The family presents to the child an environment which enables him to become a successful citizen in the future. In the absence of training of this kind the child grows up to become obstinate and criminal.

In this way, although the importance of the family from the viewpoints of religion, economy and the government has waned, it still is an important social institution. In all these spheres it assists other agents.

SOME INDIAN PRIMITIVE FAMILIES

Indian primitive families are mostly patriarchal. However, some examples of matriarchal families may also be found. In patriarchal family, the eldest male is the head, he is generally incharge of almost all the activities. His decisions are binding. He holds all the economic and social power. Every one has to obey his command. He presides over the social and religious ceremonies. The bride lives in the house of her husband and occasionally visits her parental home.

The social status of the husband is generally considered to be higher than that of wife, though the latter is not ill-treated. The situation in the matriarchal family is almost opposite of the above arrangement. In such a family the most aged woman is the head. She takes all decisions and presides over social and religious ceremonies. She commands the purse including her husband's income. Such a family is generally matrilocal. The husband, after marriage, resides in the house of his wife. Though the division of labour among sexes in patriarchal and matriarchal families is not much different, the status of woman in the latter is certainly higher than that of the male. Here we will discuss the Kharia family and the Ho family as examples of patriarchal, patrilineal and patrilocal families. The Khasi are the examples of matriarchal, matrilineal and matrilocal families.

The Kharia Family

This tribe lives in various hill ranges of Orissa adjacent to Chota Nagpur and also in Chota Nagpur itself. Family is the elementary unit of society in all the primitive societies in the West and the East. The Kharia is no exception to this rule. The Kharia family includes parents and children, own or adopted, and the son-in-law if he has chosen to reside in the home of his father-in-law. The authority is vested in the father. The descent of lineage is traced through the father. He is the master of all the property along with his sons. In some sections of this tribe joint families are found. The joint family includes the grand parents, uncles, cousins and nephews living in the same family house. Such joint families are, however, rather the exception than the rule. Most of the young men set up their own huts after marriage and live separately with their wives and children. The wife lives in the house of her husband. She occasionally visits her parental home. The family is generally monogamous though polygamy is not unknown.

The maternal uncle enjoys a special status in a Kharia family. This is generally found in the matrilineal societies. Its existence in the Kharia family shows that formerly the tribes must have been matriarchal. The maternal uncle plays an important role in exercising social control in the family.

Every primitive family aims at the satisfaction of bio-psychic drives, fundamental among which are hunger and sex. The family is contracted with an aim to perpetuate the species through reproduction. From the cultural point of view the family is the conveyer of the tribal culture from generation to generation. Economically, the family aims at the provision of food, clothing and shelter to the members. It preserves language, customs, mores and folkways. It is a link between the individual and the clan. It is an instrument of social control and education of the young. All these characteristic aims of primitive family may be found among the Kharia.

The primitive family exhibits an ideal division of labour among male and female. Both contribute to the maintenance of family. Their functions, however, differ due to obvious physical and biological limitations. Generally, the husband goes out for hunting game and fishing. The wife collects fruits, tubers and edible herbs. She draws water and cooks food. Houses are big, constructed and repaired both by male and female in cooperation. While the male builds the house, the female maintains it. Generally among primitive societies one finds a superstitious fear of menstruation. Women are considered to be impure during the period of menstruation. They are also supposed to be possessed by spirits during this period. Therefore, they are generally forbidden to participate in agricultural and other professional activities. Among cattle rearing tribes, women are forbidden to carry on activities concerning cattle rearing. This, however, does not mean any disability on the part of the women. They are considered to be important, responsible and independent members of the family. Child rearing is almost everywhere the sole responsibility of the women. All these characteristic traits of the economic aspect of primitive family are applicable to the Kharia family. A Kharia woman is not absolutely deprived of all property rights, though most of the property belongs to the male. Her personal effects like dress and ornaments are considered her personal property.

Besides the suitable status of the women, the children are also generally treated well in primitive family. They constitute an important part of the family, irrespective of their sex. Their early education is generally entrusted to their mothers. The later education in the case of the daughters, is given by the mothers, while in the case of sons it is given by the fathers. Besides the fathers, sometimes professional education is imparted to the youth by other male members of the tribe. Thus, Kharia family is an example of healthy and harmonious family relationship. In it each member has been allotted a suitable role and a more or less equal status in the family life.

The Ho Family

The Ho tribe lives in Singhbhum, in Bihar and the adjacent district. The conglomeration of Ho families is known as Kolhan. This is a government estate which is administered by the district magistrate through the heads of the tribal organisation. The Kolhan consists of clans known as killi, as units. Each killi is composed of so many families. Thus, the social organisation of a Kolhan is constituted by several killi and that of the killi by the families. In this social organisation while some functions are performed by the killi, others are entrusted to the family. The killi has a panchayat together with a sarpanch, which takes decisions in communal matters. The worship of gods and spirits, the performance of sacrifices, the observance of feasts and festivals, the ceremonies connected with marriage and death are generally entrusted to the killi since they are considered as having communal importance. The family performs functions concerning food, clothing, house, health and illness, family worship and other interpersonal matters. It consists of a man, his wife and their children. However, joint families are also found, consisting of brothers and agnates, their spouses and children. A large number of unmarried girls may be seen in a Ho family since bride price is higher and it is difficult for the parents to marry off their daughters early. The status of the male and female is almost equal though it is undeniable that the high bride price makes the status of the daughter lower than that of the son.

The Khasi Family

The Khasi tribe is found in the Khasi and Jaintia hill districts of Assam. They present an exceptional example of matriarchal society, rarely found in the present day world, anywhere else. They are matrilineal and matrilocal. They trace their descent from a mythical female ancestress. The most aged female is the head of the family. Thus, the family includes a mother, her male and female children, and her husband, sometimes her married daughters and their husbands. This is due to the fact that the Khasi marriage is matrilocal. After the marriage the bridegroom lives in the house of the bride and seldom visits his own parental home. However, if a husband can support his wife and children he is allowed to establish a house independent of his in-laws home. Most of the earnings are joint and administered by the head woman. Men have no individual right to ownership. Thus, husbands and sons have no property rights. All property is inherited by women from women. Thus, the daughter inherits the property of the mother. The role of the male, therefore, is not dominant but subordinate in social and religious matters. It is understandable since the male lives in the house of his wife's parents. It is believed that the youngest daughter holds the religion and therefore she is given the major share of parental property. In the absence of a daughter, some girl is adopted for this purpose. Thus, women enjoy high status and power. However, hard jobs like those of agriculture and other professional functions are carried on by the male. Weaving is carried on by the females. Both sexes earn money by working as porters. The women have the property rights, authority, etc. in social and religious matters. This does not mean that the husbands are not respected or loved. They also exercise some authority. The Khasi woman, though all powerful, addresses her husband as her lord.

The above examples of patrilocal and matrilocal form of Indian primitive families show that they are based upon healthy traditions and reciprocal relationships among male and female. Though the male generally dominates the family, the status of tribal woman cannot be considered as lower, particularly in comparison to her cultured sisters in civilized societies. Most of the tribal families are self-sufficient and well-to-do. However, in those areas where civilized traders have encroached their areas, their economic condition has worsened. At some places one finds prevalence of bonded labour. It is necessary that tribal societies are left free in their natural surroundings without much interference from the civilized man. If they are allowed to carry on their social institutions, unhindered and without pressure, their family lives even today may be suitably contrasted with those of any cilvilized society in the world.

23

Marriage

Ever since male and female came in each other's contact some biological and psychological reasons led to their mutual attraction and finally their intimate contact. Attraction of male and female is a biological and a psychological phenomenon. Psychologically, as well as biologically their traits and tendencies are mutually complementary. Biologically, their mating is necessary for procreation and sexual satisfaction. Hence, whenever male and female come in contact in a society there is mutual attraction, exchange, companionship, romance, recreation, friendship, mutual help, etc. Most of the males are always prepared to risk their lives to save a damsel in distress.

What is Marriage?

This male-female relationship, however, is not marriage. Marriage is a social contract for the satisfaction of physical, biological, psychological and spiritual needs of male and female leading to the formation of a family to bring up children and live together. Sexual relationship and procreation are undoubtedly the primary aims of marriage. Marriage validates sex relationships. All this is clear from the following well known definitions of marriage. Of these the last definition is the best and most integral since it covers the civil, religious, social, economic and biological purposes of marriage.

1. *Westermarck.* "As a relation of one or more men to one or more women which is recognized by custom or law, and involves certain rights and duties both in the case of the parties entering the union and in the case of the children born of it."[1]

2. *Jacobs and Stern.* "Marriage is a term for social relationship of husband and wife or of plural mates; also used for the ceremony of uniting marital partners."

3. *Robert H. Lowie.* "Marriage denotes those unequivocally sanctioned unions which persist beyond sensual satisfactions and thus come to underline family life."

1. Westermark, *The History of Human Marriage*, Vol. I. p. 26.

4. *Majumdar D. N. and T. N. Madan.* "It involves the social sanction generally in the form of civil and/or religious ceremony authorizing two persons of opposite sexes to engage in sexual and other consequent and correlated socio-economic relations with one another."

This definition of marriage lays emphasis upon its following characteristics :

(i) It is a result of civil or religious ceremony.

(ii) It is a means of contact of persons of opposite sex.

(iii) In it the male and female get the right of mutual relationship in economic, social and biological spheres.

The above definition of marriage can be summed up by saying, "Marriage is a more or less permanent association of one or more male with one or more female for the purpose of giving sociai sanction to progeny, satisfaction of biological and social needs and fulfilment of *dharma.*" This wide-based definition of marriage covers this institution as it is found among Hindus, Muslims, Christians and tribals in India.

EVOLUTION OF THE INSTITUTION OF MARRIAGE

According to social anthropologists, sociologists and historians the institution of marriage in human society gradually evolved to its present stage starting from promiscuous relationship between male and female. In this stage of promiscuity the male-female relationships were unrestrained and without control. According to the anthropologist Lewis Morgan, one finds exchange of wives, giving wives on loan and other such customs in very ancient primitive tribes which had no institution of marriage. Since there was no restriction upon sex relationships, the father was not much important in the family and most of the progeny was known by the mother. These findings of Morgan are more logical than historical. Morgan has pointed out that the institution of marriage evolved through several stages. Of these the most important stages are as follows :

1. Consanguinous marriage. This was the first stage in the marriage institution. In this stage there was the prevalence of endogamy among blood-relations.

2. Group-marriage. The next stage in the evolution of marriage was known as that of group-marriage. As is clear by the name, in this system several brothers married several women as a group among whom the sexual relationships were not defined. However, there was restriction upon sex relationship with persons of other group.

3. Syndesmian marriage. The third stage in the evolution of marriage was the pairing of the male and female which however was only temporary and not controlled by any rules and regulations. This pairing could be broken by mere desire of anyone.

4. Patriarchal marriage. In this stage a male could marry several females who would live separately from each other. The custom is known as hypergamy and polygamy.

AIMS OF MARRIAGE

The above mentioned definition of marriage clarifies its aim. The most important aims of marriage can be explained as follows :

1. Biological aim. The most important aim of marriage is biological or the satisfaction of biological needs. Sex is a natural biological need of males and females. The satisfaction of this need however leads to child birth. The human child is helpless when born and requires care for several years. Therefore, some sort of permanent institution is required for care of the human children. Hence, biological needs in human society do not function in a vacuum. It cannot be left entirely to the personal whims of males and females. At least it involves one other person from the other sex whose welfare and satisfaction is equally important. Therefore, the satisfaction of biological needs cannot be considered as the only aim of marriage. However, it cannot be denied that this is the most important aim. Young men and women enter into matrimony at least in part due to the biological need. It is hence that lack of fulfilment or consummation of sexual function leads to dissolution of marriage in almost all human societies. In spite of the availability of every other type of satisfaction and comforts, the impotence of the husband or the frigidity of the wife are generally considered as sufficient basis for divorce. Therefore, no one can deny that biological aim is the primary aim of marriage.

2. Social aim. Begetting and bringing up children is both biological as well as social function of marriage. Men naturally want to multiply. Women naturally crave tor children. Therefore, the urge to beget children and to bring them up is partly a biological need. At the same time it is also a social need since social status and communication very much depend upon the children. In India, for example, while in some tribes prestige is attached with the son, in other tribes the birth of a daughter is more welcome. In both the cases the craving for the birth of a son or a daughter is partly due to social needs. The most important function of the progeny is the continuation of the family and the lineage. Another important social function is the extension of the bonds of kinship. Yet another social function is the continuation of the cultural heritage of the society. Besides, there are some fringe social benefits to a married person, denied to a bachelor such as social respectability, easy communicability, social facilitation and more reliability in social relationship.

3. Economic aim. In primitive societies, particularly, marriage has an economic aim. In societies where the main occupation is agriculture, women are useful for light work such as sowing, etc. In such societies sometimes capable males marry several times to have several women as helping hands. Among some hill tribes polyandry is particularly due to economic reason. Due to poverty one male cannot maintain a female and therefore several males together marry a female. Due to economic reason again, the female is also anxious to marry several males to avoid economic insecurity. Among Kadar people children are welcome as providing more hands to earn a living. In most of the primitive societies the women have to bear almost equal burden in economic activities. One finds division of labour in economic activities among males and females. The economic functions of the male and female are not universally the same but both must share in economic functions.

Among the above mentioned aims of marriage different social anthropologists have given priority to different aims. George Peter Murdock studied aims of marriage in about 250 primitive societies and concluded that in human societies marriage is generally performed due to three aims : firstly, satisfaction of sexual desires, secondly economic cooperation and thirdly bringing up children. According to Murdock the first aim is not the only aim anywhere. In M.P. in India in some tribes sexual intercourse between males and females are permitted till the establishment of pregnancy. In Kuki tribe sexual intercourse is not a sufficient ground for marriage. In brief, in most of the primitive societies the aims of marriage are biological, social as well as economic. This is equally true of the primitive societies in the West as well as in India. The most important reason for this state of affairs is the hard struggle of life, lower economic status and undeveloped natural environment. Therefore, marriage is a union of the male and female not only to enjoy together but also to struggle together.

ORIGIN OF MARRIAGE

The theories about the origin of family are generally applicable to the origin of marriage as well. However, social anthropologists have sometimes separately discussed the origin of marriage and presented various theories. Most of the social anthropologists agree that the institution of marriage has gradually evolved in human societies, not only from primitive to civilized societies but also in primitive societies as well. According to Morgan, in the beginning there was no marriage institution among human beings. There was complete promiscuity and freedom in sex relationships. The theory of early promiscuity among human beings, however, has not been proved by sufficient evidence. Therefore, some other social anthropologists believe that some sort of marriage institution is always found in every human society. Evidence is available about the custom of group marriages in the primitive tribes of Brazil, Siberia and Australia, etc. However, in these societies also there is no evidence of early stage of promiscuity. Similarly, in some tribes on some occasions there may be some exchange of mates but it cannot be equated with absolute promiscuity in sex relationships. For example, even among the most primitive Indian tribes like Kadar, Pulayan, Chenchu, Birhor and the Andamanese, there is no evidence of promiscuity at any time.

However, in the evolution of marriage the stage of promiscuity appears to be sufficiently logical since everywhere human social institutions have started and evolved gradually. Therefore, in spite of lack of sufficient empirical evidence, it is natural to believe in the hypothetical possibility of early promiscuity in human societies. In fact where empirical evidence is impossible, the general laws of logic may be made the basis of suitable hypothesis. This principle is clearly in favour of the idea that the early human society must have been promiscuous. According to Morgan, from the stage of promiscuity, human society evolved to the stage of group marriages. In this stage all the brothers of a family used to marry all the sisters of another family so that every male was equally the husband of every female and *vice-versa*. Another stage in the evolution of marriage is usual monogamy with sufficient freedom to establish extra-marital relationship particularly with the female members of the bride's family. In the last stage of the evolution of marriage the male could marry more than one woman. Thus, according to Morgan the stage of monogamy precedes polygamy. Westermarck has however, vehemently opposed this view while Bachofen has supported Morgan. According to Bachofen, the early stage was promiscuous. As population increased, the means of subsistence became scarce and the numerical balance of males and females was disrupted due to killing of girls in some societies. This led to polyandry. The progress in agriculture led to the establishment of more prosperous agriculturist males permanently living at one place. They were encouraged to take recourse to polygamy. Condemning the above mentioned views Westermarck has maintained that only one type of marriage is available in animal and human societies and that is monogamy. Clearly, this is an extreme view particularly in the face of the findings of contemporary psychologists, sociologists and anthropologists about human nature.

In fact it is difficult to establish any theory in this field. However, some sort of evolution must be admitted.

AGE OF MARRIAGE

The question of age of marriage in primitive societies cannot be answered in terms of universal application. It depends on so many indigenous natural social and economic conditions. The age of marriage in primitive societies, however, is considerably lower as compared to the civilized societies. One may find boys and girls marrying at the time of puberty or adolescence in most of the primitive societies. The age of marriage is generally from 10 to 15 for the female and 12 to 18 for the male. Thus, it is much below the age of adulthood as prescribed in modern societies. Therefore, it can be said that quite a number of tribes practise child marriage. This, however, is also not true for a considerable number of other tribes, since the institution of youth dormitories has helped for providing a waiting period to the tribal male and female, to learn about married life for years before marriage and after attaining youth. In India for example, most of the tribes have the institution of youth dormitories. The young boys and girls live together in these dormitories and perform various functions together so that they may gradually mature in inter-sexual relationship before actually entering matrimony. In some tribes of Assam, for example Naga and Kuki, the average age of marriage is from 16 to 20 for the girl and 18 to 25 for the boys. This is not less in comparison with more civilized societies. In fact this is something which will be appreciated by the latest researches on the subject. Thus, it may be concluded, as has been said earlier, that there is no universal pattern about the age of marriage in primitive societies. However, child marriages as well as late marriages are rare and generally males and females enter matrimony after attaining youth and gathering some experience.

PROHIBITIONS REGARDING MARRIAGE

In every human society some sort of prohibitions are attached concerning selection of mates for marriage, considerably limiting its scope. The most universal prohibition regarding marriage is the marriage between blood relationships. The other prohibitions are known as preferential mating and the more generally prevalent customs of exogamy and endogamy.

Incest Taboo

Incest has been defined as the sexual transaction between blood relationships. Due to certain reasons this has been almost universally decried. The prohibition of sexual relationship between blood relations is known as incest regulation. Thus, in most of the societies sex relationship is prohibited between blood relations such as father and daughter, mother and son, brother and sister, etc. However, in some primitive societies exceptions to this rule are visible. For example, the Inca of Peru, and ancient Egyptians and the inhabitants of Hawaii Islands not only permit marriage among blood relations but also insist upon it to keep the family blood pure and free from contamination. This rule even in those societies was however confined to nobles, and not permitted to the commoners.

Thus, incest taboo is not universal. It is not based upon biological considerations. In fact it is impossible for the members of primitive tribe to imagine the adverse consequences of incest relationship. However, the prevalence of incest taboo in some societies has its own reasons of which the most important are as follows :

1. It is generally believed that since members of the family live together right from childhood to a considerably later age they cannot have sexual attraction towards each other. This, however, appears to be far from being true. In fact if sex attraction among close relatives is not natural, there is hardly any need of such severe prohibitions against incest. On the other hand, since these prohibitions have been prescribed in most of the societies and backed by severe punishment, it is more logical to think that there is some natural attraction between blood relatives. Sigmund Freud has referred to Oedipus complex, meaning love of the son for the mother and Electra complex involving love between father and daughter. Freud has insisted that these complexes are part of psychological mechanism of every human being. According to White, living

together increases rather than decreases sex attraction. Again, incest taboos are also applicable to those relatives who do not reside in the same family. For example, among Chiricahua and Apache people, incest taboos are prescribed about cousin brothers and sisters residing away from each other. In Navaho tribe incest taboo covers almost the entire clan. Kluckhohn has pointed out that in this tribe the male and female of a clan cannot dance holding each other.

2. Thus the causes of incest taboos are neither biological nor psychological. Linton[2] has pointed out that sexual intercourse and birth of children is in no way harmful from the biological point of view. Similarly, psychological causes cannot explain incest taboo as a universal phenomena.

3. Besides the biological and psychological explanations, incest taboos have been explained on the basis of social causes. According to Malinowski the restrictions are with the purpose of eliminating jealousy, conflict and competition over sexual affairs within the family. Thus, the prohibition is aimed at keeping the unity of family intact. Incest taboos were required to prevent familial and social disorganization.[3] This appears to be a plausible hypothesis since the primitive societies very much cared for maintaining the unity of the society at all cost. On the other hand this prohibition indirectly extended bonds of kinship since every time a male and a female had to find a marriage partner out of the family and sometimes out of the clan. This may decrease tensions between different tribes and encourage economic and social co-operation. Thus, it can be concluded that the incest taboos are primarily aimed at establishment of stable and co-operative families, free from discord and tensions. Their secondary aim must have been the social regulation of sex relationship, the extension of the boundaries of kinship relationships and the establishment of a unified family and society.

Preferential Marriage

Preferential marriage as is clear by the title, is the marriage custom in which some males or females are preferred for establishing matrimonial relationships. In such cases the marriage is a means for uniting two families for welfare of both. The preference is clearly based upon certain advantages concerning new relationships and adjustment and respect in the new family. The rules of preferential mating are however customary and not written. Preferential marriage may be seen in the following four forms :

1. Cross cousin marriage. In this type marriage between children or real brother and sister are preferred. The children among them are cross cousins. In India such marriages are prevalent in Kuki tribe of Manipur. Among Gonds this type of marriage is almost compulsory. According to Grigson, 54 per cent Gond marriages are of this type. Similar custom is prevalent in Kharia, Oraon,

2. Ralph Linton, *The Study of Man*, Appleton Century Crofts, New York, 1936, pp. 125-126.
3. Bronislaw Malinowski, "Culture", *Encyclopaedia of the Social Sciences*, The Macmillian Co., New York, 1930, Vol. IV, p. 630.

Khasi, Kadar tribes, the Mikir tribe of Assam and the Bhils of M. P. etc. In M. P. in some tribes this type of marriage is so much preferred that if it does not materialize, the other party has to pay compensation for it. Among Gonds, this custom is known as returning of the milk meaning that the bride price paid to a wife's family is returned by it. Thus, a person who marries in a family gives his daughter in marriage to that family so that the balance is restored.

2. Parellel cousin marriage. When the children of two brothers or sisters marry, it is known as parallel cousin marriage. In this sort of marriage the boy and girl are either children of some brothers or some sisters. Such marriages are prevalent among Muslims and sanctioned by their religion. It is, however, generally prohibited in Indian tribes. In Arabia such marriages are prevalent.

3. Levirate and sorrorate. Another type of preferential mating may be observed in the form of Levirate and sorrorate. In the former a man marries the sister of his wife after her death; in the latter a man marries the wife of his elder brother if she becomes a widow. This is known as junior levirate. It is however also possible between the elder brother and the widow of younger brother. This is known as senior levirate. When the marriage with the sister of the wife is performed while she is living, it is known as simultaneous sorrorate. On the other hand, if the marriage is performed after the death of the wife, it is known as restricted sorrorate. Both these types of marriages are prevalent particularly due to economic and compassionate reasons.

INDIAN TRIBAL MARRIAGE

The institution of marriage among the tribes is different from that in the Hindu society. Marriage among the tribals is not a religious sacrament but a social contract with purposes of enjoyment of sex, procreation and companionship. The forms of marriage, the ceremonies, the taboos and the laws of dissolution of marriage are different in the tribal world from civilized society.

Forms of Marriage among Indian Tribes

Normally, the tribal male marries only one woman, because he is not rich enough to maintain more than one wife and secondly the number of males and females in a tribe is usually equal. The following are the important forms of getting a mate in tribal society :

1. Marriage by purchase. The most prevalent method of securing a bride in primitive societies is marriage by purchase. This is equivalent to Asur marriage described in Hindu scriptures. According to Robert Lowie, however, the bride price is not paid as the price for the girl but symbolises her utility for the male and the compensation to the parents for giving away their daughter in marriage. Again, among some Indian tribes there is the custom of dowry, which finishes the value of bride price. This is particularly true about Santhal, Ho, Oraon, Kharia, Gond, Naga, Kuki and Bhils among Indian tribes. Like Hindus, the problem of bride price is becoming complex in tribal society. In the Singbhum district the amount of bride price in the Ho tribe is so much that very few persons can pay it, with the result that other forms of marriage are preferred.

2. Service marriage. This is a special type of marriage by purchase. While in marriage by purchase the bridegroom gives some money or gift to his father-in-law, in service marriage he pays off for the marriage in terms of service rendered to his father-in-law. This custom is particularly found among those persons who are too poor to pay any money as bride price. In the Gond tribe, a bridegroom, desirous of marrying through service, is known as Lamnai and Lamsena in Vega tribe. In Himachal Pradesh he is known as Kamaoos. In service marriage the youth has to serve his future father-in-law for three to five years. During this period if the father of the girl is satisfied with the youth, he gives his daughter in marriage to him. If, however, the father is dissatisfied, he dismisses the youth and gives this chance to another person. During the course of service, the young man can meet the girl but cannot enter into sex relationship with her.

3. Marriage by capture. An important method of securing a bride among Indian tribes is marriage by capture. This form of marriage is prevalent due to different types of causes. In the Ho tribe its cause is the excessive bride price. Another cause is the misbehaviour of the woman with her sister-in-law so that sister-in-law is always waiting for someone to carry her by force. Though the relatives apparently try to revenge for the capture of the girl but in 99 per cent cases the capture is regularized by means of marriage in which the young man has only to apply vermilion on the forehead of the girl. The custom of marriage by capture is found among the Santhal, Munda, Bhumij, Gond, Bhil and Naga tribes. Among the Bhumij tribe, it is considered to be the best form of marriage, so much so that even after the settlement of marriage the parents of the girl request the bridegroom to run away with the bride. In the Kharia and Birhor tribes of Bihar if a young man forcibly applies vermilion and oil on the forehead of a girl, she is declared his wife. Among the Nagas of Assam, a cause of marriage by capture is the death of women in their own tribe due to the evil custom of killing new born daughters. With the application of Indian Penal Code in tribal circles, the custom of marriage by capture is gradually disappearing.

4. Marriage by mutual consent and elopement. An interesting form of securing a bride prevalent among Indian tribes is marriage by mutual consent and elopement. This was known as Gandharva marriage in the ancient Hindu scriptures. Among the Ho tribes of Bihar it is known as 'Rajikhushi' marriage. In this form of marriage the girl elopes with a young man by her own consent and does not return to her parents till they consent to the marriage. Naturally, no bride price is demanded in this type of marriage.

5. Marriage by exchange. In this type of marriage when a man's son is prepared to marry another's daughter, the latter's son accepts the former's daughter in marriage; thus an exchange of boys and girls is made between the two families.

6. Probationary marriage. This system of marriage is found in the Kuki tribe of Assam. In this system the bridegroom stays in the house of the girl's father for a certain period. If during this probation period they decide to marry, the marriage ceremony is solemnized, otherwise the young man leaves after paying some compensation to the parents of the girl.

7. Anader or intrusion marriage. This method of marriage is followed if all other valid sources of marriage have been closed so much so that even the parents of the girl fail to marry her with the desired boy. In this type of marriage the girl forcibly enters the house of her lover and does not leave it in spite of bearing all types of insults and cruelties. If she does not leave the house even after a sufficient period, she is married with the young man. This custom of marriage is found among the Oraon, Ho and Birhor tribes.

8. Marriage by test. In this type of marriage the young man is allowed to marry the girl of his choice after he successfully passes the test for his bravery. A strange custom of this type of marriage is found among Bhil tribe which is known as Gol Gadhedo. In it a social function is celebrated around a tree or a high pole at the top of which a coconut and some sweets are put. The boys and girls dance around this pole or tree, the girls remaining nearer the tree and the boys forming their circle outside the circle of girls. Now a young man suddenly tries to break the circle of the girls and reaches the pole or tree, eats the sweets and breaks the coconut. The girls beat him and try to restrain him. If he comes out successful in this aim he is given a right to select any girl from the gathering as his wife.

Besides the above mentioned methods of securing a bride found among the Indian tribes there are some other methods as well. Of these the following two are worth mentioning :

1. Levirate. In this type of marriage when a person dies, his younger brother marries his wife. This custom is found in the Santhal, Gond and Kharia tribes among others.

2. Sorrorate. In this type of marriage when the wife dies, the husband marries her unmarried sister. This type of marriage is found in Gond and Kharia tribes.

Ceremonies of Marriage

The celebration of marriage in a tribe is a social occasion for much festivity and rejoicings though the marriage ceremonies are quite simple. In some tribes the mere application of vermilion on the forehead of the girl by the bridegroom is the sole ceremony of marriage. In some other tribes, the bloods of the bride and the bridegroom are mixed as a token of their intimate union. In Gond tribe the procession of marriage starts from the bride's place instead of from the bridegroom's house. There are almost no religious Sanskaras observed on the occasion of a tribal marriage, but generally there is provision for community songs, dances and feasts.

Polyandry among Tribes

Marriage is normally of two types — monogamy and polygamy. Polygamy again, has been classified into polygyny and polyandry. In polygyny a male marries several females. In polyandry on the other hand, a female marries several males at the same time. The custom of polyandry is found among the Khasi tribe of district Dehra Dun, Tiyan, Kurumb, Kot of Kerala and the Toda tribe of Nilgiri. Martin has mentioned its prevalence in Oraon tribe and Maine has mentioned it in the case of Santhals. This custom is also found among the Nayars of South India. It is also found in Laddakh, Kangra, Chamba, Kulu and Mandi.

The custom of polyandry has been divided into following two types :

1. Adelphic or Fraternal polyandry. In this type of polyandry a woman marries all the brothers of her husband. Such is the custom found in the Khasi tribe of district Dehra Dun, which has been elaborately described by D. N. Majumdar and R.N. Saxena. In this tribe, while the elder brother marries a woman, she is considered to be the wife of all his brothers. No younger brother is allowed to marry any other woman. If at the time of marriage any younger brother is a minor or he is born after marriage he is considered to be the husband of the woman after he becomes adult. But if a younger brother marries any other woman after being an adult the elder brother has an equal right over his wife also.

In the Khasi tribe though the woman is considered to be the wife of all the brothers, the eldest brother has special rights over her. She cannot refuse to cohabit with him, failing which she can be divorced. If the eldest brother asks her not to cohabit with any other brother, she has to follow his command. If the other brothers quarrel over this issue only the elder brother has a right to allow for the dissolution of the marriage. If the woman has got any child prior to marriage, the eldest brother has the sole rights over the child.

In Khasi tribe, the paternity is decided by a social ceremony. According to Dr. Majumdar if there are three brothers in a family, the children will call them by the names of Bari Babaa, Danger Baba and Bhedi Babaa respectively. According to Frazer the eldest brother is considered to be the father of the eldest son, the youngest brother that of the youngest son and so also in the case of other children.

The eldest brother is the head of the family. He has the sole rights on the house, fields, gardens, cattle, grain, etc. He is the highest authority concerning the matters of women and children. In the case of division of property, he is given the biggest share and the wife and children stay with him. The children, however, have a right in the property of all the fathers. Among these people if it is desired to marry more than one woman, generally this other woman is the sister of the first wife. This is done to ensure peace of the family. The Khasi tribe is patriarchal. The system of polyandry in it is consequently known as patriarchal polyandry.

2. Non-fraternal polyandry. In this type of polyandry, as is clear by its name, the husbands of a woman need not have fraternal relationship among themselves. Thus, the woman can also choose her husband from the males other than her husband's brothers. She successively lives in the houses of her different husbands, and while she is staying with one, the other husbands have no right over her. Non-fraternal polyandry is also known as matriarchal polyandry because in it the woman has all the rights of property. The example of non-fraternal polyandry in India can be found among the Nayars of Malabar. Among the Nayars the girl stays with her family even after marriage and visits her husbands from time to time or allows them to visit her sometimes. Sometimes the man has no relation with the wife after a certain period and the girl maintains sex relationship with several boys while living with her parents. The husbands have no right over the children or the property of the wife.

The following are the important characteristics of polyandry found in Indian tribes :

1. A woman can marry more than one husband.

2. The several husbands of a woman may be brothers or may not be so.

3. Though every husband has a right over the woman the eldest brother has the maximum right.

4. If there are more than one woman in the family, every brother is free to enter into sexual relationships with any one of them.

5. The eldest brother or the first husband has maximum rights over the property and children.

6. In matrilineal families the woman herself selects the husbands and lives with them successively. But while she is living with one husband, the others have no right over her.

7. Both men and women have equal rights of dissolving the marriage through divorce.

Normally, the following are the two important causes of the prevalence of polyandry :

1. Poverty. In Ladakh where the custom of polyandry is found, its cause is poverty. It is seen that when a person gathers sufficient amount of money, he prefers to marry a woman and live separately from his house. According to Sumner, in Tibet, where agricultural products are insufficient, several males together keep a woman. According to Lowie among Chinese several males together use a woman and meet her demands. According to R.N. Saxena, the Jaunsari woman is herself anxious to have several husbands because a single person cannot earn sufficient money to meet her demands.

2. Scarcity of women. According to Wetermarck, an important cause of polyandry is the scarcity of women. For example, among the Todas of Nilgiri, the number of women is much less in comparison with that of men and therefore polyandry is the normal custom. Now, with the increase of the number of women due to legal check on murders of daughters, the custom of polyandry is gradually diminishing. This reason advanced by Westermarck may be true in some cases, but, as has been rightly shown by Robert Briffault, polyandry can be prevalent even where there is no scarcity of women. For example, there is no appreciable difference in the number of males and females in Lahaul, Sikkim, Tibet and Ladakh and yet the custom of polyandry is prevalent there. It can be, however, safely admitted that scarcity of women though not the sole cause of polyandry, is an important cause of it.

The custom of polyandry is defective and therefore, it is gradually diminishing. The following are its important disadvantages :

1. It injures the health of women who develop venereal diseases because of sexual intercourse with several males.

2. According to some thinkers this custom encourages barrenness among women.

3. In the long run polyandry leads to population problems.

4. According to some thinkers in polyandrous marriages there is more likelihood of the birth of sons and therefore the cycle of polyandry never ends.

5. Polyandry increases the number of divorces.

Thus, the custom of polyandry does not fulfil the psychological and spiritual requirements of a marital relationship. It is not even a sufficiently legal contract. In the words of Westermarck, "The polyandrous unions of the Nayars can hardly be called marriages even from a non-legal point of view, considering that they were of the loosest and most fugitive character, that the male partners never lived with the woman and that according to some accounts the duties of fatherhood were entirely ignored." Polyandry, however, cannot be eliminated without the elimination of poverty.

Polygyny among Tribes

Polygyny is the custom of one male marrying several females. Due to several causes the custom of polygyny has very much diminished among tribes in modern times, though rich males even now marry several females. The custom of polygyny is found in Naga, Gond, Vega, Toda and other tribes of India. Its main causes are as follows :

1. Economic causes. In hills and plateaus one has to work very hard to earn his livelihood. The custom of polygyny provides free and reliable labourers to the husband. There is another economic cause of polygyny as well. The leaders of the tribes of Assam marry several females because they are capable of meeting their needs.

2. Women's consent. Among tribes because of the difficulty of daily chores of life, the woman is sometimes herself anxious to have several co-wives to help her. Psychologically, this reason does not appear to be satisfactory.

3. Other causes. Other important causes of polygyny are desire for children, increase in social prestige because of several wives and excessive lust of the male. Sometimes the scarcity of males is also a cause of polygyny.

The following are the so-called advantages of polygyny mentioned by its supporters :

1. Because only powerful and rich males marry several women, therefore it improves new generations.

2. Polygyny restricts adultery because the males get sufficient sexual variety in their own family. This also helps in bringing up the children.

The above mentioned so-called advantages are nothing before the obvious disadvantages of polygyny of which the important ones are as follows :

1. In the presence of several wives the importance of each one of them diminishes in the family.

2. Due to the presence of several co-wives, the peace of the family is disturbed because of mutual jealousy and quarrels.

3. It is difficult for a man of ordinary status to meet the needs of several co-wives and therefore, polygyny in such cases creates economic difficulties.

4. The greatest disadvantage of polygyny is that it is against the equality of the male and female. Psychologically, it is against the establishment of conjugal love among wife and husband. The woman does not receive psychological satisfaction from such a marital relationship. Therefore, a majority of thinkers are against the custom of polygyny. With the spread of education among tribals, this custom is gradually disappearing.

RESTRICTIONS ON MATE SELECTION

In every tribal society there are certain taboos and rules connected with the institution of marriage. There are different advantages and disadvantages of these taboos. The important amongst these are exogamy and endogamy.

Exogamy among Tribals

Defining exogamy, E.A. Hoebel has written, "It may be defined as a social rule that prohibits a person from marrying within a defined social group of which he is a member." According to the rule of exogamy a man may marry only outside a certain group. This group may be his caste, tribe, clan or totem. Generally, the tribals are forbidden to marry within their clan and totem group. The custom of totem exogamy is also universal among Indian tribes. Among the Khasi tribe, clan exogamy is the custom. In some tribes one finds village exogamy in which marriage cannot be contracted within the village. An example is the munda tribe of Chhota Nagpur. In South India the Erula tribe observes class exogamy. Similar is the custom among the Nagas of Assam. Different scholars have advanced different reasons for the custom of exogamy. According to Risley the reason behind the custom of exogamy is the desire for novelty. Because of his desire for novelty the male does not want to marry any woman of his acquaintance within his group. Psychologically, novelty is a factor in marital relationship but it cannot be said that novelty cannot be secured in one's own group. According to Westermarck the main cause of exogamy is the prohibition of incest. This is definitely an important factor in exogamy. According to Audrey Richards, the cause of exogamy is the scarcity of women because of the evil custom of killing daughters. It is because of scarcity of women in the group that most of the males are compelled to find their mates from other groups. This is an important cause of exogamy. But the most important causes of exogamy are prohibitions concerning totem and clan. The members of a totem and clan are considered to have blood relationships. The custom of totem and clan exogamy is therefore quite understandable.

Endogamy

Defining endogamy, Hoebel has written, "It is a social rule that requires a person to marry within a defined social group of which he is a member." Thus, in contrast with exogamy, in endogamy a man has to seek his mate within his own group. This group may be his caste, tribe, clan, etc. Endogamy is prevalent among the different classes of Bhil and Toda tribes. The following are the important causes of endogamy :

1. Fear of strangers. The most important cause of endogamy is the primitive man's natural fear of strangers. They think that the stranger may harm them by means of magic and therefore, they prefer to marry within their own group. This is the cause of endogamy in Korawa tribe.

2. Racial and geographical differences. The racial and geographical differences create a gulf among different tribes so that they fear each other and do not enter into marital relationships.

3. Protection of tribal specialities. Different tribes have a natural desire to protect their cultural, linguistic and other specialities. This is possible only in the custom of endogamy.

4. Other causes. Among other important causes of endogamy are absence of sufficient means of transport and communication, illiteracy, self-sufficient nature of tribe, etc.

Divorce among Tribes

There are no strict rules concerning divorce among tribes. Marriage is nothing more than a social contract and most of the males marry to fulfil the desire for children and the satisfaction of sex. There are different rules of divorce observed in different tribes. Among the Korawa tribe of Mirzapur, the procedure is very simple. When a dissatisfied husband asks his wife to leave him and refuses to maintain her, she leayes him and goes to her father. She is now considered to be divorced and can marry again. In this tribe the divorced women are very much respected. The woman divorced seven times is the leader in religious and social functions. Among Bhils, the husband desirous of divorcing his wife, calls the village Panchayat and publicly gives her a piece of cloth from his turban declaring that he is deserting her and henceforward treat her as his sister. The woman hangs this cloth from the roof of his father's house, where it remains hanging for a month. It signifies that her husband has no more rights over her and she can now marry again.

Among Gonds if a woman divorces her husband without his consent her second husband has to pay compensation to the former husband. Among the Muria tribe the divorce is never considered to be valid unless the amount of compensation is paid to the former husband. This amount is decided by the tribal panchayat. In the Lushai tribe of Assam when the husband divorces his wife, he has to pay off the remaining bride price to the bride's party. But if the woman is guilty of adultery or if she herself deserts her husband, she has to return the bride price paid by the husband.

The causes of divorce are not similar in different tribes. Among Gonds divorce can be secured in the circumstances of the indifference of wife towards household affairs, her barrenness, her quarrelsome nature, breaking of the marital bond, etc. In the Kharia tribe a woman can be divorced on the grounds of barrenness, adultery, refusal to live with the husband and even laziness. Among tribals both male and female have a right to divorce. The customs concerning divorce, however, are changing because of the influence of Hindu and Christian cultures on tribal people these days.

24

Status of Women

The status of women in a society is determined by the prevalent ideals and functions. These ideals and functions are however, not universal. Therefore, the status of women is not similar in all the primitive societies. The status of women is determined by the functions allotted to them, the social attitudes towards them, the behaviour of males and the social contribution of the women. An example of this criteria may be seen in the Toda tribe of South India. The Todas are pastoral. Their main economic occupation is rearing buffalloes. The buffalloes are considered sacred, and the place of dairy farming is treated as a religious place. Priests are engaged in taking out the milk of buffalloes. Women are not permitted to go near them. Even the chief priest has to remain a bachelor. The disabilities of the women concerning dairy farming are also applicable to cooking food involving milk. This, however, does not mean that the status of women is lower in every respect. They are generally treated well and respected.

The distinction of the patriarchal and matriarchal families makes significant changes in the status of women. Among Khasi tribe of Assam, the family is matriarchal. The husband has to live with the wife's family after marriage. The lineage name is given by the mother. Therefore, in terms of location as well as lineage, the status of a woman is higher than that of a man. The originator of the tribe is also believed to be female. The inheritance of property succeeds from the mother to the daughter. The mother has the right to the earning of the male before marriage and the wife after marriage. Religious functions are generally performed by a woman. Ancestor worship is prevalent and most of the ancestors are females. The Khasis believe that goddesses will protect them and keep them free from disease. In the political field also the administration is mostly in the hands of the females. This, however, does not mean that the status of males is pitiable in any sense. On the other hand, they are respected and their desires are fulfilled. Divorce requires mutual consent and both are free in their personal affairs.

Another tribe in Assam which is matriarchal, is Garo. In this tribe the descent is traced from the mother. Ancestors are females and goddesses are worshipped. Daughter succeeds to the property. The husband may use property of the wife but in succession it is given to the daughter. Polygyny is prevalent. There is no custom of bride price. Widows are not allowed to remarry. They are, however, given freedom in sexual matters. While the male is given death punishment for adultery, the women are given less punishment at least in several cases.

The description of the status of females in the matriarchal societies as given above is precisely reversed in patriarchal societies, the examples of which can be seen in almost all civilized societies. Patriarchal societies have patriarchal families. After marriage the woman has to reside in the house of her husband. The husband is head of the family and enjoys higher status in every way. The property and wealth succeeds from the father to the son. Myths and beliefs derogatory to the status of woman are prevalent. For example, in Toda tribe the women are considered impure due to the processes connected with menstruation, child birth etc., resulting in the imposition of social taboos and economic disabilities. This, however, does not mean that the status of women in patriarchal society is invariably low. For example, one may find henpecked husbands in Toda tribe as in any other primitive society.

In every society the status of a woman varies in accordance to her function in social organization. As social functions change so do social status. If the socio-economic functions of a woman are higher and more valuable in a tribe her status is naturally higher. On the other hand, if her economic functions are not very important, she does not enjoy a high social status. For example, among Todas, the functions connected with dairy farming are the most important but women are not allowed to do important jobs in dairy farming, with the result that their status is considerably lower. But, on the other hand, women get a lot of love and affection which compensates in their social status and raises it.

Social function, however, is not the sole factor determining social status. For example, in Andaman Islands women work side by side with men in social and religious functions. Hence, they have to work with men also along with their own functions. This makes their social status even worse than that of Toda women. Among Kadar people, the division of labour among women is more scientific and exclusive. Thus, the status of both men and women is equally satisfactory and comfortable.

The above examples are from patriarchal societies. The status of women in patriarchal societies is determined by the restrictions attached to their functions. The restrictions may be preventive or productive. For example, the women in Toda tribe are prevented from working in dairies as they are considered impure. This lessens their social status. But in all the patriarchal tribes the status of women is not lower to that of men. Among Gond people the women enjoy equal freedom with men. For example, they are free in the choice of mates, pre-marital relationships and divorce. But in other fields they work like labourers employed by men and most of the men evaluate their importance as labourers. Therefore, there are few bachelors among Gonds. Tharu tribe again, is patriarchal but their women dominate their men. Tharu women are beautiful and unrestrained in sex relationships. They are known to possess magical powers. In Khasi tribe there is the custom of fraternal polyandry. This naturally leads to much physical and psychological pressure upon women, but this is relieved through a strange custom. According to it though the woman has no freedom in the house of the husband, she enjoys all freedom in the paternal home and since she often visits her parents, she gets ample opportunities to relieve her tensions.

Generally, it is believed that the status of women in matriarchal tribes is higher than that of patriarchal tribes, but a survey of Indian matriarchal tribes shows that it is not so. In India among the Khasi tribe, one finds matrilocal residence and matrilineal traditions. They trace their lineage from some princess. In their mythology the creator is female. The lineage is traced through the mother. The daughter inherits the property of the mother. Man's earning belongs to the mother's family before marriage and to the wife's family after marriage. Most of the religious ceremonies are performed by women. Most of the ancestors who are worshipped are women. Diseases, death and security are mostly connected with goddesses. Women work as priests on religious occasions. They are the leaders in social and religious fields. In Khirim kingdom a woman is the highest priest and administrator. In spite of so much power of women one finds few cases of misbehaviour among men. On the other hand they are highly respected and exercise wide power after marriage. Khasi woman considers her husband as her master. Divorce is possible only by mutual consent and the non-consenting partner gets compensation. Just as the wives are free, the husbands are also free in so many matters. Thus, it is clear that the matriarchal social organization itself is not the sufficient cause for the lower status of men. It may be definitely higher in patriarchal societies and patrilocal residence.

Another example of matriarchal society is found among the Garo people. In it children are members of the mother's family. Garo people consider themselves as descendants of some women. Lineage is carried on from the mother. The daughter inherits the property of the mother. No one can transfer his property to his son though he may use the property of his wife. The proposal of marriage is made from the bride's side but the male may marry several women. However, more than three wives are exceptional. No party has to pay the price of the bride or the groom. Widows are not allowed to remarry for a sufficiently long period. This is so that the minor may get time to become major and the property of the family may remain in the family. Thus, women have to pay the price of their higher status through mental strain. The widow has to marry the nephew of her dead husband. If she fails to do this she has to pay compensation to him. In Garo tribe there is no prostitution though instances of adultery are not common. Adulterous males are given death sentence though adulterous females are given minor punishment. But if she is guilty of adultery again and again she is also given capital punishment. Divorce is possible on the basis of adultery. Divorce is also possible if the woman refuses to work.

The above discussion about the status of women in partiarchal and

Matriarchal societies shows that nowhere the status of women is compulsorily low or high. However, as a general rule, in comparison to partiarchal societies, the status of women is high in matriarchal societies. There is no custom of matrilocal residence in all the matriarchal societies. Fór example, in Khasi matriarchal society the male establishes separate residence with his wife after marriage. On the other hand, even in some patriarchal societies some sons-in-law settle in the house of their in-laws. As a general rule the more restrictions on women, the lower is their status in society. But in this respect also there is no dearth of exceptions.

In many patriarchal societies also one finds a lot of difference in the status of women. For example, the Nagas of Assam are patriarchal but among them, the status of women in Seema Nagas is higher than that among Ao and Angami Nagas. The Seema woman has a voice in deciding her mate. She enjoys a higher status in the house of her husband. In some societies where women have economic rights equal to the male rights, their status is not necessarily higher since sometimes they have to share the male activities in addition to the female burden. In fact, rights alone do not determine the status of women. It also depends upon the male's behaviour towards them. Besides this, they have also importance as mothers. Hence, in many societies barren women are very much neglected. Tribes which have been influenced by Hindu scriptures accord a lower status to women than those who were not so influenced.

In order to evaluate the status of a woman in tribal society, one has to consider her economic and political status besides her social status. The status of woman is known from her status in the family, the rights and duties of husband and wife, premarital rights and duties of a daughter, etc. If exceptions are left aside, the status of women in tribal societies is generally not lower than that of the male. The rights of son and daughter are generally the same and both enjoy freedom of movement. Among the tribes where there are dormitories, boys and girls both live in dormitories and though their functions may be somewhat different, there is hardly any difference in their status. The tribal woman has generally a free choice in the selection of a mate. Similarly the rules of divorce are similar for both the male and female. Due to the custom of couvade the male also has to suffer during the period of female's pregnancy. Concerning freedom about sexual relationships there is no distinction among male and female.

Along with the social status, the economic status of the tribal woman is also not lower than that of the male. In productive activities, agriculture, animal husbandary, etc. male and female work together. Generally, the male's work is harder than that of the female's. In hunting tribes the males go out for hunting while the females perform domestic jobs. All the work is done by mutual cooperation and if there is no love or cooperation marital relationships are dissolved. Thus, the tribal woman has no occasion to suffer and face torture within the four walls of her home living as a slave of her husband like her so many civilized sisters. Her status here is certainly better.

So far as political rights are concerned, the tribal woman's status is not lower though her rights are less than that of the male's, since in tribal life there is more emphasis upon duties than rights in the political sphere. The tribal chief has so many rights but then he has also the burden of the protection of the tribe. If he fails to carry out this burden he cannot hold the high office of the chief. In fact political power among tribals is gained by physical strength and the power of arms. Therefore, naturally males enjoy better political rights. But there are some tribal societies in which political power lies in the hands of women. In brief, the status of women in tribal societies is no less than that of men.

25

Avoidance and Joking Relationships

A particular form of kinship behaviour is known as avoidance. In this behaviour, as is clear by the nomenclature, a person avoids meeting, seeing, sitting or talking to another. Such avoidance is almost universal in tribal kinship relationships. The following are some important forms of avoidance relationships:

1. Daughter-in-law and parents-in-law avoidance. In Yokadhir tribe the daughter-in-law cannot show her face to her father-in-law or the elder brother of her husband. She cannot directly speak to them nor can she stand in their company or change clothes in their presence. Thus, she keeps her face covered before them.

2. Son-in-law and mother-in-law avoidance. Just as one finds the custom of avoidance of father-in-law by the daughter-in-law, similarly in some tribes the son-in-law avoids any type of contact and relationship with the mother-in-law. In some tribes the son-in-law cannot talk to his father-in-law as well. If he has to convey something to his in-laws he gesticulates and makes signs but never speaks.

3. Brother-sister or sibling avoidance. This type of avoidance is found in Yokadhir tribe. One cannot talk anything he likes to his brothers, sisters and even cousins. They cannot change clothes before each other, nor can they be nude in the presence of others. In the Andaman tribe a man cannot directly speak to his younger brother's wife. He can do so only through some intermediary. On the other hand, there is no restriction upon the contact or communication between a man and his elder brother's wife. In Malenesia the brother and sister cannot meet each other. Among Trobriands if the brother per chance happens to observe his sister making love to some man, all the three have to commit suicide.

CAUSES OF AVOIDANCE

Psychologists and anthropologists have tried to discover reasons behind avoidance behaviour. Of these, the most important are as follows:

1. Opinion of Tylor. According to Tylor, avoidance is particularly due to matriarchal system. In some tribes, after marriage, the bridegroom stays in the family of the wife. Since he has no definite status in the family, he is avoided. After procreation his status becomes somewhat more definite and better. In the words of R.H. Lowie, "Avoidance by the husband of the wife's family is in some way connected with his living with them, and *vice versa* as to the wife and the husband's family. In other words, matrilocalism goes with son-in-law avoidance, patrilocalism with daughter-in-law avoidance." Tylor's view, however, is not applicable everywhere. In some tribes, avoidance is not due to location. For example, Zuni and Hopi are matriarchal, and yet they have no such custom. Again, Tylor's theory does not explain the reason of avoidance among heterosexual relatives. Again, in some societies, both the types of avoidance are found. However, pointing out to the importance of Tylor's view, Lowie has said, "But Tylor's cross cultural approach remains valid. Whatever may be the explanation, the amazing parallels between the cultures of distant people cannot be ignored and with proper caution we are right in seeking possible correlates."

2. Opinion of Frazer. According to James Frazer, avoidance is due to sexual reasons. He based his theory particularly upon the brother-sister avoidance in Vedda of Ceylon and the inhabitants of Trobriand island. Among Vedda people, the brother and sister cannot live under the same roof nor can they eat together. According to Frazer this avoidance is for checking sexual contact among heterosexual relations. However, Frazer's theory does not explain the cause of avoidance among same sexes.

3. Opinion of Freud. Like Frazer, Sigmund Freud has also explained avoidance with reference to sex relationship. His theory is known as psychoanalytical theory. According to it, sex motivation is normal among persons of opposite sex. The rules of avoidance try to solve this problem. The avoidance of mother-in-law and son-in-law relationship is due to the possibility that due to attraction towards his bride, the son-in-law may be attracted to the mother-in-law or such a feeling may develop in the mother-in-law for the son-in-law. Since the daughter lives with the mother for so many years, she has natural attachment to her. This leads to rivalry since both the son-in-law and the mother crave for her love. This rivalry leads to avoidance. Freud's view cannot explain avoidance everywhere particularly among same sexes.

4. Opinion of Lowie. According to Lowie, both in-laws have different cultural and social values. It is possible that the mores of wife's side may be different from the mores of the son-in-law's side. In matriarchal family, the bridegroom is different from other members of the family since he comes from the other family. Hence, he is avoided. Similarly, in a patriarchal family the daughter-in-law is avoided.

5. Opinion of Turney High. Turney High has explained avoidance in terms of conflicts. According to him, it is the best method to achieve harmonious relationships. In a family the status of the daughter-in-law is peculiar. She has to serve the in-laws in the family. Therefore, she cannot understand proper relationship leading to conflict with the in-laws. Avoidance is an attempt to solve the problem of this conflict.

6. Opinion of Radcliffe-Brown. According to Radcliffe-Brown, the main cause of avoidance is social. Love and hate are natural among members of two different families. Hatred is harmful for the organization of family. Avoidance is a cure for this conflict. Presenting this same fact in another way, Chapple and Coon have pointed out that avoidance lessens interaction.

JOKING RELATIONSHIPS

Joking relationships are opposed to avoidance relationships. It includes relationship of elder brother's wife and the younger brother of her husband, brother-in-law and sister-in-law, nephew and aunt, etc. Joking is mostly between relationship based upon matrimony and not upon blood relationships. There may be sex relationship among relatives having joking relationship. Among Oraons joking is so much effective that sometimes the grand father marries the grand daughter. Joking relationships of brother-in-law and sister-in-law are the most popular. Sex relationships among them are equally widespread. In almost all the societies there are joking relationships among younger brother of a person and his wife. Sexual relationships among them are most widely prevalent. Among primitive societies, joking relationships are found among maternal aunt and her nephew. Among Hopi and Trobrianders it is so much prevalent that it even leads to sex relationships.

According to Radcliffe-Brown, joking relationships show friendship. Chapple and Coon maintain that joking is a means to maximum interaction. It also finishes or diminishes conflicts. According to Lowie, joking is a psychological tendency among potential mates.

26

Primitive Youth Dormitories

Besides the panchayat, the most important social institution in a tribal village in India is the youth dormitory. These are found in almost every tribe and the social life is centred around it. They are known by different names in different tribes, for example, among the Nagas of Assam, they are called 'Morung' while the female Youth organization is called 'Yo', among Angami Nagas, it is called 'Kinchuki'. In Uttar Pradesh, it is known as Rangbang, while among the Mundas and Ho tribes of Madhya Bharat, it is called Gitiora. The Oraon call it Dhoomkuriya, the Bhuiyan call it Dhangarbassa and the Gonds call it Gotul.

These youth organizations are centred in big buildings known as dormitories. They are buildings of straw and thatch. There are separate houses meant for boys and girls. All the youths of the tribe pass their night in the dormitory. The boys and girls sleep separately. In the villages where there is no dormitory for the girls, they sleep in the house of some old woman. Such is the custom in the Munda tribe. In Bastar the boys and girls of the age of 15 and 16 sleep in the dormitories. The Oraon youth has to pass his night in the Dhoomkuria situated outside the village. In the Ho tribe the unmarried boys and girls live in separate dormitories. Among the Lhota Nagas of Assam the boys can get leave from the Morung only in the case of serious illness of their mothers. Among the Miami tribals of Assam both boys and girls sleep in the same dormitory. While the girls sleep on the ground floor, the boys sleep on the first floor. Similar is the custom in the Muria tribe of Bastar. Their dormitories are situated outside the village. The unmarried boys and girls gather here at night, sing and dance and participate in other social activities and finally pass the night.

The following are the important characteristics of the youth dormitory in a tribal village :

1. While at some places there are separate dormitories for the boys and girls, in other tribes they live in a common dormitory. This is the custom in the Muria tribe. On the other hand, among the Konayak Nagas of Assam, the boys live in the Morung and the girls sleep in the Yo.

2. Normally the dormitories are situated outside the village in the forest, but they may also be near the fields as it is in the case of dormitories of the Nagas. In Oraon tribes the dormitory is situated in the centre of the village.

3. The life in the dormitory is based on certain traditions and customs which are invariably followed by all the members.

4. The age of membership of the dormitory differs from tribe to tribe. As a general rule it is four or five years in most of the tribes.

5. The boys and girls live in the dormitory till they are married when their membership is automatically dissolved.

6. If a girl becomes a widow she can again enter the dormitory as its member.

7. In the evening the members of the dormitory gather after taking their meals at their homes. At the dormitory they make a fire, sit around it, tell stories, sing, dance and play and finally sleep.

8. The members of the dormitory are divided into classes according to age — seniors and juniors. The head of the dormitory is selected from the senior group. It is his job to take care of all the members of the dormitory and maintain discipline among them. The juniors follow the command of the seniors and receive different types of education from them.

9. It is the duty of every member of the dormitory to keep everything secret about the dormitory.

10. The members of the dormitory carry out several functions together, *e.g.*, construction of a house on the occasion of marriage or helping the village-folk in harvesting the crop, etc.

THE GOTUL OF MURIA AND GOND

Among the dormitories of Indian tribe, The Gotul of the Muria and Gonds of Madhya Bharat is worth mentioning. It is raised on bamboo poles and has a roof of straw. There is no door or window in it. The members enter through a small hole sufficient to permit entry. All the unmarried boys and girls gather here in the evening, make a fire, sing and dance, tell traditional legends and sleep here. The juniors serve the seniors and receive different types of training from them. Among the members of the Gotul, different boys and girls are given different status and the corresponding roles. The head of the dormitory is known as Challan or Silledar. Under him there are Dewan, Tehsildar, Subedar, Kotwal, etc. Similar positions are also given to the girls. According to D. N. Majumdar, the purpose of the Gotul is to save the village-folk from the attack of wild animals. The youths remain waking for most of the night and sleep only in its last lap or in the day. They help their parents on the field or in grazing the cattle in the forest. In the evening they go to Gotul after taking their meals. Among the Muria tribals, the girls massage the bodies of the boys. Verrier Elvin has described the sexual life in the Gotul in detail in his book *The Muria and their Gotul*. He has pointed out that the senior girls train the junior boys in matters of sex. In *The Gondwana and the Gonds*, Shri Inder Jit Singh has denied any type of sexual activity in the Gotul. D. N. Majumdar and Hutton also agree with Singh. In fact Elvin has himself admitted and wondered that there is hardly any case of conception among the members of the Gotul. According to Majumdar and Hutton, the Gotuls are the centres of social education. In it are shown the dances imitating agriculture, hunting, gathering of honey and economic activities carried out by the village-folk. The conceptions of crime and punishment and good and bad actions are taught through different stories.

Scholars do not agree about the origin of tribal dormitory. According to one view, they are residues of the ancient communal houses when the whole village used to live under one roof and there were no individual homes. According to another view the purpose was to keep them away from the sexual relationship of their parents. According to Majumdar, the purpose of dormitory is to gather the youths of the village at one place to save the village from the attack of wild animals and the village maidens from the attack of males of other tribes. Besides it, the origin of the dormitory may be due to want of houses, the bliss of communal life and the development of tribal culture. Whatever may be the origin of dormitory, it is undeniable that it is the centre of tribal culture in a tribe. In it are taught the lessons of the traditions, norms, ideals, religious beliefs, methods of earning a livelihood and discipline to the boys and girls of the tribe. According to S. C. Roy, the tribal dormitory carries out the following three functions :

Helping in the gathering of edible things and consolidating economic organization.

Educating boys and girls in social and other duties and imparting them education in the matters of sex.

Following the principle of endogamy and keeping the movement of women limited and controlled.

At present unfortunately the institution of youth organisation is gradually weakening among the various tribes. The two important causes of this development are as follows :

1. Contact with the city. Due to contact with urban people the tribals are gradually forgetting their social ideals and institutions and following urban culture. As education is now being provided by schools, children do not go to the dormitory to receive education.

2. Influence of Christian Missionaries. The spread of Christianity among tribals and the presence of Christian missionaries among them have adversely affected their youth cultural set-up. The institution of youth dormitory is gradually weakening, which has led to social disorganization among the tribes.

In fact, as has been rightly pointed out by Elwin, the condition of the social organization of a tribal group can be rightly estimated from the condition of its youth organizations, which are the centres of the maintenance and development of its culture. The youth dormitories, therefore, should be re-established and encouraged like the village panchayats.

27

Economy

The primitive societies have passed through several stages of economic development everywhere in the world. Thus, one finds the stages of food gathering, hunting and fishing, farming, etc. among the Indian tribes. The tribes living in the forests and hills usually earn their livelihood by means of food gathering, hunting and fishing. Such is the life of Kadar of Kerala, Birhor and Kharia of Bihar and other tribes. The tribes living in dense forests, full of wild beasts, live on hunting. Such are the tribes of Naga, Kuki, Bhil, Santhal and Gond. The hunters leave the females to carry out household activities in the morning and return in the evening after hunting. In some tribes there is a usual custom of hunting collectively. The Nagas use spears and arrows and bows. The Bhils are very much specialized in shooting by arrow. The tribes living near rivers and seas usually earn their livelihood by catching fish. The hilly tribes rear the cattle, an example of which are Goojars and the tribes of Chamba. The Todas of Nilgiri rear buffaloes. Some tribes also carry out cultivation, but they are generally shifting from one place to another. Among the cultivating tribes are the Santhals and Gonds. Cottage industries, such as weaving cloths, preparing ropes and skins and utensils of different metals are prevalent in many tribes. The Kharia people are very much specialised to cottage industries.

Classification of Economic Organization

The Indian tribes can be divided into the following classes in the economic organization :

1. Hunting and food gathering tribes include Kadar, Chenchu, Kharia and Korawa etc.
2. Cattle rearing tribes such as the Todas and Bhils.
3. Cultivating tribes such as Kamar, Vega and Birhor.
4. Industrial tribes such as Kharia and Nagas.

GENERAL CHARACTERISTICS

The tribal economic organization is mainly concerned with producing such things as are necessary for their daily needs and consuming them. These activities are very much determined by the geographical environment of the tribe. Usually, the tribals have to struggle very hard to meet their economic needs. The following are the important characteristics of Indian tribal economic organization :

1. Production without technological aids. As the tribals are illiterate and cut off from the civilized world, they generally carry out production without adequate technological aids with the result that there is much loss of material with very little production. The tribals are, therefore, generally very poor in spite of working very hard.

2. Mixing economic activities with religion and magic. The tribals live in a natural environment where there is no distinction of economic, religious and magical activities. There is, therefore, a tendency to mix all these. In the economic activities also religious and magical activities are utilized to attain economic ends. Many superstitions in this respect are prevalent among the tribals, for example, among Nagas there is a custom of human sacrifice and sprinkling human blood over land in order to increase its fertility.

3. Production for consumption. In the absence of sufficient technological aids and scientific knowledge regarding agricultural and other production, the tribals generally produce only to consume. Hardly anything is left for exchange or hoarding. In the materials of consumption, food and clothing are generally given first preference, then there is the place for the home.

4. Absence of currency. The tribal people do not use currency in deciding the price of commodities and in exchange. There are no banks of economic exchanges in their societies. They hardly carry out any exchange of economic goods with outside groups.

5. Absence of regular markets. There are no tegular markets found in tribal societies and, therefore, there is no competition, monopoly, business or trade in their economic organization.

6. Absence of profiteering. There is absence of profiteering in tribal economic organization due to two important causes. Firstly, The absence of currency to fix the price of commodities and secondly, the connection of unity sentiments with economic activities.

7. Community basis of economic activities. Thus, the chief aim of economic activities in a tribal society is to fulfil the community duties. The organization of most of the economic activities is cooperative and communal.

8. Absence of specialists. There are no specialists in different branches of economic organization in tribal societies, with the result that there is no division of labour and specialization.

9. Concept of property. Some conception of personal property is found in almost every tribal society. A person is allowed a right over the things produced by him or his family. There is, however, group ownership over the ponds, the land and the forests, etc.

10. Economic backwardness. The above mentioned characteristics of tribal economic organization account for their economic backwardness. They do not know the new changes and inventions in different fields of production. Their methods and implements of cultivation, hunting and fishing are very primitive. They do not know anything about trade and commerce. The cottage industries are carried on by means of unrefined and primitive tools and methods. Hence, the economic status of Indian tribes is very much backward.

COMMUNAL OWNERSHIP

Property performs a valuable role in human society. In most of the societies it raises the status of a person. But the concept of property has been constantly changing. In modern tribes the concept of property has changed along with changes in technology and moral concepts. In primitive societies the modern concept of property is not in vogue since one does not find property in them in the sense it is found in civilized society. For example, one does not find any property in food gathering societies. People gather fruits and roots from the forest according to their needs. Among cattle rearing tribes, cattle form the property. One hardly finds property rights over land among primitive people. In fact, property in primitive societies does not mean possession of physical goods but some special prerogatives in the use of land or animals. Property rights in primitive societies are both individual as well as collective. At several places pastures are under collective possession. At other places the same land is utilised for various purposes by various people. For example, in Malenesia and West Africa, while a person is the owner of trees on a land, another has the right of cultivation on it.

The right of inheritance is connected with the right of property. Property right generally leads to right of inheritance. In Indian tribes, the wife's and children have rights over the personal belongings of a person. But since most of the property is communal, there is hardly any question of inheritance, when a person dies, there is no effect on collective property. On the other hand, the new generation constantly increases pressure upon land. Besides cattle rearing tribes, even in agricultural tribes the land is a collective property.

In primitive tribes, one finds examples of both patriarchal and matriarchal social organisation. In them the laws of inheritance are different. In a patriarchal society the son inherits the property while in a matriarchal tribe the succession of property is from mother to daughter and the sons have no share in it.

DIVISION OF LABOUR

The division of labour among primitive societies is based upon physical factors such as sex, age and physical health, etc. Besides this there is hardly any other type of division of labour. In many tribes the men and women perform different types of jobs. In some other tribes, however, there is no such division of labour based upon sex. However, even in these tribes there are taboos upon women during some periods such as those of menstruation and child birth, etc., as during these periods she is thought to be impure. In Toda tribe women are prohibited to do anything with cattle rearing. As they keep busy in bringing up children they are kept free from occupational activities. Most of the household chores is their burden. Thus, their main functions are procreation, child care, looking after the household affairs and doing light jobs concerning agriculture and cattle rearing or fisheries. This division of labour is due to the delicacy of women and their biological traits of procreation and menstruation. At some places men cook food. For example, in Toda tribe all the edibles made by milk are prepared by males.

However, in most of the tribes women have an active role in the chief occupation. In food gathering tribes they gather roots and fruits. In agricultural tribes they help in sowing, mowing, etc. Besides, light jobs such as basket weaving, making earthen wares, wearing cloth, etc., are mainly done by women. Most of the hard jobs such as big hunting games, felling big trees and the jobs of carpenters and blacksmiths are done by males. Both male and female work as labourers in agriculture and industries. The tribal women work in tea gardens and mines. Tribal males work in iron factories, coal mines and tea gardens. In tribal areas there are no labourers, everybody performs his own job. The jobs of labourers are done in civilized areas.

The above discussion of tribal economy shows that there is a predominance of division of labour and collective ownership in tribal economy. Most of the methods, techniques and procedures of agriculture and vocations are undeveloped and inefficient which involve a lot of waste. There is no provision for currency. Banking is conspicuous by its absence. There is the institution of profit. Most of the functions are cooperative. There is stability due to simplicity. There are no regular markets. Bazars are held on festivals in which there is barter of things of everyday use. There is hardly any specialization.

PRINCIPLES OF PRIMITIVE ECONOMY

Anthropologists study the economic activities of primitive societies. They study activities of food gathering tribes. They find that the agricultural system, handicrafts, etc., and the functioning of cooperative credit institutions and values are different from those of civilized society. For this purpose the economic anthropologist has to make a wide use of economic principles, as he is studying a society where money is not the medium of exchange. He faces a lot of difficulties in determining economic values. He has no standard and measurement to determine the economic system. Hence, he has to understand labour hours and labour wages, etc. He studies the production and its relationship to exchange. Keeping all these things in view he studies principles of primitive economy.

Every society has to fulfil unlimited human desires by means of limited resources at its disposal. The primitive societies use natural resources unsystematically due to a paucity of modern machines and tools. For example, primitive tribes in India practise shifting cultivation. Therefore, they fulfil even minimum needs by means of maximum labour. However, they do have some economic surplus. In brief, the principles of primitive economy are as follows :

1. Economic relationships are based on barter and exchange. There is no provision of currency. There are no banks and other credit societies.

2. Economic system is based upon social customs, physical conditions and faith in ancestors. Almost no primitive crosses their limits. Profit is seldom the motive of economic activities. Mutual obligations and unity perform the function of motivation. Give and take among primitives is the basis of economic system.

3. Mutual cooperation and collective enterprises are characteristics of primitive economy. According to Thurnwald, the Indian tribes depict a strong communal organisation.

4. There are no regular markets. Weekly moving markets are the bases of exchange. There is no monopoly and cut throat competition characteristic of civilized society.

5. There is no institution of private property. All the land is collectively owned. Land is equally divided among families and each family cultivates land allotted to it. There is more consumption than production. Consumption includes food, clothes and housing.

6. Economic values change in decades. Mostly, stability, equality and simplicity are the hallmarks of primitive economy. This is particularly true about procedures and techniques. There is no specialization. Division of labour is generally based upon sex distinction. In the words of Majumdar and Madan, "Specialization based on specially acquired specific technical abilities is absent in pre-urban societies. However, a division of labour based on factors other than specialization, like sex for instance, is widely prevalent."

In modern times tribal economy has been widely influenced by rapid industrialization in tribal areas. In the words of Majumdar and Madan, "The impact of industrialization has effected both men and women. Tribal men work in iron and steel factories, in coal mines and tea gardens. Tribal women workers are engaged in mica and coal mines, in tea gardens, in quarries and so on."

CONCEPT OF PROPERTY

Property and wealth are found in every society, but their meaning is different everywhere. Similarly, in tribal society also they have peculiar meaning. Modern man is engaged in earning wealth. This was not the case with his primitive ancestor, or the primitive counterpart. Property played its part in man's origin. But gradually social life evolved and different type of goods are used. Thus, the meaning of property changed gradually. In a single country itself the meaning of property differed from place to place. In the words of Philbrick, "The concept of property never has been, is not and never can be a definite content." Modern man uses the word property in the sense of capital, interest, rent and wages, etc. These were not the meaning in ancient times. The study of property in different tribes reveals different meanings. Hence, property has not a single meaning for the anthropologist. It is generally collective and rarely individual. Both the types of movable and immovable properties are available in primitive societies. In Newzealand and Melanesia, besides collective and personal properties, one finds multiple possessive rights. In this condition several owners use the property in different ways.

CONCEPT OF WEALTH

Wealth in primitive societies, does not mean gold, silver or currency notes. They are ignorant of means of exchange. Their needs are fulfilled by barter. Wealth is a public property which can be easily divided. The north pacific tribes conduct exchange known as gift exchange. Societies in which saving is not much do not have much wealth. Wealth first of all accumulated in food gathering tribes such as Kadar in India. In simple peasant societies the means of exchange of surplus goods gradually developed. As specialization increased wealth also increased. Many of the valuable products of sea such as cowries and beads, etc., were used as wealth. Thus, the meaning of property and wealth in primitive societies has been much different from that in civilized societies.

28

Religion and Magic

The phenomenon called religion is extremely variegated, complex, intricate and full of paradoxes. It includes such facts as celebration, despair, ethical vigour, mystery, retreat, social activism, monastic quietude, contemplation, animal sacrifice, rituals involving pain and terror, images of hope, symbols of fear, the affirmation of life and struggle against death, creative growth, unthinking superstitions, beliefs and dogmas about natural and supernatural etc. At first glance it looks pretty certain that such a protean phenomenon, such a closely knit mass of fact and imagination is intractable and cannot be studied either empirically or analytically. But of late, scholars from diverse disciplines like psychology, sociology, anthropology, history and linguistics have succeeded in bringing the unbounded phenomenon of religion under some system and order and have also evolved methods and techniques for its study which have yielded impressive results. Accordingly, in order to understand and appreciate the phenomenon of religion in its anthropological perspective, we must briefly know the various scientific and empirical approaches to the study of religion which are being made today. Broadly, these approaches can be divided into two groups : 1. which consider the question of origin of religion to be of paramount importance, and 2. according to which not origin but description is important.

ORIGIN OF RELIGION

In the early years of present century, the sociologist, the anthropologist and the psychologist greatly widened his horizons and laid the net of his investigation rather wide. In the process each investigator, irrespective of his personal attitudes, encountered the ineluctable fact that no account of human behaviour and social change is adequate which ignores the singular role and value of religious ideas and motives, dogmas and beliefs, faith and superstition in human behaviour. The primary interest of the early pioneers in the fields of social, anthropological and psychological research was to discover the origin of religious ideas in man rather than to describe them.

Intellectual Origin Theories

(i) *Nature-Myth School.* According to scholars subscribing to this view all the great symbols of the world's religions were personifications of natural phenomena; the sun, moon, stars, storms, the seasons of the year. One branch of this school maintained that solar myths were most important and that primitive rituals and myths were primarily concerned with man's relation to the sun.

(ii) *Animism.* According to the great anthropologist Edward Tylor, religion had its origin in primitive man's belief that non-physical substances like soul inhabited the physical and inanimate objects like stones, trees etc. Animism, derived from the Greek word Anima, meaning soul, is a belief in the non-physical, transempirical substance existing independent of body. This fact was seen confirmed by dreams in which man saw somebody talking to him, who had died recently. Thus, dreams convinced the primitive man of the existence of spirits and this conviction became, according to Tylor, the basis of religious beliefs.

(iii) *Ancestor worship.* The philosopher Herbert Spencer traced the origin of religion in the respect given to ancestors combined with beliefs in ghosts and fairies caused by dream experience. According to Spencer the ghosts of ancestors were transformed into gods.

(iv) *Magic Theory.* According to Sir James Frazer, religion developed out of an original magical stage of human culture. As the magician believes that nature can be overwhelmed and instrumentalized for personal benefit through magical spells, in the very same manner, religious man believes in the existence of spirits that must be pleased and cajoled by prayers, rather than overwhelmed by magic formulas, though religionist, like magician, seeks to understand the mechanism of nature and control it.

Emotive Theories

The above four theories are known as intellectual origin theories, because they assume that the primary source and value of religion is seeking answer to some questions. But as R.R. Marett argues, religion is not so much an intellectual endeavour as a set of profound emotional responses to various aspects or consider emotional factor to be called emotive theories and these are discussed below :

(i) *Fear.* According to the celebrated psychologist Wilhelm Wundt, religion is simply projection of fear into the environment, and according to Otto religion is identical with numinous feeling. Though Otto did not call this numinous feeling an emotion, other psychologists have identified religion with the sense of mysterious, the uncanny, and the sacred and termed it as numinous emotion.

(ii) *Unspecified emotion.* Psychologist William James refutes the theory that there is in man a specific emotion which may be considered either a cause of religion or religious experience *per se*. But he also admits that religion has profound emotional basis.

(iii) *Fetishism.* Fetishism implies undue emotional attachment to some object. In early phases of religion we find stones, trees and such objects given extreme reverence and worshipped. Thus, according to some scholars religion is nothing but a form of fetishism.

Ordinarily, it is believed that evolution of religion takes the form of a steady decline in number of gods that is a movement from polytheism to monotheism. However, according to Wm. Schmidt and Andrew Lang religion began with a primordial monotheism which later changed (either developed or degenerated) into polytheism, animism and magic.

Psychological Theories

Apart from theories which seek to explain religion with reference to some stable characteristics or traits in man, whether intellectual or emotional, there are theories which instead of considering any particular factor or trait lay stress on laws, whether social or psychological.

According to Emile Durkheim religion is one of the ways of accomplishing socialization, that is, integration, accommodation and adjustment of social and personal needs. The symbols of religion appear to their users to be about a realm of supernatural powers and forces. They are really about society and its claims upon the man. The divine laws are as a matter of fact the most crucial laws of a given society.

According to the father of psychoanalysis, Sigmund Freud, the origin of religion can be traced back to the problem of child seeking to work out adequate relationships with his parents, particularly his father. The child regards his father a figure of absolute power, but as he grows the supremacy of father becomes untenable. Religion comes in as a substitute to fill up the vacuum created by displacement of the father. Religion, therefore, has its origin in man's attempt to project into the universe a belief in a cosmic father or God to give him support he once had from his human father.

Freud suggested that primitive man originally existed in a patriarchal society where the father had absolute right over all desirable females. At some point in history, sons rebelled against the father, killed him and distributed the females among themselves. However, this primal act and ensuing guilt are the psychological causes of belief in father-god whose wrath has to be placed through sacrifice. This patriarchal society theory is stoutly opposed by those who consider that the original society was matriarchal and that is why mother-worship is so central to every religion.

As a matter of fact all these theories are highly speculative and conjectural and there are no adequate methods of verifying or disverifying them. Therefore, modern scholars have abandoned the approach of tracing the origin of the religion. Instead, they prefer objective or careful observation of what men actually do while engaging themselves in various religious activities. This is the descriptive approach towards religion and this is precisely the approach being followed by modern psychologists of religion.

Sociological Theories

Auguste Comte is regarded to be the father of sociology. He organised and classified the social thought prevailing before his times. Comte gave birth not only to a specific methodology of studying knowledge but also analyzed the evolution of human thinking and its various stages. The principle evolved by Comte in the study of human thinking presumes gradual evolution and development in human thinking and is known as the law of three stages because, according to it, human thought has undergone three separate stages in its evolution and development. The main importance of this principle is that it provides the basis of sociological thinking.

Stages of Evolution

According to Auguste Comte, human thinking has passed through the following three stages. There has been an evolution in the human thinking so that each succeeding stages is superior to and more evolved than the preceding stage:

1. Theological or Fictitious stage.
2. Metaphysical or Abstract stage.
3. Scientific or Positive stage.

Auguste Comte has explained his classification of human thinking into various stages in the words, that each of our leading conceptions, each branch of our knowledge, passes successively through three different theoretical conditions — theological or fictitious, the metaphysical or abstract, and the scientific or positive. In the following pages we shall discuss these stages briefly.

1. Theological or Fictitious Stage. The first or primary stage of human thinking is theological or fictitious. This type of thinking of children is also at this level. At this level of thinking there is marked lack of logical and orderly thinking. The primitive man and children do not have the scientific outlook. Therefore, theological thinking is characterized by non-scientific or unscientific outlook. The main subject matter of theological thinking is natural events. The usual and unintelligible events of nature tend man towards theological or fictitious interpretation of these events. Unable to discover the natural causes of the various happenings the primitive man attributes them to imaginary or divine forces. The explanation of natural events in non-natural, divine, or imaginary conditions is known as theological or fictitious thinking. For example, if we explain and understand the excess or deficiency of rain due to godly wrath, such a causal explanation would be in terms of theological or fictitious explanation. The theological thinking implies belief in another world wherein reside the divine forces which control the events in this world. Thus, it is clear that theological thinking implies a belief in divine and extra-terrestrial forces. Comte has classified the theological stage further into three loud stages. These are :

(i) Fetishism, (ii) Polytheism, and (iii) Monotheism.

(i) *Fetishism*. The first and primary stage in theological thinking is that of fetishism. Fetishism is a belief that there is some living spirit in the non-living objects. This is also known as animism. As the very term animism signifies it means that the so-called inanimate objects are not dead and lifeless but are informed by a living spirit. The examples of fetishistic thinking can be seen from the widespread belief among rural people in India that some deities reside in trees. They are, therefore, seen to engage in the worship of trees etc.

(ii) *Polytheism.* With the gradual development in human thinking there occurred a change in the form of thinking. The more evolved and developed form than that of Fetishism is known as Polytheism. At this stage man had classified gods as well as natural and human forces. Each natural or human force had a presiding deity. Each god had some definite function and his scope and area of action was determined.

(iii) *Monotheism*. The last and most developed form of theological thinking is seen manifested in monotheism. As the very term monotheism implies, at this level of human thinking a belief in one God had replaced the earlier belief in many gods. The monotheistic thinking symbolizes the victory of human intellect and reason over non-intellectual and irrational thinking. In monotheism it is believed that one God is Supreme and that he is responsible for the maintenance of order and system in the world.

2. Metaphysical or Abstract Stage. The metaphysical or abstract thinking marks the second stage in the evolution of human thinking. According to Comte each successive stage is an improvement upon the earlier stage. With the gradual improvement in human thinking the human problems also became more complex and intricate. The theological thinking was not adequate to tackle these efficiently. The appearance of conflicting and opposite forces in the world presented problems which could not be successfully tackled by monotheism. It was difficult to believe that the same God was responsible for primordial creation as well as destruction. A personal and concrete God could not account for the simultaneous creation and annihilation. In order to resolve this intellectual puzzle or riddle metaphysical thinking was invented. Under metaphysical thinking, belief in an abstract transcendental entity or Absolute replaces the belief in personal concrete God. Under metaphysical thinking it is believed that an abstract power or force guides and determines the events in the world. Metaphysical thinking discards belief in concrete God.

3. Scientific or Positive Stage. After theological and metaphysical thinking comes the next stage known as scientific or positive stage. All metaphysical knowledge is based upon speculation and is at best inferential knowledge. There are no direct means to confirm the metaphysical knowledge. In the last analysis it is a matter of belief or temperament. The modern temper of man is such that it cannot remain satisfied with mere guess work; it craves positive knowledge which can be scientifically confirmed. The positive or scientific knowledge is based upon facts, and these facts are gathered by observation and experience. The observation and classification of facts are the beginning of the scientific knowledge. From the facts we generalize and draw conclusions. These conclusions in turn are subjected to verification and once verified these become established laws, which can be relied upon in gathering and classifying the facts. The scientific thinking is thoroughly rational and in it there is no place for any belief on superstition.

Auguste Comte is of the opinion that all human thinking before reaching the stage of positivism must have passed through the two earlier stages of theological and metaphysical thinking. Even in scientific thinking some traces of earlier types are to be usually found.

TRIBAL RELIGION

Tribal religion is the most primitive form of religion found in human society. The following are the important characteristics of the Indian tribal religion :

1. Mana. Defining faith in Mana found in tribal society, R. H. Codrington has pointed out that Mana is, "A force altogether distinct from physical power, which acts in all kinds of ways for good and evil, and which is of the greatest advantage to possess or control." Thus Mana is supernatural power which is useful to man in the control of many natural phenomena beyond his power. According to Majumdar and Madan, ' Entire religious life of the primitives is born out of their belief in certain understandable, impersonal, non-material and unindividualized supernatural power which takes abode in all the objects, animate and inanimate, that exist in the world." According to Max Mueller, Mana is an attempt to define certain natural phenomena in terms of an impersonal power. The high mountain, the river, thunder and all other natural phenomena, according to the tribal people, act with the power of Mana. This power acts both for good and for evil. It is connected with the soul, ghost of the departed man and the living being. The Ho and Munda tribes of Chhota Nagpur call it Bonga.

2. The concept of Bonga. According to these tribes, Bonga is a mysterious and impersonal power at the back of rains, tempests, cold, floods, epidemics and the wild animals. Everywhere activity is due to the power of Bonga. Thus, Bonga is a form of Mana.

3. Animism. Another important characteristic of Indian tribal religion is animism. According to Risley, tribal religion is animism. The tribal people believe in the presence of supernatural powers in high mountains, flooded rivers, big trees and epidemics. They try to please these powers by means of different types of propitiations and worships. Sometimes, they are worshipped even without being given any name. An important type of animism is ancestral worship which is found among the Santhals and Oraons. The Santhals worship family deities and villages deities. Among the Korawa tribe, there is a goddess of crop, one of animals and a deity presiding over rains. The tribal people try to please these gods and goddesses by offering the sacrifices of different types of animals and birds to them.

The principle of animism is based on the following two beliefs :

(i) There are powerful souls besides powerful gods. The souls are connected with men and feel pleasure and pain through them. They influence the events in this world and also control them.

(ii) The soul of man survives even after his death. The word 'animism' was used for the first time by E. B. "Taylor in anthropological literature. Animism, according to Taylor, is the groundwork of the philosophy of religion from that of savage upto that of civilized man".

4. Animatism. According to animatism there is some impersonal power behind every material object besides the living beings. Thus, in the tribal religions is found faith in the presence of supernatural power in bones and feathers etc. This impersonal power is worshipped to maintain peace and prosperity in the group. It is difficult to distinguish between animatism and animism. The following distinctions, however, have been pointed out between the two. While according to animatism there is some mysterious unknown impersonal power underlying all living beings and things, according to animism there is animal spirit found in all movable and immovable things. An example of animatism is found in the tribes of Bihar. They consider the bones beads, stones and feathers to have living and magical powers. The stones are considered to be the children of mother earth and worshipped. The tribal people worship only those powers which can do some harm to them, but sometimes such powers are also worshipped which cannot do any harm for example, the Sing-Benga of the Munda tribe. Though it is difficult to say as to which type of nature worship is found in a particular tribe in India, generally one finds animism as well as animatism in most of the tribes. From the comparative point of view, however, animatism is more widespread than animism.

5. Naturalism. A universal characteristic of tribal religion is naturalism or nature worship. The Garo tribe of Assam worships sun and moon. The Munda people worship sun god. Besides, other tribes worship rivers, mountains, stars, trees and other natural objects.

6. Faith in the immortality of soul. Among many tribes there is a custom observing funeral rites twice. This is because of their faith in the immortality of soul. Sometimes the second rite is considered to be more important than the first. The tribals believe that the soul is not destroyed on the death of the body and requires food etc., for a sufficiently long lime. Among the Nagas and the tribals of the Nicobar Island, the skull of the dead man is placed on a wooden statue believing that the soul of the dead man will pass from the skull to the statue. Now the statue is served like a living human being and efforts are made to fulfil all its needs. Sometimes the statue is made of brass. Such is the custom among the Garo tribe of Assam. In Kerala in South India the statue of a dead person is worshipped at least once a year. The tribals believe that the soul matter can increase the fertility of land and produce life. In the Naga tribe there is a custom of worshipping souls of the ancestors at the time of sowing and when rains are needed.

7. Faith in rebirth. Most of the Indian tribes believe that after death the soul of a man survives the body and enters into the body of some animal, bird or other living being. Among the Bhils efforts are made to find out as to which body will be entered into by a particular soul. Similar beliefs are found among Nagas of Assam, Abhirs of Bengal, Kamar and Gond tribes.

8. Faith in magic. The most important characteristic of tribal religion is faith in magic. According to M. F. Keesing, "In its technical sense, magic is a term which summarizes a variety of methods by which man purports to influence automatically the course of events by that touch of supernatural. A magical act is a rite carried out to twist Nature in a specific way to satisfy human desire." Different types of magical acts are prevalent in different tribes. The tribals believe in magicians and witches. If a woman is declared a witch by the magician of the village, she is given all types of tortures. A strange type of magical act is found among the Bhils to contradict the effect of epidemic. In the event of the spread of epidemic, some people hang some pitchers and baskets on a bamboo pole and run on the main street crying 'Toraka, Toraka'. Hearing them other people of the village help them in carrying this load out of the village. The load is carried to the nearest river or jungle and throwing it the people believe that the epidemic has been thrown out of the village in the river or the forest.

9. Totem and Taboo. The custom of totem is an important characteristic of tribal religion. Different Indian tribes believe in different types of totems. The totem is considered to be the originator of a particular tribe. Its killing and eating is a taboo for the people of the particular tribe. It is worshipped and respected everywhere. Marriages cannot be contracted among the male and female of the same totem, because they are thought to be having blood relationship.

In fact, tribal religion is the most primitive form of human religion. Thus, it exhibits that unrefined purity characteristic of the primitive form. It is the beginning of religious evolution. Hence, in it one finds magic, religion and ritualism all in one. In it there is no distinction of unity and religious sanctity. Mostly, the latter depends on the former. The tribal religion is not merely a particular part of the tribal life, but enters in life everywhere. The religious and social activities of the tribal people are closely inter-connected.

RITUALS AND SYMBOLS

What are Rituals ?

Rituals and symbols have much importance among the homo sapiens. In almost all ancient or modern societies different special occasions warrant the observance and performance of specific rituals. And particularly in the case of marriage the performance of some rituals is almost inevitable in all societies. Besides this important occasion, all other occasions that may conceivably and profoundly influence the life of an individual are usually marked by the performance of some or the other rituals at their inception. Some such occasions would be the construction of a new house, starting any new work, some activity concerned with agriculture, and many other such occasions. Rituals have the recognition of society. They are modes of behaviour and methods that reflect the individual's awareness towards society. In this way, rituals are modes of behaviour recognised by society that are performed on particular occasions.

Religion and Rituals

One may observe a great difference between the rituals performed by different societies on a certain occasion. In the tribal societies many of the rituals are of a very cruel and painful nature and sometimes even involve human sacrifice. But what is universal is the deep relationship between religion and rituals that is to be seen in almost every society. Some thinkers, among them Durkheim, have interpreted this relationship to mean that religion is the origin of rituals. But the majority of thinkers do not subscribe to this viewpoint because the sphere of religion does not coincide with the field of ritualism. Rituals are undoubtedly an aspect of religion but religion is also something much more than performance and observance of rituals. And looked at from the other side, rituals are not restricted only to the field of religion. Ritualism includes many of the aspects of art and culture. Consequently, it is not correct to say that rituals are invariably religious in nature. One finds the existence of rituals in circumstances which have no connection whatever with religion. There are, of course, social occasions on which there are religious rituals. But nevertheless there can be no doubting the fact that religion does give meaning and existence to a great number of rituals. For example, in India, among the Hindus one comes across so many rituals that grace religious and other purely social occasions. In fact one may discover rituals in any field of behaviour.

Ritual and Art

Despite its predominantly religious flavour, rituals also have a profound relationship with art. According to Harrison, art has originated in religious ritualism. But as we have had occasion to observe earlier, rituals are not exclusively of a religious nature and similarly art is also not always religious. And particularly in the modern age religion and art are far removed, one is almost tempted to say that they have nothing in common and even to deny that there ever existed any common grounds between them. Hence, the idea that art originated in religious rituals is a one-sided theory. The truth of the matter is that there is no inevitable relationships between art and rituals.

Social Importance of Rituals

Rituals are found in the social life of masses. It is only natural therefore that the greater importance that attaches to them should concern the social life. In a country like India, all the rituals that are performed on various occasions have as much social as religious importance that attaches to them. Rituals help in social control. For example, the rituals that are performed on the occasion of marriage help to strengthen the bonds that are inherent in this social institution and also to grant it social recognition. The rituals contiguous with this occasion are both social and religious. The rituals that are performed on the occasion of 'Yagyopavita' observed by the Hindus, exercise considerable control on the individual. In Hindu society much importance is attached to the performance of rituals. The rituals observed at the time of marriage are intended to socialize the individual because he takes oath to prolong the life of community through procreation. In Hindu society, the performance of each ritual clearly indicates that from the point of view of both individual and social benefit some new responsibilities are being placed on the individual, the faithful observance of which is his main duty. Upanayana, marriage, etc., are rituals that are not intended merely for the individual's edification but also for awakening him to his responsibility towards the society. In this way, rituals serve to maintain the synthesis and adjustment between the society and the individual.

Rituals and Symbols

Symbols and rituals are closely related. Symbols have much importance and significance in both individual and social life. For example, the flag is believed to be the symbol of the country and hence it is held in great respect. Modern art utilises all kinds of symbols to give expression to the various postures, situations, emotions, etc. And symbols are to be seen in every aspect of man's life. It is conventional to fold one's hands and leave the chair when a senior person approaches.

Types of Symbols

It is evident from the study of symbols, that their real meaning is far more comprehensive than their explicit meaning, and the meanings of symbols are continuously determined. Symbols may be classified in the following categories:

1. Referential symbols. As is evident from the term applied to this particular form, this symbol serves to provide information concerning some person or object. For example, the red light is a symbol of danger.

2. Condensed symbols. These symbols are utilised to express in compressed form something that is too detailed to admit of economic or environment transmission or expression. An example of this is shorthand or the Morse Code.

Symbols in Human Life

Symbols are to be seen in every field of human life. Two of the more important fields in which symbols abound are politics and religion. Some examples of the symbols that are employed in the field of politics are flags, vociferous slogan shouting, party symbols, etc. In social life the etiquette is purely a matter of symbolic expression. Social behaviour such as moving in society, casual conversation, mutual behaviour, are all expressed through the medium of symbols. Another field of social life in which symbols find abundant use is education; the degrees that are given to candidates who succeed at examinations are symbolic expression of their respective educational status. Human life and conduct are both subject to constant change. Due to this fluctuation no object or form of conduct has the same value or meaning at all times and places. The symbolic meaning and expression of many things change at different times.

MAGIC

What is magic?

While in religion one prays for help, in magic he tries to force supernatural powers to help him. In the words of R. Piddington, "Magic produces results directly, that is without the intervention of spiritual beings, is essentially and often secret; has a definite objective in view and is often malicious and therefore socially condemned." Magic is based on the conviction that cause-effect relationship is universal and invariable. In other words, some definite causes lead to definite results. According to Beals and Hoijer, "Magic is a body of techniques and methods for controlling the universe, on the assumption that if certain procedures are followed minutely certain results are inevitable. It presupposes an orderly universe of cause and effect." M.F. Keesing has maintained, "A magical act is a rite carried out to twist nature in a specific way to satisfy human desire."

Magic is Pseudo Science

According to some scholars magic is pseudo-science. This view is based on the logic that both science and magic believe in the supremacy of the law of causation. In the words of Hoebel, "Magic is thus in some of its aspects pseudo-science. When the magician proceeds on the mechanistic assumption that the magical formula is a cause that must produce a given effect, his thinking parallels that of the scientist." In brief one may find the following similarities between magic and science.

1. Mechanical procedure. According to Majumdar and Madan, "Science and magic both depend on mechanistic procedures. The magician must follow the same type of process as is done by the scientist."

2. Definite aim. The magician and the scientist both act with a definite aim and purpose.

3. Faith in causal relationship. Both magic and science are based upon the universal invariable law of causation.

4. Following special rules. Both science and magic follow the special rules very minutely.

In spite of the above similarities, magic and science are very much different.

Pointing out their distinctions James Frazer has written, "The principles of association are excellent in themselves and indeed absolutely essential to the working of the human mind; legitimately applied, they yield science, illegitimately they yield magic, the bastard sister of science." Science is connected with the natural world, magic with supernatural. Science is valid, magic is invalid. Science is legitimate, magic is illegitimate. Hence, magic is not science. At best it only appears as science. In other words, it is pseudo-science.

MAGIC AND IMITATIVE MAGIC

Types of Magic

Magic has been classified into two types: Imitative magic and Contagious magic. Imitative magic is based upon the law of similarity. In the words of James Frazer, "Magic involves two basic assumptions; first, that like produces like, or that an affect resembles its causes; and second, that things which have once been in a contact with each other, continue to act on each other at a distance, even after the physical contact has been severed." Of these laws, the first has been called the law of similarity. The law of similarity is: like produces like. Hence, in imitative magic the magician performs action similar to the result desired or a cause similar to the desired effect is produced. For example, if the aim of magic is to bring rains, the magician creates smoke which resembles cloud in the hope that like cloud it will bring rains. Similarly, if any enemy has to be destroyed, his statue is ceremoniously broken or destroyed. Among Khonds some human being is sacrificed to bring rains since there is similarity between rains and incessant tears of the dying person. All these are examples of Imitative magic.

Shamanism

Among primitive people some persons are considered to have special powers of acting as middle men between man and gods. Such persons are called Shamans. Among Tharu tribe of India Shaman is called Baiga. In the tribes of Uttar Pradesh he is called Anghad. Shaman performs certain rituals concerning magic and religion to save the tribe in times of crisis. Therefore, he enjoys a high social status and he is respected by all the members of the tribe. They present gift to him on particular occasions. Added with political power it is known as Shamanism. Generally each tribe has three or four Shamans.

Taboo

Taboo is a Polynesian term. It means prohibited. Thus, taboo is a prohibition. It prevents from so many activities. Its disobedience is not a crime but a sin. Therefore, the society or the state cannot punish him but his own conscience pricks. And yet the power of taboo is more than that of law. Man does not so much fear law as the abstract power behind taboo. At the back of law is the power of the state, at the back of taboo is the sanction of religion. Therefore, taboos are more strictly observed. Its non-observance is supposed to lead to the wrath of gods.

Taboo is an important part of magic. According to Majumdar and Madan, "The woof and warp of magical beliefs and practices is made up of positive and negative strands, and taboo is latter. Its purpose is three-fold — productive, protective and prohibitive." The productive purpose of taboo is the growth of cultivation and other occupation. Its protective purpose is the safety of the individual, family and tribe. Its prohibitive purpose is to prohibit the members of tribe from doing some specific activities.

Magic, Science and Religion

Explaining the relationship of religion, science and magic some anthropologists have presented functional theories. Of these the theories of Malinowski and Radcliffe-Brown are worth mentioning. According to Malinowski religion performs many important functions in economic field among tribes. For example, one finds the fishing trade among Trobriand islanders. Most of the magical and religious activities among them are connected with this. Their scientists are efficient in manufacturing arms, instruments and boats but there are ebbs and tides on the sea and their fear leads to the need of religion to maintain the mental balance. Thus, religion also is an instrument of adjustment. Its purpose is to save men's minds from so many tensions. It makes for man's adjustment with supernatural powers which results in mental peace and tranquillity.

According to Radcliffe-Brown the aim of religion is not only to free man from all kinds of fears and tensions but to create a consciousness of depending upon supernatural powers. The existence of the group is much more important than that of the individual and hence he has to make sacrifices for the group. This sense of duty and sacrifice is created by religion. On the one hand, religion makes the individual dependent upon the society, on the other hand he teaches him to live according to social norms. Thus, religion helps in maintaining social life. As D.N. Majumdar has pointed out, in fact the views of Malinowski and Radcliffe-Brown are complementary since both the individual and society are equally important and religion is equally useful for both. According to Durkheim, religious conceptions are the product of collective situations. Religion gives priority to the moral and physical status of the collectivity over the individual. It includes beliefs and activities. Beliefs are its stable aspects while ritualism is the dynamic aspect. On religious occasions the beliefs are converted into activities.

In fact, not only religion, but even magic and science are the means of adjustment of man with his environment. The primitive man takes recourse to magic to use supernatural powers and uses religion also for precisely this purpose. In civilized societies such functions are done by science. In primitive societies many activities connected with agriculture, animal husbandary and fishing require the help of science, religion and even magic. On which occasion, which of these is used, depends upon the beliefs of the individual. Both magic and science depend upon mechanical activities. But while science is concerned with the natural world, magic is concerned with supernatural. Similarly magic and religion are also closely connected. Both create a symbolic environment. Both give importance to rituals. Both are means for the achievement of man's purpose. But while religion explains things with reference to gods and goddesses, magic explains with reference to supernatural powers.

29

Language

Theory of Evolution

The anthropologist also studies the evolution of language. He must know the language of the field in which he works. Without a working knowledge of local languages he cannot succeed in his research work. The languages of civilized societies are generally taught in the schools. The study of tribal language, however, is possible only with the help of a member of a tribe. The study of language starts with the study of its origin and proceeds to the study of its evolution. There are the following important theories about the evolution of language :

1. Inter-sectional Theory. Propounders of this theory believe that language evolved out of stimulations. Many sentiments take the form of gestures, sounds and words when stimulated. Darwin has supported this viewpoint. This view has been generally rejected.

2. Divine Origin Theory. This is the oldest theory. According to it language has originated from and evolved in Divine power. Such has been the explanation of Vedas in India. Most of the religions assert the divine origin and evolution of the language of their scriptures. This, however, fails to explain the wide variety of languages created by the same God.

3. Theory of Roots. This theory was first presented by Maxmuller Heyes. According to him, sound was a natural reaction of man to things and events in his environment. This sound gives rise to roots of words. This theory does not consider the contribution of human brain to the evolution of language.

4. Theory of Evolution. According to this theory, like all other animals man also used to emit certain sounds in the beginning. Gradually due to the sharpness of his brain he developed language. He developed language by imitation, interjection and symbolism. This theory fails to explain the relation of sound and meaning,

5. Gesture Theory. According to this theory, in the beginning men made and used to express themselves by means of gestures like dumb persons. Gradually, they developed certain sounds which evolved into so many words.

This was done by collective decision. Here, it is difficult to understand as to how human beings could take collective decision in the absence of language and words.

6. Theory of Symbolism. According to this theory men assembled and fixed symbols for different things and events and thus evolved language. It is, however, difficult to understand how people in a group could communicate to fix symbols in the absence of language.

7. Theory of Yo, ho, ho. According to this theory language has its origin in labour. Labourers emit certain natural sounds which help them in performing labour. These sounds of yo, ho, ho etc., gradually developed into words. These words, however, do not have any important place in any language. Therefore, it is improper to explain the origin of language with particular reference to these sounds.

8. Ding Dong Theory. According to this theory men imitated sounds emitted by natural objects and animals such as in the case of words like Dazzle, Gazz and Thunder, etc. All the words in any language, however, cannot be explained like this.

9. Onomatopoetic Theory. According to this theory words have their origin in imitation of the sounds emitted by natural objects, animals and birds, etc. This theory fails to explain the origin of majority of words.

10. Synthetic Theory. According to this theory, as is clear by its name, almost all the above mentioned theories have some element of truth, which is arrived at by a synthesis of all these theories. This synthetic theory is the most widely accepted theory today. This will be clear by the following discussion of the elements of language. Language and culture, power of words, importance of language and development of language in the human child.

ELEMENTS OF LANGUAGE

Social interaction depends upon social stimulation. It is necessary that there should be some direct relation between two individuals. Social stimulation is of two types, which are as follows :

1. Primary social stimulation. Primary social stimulation is that in which individuals directly and mutually stimulate each other. The main among these are gestures, emotional facial expressions, postures and movements; interjections articulate speech, physiognomy or facial expression in repose and laughter.

2. Secondary social stimulation. This type of social stimulation comprises those forms in which the relationship between individuals is of an indirect nature. At this stage, having got over the preliminary description of the various forms of social stimulation it would be proper to go into details about them.

3. Gestures. As a general rule almost every individual has recourse to gestures in the course of conversation in expressing or clarifying his idea. A dumb man may talk only through the media of gestures. Even the normal individual may use a variety of gestures such as winking, lowering the eyes, glaring, raising the hand, distorting the mouth, stamping the foot, furrowing the brow, etc., in order to give expression to his feelings and emotions. Evidently, all the various physical organs work in the process of manifesting emotions through the media of gestures. It is often said of women that their eyes talk more eloquently than their tongue. They may even make their hands talk. And it is said about the legendary Sherlock Holmes, the wonder detective, that he could discover the truth or untruth of a statement by merely studying the manner of the moving of lips of the speaker. This tendency to make the most of the body is fully exploited in literature where the signs and gestures made by the eyes for expressing some subtle emotions are a regular stock in trade.

Allport has classified gestures according to their respective bases and their nature. The following are its various classes :

(i) *Emotional gestures.* As is evident from the name, these gestures give expression to emotions and they are also born out of emotions. Some examples of this type of gestures would be grinding of the teeth, stamping the feet, making fists of the hands and shaking the head violently. There are different gestures for different emotions and in specific cultures these gestures differ from individual to individual within very narrow limits. And from these gestures, it is possible to deduce the internal emotional state of the individual.

(ii) *Demonstrative gestures.* This particular type includes those gestures by means of which an individual points to something. For example, the index finger is used to point out things or persons. People raise the arm to indicate a particular route. Similarly, the eyes are also used for the purpose of expression.

(iii) *Graphic gestures.* Herein are included all those forms of gestures whereby imitation is effected. For example, it is not necessary to call someone fat, since the same effect can be achieved by making an expansive gesture of flinging the arms out, or by twiddling the fingers to point out the thinness of a person, or to draw in the cheeks to indicate an undernourished person and other such caricaturing. This gesture serves a dual purpose in as much as it not only helps to describe the individual but also to form a picture of him in the mind of the listener.

(iv) *Symbolic gestures.* Many of the thoughts and feelings of the individual are expressed by him through the use of symbols. When a gesture is used to indicate these symbols it is called a symbolic gesture. One very good example of this would be the dance form called ballet in which a story or incident is enacted on the stage in the form of a dance. The dance rhythm, the various parts of the body and the expressions on the face express the incident to which expression is to be given.

(v) *Habitual gestures.* In some cases it is seen that people develop a habit of making a gesture and then they keep on repeating it from a sheer force of habit rather than any inherent necessity. Evidently, it is not possible to make any sense from such gestures though they may mislead any person who is not acquainted with the person who makes them. For example, some people keep on furrowing the forehead, or moving the shoulders while some others have a habit of shaking the head.

(vi) *Autistic gestures.* These gestures can be said to be autistic in two respects; one, that the person who makes the gesture is not aware of his intention in so doing while in the second respect the person observing them cannot make any head or tail out of them. In order to find out their meaning it is necessary to analyse the causes buried in the unconscious. This function is performed by psychologists and psychiatrists. Some of the gestures of this kind are biting nails with the teeth, biting pencils or any other objects held in the hand, etc. It is generally believed that such gestures arise from some mental conflict or restlessness.

4. Emotional facial expression. It is a commonly known fact that people can guess the mental state of the individual from his face. It is a proverbial saying that the face is an index of the mind. Not many people can successfully conceal their emotions because their feelings are expressed by their faces. The facial expression is altered when a different emotion becomes prominent in the mind. For example, the face lights up in happiness, becomes elongated and haggard in distress, red in embarrassment, etc.

5. Postures and movements. Posture implies the position of the body and its various parts such as standing upright, or standing bent, lying in horizontal position, preparing to run, etc. Movements of the body include such activities as running, shivering, falling, etc. These different postures and movements also perform the function of gesture and serve to indicate some definite state of mind. For example, standing straight and upright indicates the intention of opposing another person.

6. Interjections. The emotion of awe, fear or wonder spread on the face of an individual indicates his mental state concerning some object person or circumstance.

7. Articulate speech. Man used the instrument of speech in order to express his feelings and even resorts to oratory. This mode of expression in language makes adequate use of symbols and gestures.

8. Physiognomy or facial expression in response. The expression on an individual's face even when he is not excited by any motion seems to manifest his feelings.

9. Laughter. Laughter is a social stimulus. We feel like laughing when we observe a person who is amused but what is even more amusing is the eccentricity of other individuals. While laughter is a means of relieving internal tensions, it is also a mode of expressing one's feeling for another. The meaning that is inherent in laughter is derived from the context in which it arose since laughing when the occasion does not seem to demand it, is indicative of either foolishness or animosity. When two or more people laugh at the same thing, it is possible to assume that their viewpoint concerning it is similar.

LANGUAGE AND CULTURE

One major reason for the present state of human culture and civilization through constant development is the dexterity that man has achieved in the use of language. Men have evolved a medium through which ideas and thoughts may be expressed and exchanged. Animals are so much underdeveloped because they do not have the facility of language. Now what is language? It is comprised of words, symbols, signs, etc. The name that we give to any particular object exists in conjunction with all its various qualities. The moon will radiate its coolness whatever the name given to it. But can the name sun be designated for the moon? If not, why ? The reason is that in different cultures different names are given to indicate different objects and though these names are susceptible to minor variations, they cannot be changed completely. If this permance were not there, the language would have been deprived of all its purpose and meaning. Hence, it is considered necessary to determine the meaning of any term before entering into any discussion upon it. If two persons are interpreting the same term in two different senses their discussion upon it is a waste of time and energy.

The Power of Words

There is practically no limit to the power that words can wield. When the words are given the Shape of slogans they become even more powerful than the bullets fired from a gun. When Karl Marks gave the working class of the world the slogan; "Workers of the world unite!" many of the countries in the world were left with a crisis and a revolution on their hands. In democratic states the three words, equality, fraternity and liberty have immense importance which was first attached to these words at the time of the famous French Revolution. What is there in the word 'thanks' that it pleases the hearer? The word is used to express the recognition of an obligation bestowed on one. Concerning the importance of words and the power that is inherent in them Stuart Chase has rightly said. "A Japanese word, *mokusatsu*, may have changed all our lives." The word has two different meanings : taken in one sense, it means disregard or infringement, while understood in another sense, it means abstaining from commenting upon. In 1945, the Japanese Cabinet adopted the policy of *mokusatsu* in the latter sense in reply to the challenge thrown to them by the Allied Nations. But in its translation it was interpreted in the former sense. The result was that atom bombs were dropped on Hiroshima and Nagasaki killing thousands and rendering many more homeless.

Importance of Language

The importance and the power of words also, by implication, indicates the importance of language. As has been indicated earlier one main cause of man's superiority over the animal world is his skill in using language. The following are the main facts concerning the importance of language :

1. Language is the basis of intellectual development. Julian Huxley has written, "The evolution of verbal concepts opened the door to all further organization and achievement of man's thought." There is no gainsaying the fact that the present development of man was possible only because there has been language.

2. Human culture is based on language. In the words of Kimball Young, "Language is surely a *sine qua non* of human culture and without language culture could not exist or operate." In any country in human society language has developed to the same extent to which the culture has developed because in the absence of development of language there can be no development of culture.

3. Language is the basis of social interactions. In the absence of language all the day-to-day business of man would come to a standstill. Social interactions such as co-operation, competition, conflict, etc., would become impossible. Concerning the importance of language in the mutual relations between persons in the human society, Sherif and Sherif have observed in their treatise, *An Outline of Social Psychology*, "Human interactions and social life as we know it depends upon the use of words or gestures which are understood by the individuals taking part."

Development of Language in the Human Child

Almost every one is cognisant of the fact that the human child takes its own time in learning language. In the beginning he only makes a loud noise. At a later stage he learns to make some different types of noise and then learns to talk through imitating other people. Most thinkers have conceived of the following four stages in the development of language :

1. Prelinguistic. In this stage the child cannot make any articulate sound. He can only cry and make a lot of sound.

2. Babbling. This stage starts after the child has attained the age of three months. As is evident from the name given to it, the child can now make some simple sounds.

3. Simple imitation. In this stage the child starts imitating the older people around him and learns to make the simpler forms of sounds that they make.

4. The rise of true language. This stage sets in after one year or a year and a half. Now the child may speak some words and his vocabulary improves slowly and steadily.

All the above mentioned four stages in the development of language do not start at the same time in case of each and every child. Some children take less time than others to pick up language. And some falter less than others. But nevertheless, all these stages can be seen in the evolution of language in the case of almost every child.

30

Art, Mythology and Literature

Dance, folk-songs and other kinds of art are found everywhere in primitive societies. Dance and folk songs are inseparable parts of the life of the primitive people in India. None of their social or religious functions is complete without dance and folk songs. Primitive people generally dance in a group accompanied by band-music. Different kinds of musical instruments like drums and pipe, etc., are used. They generally dance in a circle. Men and women, all take part in a dance. A difference in dress of dancers, their styles and gestures etc. is found in different primitive people. People wear masks of various kinds at the time of dancing in certain places. They decorate their heads with horns, peacock feathers and many other things of the kind. The importance of dance in the cultural life of primitive people is very great. Boys and girls in every tribe are therefore given training in dancing. Dancing is taught in children-nurseries among Gond, Muriya and other primitive tribes.

Folk-songs are in vogue everywhere among the primitives. Just as no social and religious function is complete without dance, in just the same way, they include also the folk-songs in their functions. On different occasions, different folk-songs are sung according to the occasion. For example, on marriage occasion, songs connected with the married-couple are sung, on religious functions, songs connected with deities are sung. Women sing folk-songs in their houses while they are working. Men sing folk-songs while working in the fields. The thoughts and sentiments of the primitives are expressed clearly in these folk-songs. Boys and girls are given practice in singing folk-songs of their tribe as is done in dancing. The effect of the geographical situations of their places on their lives is very great. Their lives are tied to the soil and nature of the place where they live. All these impress their folk-songs also. These folk-songs also help in getting knowledge about the culture of the primitive societies.

Dance and folk-songs have great importance in social life, group-feeling in primitives is maintained by taking part in them and their unity remains firm. It is a means of recreation for them and their sentiments are displayed. It increases their enthusiasm for social functions and it brings joy to life. Folk-songs remove their tiresomeness at the time of work and make the singers fresh. The culture of the tribes is communicated from one generation to another through dance and folk-songs. Men and women get a chance to come into contact with one another by participating in them and it also gives strength to their collective organization. It is an inseparable part of primitive life.

FOLK-LORE

Folk-lore has an important place in every primitive culture. It is through the medium of folk-lores that the culture of a primitive society is transmitted from one generation to the other. The folk-lores contain the philosophy of the primitive people. How the world was evolved is a theme of many folk-lores current in different tribes. In most of the folk-lores, a reference to the mutual relation of the people and their gods is given. Many folk-lores aim at socialization and point out how different offences are punished by the supernatural powers in different ways. Descriptions about birds and beasts and also the trees, besides human beings, are given in these folk-lores. In various primitive folk-lores of India it has been shown how man depends on plants, trees, animals, birds, etc. Very interesting folk-lores about the origin of different tribes are current. One of the interesting folk-lores of this kind is found in the Ho tribe. In this folk-lore it is said that Sing Bonga and Oteborom were self-created and they made the earth with grass and trees. Next they created animals. First, they created domestic animals and later they created wild animals. Then they created a boy and a girl and put them in a cave to bring forth progeny. They were too innocent to copulate. Sing Bonga then taught them how to make *illi* (rice-bear) which excites passion. *Illi* had its effect on them and in course of time they brought forth twelve sons and twelve daughters. When all these children had been born, Sing Bonga arranged a feast at which the flesh of buffaloes, bullocks, goats, sheep, pigs and fish and fowls and vegetables were served. Sing Bonga divided twenty-four siblings into twelve pairs of brother and sister and asked each pair to choose the flesh of bullocks and buffaloes and they became the originators of Ho and Bhumij. Those pairs who chose vegetables became the progenitors of the Brahmins and the Kshatriyas : those who chose fish and goats became the ancestors of Sudras; those who chose fish gave birth to Bhuiya; and the present day Santhal were descendants of those who chose the pigs. One pair got nothing and seeing this, the Ho gave them their surplus, and the descendants of this pair became the Ghasi, who have for long worked as menials in Ho villages. There are various versions of this myth in different tribes. According to one of them, the first human pair was born out of a swan's egg. But all of their progeny were one day burnt to death by Sing Bonga in his fury. Later he repented on seeing the earth desolate, but was delighted to find that Naga bonga (the water deity) had concealed a brother and sister under water. What happened after that has already been stated above from the folk-lore prevalent among the Ho people.

The folk-lore relating to the origin of creation is prevalent in a different manner in Kamar tribe. God Mahadeo was once so annoyed by a mad jackal that he ordered the destruction of the world. An old woman overheard the curse, told her husband about it, and the two together went to a forest and hastily improvised a houseboat and loaded it with all necessities of life to last for twelve years. Then they placed their young son and daughter in the boat. Soon after a deluge overtook the world drowning the whole of mankind and also the earth. After twelve years, Mahadeo's anger subsided and he sent out his attendants to recreate the word. The young boy and girl were discovered and Mahadeo adopted them as his children. Some earth was procured from the teeth of an earth-worm and the earth was created again. The boy and the girl were left on this earth. Mahadeo had to try several tricks before he could make the boy and the girl engage in copulation. Several children were born out of the union, and their mother died soon after due to shame. Mahadeo divided these children into various pairs, and each pair became the progenitor of a caste or tribe.

The Hill Kharia people have presented a different story about the world's creation. According to the Kharia folk-lore, God created the sky in the beginning and then a pea-fowl. The fowl laid an egg which burst. Out of the broken shell came forth the first Kharia, out of the white of the egg the first Purana, progenitor of a Hindu caste, and out of its yolk came out the ancestor of the ruling Bhanja family of Mayurbhanj.

It becomes clear from the folk-lores described above and prevalent in various Indian tribes, that the folk-lores are more imaginative and entertaining than awe-inspiring. Their main function appears to entertain their listeners. Some folk-lores are like the short stories but the others are long like the novels. They deal with human situations in which suspense, ghosts, genii, heroes and heroines have their due place. A good number of similarities are found in most of the folk-lores of the world and their subject matter is very much alike. Many hundred events are described in different ways in different folk-lores. Many folk-lores like the story of Oedipus and Cinderella found in western tribes, are also found in primitive societies of India.

Folk-lores are tribal literature and contain the ideas of primitive people about the various natural objects, birds, beasts, trees and plants, planets and stars, about the creation of the world etc. A comparative study of the folk-lores of different countries reveals that the ideas of the people about the creation of the world are, similar to a great extent, everywhere in the world. It shows a similarity of the factors working in human thought, feelings and imagination everywhere in the world. Man's reaction towards nature is clearly depicted in folk-lores. They indicate the ideas of the primitive man about the environment around him, his problems and their significations. In this way, folk-lores are important means to understand human culture.

PRIMITIVE ART

Although no systematic studies about arts of the Indian tribes have been made, yet a sufficiently high standard of art is perceptible in different tribes. After the Indian independence, the Indian government have given an important place for the exhibition of the tribal art among the cultural programmes on the occasions of national festivals. Among the development programmes of the tribes, attention is regularly paid to see that their primitive arts do not come to an end as a result of their contact with urban civilization. Many experts who have worked in the tribal field, have praised their arts of music and dancing. Karma dance of the Gond people and the Bihu dance of the Assam tribes need special mention. Among the musical instruments used by Indian tribes on dancing occasions, mention may be made of drums of various types, pipes, flutes, horns, anklets, brass plates, khartal, jhanjh, etc.

Making of wooden and stone statues and even paintings are seen among Indian tribes. They decorate their bodies with different colours and make paintings on them. Their ornaments made of cowries are samples of their art. Different dresses and head-dresses are embellished. Artistic paintings on various things, used at the time of a marriage, are made. Their artistic representations do not include gods. They represent demons. Paintings are also found on funeral pillars. Some fine examples of art can be seen on the doors of dormitories among the tribes. Stools and chairs and cots are also decorated. Totemic flags are also products of artistic efforts. Erogenous parts of the body receive special attention in painting. In dances, musical instruments and masks of various designs are widely used. Animals, birds and hunting scenes are also depicted in painting and engraving, besides those of men and women. Various paintings can be seen on utensils and other articles of daily use in their houses.

The above description of primitive art justifies Hoebel's statement that "The art of primitive people runs wide gamut from technical clumsiness to high skill, from child-like simplicity to confusing complexity, from naturalism and realism to conventionalized abstraction." One of the chief specialities of primitive art is that primitive art is not for the sake of art but for life. Most of the art products are the necessary articles of daily life. A wonderful mixture of art and technology is found among many primitive people.

The main art forms of primitive tribes are given below :

1. Sculpture. Images of superhuman powers are found engraved on wood and on rocks of stones among primitive people. Such engravings at certain places are seen even on articles made of metal. The religious character of their sculpture is specially conspicuous, although demons are depicted in their engravings more than their gods.

2. Painting. Animals, birds and hunting scenes are shown depicted on the doors and walls of their houses, on clothes, floors. and even on their utensils among the primitive societies.

3. Music. Music, which is found in primitive societies shows that the people of primitive societies, possess a sufficient knowledge of rhythm and sound. They attach special importance to music on religious occasions and music is considered necessary before the commencement of every function. Besides the religious functions, music is specially arranged on social occasions. Some people are professional musicians, but generally, men and women, all take part in group programmes of music. Along with vocal music, instrumental music is also found.

4. Dancing. Almost, in all primitive societies, some sort of dance is arranged on various social and religious occasions and, men and women, all take part in dancing. Group dancing is taught in dormitories in most of the tribes. The custom of group dance is very common in primitive societies. Dancing is a social activity and gives entertainment to all men and women.

5. Oral Literature. Written literature is not available in primitive societies. Literature is found among them in the form of folk-lores. These folk-lores show that they possess a good knowledge about the subject matter, characters and style of a story. In dormitories, young boys and girls listen to various kinds of folk-lores which contain important information about the origin of their tribe; about the origin of creation; about the mutual relations among men and women; about the origin of various social institutions and about so many other things. It is through the medium of these folk-lores that the folk literature of the primitive societies is verbally communicated from one generation to another.

Primitive art is a social art, although it also statisfies an individual in so many ways. Music and dancing are mostly performed in group form. Art is the medium of entertainment. In primitive life, people have to spend so much of their time in supplying the very needs of their life that no time is left for art exclusively. Art and life are, therefore, closely related and go together in a primitive life. They make artistic designs on the articles of their use, such as utensils, weapons and their dresses. The influence of their environment on their art is clearly seen. Trees and plants, animals and birds shown in their paintings are mostly those which are found in their particular environment. In primitive society also, like the civilized society, an artistically made article is considered to be more valuable in comparison to an ordinary article; and, in this way, the time spent in giving an artistic shape to an article is not supposed to be wasted. The aim of art is the creation of beauty along with the self-expression of the artist. Things are made more beautiful through art productions. Art productions are also expressions of the imaginations or ideas of the articles.

PRIMITIVE MYTHOLOGY

When an individual is born in a society, there are many things that accrue to him in the form of cultural heritage. The cultural heritage includes all those elements of culture that a man receives from tradition. Some myths are prevalent in every society. Many of the myths owe their origin to the beliefs and ideals that are associated with leaders, patriots, national heroes, institutions and individuals. For example, in our own country many myths are current that have originated in connection with Tulsidas, Krishna, Bhisma and many other famous personalities. The myths are handed down from one generation to another and the examples set by them guide the people in their day-to-day business of life. Hence, dispite their admittedly imaginative and unrealistic character myths are very important. Besides myths, many legends also circulate in society. The function that these legends perform is much the same as that performed by the myths, *viz.*, lending guidance to people in their life and its various complexities. Every society evolves in a definite and unique geographic environment. And the people tend easily to generalize upon the experience that they acquire when they come into contact with Nature. On the basis of these generalizations the people form all kinds of superstitions concerning Nature. These superstitions, as is evident from their name, are illogical, unreasoned and blind. And yet, many are the activities of the human beings the patterns of which are determined by these superstitions. Similarly, in every society all kinds of proverbs are also circulating, having originated in the observations of the behaviour of various kinds of individuals, animals, races, etc. This is also equally true of India, just as much as it is true of any society in the world. In India many of the proverbs and myths originate in the peculiar social system that prevailed here some hundreds of years ago. Whatever the defects in these proverbs and whatever the element and degree of falsity that they may harbour, they nevertheless do to some extent guide the conduct of many individuals. In this way, myths, legends, superstitions and proverbs are received by the individual in the form of his cultural heritage and they guide and formulate his behaviour.

What Are Myths?

In every society many imaginary stories circulate in connection with the famous and great persons of particular areas or of the society as a whole. These stories do not do much in the way of providing any useful knowledge about the persons whom they concern but they do, to a considerable extent, reflect the belief and values of the people concerning them. In this way, myths do not present factual knowledge but they rather represent the fundamental beliefs of a particular group. As Kimball Young has written, "...as stories and descriptions of an imaginative nature which provide a group with the meaning of their life and culture, myths represent the fundamental beliefs, convictions and values of group." Evidently then, myths are a very important part of the social and cultural heritage. These myths pass to the individual from his family and society. In the family, the older members tell stories. And in times of crises the people have recourse to these myths which guide their conduct. In their passage through time the form of the myths is modified considerably. They also form the basis of folk songs. In his book, *Myths in Primitive Psychology*, the famous anthropologist Malinowski rightly refused to consider myths as imaginary. In fact, had they been based completely on the imaginary beliefs of the people the myths could not have so credulously stood the test of time and continued into the future. The fact is that various myths arise out of different social conditions and express the religious and cultural beliefs of the society. For example, in the Hindu society of India, myths concerning speaking truth have been circulating in connection with Kings Harishchandra and Yudhishthria.

Myths are not identical with legends. They possess greater degree of truth than the legends. Legends are a form of social myths that are related to some heroes and incidents. Both are part of the cultural heritage, and both help to maintain the continuity of the cultural life of a society.

As has been pointed out earlier, myths are not imagined stories. They have a sound psychological basis. In India, the stories of *Hitopadesha* are a very important part of the cultural heritage of society. A great majority of the people consider them to be true consequently imitating them. As Kimball Young has written, "With us, as with primitive people, myths are real and actual part of the social cultural environment. Specific experiences of the group inhere in the myths. They also reflect the interests of the group. They have considerable and profound influence upon the following generations. These successors are attached by them, encouraged by them and led to imitate the examples represented in them. Myths are unique, interesting and even shocking". According to Malinowski, they directly express the object to which they relate. Because these myths pass from one generation to another they are only too likely to be distorted and modified during this transition. One main factor in their impermanence is the fact that they are usually verbally communicated from one to another and hence derive their authority only from the strength of the memory of the person communicating them. In this connection, the observation made by Kimball Young is only too trenchant. "Memory of past experiences is not an accurate photographic reproduction of perceptions and actions. It is also affected by other images, other perceptions and emotional states and by the lapse of time. The process of forgetting and recalling is as dynamic as perception or any other anticipatory response."

As has been indicated earlier, myths are born in society and they also mould society. Upon the subject of their importance, C. Kluckhohn has written, "Myths and rituals jointly provide systematic protection against supernatural dangers, the threats of ill-health and of the physical environment, anti-social tensions and the pressure of a powerful society."

Social Functions of Myth

Concerning the importance of myth in society, Kimball Young writes, "Without them the past and the present as well as the future would seem chaotic. With them the world takes new meaning and form and does not need to be constantly recast by or for us. They make our social-cultural reality stable, predictable and capable of being endured." In this way the myths perform the further function of maintaining the relationships between the past, present and the future. Myths also help to achieve a certain degree of synthesis in the social environment. They induce the feeling of security and assertion of one's beliefs. They are also good introduction to culture. They determine the social values that serve to maintain the social control. They also serve to boost one's morale at times in one's life that try the soul to the utmost. As these myths are often related to the great people in one's society they are also an additional source of knowledge concerning these great figures. Through the influence that they wield upon the children, they maintain the necessary degree of social control. And these children growing up do not experience any burden in bearing the control that the society exercises upon them.

31

Legends

What is Legend ?

The term that is used to denote them tends to give the impression that legends are some kind of religious tales and there is no doubt that most of the legends do have a pronounced religious flavour but much of their importance attaches to their social and psychological aspect rather than the religious implication that they may have. They, too, are an important element of the cultural heritage. Despite their containing little in the way of any genuine information or truth, they profoundly influence the cultural behaviour of the people. Defining legends Kimball Young has called them, "a form of social myth based, in part on historical fact, dealing chiefly with heroes and events related to the successes and failures of a group of society." In this way, legends are connected with events and heroes. And these heroes, in the majority cases, are religious or at least, believed to be so. And these events which deserve to have place in legends said about them are usually of a divine, supra-social or extra-social nature. As in the case of myths, the legends are also of an imaginary nature and in their transition from one generation to the following, they are apt to be modified considerably. Besides being of a religious nature, they are related to historical events and heroes. These heroes to whom legends are attached command great respect and influence in society even if they are only imaginary figures. Often the mass of humanity attempts to mould its life along the lines of the lives led by legendary heroes. For example, there are so many legends attached to the life of Shri Krishna in India that he is now considered God with the result that there are few if any cultural or social spheres of Indian life that are immune to his influence. Folk tales and folk-songs arise out of these legends. The common sense folk philosophy is based on these legends. These legends also communicate many superstitions in society of which most are of a religious nature.

Kinds of Legends

Generally legends may be divided into the following classes :

(1) Religious legends

(2) Political legends

(3) Economic legends

(4) Social legends.

Evolution of Legends

Kimball Young has enumerated the following points in the evolution of legends :

(1) The development of legends takes place in the affective or emotional state of the people.

(2) The sequence of legendary stories is apt to be marred by defects through imprecise narration in communication.

(3) The retelling of legends further modifies and changes them.

(4) In these legends, certain preconceptions about the subject of the legends are also formed.

(5) In legends, the individual relating to them may misrepresent them.

(6) In legends there is a tendency to simplify the objective situation.

(7) In legends imagination is expressed in the form of stories and tales.

(8) In legends, there is an effort or desire to influence the audience.

(9) Legends are purposely and intentionally composed artificially.

(10) They are also influenced by the time period that passes between their actual creation and their being retold.

In this way, then, the form of legend changes continually as it passes through its various stages of evolution and development, and yet, in spite of this, most of the people place such implicit faith in it that they are never tempted to think about its propriety or veracity and they accept it unquestioningly. Legends differ from religious stories. Religious tales are usually of a traditional nature and are limited by customs. The mind attains peace after one hears a legend, as is apparent from the telling of or reading of the Bhagvat, the Ramayana and the Satya Narayana. In connection with the origin of legends, Kimball Young has written, "'The more common situation in which myths and legends have arisen and still arise involve religion and supernaturalism, economic matters and political problems."

Importance of Legends

The preceding description of legends is sufficient to illustrate the social function of legends. They help the man to understand the events of nature and to elucidate them besides helping him in his adjustment with Nature. They represent the ideals and values of society. In this way, they also provide the opportunity of acquainting oneself with the culture of the society that existed. The profundity of their influence is amply reflected in the fact that because of them it is possible to predict the behaviour of the individuals of a particular society. To them are attached the emotions, feelings and assumptions of the individuals of a particular society. Customs and traditions evolve on the basis of legends. Correctly gauging their importance, Kimball Young has written, "We must remind ourselves that man does not live alone in a colourless universe of passive objectivity but in a subjective, emotionally toned world of attitudes and images, and that myth, ideology and legend determine his conduct more than does the purely physical universe."

32

Government and Law

Government is the institutional form of the state which is a sovereign political organization of the people settled in a particular country. The government runs the administration. It performs the functions of the state. The functions are generally of three types — legislative, administrative and judicial. Corresponding to these three forms of functions, the government has three parts — legislature, executive and judiciary. As has been already said in connection with other primitive institutions, here also only rudimentary forms of different aspects of government are found in primitive societies. In rudimentary form of the government these three functions are not distinct; it is a later development. Therefore, in most of the primitive societies, the legislature, the executive and the judiciary are not distinct but homogeneous. In Australia, the same tribal council formulates laws, applies them and awards punishment for their violation. The same is the condition concerning most of the primitive societies in the world. According to Robert H. Lowie, a significant characteristic of the primitive government is that, in comparison to government of more civilized and developed societies, it performs very few functions. It seldom formulates laws which are generally customary.[1] The tribal life is generally regulated by customs and traditions in social, economic and political fields. Therefore, the function of the government is not to formulate laws but to see that customs and traditions are followed. Again, primitive life is simple and plain and does not require control through so many rules and regulations. Hence, also it is not necessary that laws may be formulated. The tribal chief is generally a despot. His dictates are the laws, and he does not care even for the customs and traditions. In that case too the legislative function of the government is not important. However, lack of legislation is not so much due to the despotic ruler but rather due to the regulation and control through customs and traditions. According to Morgan, Maine and others, primitive societies neither require nor have any type of government. The only bond of kinship among them is the blood relationship. Therefore, kinship itself regulates social life. It hardly requires any form of government. The formation of government was a later development. Most of the contemporary social anthropologists, however, do not agree with this view-

1. Robert H. Lowie, *Primitive Society*, London, 1953, pp. 344-45.

point. According to them every primitive society has some sort of government and administration.

TYPES OF GOVERNMENT

Types of government have been classified as oligarchy or the government by a few, monarchy or the government by hereditary kingship, gerontocracy or the rule of the elders, democracy or the people's government and theocracy or the government of the priests or religious authority. Of the above mentioned types of governments, monarchy is the most popular among primitive societies. However, it is seldom found in a pure form. Generally it takes the form of oligarchy and even democracy since the ruler almost never violates the voice of the people. Examples of monarchy can be found in Uganda in East Africa. Oligarchy is generally found among some tribes in Australia and India. Theocracy may be seen in some tribes of Oceania. Democracy may be found in some North Indian tribes. Gerontocracy is found in some Australian tribes.

Local Self-Government

Some sort of local self-government is also an essential part of primitive political organization. The village is the unit of administration. Most of the villages are self-sufficient and carry out local self-government. This is run by a council of the elders like the Panchayat in Indian tribal villages. This council has all the rights in internal affairs. This system can be found in most of the tribes of Australia and India. The most important functions of the council include the protection of public property such as pastures, forests and land, etc. Most of the villages are constituted by twenty to one hundred persons, closely related by blood relationships. Therefore, each village has a strong community consciousness with the result that each member of the community participates in collective defence and leaves no stone unturned to maintain the prestige of the village. As the population increases the village is further sub-divided and bifurcated into two or more villages which maintain contact and sometimes carry on unified political administration. Administration based on kinship relationships is the most rudimentary form of primitive government.

The Chieftain

The chieftain is the highest office bearer in the primitive political organization. He may be hereditary or otherwise. Sometimes he is also elected by the people. In different societies the powers of the chieftain are different. In some societies there are two chiefs, the peace chief and the war chief. The peace chief is the head of the tribal council which regulates internal relationships. It also decides some cases of crime. In some tribes he is elected for a definite period. The war chief guides the war. This status may be given to anyone having special abilities in matters of war.

The Headman

The most ancient office bearer in the political organization of the primitive societies is the headman. The headman is generally hereditary, respected and influential. He takes care of almost all the matters concerning his group and issues instructions on every occasion. In some societies he even leads hunting expeditions. He settles the disputes and his judgment is honoured. However, he is seldom a despot and is generally a democratic administrator.

The Council

An important part of the political organization of the primitive society is the council of elders. It is almost universally available since a single person cannot run tribal administration anywhere. Even a despotic king has to seek help from the advisers. In some tribes the royal council elects a successor to the king every time a king dies. This selection is based upon certain customs and traditions. Most of the members of the council are the elders of the society. The council decides by majority votes; however, in some American Indian councils, the decision is always unanimous. The main function of the council is to advise the ruler particularly in more complex matters. The council is constituted on the basis of the villages, the clan or the tribe. Council of a clan includes representatives of every sub-group. The same type of arrangement may be found in the case of other types of councils. In some tribes members of the council are elected. The advice of the council is respected even by the despotic kings. The king generally respects the opinion of the royal elders. Those often violating the advice of the council cannot retain their office for a long time.

PRIMITIVE GOVERNMENT AND LAW

The institution of law is run by a government association. In other wolds, government is that society (of administrators or representatives) which is appointed in a region to establish and maintain the legal order. The work of the government is to make laws to carry on administration according to them and to arrange for justice when the laws are disobeyed. In this way, the three main functions of government are legislative, judicial and executive. Is there a government among primitive societies? Different anthropologists have answered this question in different ways. Morgan, Mairie and other anthropologists have not accepted the existence of any form of government in primitive society. According to Dr. D.N. Majumdar, a government association can be seen among many tribes. For example there is an institution of chieftainship in most of the tribes, and this chieftain performs all the functions of the government. The institution of chieftainship is found in many tribes of Assam in India. They establish law and order in the tribe with the help of village councils. After the establishment of the British administration local political institutions began to lose their influence, but they could not be completely wiped out of existence. After the establishment of village panchayats in tribal areas, tribal governments have been re-established. There are generally two kinds of government, republic and non-republic.

1. Republican government. This form of government is mostly found among those primitive societies where people carry on the work of collecting fruits. Among these people, old and experienced persons define law and organize justice. Panchayat leaders are generally elected and the government is run by majority votes. An example of such a type of government is found among American Indians.

2. Republican administration. This class of government includes all those administrative organizations which do not depend on a republic. Republican governments are found in societies of simple farmers and among primitive societies of low economic standard. There are non-republican governments among societies with complicated economic organization. Examples of such administrative organizations are seen among the tribes of Africa. Some of these tribes have a strong monarchist administration and there is no leader on special occasions in certain tribes. Such occasions are often the occasions of hunting or of war. Examples of monarchic administration are found among Nagas of India. In many tribes there are chieftain-administrators. The chieftain is hereditary in some cases and elected in others. In various tribes, his rights and duties are different. Most of the chieftains are hunters and warriors and lead the tribe on the occasions of hunting and war. These chieftains are often like kings. In certain tribes, there are many chieftains under one king. Many tribes in the Uganda region of Africa live under the control of one king. Uganda province was divided in ten districts with twelve chiefs. Every district was under one chief and the remaining two chiefs acted as the king's ministers. The government is run by the chieftains elected by the members of the tribe in most of the Indian primitive societies. In some tribes, old persons, elected by the members, together form a panchayat which runs the government. Therefore, examples of both the types of government, republican and non-republican, are found here. After the establishment of British administration, the remaining governments among Indian tribes are only republican governments.

Primitive Law

Some sort of political organization is necessary to keep a control over the behaviour of the members of every society. This political organization makes laws of different kinds for controlling and directing the behaviour of the members. Their own behaviour is also regulated by these laws. This very political organization is the state. The state controls the behaviour of its members within its territory, and permits the use of force when it is necessary. Laws are those rules which are recognized by the state. The state asserts its authority by prescribing punishment for those who disobey the laws. In this way laws are distinguished from other kinds of rules through their confirmation by the state and through the provision of a penal code. Those who disobey these laws are fined, awarded physical punishment and are sometimes even hanged. No other association inside the state exerts such a widespread authority over its members. The rules of other associations have to be sanctioned by these laws. If the rules of some associations are not in conformity with these laws, they can be abolished with the help of the state. In this way, law is the only authority, within the territory of the state, which helps in the organization of other associations.

Law is called an institution because it has a sanction behind it. Law is not merely a custom. Any custom can become a law when it receives a sanction from political authority. In most of the countries, laws are enacted and the state obtains their compliance through police aid. Laws are defined in courts and it is through courts that punishment for those who disobey the laws, is legalized. There are many kinds of high and low courts in civilized countries. Appeal against the judgement of a law court can be made in a High Court but the judgment of the Supreme Court is final.

From the discussion of the aforesaid definition of law, a question arises as to how law and justice are enforced in primitive societies where there are no police and no courts. It is true, but it only demonstrates the fact that the form of law in a primitive society is different from the form of law in civilized society. Coercion for the maintenance of law or justice does exist in a primitive society but it is not in the shape of a police force nor does it need to be defined by a judge. In many primitive societies, the word of the chieftain is a law and the chieftain himself is the judge. This position is sometimes occupied by a priest because law in a primitive society is considered to be a part of natural or supernatural principle.

Nature of Primitive Law

Some people thought that since primitive people mostly kept quarrelling among themselves there must have been only criminal law applicable to them. But an anthropologist, Lowie, has shown that, in primitive societies there are civil laws also along with criminal laws, because there are some working principles in primitive societies about their mutual relations, rights of property and many other things due to different social situations of different individuals. According to Lowie, there are three main differences between primitive laws and the laws of a civilized society. They are given below :

1. Primitive law depends on the bond of kinship and not on territorial relations. On the other hand, modern law is related to a specified area.

2. Primitive law is very much similar to moral principles and public opinion, whereas modern law can also be immoral and against public opinion.

3. Primitive law makes no distinction between public and private crimes. Such a distinction is found in modern law.

In this way, kinship bond is the basis for primitive law. It is the kinship bond which keeps the different members of primitive society united. It does not require a territorial relation. As a matter of fact, kinship bond is more important in the primitive social organization than the residence at one place.

The other main basis of primitive law is public opinion. Most of the problems in primitive society are solved through public opinion. Since a primitive society is small, it is easy to know the opinions of all the members about a particular matter. Individuals are often known to one another and public opinion generally reflects the collective opinion. Since there are no party politics, public opinion is one and the same and it has therefore the strength of the whole society behind it. Public opinion is not opinion of any particular individual, or group, and therefore all the members of the society consider it their duty to act according to it. Public opinion depends on considerations of good and evil and every member of the society wants to see that current moral principles are obeyed. It is clear that no police force is needed for this. What a police force cannot do in a civilized society is done in a primitive society, by itself because in a primitive society, morality and law are not two different things. Besides this, in a primitive society, an individual has no power when separated from the group nor does he possess any moral views of his own. It, therefore, becomes necessary to obey the rules of the society.

Since, in a primitive society, law does not depend on territory, an offence, instead of being a wrong act against the state, is a wrong act against an individual. The individual offended is somebody's kin and so is the offender. The kins of the individual offended avenge themselves on the offender and his kins. There is a direct dealing between the two parties and the society as a whole has no part to play in this matter. But there are certain instances when the society has to intervene, specially in the cases where a breach of norm is likely to affect the whole society. For example, the Eskimos do not bother themselves as a group over homicide. But, if witchcraft or sorcery is suspected, they act as a group, even without caring for any kinship ties, because an act like that is supposed to be harmful to the whole society. The same thing can be said about other primitive societies. It is a common belief in most of the primitive societies that if heinous crimes by society as a whole are not punished by the society, the whole society is punished by supernatural power. They, therefore keep an eye on such crimes, and the moment they are detected, the offenders are severely punished.

There is yet another difference between primitive and civilized law, that is, whereas the intention of the offender under civilized law is taken into consideration while giving judgment attention is not paid to his intention but to the crime itself in a primitive law. Among civilized societies, even the most heinous crimes, if the intention is correct, are punished very lightly or the case is dismissed after giving a warning only. But in a primitive society, whatever may be the intention of the offender, he cannot escape punishment for his misbehaviour and in this way more attention is paid to the crime than to the intention; although it does not mean that intention has no importance in primitive law.

Another difference between primitive and civilized law is related to responsibility. There is collective responsibility behind primitive law because it rests on the principle of kinship bond. On the other hand, such a collective responsibility is not accepted in civilized society and therefore an appeal can be made in a law court against the state actions.

While in civilized societies the judges are in no way connected with an offender, the judges in primitive societies are from among the kins of the offender. The village associations decide the criminal cases and there is always a representative of every kin group of the tribe in every village association. Where decisions are taken in criminal cases by the chieftains of primitive societies, most of the chieftains give judgments only after due consultations with the family chiefs, village chiefs or with the representatives of the kin-group.

Evidence

There is some difference in the nature of evidence in primitive and civilized law. The following two kinds of evidences are called for in deciding the criminal cases in primitive societies.

(a) *Oath*. The offender has to take an oath and then he is asked to state whether he has committed the offence or not. It is generally believed that, if the offender tells a lie, he falls a prey to the supernatural anger for taking a false oath.

(b) *Ordeal*. Sometimes the persons accused are put to torture in primitive societies before the declaration of judgment in criminal cases. If the accused persons escape without injury, they are acquitted as they are supposed to be not guilty. In some cases, for example, the accused is asked to put his hand in boiling water or oil; and if he can do so without causing an injury to his person, he is let free. But if his hand gets burnt, he is believed to have committed the said crime. The belief behind this kind of treatment is that the supernatural powers help an innocent person and therefore his hand, even when it is put in boiling water or oil, does not get burnt.

Punishment

While punishment is meted out in the shape of imprisonment or fine in a civilized society, there are no such prison institutions in primitive societies. In most of the primitive societies there are provisions for mutilation which often result in the death of the culprit. Capital sentence is generally given in a case of homicide; but sometimes the death penalty is given to one of his family members or to one of his kins instead of inflicting it upto the person who has actually committed homicide. They believe that it is not the individual who is regarded to have been wronged but the whole kin-group to which he belonged and his kin-group, therefore, avenges itself on the kin-group of the accused and not necessarily on the accused himself. In primitive societies all the persons who have committed a similar crime are not punished in a similar manner. The same crime may be differently punished according to who has been wronged. The misbehaviour done to an ordinary individual is lightly punished, when the same misbehaviour done to a chieftain is punished severely. For example, adultery with the wife of a king or chieftain is a capital crime and punished with death whereas adultery with some ordinary individual is not punished so severely.

The punishment of imposing a fine is not found among the punishments for crimes in primitive societies. Where fines are charged in a primitive society, they are paid by way of compensation to the aggrieved party. The accused, very often, has to give a feast to the whole village in compensation for his crime. Even in case where fines are paid by way of compensation for the wrong done, attention is paid to the person who has done the wrong as well as to the person who has been wronged, if a person of a low standard offends a person of a high status, the fine imposed is very heavy. But, if a person of a high status offends an ordinary person, the amount of compensation is very small.

From the above discussion, it is clear that primitive law is obeyed naturally, knowingly and blind-folded. Why is it so ? As has been said before, primitive law depends on public opinion, moral principle and religious principle. In this way disobedience to law is not only a crime, but is also a sin and an improper act. If an offender is not punished for his offence, it is supposed that supernatural powers would punish him for his sins, and sometimes the members of his family and even his kin-group are victimized by the wrath of supernatural powers along with him. All relations among people of primitive society are natural. Every member knows very well that if he himself wants to be treated well by others, he will also have to treat them well. In this way their duties are reciprocal and it becomes the religious duty of every individual to fulfil them. These reciprocal duties are primitive laws and obedience to primitive laws, therefore, goes on in a natural way.

Examples of Primitive Law

By studying various primitive tribes, the form of primitive law will become all the more distinct. In this connection examples of the Ho tribe of Chhota Nagpur, the Kamar of Madhya Pradesh, the Kharia tribes of Orissa and Bihar and the Rengama Naga of the Eastern Frontier Province are given below :

1. The Ho. The economic and cultural standard of the Ho tribe of Chhota Nagpur is sufficiently high among the Indian tribes. A reconciliation of the past and the present can be seen in this tribe. The administration of government officials in the tribal area is carried on through some chosen workers from the village. With the advent of modern law and justice, the influence of traditional primitive laws among the people here is on the decline, but the number of crimes and law suits are proportionately on the increase. The individuals among the Ho people who mediate between government officials and the tribal members are known as 'mankis' and 'mundas'. These tribal workers are inefficient and corrupt. They can neither help the government nor safeguard the tribal interests. The result is that they generally become self-seekers. Their activities have been very harmful for the local panchayat. However, the government has been making attempts to maintain the traditional machinery of the panchayat. There is a tribal inspector for the tribal organization and a Kolhan superintendent of a Deputy Collector's rank to look into the panchayat decisions. The superintendent attends the final sitting of the panchayat, tries to understand the whole suit and examines the panchayat's decision in that connection. The panchayat has to consult the 'munda' and the 'manki' of the kin concerned for their opinion before deciding a dispute. Whenever a chieftain fails to settle a dispute the Kolhan superintendent himself proceeds to question the parties and the chieftain about the details of the dispute and gives a decision.

2. The Kamar. The Kamar tribe also, like other tribes, has to follow its own customary laws along with the laws of the Indian government. The people of this tribe rarely go to a law court for justice because they are not acquainted with the functioning of the court nor is there a tradition of going to the court. There are different laws to deal with different climes among these people. The punishments for crimes, according to their own laws, are not the same as suggested by the government laws, because the conception of a crime among these people is different from the government conception. For example, stealing of grains and other things from government stores for their tribe is not considered to be a crime among the Kamar people. Personal disputes are personally settled through an exchange of blows. In case of a homicide, the murderer's crime is pardoned when he invites the whole village to a feast. The provision of punishment in such cases, according to Indian laws, is clearly different. The crimes are decided by the panchayats and they alone are responsible to execute the punishments awarded. They do not award punishment in crimes in which there is provision of punishment by the supernatural powers, because it is believed that if a criminal is not punished by the supernatural powers in his life period, he will surely be punished for his crime in the after world. Incest is one such offence among the Kamar people which need not be punished, as supernatural wrath is sure to be visited upon the offending pair. The bad name which the pair earns for the crime in the society is in itself a punishment. In some cases, the offenders are outcast or driven out of the village. Negligence in religious duties is not punished in the hope that the gods themselves will take revenge. There are automatic supernatural punishments for some ordinary breaches of various taboos. For examples, if a menstruating woman violates any of the taboos imposed on her, it is expected that not only she, but the whole of her family will be punished by supernatural powers.

The panchayat does not settle all kinds of crimes. In many cases, social disapproval expressed by the elders of the local group is considered to be enough, while others are left for their settlement to the supernatural powers. The panchayats settle only those cases in which the crime committed is of a very serious nature or where there is a serious breach of law. The panchayats enjoy wide powers in socio-religious matters. They depend on officials for their work. The Sarpanch presides over the panchayat meetings. There is a chaprasi who runs errands and informs the people about the date, place and purpose of the panchayat meetings. The village chief helps the panchayat in deciding criminal cases. But all those officials have no voice in the decisions of the panchayat. They only help the panchayat in its work. Only elderly men can be members of a panchayat. Children, young men and women are excluded from this membership. The decisions taken by the panchayat are either unanimous or majority decisions. The people assembled can express their views but their opinions are not counted in reaching decisions. An appeal against panchayat decisions cannot be made. The panchayat hears both the sides along with their witnesses and the persons accused are also given an opportunity to explain their positions.

Intentions and motives are subordinated to the consequences of an act. The punishment awarded is one and the same in wrongs committed deliberately as well as in those committed unknowingly. Penal feasts are given as penalty in most of the offences. The details of such feasts are fixed by the panchayat itself and the expenses can be reduced on the request of the accused. Enough time is sometimes allowed to an accused for the arrangement of the feast, during which time he has to bear with the punishment awarded to him and has to remain outside the social life of the tribe at least.

After the establishment of the government administration in the tribal areas, such offences as homicide, grievous bodily hurt and thefts of a very serious nature are taken to the Indian courts for decision. For other offences, not considered as such according to the Indian Penal Code, the punishments are awarded by the panchayat. Examples of such offences in the Kamar tribe are adultery, witchcraft, touching or riding a horse, eating with the people of low castes, black magic, killing of a cow or bullock, being beaten by a low caste person, having vermin in the wound, marrying a fifth husband after changing four, elopment and breaking of the rule of clan exogamy, etc. Offences against property are given special importance among the Kamar People. Few people conceal their offences and the evidences are generally true. Most of the offences are considered as sins which can be expiated in most of the cases by giving a tribal feast or by paying a fine. The elders are the guardians of law and it is they who define the law.

3. The Kharia. In the matter of law and justice in the Kharia tribe, the village headman is the most important person. The headman consults the leaders of influential families in giving justice. The leaders, taken together, constitute the village panchayat. The village panchayat deals with all violations of social, religious and political principles. The headman and the panchayat members attend the public worships, marriages and funerals. Different offences are punished differently. Excommunication is the severest punishment which a panchayat can inflict. This punishment is inflicted for offences such as sexual union with a non-Kharia, sexual intrigue within the clan, killing, intentional or accidental, of a cow, calf or bullock and so on. In offences of minor gravity, there is a custom of sacrificing a white cock or a he-goat in the name of sun god.

There are customary laws among the Kharia people pertaining to inheritance of property. Ordinarily a son inherits the property of his father; but if there is no son the widow inherits the property of her dead husband. Contact, sexual intercourse or eating of food with non-Kharia people is also regarded as social offence and certain rites are performed to purify the polluted, without which they cannot be re-admitted into social life. Witchcraft is considered to be a serious offence. Those who practise witchcraft are regarded as enemies of the society and its good and such persons are excommunicated.

4. The Rengama Nagas. Before the introduction of British rule the village government of the Rengama Nagas rested on the institution of chieftainship. The chief was assisted in his work by able men of different clans. His office was hereditary in the clan but not in the family. The power of the chief was supreme but he could also be removed if he proved very inefficient. The penalty for disobeying a chief was destructing of the offender's house. After the establishment of British rule, the chief lost this power, but in the matter of inheritance of properly and in many other matters their customary laws prevail even today. The right of inheritance goes from father to son, but, in the absence of a son, the widow is entitled to maintenance till her remarriage or death. For serious offences like homicide and arson, the accused is exiled and his house is destroyed. They also distinguish between murder and accidental homicide and the offences committed knowingly are punished very severely. An example of such an offence is putting a jungle to fire which makes the jungle useless for many years. Stealing of grains is considered a serious crime. Fines are imposed in such cases but the amount of the fine is realized from the property of the accused only after his death. Sexual relation with an unmarried girl, if not against her will, is no offence but the parents may claim a fine. The amount of fine in such cases is distributed among the poor. Oaths are sometimes administered to find out the truth. According to the belief prevalent among them, many kinds of offences are punished by supernatural powers. Men and women have equal status in the eyes of law.

In some of the main Indian tribes, as is clear from the above description, there are some common factors existing in their administration of law and justice. Many kinds of offences in Indian tribes are left to supernatural powers for their punishment. Decisions in criminal cases are taken by the panchayat and there is no appeal against such decisions. Many of the offences are expiated by inviting the whole village to a feast. In many cases, the offenders are exiled. The administration of law and justice in most of the cases depends on customs and traditions. The work of administering law and justice is entrusted to elderly people of the tribe, and the punishments are awarded by them in common interest. Witchcraft is considered a serious crime everywhere. The panchayat members take the statements of the witnesses besides the statements of both the parties in arriving at their decisions in criminal cases.

33

Justice and Punishment

Like other social institutions one finds a rudimentary system of providing justice in primitive societies. The organisation for provision of justice is vague and lacks the complex structure found in modern societies. The basis of this system is generally the kinship group. The responsibility for identifying and punishing the criminal in primitive societies lies with the kinship group collectively. Since in most of the primitive societies, the hereditary chief represents the collectivity, he is therefore the leader in carrying out the system of justice. He performs this function generally with the help of a council of elders. This council is constituted by representatives of different sub-groups, within the particular primitive society. The council of elders advises about the type and quantum of punishment given to the offender.

The rudimentary organisation of justice, in primitive society is due to the fact that the society is a simple and small group based upon kinship relationships, and face to face relations generally devoid of much external contact. The customary laws are generally followed due to the fear of public opinion. Most of the social rules are not violated since it will make the offender an object of laughter and his social status will be considerably reduced. Since a primitive society is generally a small community where each one knows everyone else and everyone has to pass his life in contact with others, social mockery is the biggest punishment. Therefore, the entire primitive system of social justice is very much facilitated due to the effectiveness of public opinion.

COLLECTIVE RESPONSIBILITY

It is clear from the above discussion that the system of social justice in primitive societies is carried on by collective responsibility. For example, in a clan organisation, the members consider themselves blood relations. Therefore, if someone misbehaves with some other members of the clan, the rest of the members oppose him. This social consciousness is clear in the saying "strike my clan brother and you strike me". Thus, every wrong act within or out of the clan is avenged collectively. Another significant aspect of collective responsibility is the collective feeling of shame and fame. The bad name for a bad act is not applicable to the doer alone but is felt by the total group. Thus, others will not allow him to carry on his nefarious activities. This is not only applicable to clan groups but even to the tribes outsides the clan. For example, in Hupa tribe if a member is killed by someone, the other people kill some or the other member of the murderer's family. It is so since the crime of a person is considered not only against an individual but against the whole group. It is due to this sense of collective responsibility again that the group has a collective responsibility to punish the criminal member. In Ifugao tribe sometimes a murderer was left without punishment, but he was punished by other members of the group. Since collective responsibility is useful for everyone, it is in everyone's interest to maintain it. Sometimes the reprisal is small while at other times it ends in almost a war. Thus, the responsibility is closely linked with the question of survival. Therefore, if A harms B, A's group tries to restrain him and arrange for compensation to B.

DETERMINATION OF CRIME

Crime is determined in several ways in primitive societies. The direct perception of the act of crime is sometimes not necessarily available. In the absence of such evidence, the determination of crime is left to the supernatural powers and the person concerned has to undergo severe tests. If he passes through the tests satisfactorily he is declared innocent, otherwise he has to face punishment. In Africa, in some tribes if it is suspected that a woman has committed some sexual crime and she does not admit it, she is thrown from a high hill to determine whether she has committed the crime or not. After rolling down the hill if she is unhurt, she is declared innocent, otherwise she is punished. In some other tribes the suspected person has to put his hand in fire or boiling water to prove his innocence. This is what is known as retributive theory of punishment which is based upon fulfilment of moral justice. It is like the Hindu law of *karma* according to which the good must be rewarded and evil punished even if they evade determination by the law. Since the primitive people believe that offenders are punished by Nemesis, the goddess of retribution and punishment, the criminal is put to severe tests.

In primitive societies it is generally believed that the priest or Shaman or the magician possesses a supernatural power. Therefore, sometimes the determination of crime is left to them. They follow traditional methods to determine the crime. In some other primitive societies there is a very mild way of determination of crime. The suspected person is asked to solemnly declare whether he is innocent or a criminal. If he denies to make a statement on oath, he is held to be the criminal. On the other hand, if he unhesitatingly declares his innocence on oath, he is freed. Similar custom may be found in case of Panchayat System in Indian tribes. The oath is taken in the name of God, one's children or the Ganges water. This type of determination of crime is prevalent due to faith in the supernatural power of oath. It is generally believed that if a false oath is taken, the offender is punished severely by the supernatural powers, as nothing can be hidden from them. This way of determination of crime is quite popular. However, in some tribes in Africa and America the plaintiff and the defendant respectively present their arguments before the council of elders and the final decision is left to the majority vote of the elders. This type of arrangement may be seen in most of the Indian tribes. And generally justice is done.

EVIDENCE

According to Hobhouse, evidence is not only due to the need of testing the suspect but also to prevent the reactions of the group against him. Therefore, some sort of evidence counts in the determination of crime in almost all the primitive societies. In some tribes evidence is mostly gathered through religious and magical practices. Therefore, direct evidence is not always necessary. This evidence may be in the form of oath or ordeal. In the former case different methods are adopted in different tribes. For example, among Crow tribe the suspect repeats some words of oath, taking the sun as a witness and keeping a knife in the mouth. In Samoid tribe the oath is taken keeping one hand on the nose of a pig. Among Negroes of Africa an oath is taken keeping one hand on the forehead of the chief of the group. In Kirgiz tribe the suspect has not to take an oath to prove his innocence but such oath is taken by some other person intimately connected with him. The reason for this custom is that few persons would like to risk the life of their dear ones since a false oath may cause the wrath of the supernatural power.

Similarly, a variety of customs may be found in the ordeal test of evidence. In Chukchi tribe, the two persons fighting with one another are required to compete to decide about the offender and the looser is the offender. In Ifugao tribe both the plaintiff and the defendant have to put hands in boiling water to prove their innocence. Any one who does it in haste or whose hand is hurt is declared offender. In Ewy tribe of Africa boiling water is poured over the head of the suspected person. If he tolerates it without flinching he is declared innocent. It may be observed that in most of the ordeal tests, the natural result is the establishment of crime unless by chance or by some unknown reasons the offender comes out unhurt. By the natural laws the suspect must be hurt. If he is not hurt it is presumed to be due to the interference of some supernatural power. This is hardly scientific but is based upon a faith in the moral order in Nature. It is possible that in most of the cases the suspect is declared criminal through the ordeal test. The tests by oath are certainly better and more humane.

CRIMINAL INTENT OR MOTIVE

A criminal is not only punished for his action but more for his intention or motive. Without intention or motive so many wrong acts are left without much punishment since responsibility goes with intention. If by mistake a person kills another or does it in self-defence he is not punished. On the other hand, if criminal intent is proved severe punishment is awarded. In primitive societies, however, criminal intent or motive is not very important. They believe that if a crime goes unpunished the supernatural power may punish the whole group for it. Therefore, every rule and regulation is considered sacred and the supernatural power punishes the criminal. An interesting example has been given by Goddard concerning Hupa tribe in this connection. A woman prepared fire to heat water to wash clothes. A child got entangled in the fire, was burnt and died. Though there was no intent on the part of the woman, even then she had to sacrifice the life of her son in exchange. In the Jaggi tribe the intent is meaningless in the case of murder. It is considered necessary that blood must flow in return for blood since it is believed that the soul of the murdered person thirsts for revenge. Therefore, it is necessary that the murderer must be given death punishment, otherwise the murdered soul will seek revenge from the whole group.

Though it is true that intent is not very important in the consideration of punishment, in tribal society, however, this does not mean that it is not considered relevant anywhere. For example, in Ifugao tribe distinction is made between wilful and accidental actions in order to decide responsibility. If the crime is due to carelessness or wilful action, the criminal is invariably punished. On the other hand, if the action is accidental, the accused is not punished even if he has caused loss to others. For example, if by accident the eyes of a person are injured by another, no compensation is demanded. On the other hand, if a person shoots an arrow and it kills a boy passing on the way, the person concerned has to pay half of the usual fine fixed for a murder, since the death is not by intent but by carelessness. Similarly, if mistaking a person as an enemy, someone kills him, he has to pay the fine since the crime is due to carelessness. However, there is one occasion when intent is disregarded in punishment in Ifugao tribe. If some mishap occurs in a grand feast, the host and the priest are held responsible for it. The host is held responsible since if he had not given the feast, there would not have been any mishap. The priest is guilty since it is believed that the mishap has happened due to some error in the performance of religious rites and the consequent sin. In Bantu tribe each murder is a crime, whether it is by intent or otherwise. The murderer has to pay compensation to the chief of the group since an active member of the group has been lost, which is represented by the chief. On the other hand, if a person has incurred monetary loss due to some individual, it is not considered a crime and no compensation has to be paid. In this example the crime is considered a wrong act against the group. A wrong act against an individual is not a crime requiring punishment.

PUNISHMENT

The most usual criteria for punishment in primitive societies is the principle of "eye for an eye". According to this principle if a person has taken the eye of another the chief orders that the eye of the criminal should be taken. Blood for blood is the ancient principle of retribution in primitive societies. Thus, punishment is based on retributive principle. This is so since most of the tribal people believe that crime is a violation of divine system or rules. Hence, it is believed that the criminal is evil and should be given suitable punishment so that he may become free from evil. The evil souls must be punished. Besides retribution, another basis for punishment is compensation of the loss. Punishment in the form of fine is usually based on this principle. A fine is imposed since it compensates the loss.

But the most important principle in the primitive system of punishment, is the principle of collective responsibility. According to this principle punishment is not necessarily awarded to the individual who has committed the crime but his family, clan and local group may also be punished. For example, punishment of death is given for a murder, but this punishment may not be awarded to him who has murdered. In his place some other member of his family, group or clan may be killed since the group is collectively responsible for the criminal act of each member.

Different types of punishment are prevalent in different primitive societies. While in some societies compensation and social extermination are the more usual punishments, in other societies different types of physical injuries are inflicted as punishment. Similarly, in some societies fines are imposed and community feast is demanded to wipe off the crime. In some other societies the criminal is publicly insulted by blackening his face and carrying him through the entire village seated on a donkey. In America, in a tribe an unfaithful wife is given the punishment of death by drowning in water. In an Uganda tribe there is provision of jail for the criminal. The criminal, however, can be set free for a night. If the crime is very serious the criminal is fixed to a pole till he dies. Murder is usually punished by capital punishment but most of the tribes do not have the provision for hanging till death. The provision for jail, however, is very exceptional. Usually, one does not find prison houses in tribal societies.

While deciding punishment the tribals take into consideration the social status, sex and other distinctions of the criminal. For example, in Garo tribe in India an adulterer is punished by death but an adultress is given the milder punishment of piercing of the ears. However, if she repeats this crime several times she is punished by death. Similarly, there are some criminal acts which carry no punishments if done by the chief while every other person is punished for them. Similarly, punishment may be varied in proportion to the social status of the criminal. The higher status sometimes carries lower punishment while at other times it is the reverse. For example, in some African tribes adultery by a common woman is considered a minor crime while death punishment is awarded for the same crime to the wife of the chief. In some tribes punishment is not given to the individuals but rather to the groups, families or clans. A village is punished for the crime of a member of the village. Revenge also is not sought by an individual against another individual but by a family against another family, a village against another village and a clan against another clan.

COMPENSATION

Like the civilized societies, most of the primitive societies have provision for compensation for the loss due to crime. In some societies the compensation has to be paid by the criminal according to definite customs. The list of crimes carrying definite compensation is different in different tribes. In Ifugao tribe most of the crimes are decided by compensation. The compensation for life, however, can be life, blood for blood. In such cases the criminal is killed and no other compensation is accepted. The amount of compensation often varies according to economic status of the criminal. In Kirgiz tribe compensation is fixed according to economic status. Among Red Indians of U.S.A. compensation in sought by destroying some valuable possessions of the criminal. This policy is particularly practised in the cases of adultery. In Samao tribe the criminal has to give valuable presents as compensation. By this he means to show that he has surrendered and is prepared to face any punishment given to him. Such presents and surrenders usually do not go waste since the aggrieved party usually accepts the presents. In some other tribes other forms of compensation are prevalent. One way is to give a feast to the whole village. In some tribes if the offender is unable to pay compensation himself the compensation is paid by the chief of his group.

TRIAL

As a general rule one finds some rudimentary form of trial before the award of punishment to the primitive criminal. Both the plaintiff and the defendant present their cases before the chief and the council of elders who carefully hear them and sometimes cross questions are put by them. Examples of this arrangement for trials may be found in most of the Indian tribes.

From the above discussion of the system of justice and punishment in tribal societies it is clear that they exhibit almost all the elements of the system of justice in rudimentary form. The main distinction between the primitive and civilized societies concerning crime and punishment is that while in civilized societies it is absolutely concerned with the individual, in primitive societies it is a collective affair. This is applicable to crime, punishment and compensation. While in the civilized society it is the concern of the individual, in primitive societies it is the concern of collectivity. It may be said that the latter arrangement is more humane and better measure for the prevention of crime. In its absence crime increases both in quality and quantity with the growth of civilization.

34

Criminal Tribes

A person who violates established law for some personal end is called a criminal. And a person who habitually offends and defies the law and has made law-breaking the source of his livelihood and who feels little or no remorse for his misdeeds, in fact, ceases to regard them as misdeeds, is a professional criminal. There are certain tribes in India which had been considered habitual offenders or professional criminals for a pretty long time. A criminal tribe is one, the majority of whose members earn their livelihood by practising crime. The members of these tribes do not look down upon or condemn crime but accept it as a part and parcel of their lives. As a matter of fact, right from the cradle they start teaching their children the tricks of the trade and by the time they grow up they become expert criminals who, therefore, feel nothing easier than law-breaking for personal profit. Some criminologists believe that crime has become the hereditary property of these tribes and that whosoever is born in such a tribe automatically inherits the predisposition to crime. But there are many scholars of eminence who reject the hereditary theory to account for widespread tendency to crime among the members of criminal tribes. As a matter of fact, it is not so much of a genetic heredity but is certainly a case of social heredity. As the parents of these children are practising crime and, since they feel no shame about what they do, their children are exposed at a very impressionable age to crime and pick it up by imitation and learn through experience and trial and error the tricks of the trade. As it is common knowledge that children generally adopt the professions of their parents, it is small wonder that children of the parents who are professionally criminal take to crime.

ORIGIN AND DEVELOPMENT OF CRIMINAL TRIBES

There are a number of criminal tribes in India. The majority of these tribes are nomads and keep moving from place to place. Like gypsies of Europe they have no fixed abode. It is due to this nomadism that it is difficult to collect authentic information about the origin and development of these tribes. Therefore, there are a variety of views among scholars about their origins. According to one view, as the Indian tribes belong to original gypsies of Europe, the Indian criminal tribes also belong to gypsies. According to these scholars the gypsies of Europe spread all over the world and the Indian tribes are therefore European gypsies who migrated to India. There are quite a few scholars who support this view; but there is little scientific evidence in its favour. This view is at best a conjecture.

The second view about the origin of these tribes is that they are actually offshoots of the primitive Indian races. Those members who found a fixed abode and kept pace with the development of civilization and successfully adjusted themselves to changes got amalgamated with the main current of national life. But those individuals, who, for some reasons, could not make adjustments and kept moving from place to place and failed to find a permanent home became nomads and that these nomads are the real ancestors of modern tribes. On account of economic hardships and social organisation these people gradually took to crime to keep themselves going and this has become their habit.

The third view is quite different from the other two views. According to some scholars, these tribals are neither migrants from foreign lands nor have they sprang from primitive races. As a matter of fact, the ancestors of these people belonged to royal households but were forced into exile for some serious crime. In order to escape persecution they kept moving from place to place. It is also claimed that they took to crime as a revenge against their persecutors. In this connection there are many legends and romantic tale about tribals of Rajasthan. It is said that when Maharana Pratap was vanquished, he decided not to settle down anywhere permanently till the defeat was avenged and that his followers kept this vow till recently.

The history of criminal tribes is very old; but the name and classification of these tribes is due to British Imperialist government in India. The British Government passed an Act in 1871, known as Criminal Tribes Act. Between the years 1897 and 1911 the Act was amended twice. According to this Act all the criminal tribes are born criminal and therefore anyone born in this tribe is bound to take to crime. Accordingly, all children born in these tribes were listed as criminal in police records so that a strict surveillance and supervision was kept over their activities. With the dawn of independence there was great hue and cry against this Act and, as a result, this Act was modified and finally repealed in 1952. However, the long record of criminal activity and propensity could not be abolished by the repeal of the Act. Therefore, to fill the vacuum created by the repeal of the Act, another Act was passed, known as Habitual Offenders Act. About these tribes, T.V. Stephens has written: "The special feature in India is caste system : a family of carpenters will be carpenters, a century or five century hence, if they last so long. Keeping this in mind the meaning of professional criminal is clear, it means a tribe whose ancestors were criminal from time immemorial, where descendants will be offenders against law until the whole tribe is exterminated."

In modern India, the population of the so-called criminal tribes or habitual offenders is about 4 millions. According to a recent survey, the break-up for various states is as follows:

Sr. No.	Name of State	Population
1.	Uttar Pradesh	16,68,845
2.	Maharashtra	6,23,809
3.	Karnataka	2,10,321
4.	Tamil Nadu	5,94,440
5.	Madhya Pradesh	76,721
6.	Orissa	74,762
7.	Andhra Pradesh	69,602
8.	Bihar	13,311
9.	West Bengal	4,598
10.	Punjab	76,564
11.	Rajasthan	65,440

CHIEF CRIMINAL TRIBES

In India, there are a number of criminal tribes. The same tribe is known by different names in different parts of the country. In Northern India, the chief among criminal tribes are Sansi, Meena, Kanjar, Bavaria, Boria, Bhedkoot, Bhatoo, Dom, Haboora, Biloch, Karwal, Mahatam, Pakhiwara, Togco, Harni, Badhak, Bhagaria, Bhil, Bahelia, Aheria, Tootia, Bakhar and Nath, etc. The chief tribes of Western and Southern India are Bavaria, Chohara, Pardhi and Kanjar. Now we discuss in detail the more important of these tribes.

1. Sansi or Sansia. Sansi is an extremely well-known criminal tribe. Their areas of origin are believed to be Ajmer and Mewar in Rajasthan. The Sansis are broadly divided into two groups — Kalka and Mali. Further, these have many sub-classes amongst them. There is another basis for the division of Sansis; those who are settled in some place permanently and the others who are nomadic and move bag and baggage from one place to another, taking no fixed residence anywhere. In the nomadic Sansis, one group is known as Birthwar and the other group is known as Rheluwala. An interesting feature about these groups is that though they are generally indifferent to moral values, they strictly observe the prohibition against inter-caste or inter-group marriage. Some Sansis are settled in Rajasthan. It is believed that they are descendants of the notorious dacoit and robber Sahasmal. Some Sansis have settled down in Bengal, too. However, the most famous of all Sansis are the Sansis of Punjab. There is a romantic tale about their origin. It is said that a daughter of a certain King was extremely beautiful and passionate. Her sexual adventures led her to commit a sexual offence — coitus with an outsider, not belonging to royal household. As a result of this she was exiled from the kingdom. In the jungle she gave birth to a child who was named Sansi. This bastard child is supposed to be the ancestor of the Punjab Sansis. As a matter of fact, Sansis include persons from all tribes. Some Sansis observe the rites of Moslem religion, while others are Hindus. However, they are considered outcastes by Hindus.

2. Haboora. According to some scholars, Habooras are only a branch of Sansis. The word haboora is connected with Sanskrit word 'hori' which means a dishonest person. Some Habooras trace their origin to Rana Pratap who had taken the vow not to settle down permanently till his defeat of Haldighati was avenged. His followers kept roaming from jungle to jungle and on account of economic pressure felt compelled to take to crime. According to some scholars there are twenty sub-castes among Habooras.

3. Dom. Dom is also a criminal tribe. Their origin is traced to a low Dravidian tribe. Doms are extremely insolvent and slatternly. They are so filthy that no one wants them to come near. Mostly they live outside the cities. It is said about Doms that they are in fact an amalgam of individuals excommunicated by other tribes. The Doms of U.P. try to trace their origin to King Ben; and it is said of Punjab Doms that they belong to a Brahmin tribe which had corrupted itself. It is said that Raja Harischandra had to do the task of a Dom once.

Broadly, there are three categories of Doms. The first type of Doms are nomads; they roam about the jungles of Bihar and Bengal. The second type of Doms are those who live in hills. The third are those who are fond of music and entertain by song and witty talks. They sell small toy musical instruments. They are also known as Dom-Mirasi whose main function was to serve and entertain royal families. According to some schools Dom-Mirasi and Criminal Doms are different peoples.

4. Kanjar. Kanjar is also one of the most notable criminal tribes. Kanjar are further sub-divided into, in some areas, in twelve and, in other areas, 23 sub-castes. In earlier days Kanjars used to perform the task of folk entertainers. They were adept in dance and music, and used to entertain feudal lords and royal families by their skills in music and dancing. Later on they were replaced by more skilful entertainers and were forced to seek other avenues of earning livelihood. Some Kanjars believe that their ancestors are a sylvan couple residing in the woods. This couple was their guru Man and Kanjarani Nathia. They were hunters and dancers and also outlaws. There are many folk-tales about the ancestors of Kanjars and all of them emphasize their dancing skill. In Punjab a nautch girl is called Kanjari. A Kanjari entertains and a Kanjar acts as an escort. Regarding the origin of Kanjar there is a legend that there was an excellent dancer named Majori. She was the very perfection of dancing skill and was so agile and nimble footed that she could dance expertly on a tight rope. Her fame was such that many a king was enamoured of her. A certain King offered her the status of Queen and half the kingdom if she could dance blind-folded on the rope and catch the bangles thrown by him. The performance was arranged and as Majori was about to hold the bangles another nautch girl, green with jealousy, severed the cord and Majori came tumbling down, and was badly hurt and died. But before dying she cursed her rivals that their progeny may be corrupt and being unable to make a living off dancing be condemned to practise prostitution.

FACTORS OF CRIME IN TRIBES

Many a tribe in India is generally regarded to be criminal. From legal point of view these are the ex-criminal tribes. There is not enough evidence, scientifically established or ascertainable, about the origin and development of these tribes. Their origin is shrouded in mythology and folklore. As regards the question as to when a group as a whole takes to crime as a profession divergent views have been expressed by scholars. According to one point of view the tendency to commit crimes is hereditary and by virtue of being criminal the parents pass on this tendency to their offspring. However, this possibility of genetic heredity of crime is contested by other scholars. The truth of the matter appears to be this : the children who are born in an atmosphere replete and suffused with criminality are bound to be affected. At a very impressionable age they learn the various criminal operations and by the time they mature they are expert in criminal techniques. Now nothing appears to them easier than the profession of crime. Being usually illiterate and uncultured they are not suited to any good profession. Little wonder, then, they are so heavily drawn to crime. Dr. Haikerwal has aptly observed. "The day a baby is born, its parents and others begin to teach it the tricks of trade."

On account of their promiscuous sex life the criminal tribes are of highly mixed character and if the genetic theory of crime were true these people should not be criminal because children born of these people are usually a cross because women of these tribes are inveterate prostitutes. We discuss below some of the factors usually considered important for production of criminality in criminal tribes.

1. Social and economic causes. The social and economic causes play an important role in the production of criminality in the criminal tribes. The individuals or groups which are neglected by the society and are not given their due share in its achievements or accomplishments, move away from society and become apathetic to it. If this apathy is not countered by positive social response it turns into hostility towards society in general and those groups or persons in particular who are directly responsible for the neglect. In order to settle their scores with society such groups operate underground and keep moving. Besides social factors, economic factors, too, play an important part in helping tribes toward criminality. With the advance of civilization a number of economic problems also crop up. It is well known that with the advancement of civilization, social organizations also become more intricate and complex. As a result, only intellectually and technically resourceful people can find important gainful roles in society. The social changes moreover render many hitherto important and useful persons superfluous. Their skills are no longer worthwhile.

Due to these social upheavals many persons and groups become economically sterile. They may go to jungles to lead the life of primitive men — hunting and eating jungle fruits. They may take to begging or singing and entertaining in bazaars. In extreme situations they may live off the income from the sale of the bodies of their womenfolk and lastly they may become out and out criminals. Thus, we see that economically sterile groups are driven by the society in a phased manner, from vegetation in jungle to prostitution and crime. What is more, well-to-do groups find in them an easy prey to appease their lust.

2. Extinction of traditional professions. The social change has the effect of rendering many a type of services, worthless. The persons dislocated from their trade find it extremely difficult to adopt alternative trades, particularly if they are past middle-age. For example, with the construction of bridges, the jobs of boatmen have become superfluous with the advent of radio, the street singers are no longer in demand; with the downfall of feudalism and popularity of cinema, the nautch girls are no longer in great demand. Some such tragedy must have overtaken the criminal tribes. The eunuchs provide a good illustration. The eunuchs at one time enjoyed a place of pride; they were guardians of Zenana or women of royal families or aristocrats. They were privy to many secrets and wielded unusual power. But now they are reduced to the task of putting up grotesque and obscene performances at marriages or births; their status is no more than that of a high class beggar. What is worse they are unable to make both ends meet. In order to support themselves they act as sodomists, fellators and commit sex perversions. As a matter of fact, they are a source of perverse sex. Being sharp-witted, they enjoy patronage of both men and women in matters of sex. It will not be surprising if they become one day only purveyors of perverse sex.

3. Family disorganization and degeneration. There are in every society many degenerate families which are morally and culturally so lost that what are considered disvalues by normal persons are regarded as values by them. For example, they like to have sons who can dishonour women and disrobe them. They encourage pickpocketing and minor thefts. They are proud if their daughters manage to live off a number of men simultaneously, even if it leads to mutual destruction among suitors. Such families are breeding grounds for criminality.

4. Caste system. Each criminal tribe has a specialized organization. This organization is like a Panchayat and this body is usually performing the function and role of a crime polytechnic, that is, it trains its members in the advanced operations of crime. They are imparted expertise in successful cheating. If any of its members is trapped by police and either imprisoned or killed, the members of his family are properly looked after by the Panchayat during the absence of the member.

5. Corruption among officials. The government normally appoint a high official with numerous subordinates to supervise the activities of criminal tribes. In each sector there are departments which are supposed to maintain a detailed record of each criminal and the nature of his activity. But there are a number of government servants who are corrupt and become accomplices of these criminals and share the booty of crime. The register of crime record is left unfulfilled and the criminal activity is not reported. Some government servants are successfully trapped by women of these tribes and the lure of free sex deflects many of them from carrying out their duties properly.

From the above discussion it is clear that there are many factors responsible for the inherent criminality of the criminal tribes. Many social and economic factors induce criminality among them; and since they carry the stigma of criminality, society is initially prejudiced against them and considers them beyond help and redemption. Accordingly, neither government nor any other public agency thinks about them in constructive terms to draw up some elaborate plan of their rehabilitation. They are at best given lip service by the influential members of government and the public. As a matter of fact, certain political and social groups have developed vested interests in their continuance and perpetuation. They consider them a section of well-trained criminals who can be hired to advance personal motives of the hiring agencies. They also function as receptacles of the overfill or spillover of sex needs of many persons. Their lack of a sense of shame provides opportunity to some enterprising film-makers to produce blue movies. But, above all, they are, utterly deficient in a desire to reform or improve themselves.

6. Social life. Almost all criminal tribes lead an abnormal social life; there are no sets of social and moral values governing their life. Being mostly nomadic there is little fixed social structure and no set of social customs or traditions. As a rule they abide by no fixed laws and perform no definite rites and ceremonies with regard to marriage, birth, etc. Their food habits are also not fixed; they have no taboos regarding food and sex. In food, the animal food and liquor are important items. However, they can eat intestines and other parts of animals which are normally eaten by dogs. They usually eat every variety of meat and drink hard liquor. Their sex life is promiscuous. Young boys and girls freely indulge in sex play under the very nose of elders. Most women function as veritable prostitutes. Their economic life is fluid and uncertain; only one thing is certain, they steal whenever possible. Their children are born in open and the function of mid-wife is performed by neighbourhood women. They suckle their young till another is born and are unmindful of suckling two children at the same time. A notable feature of these women is that they are constantly suckling young ones.

7. Economic life. The economic life of these tribes is both irregular and uncertain. The members of criminal tribes have no definite means of livelihood and therefore their spending is also erratic. If they somehow are able to lay hand on a handsome amount of money, they usually gamble, drink and prostitute. They are fond of spending extra money in feasting on meats and hard liquor. There are many small occupations carried on by these people. They collect various materials available in jungle and sell them in towns. These include honey, wax, gum, resin, animal skins and various herbals and animals which are supposedly aphrodisiac and also possess some other medicinal values. There are some criminal tribes which earn their livelihood by putting up public display of monkey-tricks, bear-shows or performances by honourable means and should not therefore be referred to as criminal. As a matter of fact, all tribals do something or the other. Quite a few of them make sufficient money by their small avocations and are satisfied. They refrain from stealing or other criminal acts. However, there are many who, not content with the meagre earning, are lured into crime to earn easy money. As their moral fabric and sense of social values is weak, being illiterate and exposed from early life to criminality, they are unable to resist the lure of easy money which can be made by theft. Whenever they visit homes of townsmen to sell some articles or repair some ironwares, they would not lose the opportunity of making off with some utensil or other article which they sell for small price. Some of them are really vicious and indulge in child-lifting and extorting regular payments from villagers and petty shopkeepers. Some of them run brothels in their huts and offer their females for gratification against money. In short, they can do any fair or foul thing to make money.

COLLECTIVE SOCIAL LIFE

The tribals operate as a well-knit unit. This is an imperative for the success of their criminal operations. They have a central organization called Panchayat, where all powers are vested in the headman or tribal chief. The Panchayat organizes training in crime expertise of its members. It also provides them with legal and professional aid in the event of abortive criminal attempt. In the event of the death of a member, his family is economically provided for and protected by the Panchayat. The headman is empowered to punish any member if he violates the code of Panchayat. There can be excommunication and even extermination if the headman is satisfied that the presence of a particular member is a threat to the whole tribe. The headman also enjoys special privileges. He must get whole of the booty of the crime and also have access to every woman.

FAMILY AND PROFESSIONAL LIFE

The homes of criminal tribes are the training centres and prepare the children for their future life of criminality. From early childhood the children are trained into crimes. Their ears are filled with heroic criminal exploits of their elders and their hearts stuffed and suffused with hatred of other people. They are asked to be brave and courageous and are trained to kill animals and birds mercilessly and without compunction. They are told that they belong to a grandfather who had a lifelong record of murder, dacoity and kidnapping but could ever throw dust into the eyes of policemen; the police was even terrorized and badly afraid of him.

From early youth they start a course of practical training and undergo various tests of steeling their nerves. They are trained how to disguise and how to cheat; how to rob; how to throw acid; how to escape detection; how to wield knife and firearms. They are also trained to be masculine and remove necklace and ornaments off women. Another important feature of their training is to operate secretly, be loyal and faithful to the superior and cooperate among themselves. The girls are trained how to use their charms for criminal purposes. Wrestling, mock-fight, knife-throwing, etc., are their popular sports. Their first training ground in practical crime is fairs, festivals, crowded railway platforms, etc. Thus, by phases, the child becomes a full-fledged, well-trained criminal.

There is also training in strict discipline in these tribes, though intra-tribal quarrels are not infrequent and they are settled by the headman. But if an outsider clashes with any members of the tribe, the whole tribe fights against him as a man, sinking their mutual differences.

MARRIAGE AND MORALS

On account of their nomadic existence and criminal life, the institution of marriage is rather weak, the stable marital arrangements are few and divorce is fairly common. There is no fixed age for marriage; but child marriages are not uncommon. The marriages are usually ceremonized without the assistance of priest. This primarily is due to the fact that Hindus regard these tribes as untouchables. However, tribals celebrate their marriages with great pomp and show; and though, in different tribes different customs are observed. One thing common to all tribal marriages is feasting on meats and hard alcohol. Among some gypsies of the middle-east, marriage is an occasion of great merry-making; and in Turkey all guests have sexual intercourse with the bride. However, such licentiousness is not to be found among Indian tribals, though dancing is quite common.

In a majority of tribal societies, marriage is by purchase, that is, the bridegroom is required to give bride-money to his father-in-law. There is usually hard bargaining for the price of a bride between the bridegroom and the parents of the bride. The bride-money, as it is called, varies in quantum from one tribe to the other. As may be expected, a pretty young girl fetches higher price than a fat unseemly one. In order to exercise a restraint on the tendency to charge exorbitant prices for brides, various tribal panchayats have fixed such an amount. Bantu Panchayat fixed the price of Rs. 600 maximum for girls of Dholi, Gaddi, Marwari sub-castes and Rs. 500 maximum for girls of Dhapo, Kodan and Charralia sub-castes. Among Sansis there is a flat rate of Rs. 78 and in Doms it is a paltry Rs. 15. In spite of the Panchayat there is bargaining, particularly if the bride is passionately attractive and adept in sex techniques.

Besides abnormal marriage practices, the moral laws followed by criminal tribes are cock-eyed; these are in fact topsy turvy. What is moral or valuable in normal society is considered to be of no consequence by tribals; they are completely indifferent, even contemptuous of morals. Thieving, dacoity and killing are perfectly normal for them. Their sexual morals are equally perverse according to conventional morality. Generally, most females of criminal tribes are extremely passionate and fond of sexual intercourse. They indulge in extra-marital sex for money or pleasure. They are usually scantily dressed and particularly while suckling, they are completely topless. Usually they are unmindful of covering while bathing. etc. They are so unashamed of their bodies that they may be called children of nature or born exhibitionists. Besides normal sex many of them are fond of sodomy. They use their skill at body display and entertainment for espionage for their tribes and thus help in theft and dacoity. Thus, one may conclude that the morals of tribals are at a low level.

RELIGIOUS BELIEFS AND SUPERSTITIONS

Some tribals subscribe to Moslem faith and others to Hinduism. Those subscribing to Hindu faith are, however, considered to be untouchables by the caste Hindus and not allowed entry into Hindu temples. But the Hindu tribes have fashioned out or developed in course of time many deities which are to be placated and whose grace is sought through adulation, etc. For example, Bavaria tribals believe in the transmigration of souls and they dutifully set apart a certain portion of the booty or looted wealth for the deity. Some tribals are known to worship a deity known by the name of Goodar Por. The water of river Ganges is regarded holy and sacred and plays an important part in the lives of the tribals. The swearing by *Ganga-jal* (Ganges water) is regarded to be final and unalterable commitment. Whenever any ceremony or worship is to be performed, a bottle of *Ganga-jal* is kept as a divine witness. At the time of epidemics a ceremonial worship of Kali Devi with elaborate paraphernalia is duly performed. The Bavarias also worship a deity known as Dat. Bantus attach great importance to the worship of Kali Devi; they are also sun-worshippers.

The tribals entertain plenty of superstitions, some ludicrous and some strange and interesting. Like all primitive tribes, the Indian tribals attach great importance to the dream phenomenon. Whatever they happen to see in dreams is loaded with meaning for their day-to-day life. They regard the intimation of dream as realities bound to happen and therefore their dreams determine their attitudes and responses to life. The dreams may be auspicious or inauspicious depending upon the object seen in the dream. Thus, for example, the sight of a beautiful woman in a dream is taken to be extremely auspicious and this may indicate good luck and bring money for feasting and merry-making or may indicate that the man will marry a damsel soon. But if a fall of a tooth is seen in a dream this is most inauspicious as it foretells certain death of a youth of the tribe. As they launch upon criminal operations the Bavarias carefully watch the initial symptoms. The sight of the bird 'Neelkantha' indicates sure success of the operation and is very auspicious. Again, a suckling calf or baby is an auspicious sign; but the howl of jackals and sight of menstruating woman is very inauspicious, and the plan is abandoned. Bantus regard the bleating of lamb an auspicious sign; but they regard the sight of a urinating woman a bad omen, the sight of the backside is less ominous than the sight of the front portion. The sight of a pregnant woman may indicate big success or total failure. The sight of the barber, oil-vendor, one-eyed person or a policeman in the early morning is regarded very inauspicious. Thus, it is clear that the tribals entertain plenty of superstitions and are guided in their behaviour by these.

ACTS CONCERNING CRIMINAL TRIBES

There are a number of criminal tribes in India. Some of them are exclusively engaged in criminal activity, while others are doing some odd jobs but also miss no opportunity to steal and cheat. The latter may be called "partially criminal" and the first "wholly criminal". The wholly criminal tribes do no honourable job for making a living. They are most of the time committing crimes or else planning for future crimes. They are always on a lookout for potential centres of crime and are mostly found on crowded railway platforms, fairs and other crowded places to pursue their ends. But partially criminal tribes are either engaged in entertaining by song or dance and animal circus. They also make musical drums, bamboo baskets or small iron wares. There is a legislation regarding all these people, known as the Criminal Tribes Act. In India an ordinance known as Indian Penal Code was first promulgated in the year 1760, in which crimes and respective punishments were given in details. Shortly afterwards, Regulation 27 was passed by the East India Company which pertained to criminal tribes. By virtue of this regulation the so-called criminal tribals could be engaged against payment in the construction of roads; and in case any of them deserted duty, he could be sentenced to imprisonment for 6 months. During these days Pindari Thugs were very active and posed a serious menace to travellers. In 1839, Government of India established a department known as Thugee and Dacoity department. At the same time the activities of criminal tribes came to official notice and various laws regarding them were passed from time to time. The important acts are listed below :

(a) Criminal Tribes Act 1871

(b) Criminal Tribes Act 1911

(c) Criminal Tribes Act 1924

(d) Habitual Offenders Act 1952.

Criminal Tribes Act 1871

The main aim of the 1871 Act was to keep an eye on the activities of the criminal tribes. A constant surveillance over and vigilance about their activity was planned; but it was not the intention or object of this act to check the nomadism of these people, as nomadism or moving from one place to another was not regarded in any way objectionable and harmful to the society. It was considered a normal way of life as is the settlement at some fixed abode. The aim of the Act was to control the crime and help the members of criminal tribes to reform and rehabilitate themselves. This Act gave wide-ranging powers to the provincial governments. The provincial governments were authorized to declare any group of people who were incorrigible criminals as Criminal Tribe.

This Act provided for maintenance of a register in which the names and other particulars of all the adult members of a tribe were written. Further, they were required to register the information about births and deaths. Some of them were required to report at regular intervals to the police station. From time to time policemen used to take a round of their colonies and take roll-call of all the members. The 1871 Act had no specific plans for the reform of these people.

In 1879 this Act was amended and it was provided that the government could take the custody of all children of the age 4 and keep them in government schools, away from the pollutant atmosphere of the tribe, upto the age of 18. There were, however, many flaws and loopholes in the Act. Therefore, in the year 1911, it was replaced by a new Act, known as Criminal Tribes Act, 1911.

Criminal Tribes Act, 1911

On account of the lack of success in the control of crime by the criminal tribes and the lack of any improvement in the state of affairs in spite of the 1879 amendment in the Act, the government set up a committee to go into the matters afresh and review the whole thing in all possible aspects. In 1902-03 a high powered Police Commission went into the matter in minute detail. On the basis of the report submitted by the Commission, the Government of India passed a new Act regarding Criminal Tribes in the year 1911. In accordance with this Act schedules were prepared for various criminal tribes and these schedules were complete in each respect. In these, there were personal identification marks and the thumb impressions of each of the members of the Tribe. This was done with a view to track down the criminals with ease. Besides, the more notorious members of the tribe were put under very strict observation; their activities were minutely watched. The government could remove any child of the age 6 or above from the criminal parents and give him education and training in governmental institutions. Under this Act provincial governments were given special instructions for the control of these tribes. The provincial governments were given powers to make suitable amendments in the Act in the light of their experience.

Criminal Tribes Act, 1924

In many aspects the 1911 Act was defective and contained many loop-holes. Basically in aim and intent it was preventive and not corrective. There were virtually no attempts in it to reform and rehabilitate the present criminals. Of course, there was provision for taking away children and giving them proper education. But there were practical difficulties here, too. Therefore, the 1911 Act was replaced by a new Act in 1924. The 1924 Act empowered the provincial governments to declare criminal tribes and prepare a list of their members, having identification mark aud thumb impression of each member. Besides, a check was put on the migratory instinct of the tribals. They were not to leave their places without prior permission of the police.

However, the most significant part of the 1921 Act was the provision of the reform and rehabilitation of the criminals. The provincial governments were issued express instructions to draw up elaborate plans to provide relief and rehabilitation to the tribals. They were to be attracted to useful professions and attempts were made to preserve the integrity of their traditional profession and skills.

Habitual Offenders Restriction Act, 1952

Beginning from the year 1871 to the dawn of independence, a number of Acts regarding Criminal Tribes were passed and many amendments thereto made to make them effective and help in checking the crime and control of activities of the tribals. However, they met with little success and the criminality of the tribes, instead of being controlled or eliminated, was being perpetuated and the number of crimes and criminals went up with the population growth of tribals. The idea of checking birth rate among them was alien at that time. After 1947, the national government paid serious attention to the problem and a number of committees were set up to go into the matter. The basic theoretical and practical drawback in all previous thinking on the matter was the fact that these persons were deemed criminal by birth and it was believed that no matter what their opportunities or facilities they could not help being criminal. Therefore, nothing could be done to bring them back to normal life and wean them away from criminality. In this connection U. P. Government set up a high power Committee under the Chairmanship of Shri V. N. Tewari to go into the various aspects of the life of the criminal tribes. After discussing the pros and cons of various proposals it came to the conclusion that the first and foremost imperative for any possible improvement in the condition of tribals is that the appellation "criminal" should be dropped. This unnecessarily stigmatized these people and prejudiced others to them. In the words of the Committee : "The removal of the appellation 'criminal' will have salubrious psycho-social impact upon the children of these tribes. This will help to eliminate from the minds of these people anti-social feelings and sentiments, because they will be relieved of the stigma and evil of considering themselves criminals and also relieved of the painful obligation of registering themselves with the police as soon as they attained the age of 15." On the basis of this and many other reports of the committee and recommendations of social scientists and criminologists, the Bombay Criminal Tribes Act was repealed in 1949. This proved a pace-setter and soon after all states repealed the Criminal Tribes Acts from the respective jurisdictions.

Consequent upon the repeal of the Criminal Tribes Acts, a lacuna, rather a vaccum, was felt. It was found that the police were unable to track the criminals on the basis of their records, because these were outdated and the sources of fresh information had dried up. Therefore, the Criminal Tribes Act was replaced by the Habitual Offenders Restriction Act, 1952. This filled the gap left by the repeal of the Criminal Tribes Acts. But this also removed the most glaring deficiency of the previous Acts insofar as the term "Criminal" which was a source of stigma against many people and tended to unfairly prejudge them, was removed; and yet a mechanism was evolved to maintain strict supervision over the activities of those who, for historical and psycho-socio-economic reasons were predisposed to criminality.

35

Tribal Problems and Welfare

Modern Trends in Tribal Culture

Due to contact with Hindu and Western culture, the tribal culture has constantly changed. This cultural change has been effected by the following processes:

1. Simple adoption. In this process of cultural change a tribe simply adopts the culture of another tribe, for example, the Warli tribe of Bombay state, formerly used to wear only a cloth. Now they use shirt, turban and dhoti due to the influence of Koli tribe.

2. Acculturation. Where a culture almost engulfs another culture and changes it, the process is known as acculturation. This involves a wider and deeper cultural change. For example, the Indian tribal culture is being constantly influenced by Hindu culture, so much so that some tribes are almost Hindu in culture. An example of this type of cultural change can be found in Gond tribe.

3. Assimilation. In this process of cultural change, a culture is not only adopted, but also assimilated and therefore becomes an integral part of the adopting culture. This process is seen in the tribes who, leaving their difficult mountain tracks and deep forests, come to plains and stay there. Such tribes in India have been assimilated in Hindu culture in almost every aspect of their social and cultural organization.

According to D. N. Majumdar, the Indian tribes can be classified into two groups on the basis of processes of cultural change. Firstly, there are assimilated tribes whose culture has been completely assimilated by some other culture. Secondly, there are adaptative tribes whose culture is gradually adapting the modes of some new culture.

IMPACT OF HINDU AND CHRISTIAN CULTURE

The impact of cultural contact with Hindus and Christians has resulted both in evil as well as favourable consequences. This cultural contact has removed many superstitions and evil customs from the tribes. The Christian missionaries have opened hospitals and schools for the benefit of tribal people. These have decreased the influence of diseases and illiteracy. The Christian missionaries are also running several orphanages in tribal areas. They are giving monetary help to the needy tribals and helping in the improvement of the levels of health and education. These favourable influences, however, are nothing before the evil consequences of the cultural contact. The following are the most important evil consequences in this connection :

1. Degeneration of collective life. Due to the influence of Western culture many of the tribals have begun to hate their traditions and customs which are gradually disappearing with the result that collective life is degenerating.

2. Social disorganization. This has led to disorganization of family and social institutions. The tribals who have been converted into Christian religion, try to imitate European culture and hate their tribal brothers. This has led to social disorganization everywhere.

3. Economic exploitation. The civilized traders, contractors and religious missionaries have also economically exploited the tribal people. Misusing their ignorance they have caught them in the net of indebtedness and robbed their money and land.

4. Moral degeneration. The civilized people have spread gross immorality in tribal society. The poor women have been made to prostitute themselves. The evil of drinking and using all sorts of intoxicants has increased among the tribals. Prostitution has led to increase of venereal diseases. The tribes living near the city are very much morally degenerated.

5. Gradual disappearance. The above-mentioned evil consequences of tribal contact with other cultures have led to gradual disappearance of some tribes, as it is in the case of Andmani, Korawa, Toda and Chenchu tribes.

TRIBAL PROBLEMS

The Indian tribes at present suffer from mainly two types of problems. Firstly, those which are also found in other people of the country and secondly, those which are peculiar to tribal people. In this latter type of tribal problems the following are the most important :

1. Cultural problems. Due to contact with other cultures, the tribal culture is undergoing a revolutionary change. Due to the influence of Christian missionaries, the problem of bilingualism has developed which has led to indifference towards tribal language. The tribal people are imitating Western culture in different aspects of their social life and leaving their own culture. An important influence of culture contact is seen in the form of disappearance of youth dormitories. Imitation of the Western dress and modes of living has led to the degeneration of tribal life and tribal arts, such as dance, music and different types of crafts.

2. Religious problems. Due to the conversion of many tribal people to Hindu and Christian religions, the tribal groups have been divided into several sects on the basis of religion. This has shattered their collective life and conflicts and dissensions are increasing. The tribal people are gradually forgetting their tribal religion. This has led to social disorganization.

3. Social problems. Due to the influence of Hindu community, the tribals are facing the problem of increasing bride price. This has encouraged elopement of girls and their forcible lifting by males. Another social problem created by the tribal contact with Hindus is the evil custom of child marriage. The contact with the civilized society has increased the number of premarital and extra-marital sexual relationships in tribal society and the number of dissolution of marriages. This has also increased the incidence of prostitution and venereal diseases.

4. Economic problems. The contact with the civilized world has disintegrated the entire economic system of the tribal people. They have forgotten their ancient crafts, most of them are working as labourers in plantations, agricultural farms, factories and other jobs. The employers everywhere misuse the ignorance of the tribal people, take maximum work from them and give them minimum money in return.

CONSTITUTIONAL SAFEGUARDS

The Indian Constitution prescribes protection and safeguards for the scheduled tribes, and other backward classes either specially or by way of insisting on their general rights as citizens with the object of promoting their educational and economic interest and of removing the social disabilities. The main safeguards are :

(i) the promotion of their educational and economic interests and their protection from social injustice and all forms of exploitation (art. 46);

(ii) the throwing open by law of Hindu religious institutions of a public character to all classes and sections of Hindus (art. 25);

(iii) the removal of any disability, liability, restriction or condition with regard to access to shops, public restaurants, hotels and places of public entertainment or the use of wells, tanks, bathing ghats, roads and places of public resort maintained wholly or partly out of State funds or dedicated to the use of the general public (art. 14);

(iv) the curtailment by law, in the interests of any scheduled tribe to settle in, and acquire property [art. 19 (5)];

(v) the forbidding of any denial of admission to educational institutions maintained by the State or receiving aid out of State funds (art. 29);

(vi) permitting the State to make reservation of the backward classes in public services in case of inadequate representation and requiring the State to consider the claims of the scheduled tribes in the making of appointments to public services (art. 16 and 335);

(vii) special representation in the Lok Sabha and the State Vidhan Sabhas to scheduled tribes till 25 January 1990 (arts. 330, 332 and 334);

(viii) the setting up of tribal advisory councils and separate departments in the states and the appointment of a special officer at the centre to promote their welfare and safeguard their interests (arts. 164 and 338 and Fifth Schedule);

(ix) special provision for the administration and control of scheduled and tribal areas (art. 244 and Fifth and Sixth Schedules); and

(x) prohibition of traffic in human beings and forced labour (art. 23).

TRIBAL WELFARE

Thus, it is clear that the Indian Constitution has made important provisions for the welfare of tribal people. Posts have been reserved for them in public services, in States and Centre. Seats have been reserved for their representatives in the Legislatures of different States and in the Indian Parliament. Special provisions have been made regarding their administration. District and regional councils have been established to carry out their welfare. The government have given special attention to their education and economic development. This has not appreciably improved the condition of tribal people. The following suggestions can be made in connection with tribal welfare :

1. Economic reforms. Efforts should be made to encourage tribal people to permanently establish for cultivation, because the shifting cultivation practised by them results in much wastage. The co-operative forests utilization societies can help the tribals in utilizing the forests in which they live. The government should arrange for technical help and education to improve the condition of tribal crafts and provision should be made for the marketing of the goods produced by them. Laws should be strictly imposed in tribal areas to solve the problem of indebtedness and to restrict exploitation. Co-operative credit societies can be organized to provide money for small scale industries. Labour laws should be strictly enforced in tribal areas.

2. Educational reforms. At the base of the fallen state of tribal society is their widespread illiteracy. Educational expansion, therefore, should be given primary consideration. The tribal education should be given through their own language and in their own cultural background. Colleges should be established to safeguard the tribal fine arts. Provision should be made for technical and commercial education in the tribes, Along with education, the tribal music, dance, plays and recreation should be encouraged. Religious dogmatism and superstitions should be removed through scientific education.

3. Reform in the level of health. Efforts should be made to improve the level of health of tribal people. This will require provision of medicines, pure water, nutritive food, clean and properly ventilated houses and generally healthy atmosphere.

4. Social reforms. Whatever may be the opposition from certain vested interests, efforts to carry out social reforms in tribals must be realized. The evil customs of bride price, magic and ritualism, child marriage, prostitution etc.

should be removed. These social reforms can be carried out only after economic reforms.

5. Political reforms. It is a pity that the Government officials posted in tribal areas misuse the ignorance of tribal people and exploit them for different purposes. They scorn the tribal culture and are completely indifferent to their welfare. The Government should appoint such officials as are conversant with tribal culture and intend to improve the condition of tribal people.

In free India the State and Central Governments have made incessant efforts in the direction of tribal welfare. At the central level a Commissioner attached to Home Ministry takes care of tribal welfare. Under him there are several regional Assistant Commissioners whose number has now increased to 16. In the States, there are special Directorates of tribal welfare. In Assam five District and Regional Councils have been established for tribal welfare. Tribal Research Institutes for the study of tribal culture and language are working in Bihar, Madhya Pradesh, Orissa and other states. Efforts are being made to expand educational facilities in tribal areas. Thousands of scholarships have been granted by Central and State Governments. Provisions have been made for special seats for tribal people in medical, engineering and technical colleges. Posts have been reserved for them in public services. Primary and secondary schools have been established in tribal areas where there is provision for free education.

In the political field the tribes send their representatives to State and Central Legislatures, some of whom have risen to the rank of Deputy Ministers and Ministers. Some tribal youths qualify in All India Services and their number is gradually increasing.

For the economic regeneration of the tribes, the government has enforced rules regarding land ownership and utilization of land. Crores of rupees have been spent for the development of cottage industries. The Community Projects have been established everywhere. Grain shops have been opened which provide improved type of seeds. Laws in connection with debt have been enforced. Special multipurpose tribal blocks have been created. Shifting cultivation is restricted and tribal families have been made to settle permanently on suitable land. Efforts have been made to provide housing facilities in some tribal areas. Hospitals have been opened which provide free medicines, check epidemics and cure all types of diseases. Research Institutes have been opened for the study of tribal culture and language. New roads have been made and old roads improved in the tribal areas. Personnel working for tribal welfare are given special training for this purpose. Institutes for their training have been established in Madhya Pradesh. West Bengal, Assam, Rajasthan, Maharashtra and other States.

The above brief outline of the State and Central Government efforts in the direction of tribal welfare show the extent of work that has been done in different Five Year Plans. This has definitely led to some improvement in some directions. The solution of tribal problems, however, requires a multisided planning. To quote D. N. Majumdar, an authority on Indian tribal problems: "There is no one solution to tribal problems, there is no common platform to demand it. There are levels of cultural development and there are different patterns of life that the tribes own. In any scheme of rehabilitation of tribal life, the attitudes and configurations of culture must be known to work out plans, as what is true of one culture area may not be so for a second."[1]

ADMINISTRATION OF TRIBAL AREAS

The tribal areas in the State of Assam and Meghalaya and the Union Territory of Mizoram are administrated subject to the provisions of the Sixth Schedule to the Constitution. Under the Schedule, they are divided into autonomous districts. There are eight such districts, namely, North Cachar Hills and Mikir Hills districts in Assam, United Khasi-Jaintia Hills, Jowai and Garo Hills districts in Meghalaya and Chakma, Lakher and Pawi districts in Mizoram. Each autonomous district has a district council consisting of not more than 30 members of whom not more than four can be nominated and the rest are to be elected on the basis of adult suffrage. The councils are vested with certain administrative, legislative and judicial powers.

Measures to Check Atrocities Against SCs/STs

With a view to effectively deal with crimes against scheduled castes and scheduled tribes and to tone up administrative machinery to tackle this vital issue, comprehensive guidelines containing precautionary, preventive, punitive and rehabilitative measures exist which States/UTs have to follow. Still these communities continue to be vulnerable and atrocities are committed against them in one form or other. Government enacted the Scheduled Castes and the Scheduled Tribes (Prevention of Atrocities) Act, 1989. It came into force from 30 January, 1990. It specifies offences which are considered as atrocities and provides for deterrent punishments for commission of the same. It also envisages preventive measures and states have to evolve schemes, among other things, for economic and social rehabilitation of such victims. All States and UTs except Arunachal Pradesh, Mizoram and Nagaland have specialised courts for trial of offences under this Act.

Machinery for Safeguards of SCs and STs

By virtue of the Constitution (Sixty-fifth Amendment) Act, 1990, the 'Special Officer' post under Article 338 of the Constitution has been substituted by the National Commission for Scheduled Castes and Scheduled Tribes. It shall consist of a chairperson, vice-chairperson and five other members to be appointed by the President under his hand and seal. It shall be the duty of the Commission : (a) to investigate and monitor all matters relating to the safeguards provided for the scheduled castes and scheduled tribes under the Constitution

1. Majumdar, D. N., *Social Anthropology*, Asia, Bombay, 1957.

or under any other law; (b) to enquire into specific complaints with respect to the deprivation of rights and safeguards of the scheduled castes and tribes; (c) to participate and advise on the planning process of socio-economic development of the scheduled castes and scheduled tribes and to evaluate the progress of their development under the Union and any State; (d) to present to the President annually and at such other times as the Commission may deem fit, reports upon the working of these safeguards; (e) to make in such reports recommendations as to the measures that should be taken by the Union or any state for the effective implementation of those safeguards and other measures for the protection, welfare and socio-economic development of the scheduled castes and scheduled tribes; and (f) to discharge such other functions in relation to the protection, welfare and development and advancement of the scheduled castes and scheduled tribes as the President may, subject to the provisions of any law made by Parliament, by rule specify.

The President shall cause all such reports to be laid before each House of Parliament alongwith a memorandum explaining the action taken or proposed to be taken on the recommendations relating to the Union and the reasons for the non-acceptance, if any, of any of such recommendations. Where any such report or any part thereof, relates to any matter with which any State government is concerned, a copy of such report shall be forwarded to the Governor of the State who shall cause it to be laid before the Legislature of the State.

The Commission shall while investigating and monitoring any matter relating to safeguards provided for scheduled castes and scheduled tribes under the Constitution or any other law for the time being in force or under any order of the Government have all powers of a civil court trying a suit and in particular in respect of the following matters, namely : (a) summoning and enforcing attendance of any person from any part of India and examining him on oath; (b) requiring the discovery and production of any document; (c) receiving evidence on affidavits; (d) requisitioning any public record or copy thereof from any court or office; (e) issuing commissions for the examination of witnesses and documents; and (f) any other matter which the President may, by rule, determine.

The Union and every State government shall consult the Commission on all major policy matters affecting scheduled castes and scheduled tribes.

Welfare and Advisory Agencies

The Ministry of Welfare is the nodal agency for overall policy, planning and coordination of programmes of development of scheduled castes and scheduled tribes. Each Central ministry and department is the nodal agency concerning its sector.

Parliamentary Committee

Government had set up three Parliamentary Committees, first in 1966, second in 1971 and the third in 1973 to examine the implementation of the constitutional safeguards for welfare of scheduled castes and scheduled tribes. The Committee has since been constitued as a Standing Committee of Parliament, the tenure of its members being one year.

Welfare Departments in States

States and UTs have separate departments to look after the welfare of scheduled castes and scheduled tribes and other backward classes. Administrative set-up varies from state to state. In Bihar, Madhya Pradesh and Orissa, separate ministers have been appointed to look after tribal welfare as prescribed in Article 164 of the Constitution. Some other states have set-up committees of members of state legislatures on the pattern of Parliamentary Committee at the Centre. All the states having scheduled areas including Tamil Nadu and West Bengal have constituted Tribal Advisory Councils as per the provision in the Fifth Schedule to the Constitution to advise on matters pertaining to welfare and advancement of scheduled tribes.

Voluntary Organisations

A number of voluntary organisations also promote welfare of scheduled castes and scheduled tribes. Among them, the important organisations of all India character are : Harijan Sevak Sangh, Delhi; Indian Red Cross Society, New Delhi; Hindu Sweepers Sevak-Samaj, New Delhi; Ramakrishna Mission, Narendrapur; Bharatiya Adimjati Sevak Sangh, New Delhi; Andhra Rashtra-Adimjati Sevak Sangh, Nellore; Ramakrishna Missions, Cherrapunji, Ranchi, Puri, Silchar, Shillong and Purulia; Bharatiya Samaj Unnati Mandali, Bhivandi in Maharashtra, Thakkar Bapa Ashram, Numakhandi, Orissa; Servants of India-Society, Pune, Maharashtra, and Social Work and Research Centre, Tilonia, Rajasthan. The Government also provides grants-in-aid to non-official voluntary organisations working among scheduled castes and scheduled tribes. During 1994-95, 313 voluntary organizations were given grant-in-aid to the tune of Rs. 11.60 crore upto 31 December 1995.

Special Central Assistance

Special Central Assistance (SCA) to Special Component Plan of the states/ union territories for scheduled caste people is linked to Government of India strategy for the socio-economic development of these people. The Centrally sponsored scheme is the most important programme of the Ministry of Welfare for the alleviation of poverty among scheduled caste people. The underlying objective behind SCA which provides hundred per cent grant to states and union territories as an additive to their Special Component Plans is that it would be used to give an added thrust to the development programmes for scheduled caste people with reference to their occupational pattern and the need for increasing the productivity of and income from their limited assets by taking up family-oriented schemes for them. The SCA is used to fill the critical gaps and vital missing inputs in family-oriented income generating schemes and through non-recurring items so as to make the schemes more meaningful and effective. This scheme was started in 1979-80 with a token provision of rupees five crore. The state governments and union territory administrations are required to disburse Special Central Assistance to various sectors and agencies including SCDCs which are involved in the implementation of economic development programmes for SCs. A provision of Rs. 1,125 crore has been made for Eighth Five Year Plan.

Coaching and Allied Scheme

Under this scheme the Central assistance is provided to the state governments/union territory administrations on 50:50 basis for providing coaching to SC/ST candidates through pre-examination recruitment training centres to improve their representation in various services under the Central/ State governments and public sector undertakings. In the case of universities and private institutions cent per cent Central assistance is provided for running the pre-examination training centres for SC/ST candidates who intent to appear in the various competitive examinations. There are 101 pre-examination coaching training centres. Some of the coaching centres have made considerable contribution in enabling the SC/ST candidates getting into IAS and allied services, medical, engineering and banking services. During 1995-96, a provision of Rs. Three crores has been made.

National Scheduled Castes and Scheduled Tribes Finance and Development Corporation

National Scheduled Castes and Scheduled Tribes Finance and Development Corporation has been set up by the Government of India under Section 25 of the Companies Act, 1956 and is functioning with effect from 8 February 1989. The objective of the corporation is to stimulate economic development of scheduled castes and scheduled tribes and also identify and fill in the critical gaps in the programmes of state-level scheduled castes development corporations and other agencies. It is also to function as an apex institution for the agencies engaged in the economic development of scheduled castes and scheduled tribes. The corporation also plays a catalystic role in developing schemes for employment generation and financing pilot programmes which can later be taken up by the state-level corporations and other agencies engaged in this field. So far it has sanctioned 761 schemes costing Rs. 569.11 crore benefitting 1,85,027 SCs/STs entrepreneurs.

Book Bank Scheme

Book Bank Scheme is intended to provide text books required for the students belonging to SCs/STs pursuing medical and engineering degree courses from 1991-92. Agricultural, veterinary and polytechnic courses have also been included under the Scheme. A group of two students are provided one set of text books. During 1994-95, an amount of Rs. 3.50 crore was released to 37,827 SC/ST students. An allocation of rupees 3.60 crore has been made for 1995-96.

Pre-Matric Scholarships

Beginning in 1977-78, this scheme is for educational development of children of those who are engaged in the so-called unclean occupations, *viz* scavenging of' dry latrines, tanning, flaying and sweeping. The scheme as modified with effect from 1 November 1991 provides a scholarship of Rs. 25 per month in class I to V, Rs. 40 per month in class VI-VIII and Rs. 50 per month in class IX-X in respect of day scholars. For hostellers scholarship of Rs. 200 per month in classes 111 to VIII and Rs. 250 per month in classes IX-X is provided. An ad hoc grant of Rs. 500 per annum is also provided to day scholars as well as hostellers. The income ceiling is Rs. 1,500 per month. A provision of Rs. 6.25 crore has been made under the scheme during 1994-95.

Post-Matric Scholarships for SC/ST Students

The scheme of post-matric scholarships to SC/ST was introduced in 1944-45 with the objective of providing financial assistance to students studying at post-matriculation stages in different schools and colleges so as to enable them to complete their education. Beginning with a mere 114 awards to scheduled caste students in 1944-45 and 89 for scheduled tribe students in 1948-49, number of awards to them had reached over 14 lakh in 1990-91. Keeping in view the rising cost of living and other factors, rates for all courses and income limits of parents/guardians awards for eligibility of scholarships have also been revised from 1 July 1989. From 1988-89, employed students with a total income of Rs. 1,500 per month are made eligible for scholarships, restricted to reimbursement of compulsory non-refundable dues/fees etc. There is an allocation of Rs. 145 crore during 1995-96, the anticipated number of scholarships for these categories is expected to increase substantially during this period.

National Commission for SCs and STs

In pursuance of the Constitution Sixtyfifth Amendment Act, 1990 a National Commission for Scheduled Castes and Scheduled Tribes replacing the erstwhile Commissioner for Scheduled Castes and Scheduled Tribes, has been constituted with effect from 12 March 1992 with wider functions and powers. The National Commission consists of chairperson, vice chairperson and five other members. The main function of the commission is to investigate and monitor all matters relating to the safeguards provided for the scheduled castes and scheduled tribes, participate and advise on the planning process of socio-economic development of the SCs and STs, discharge such other functions in relation to the protection, welfare, development and advancement and to make such reports/ recommendations as to the measures that should be taken by the Union or the state(s) for effective implementation of the safeguards. It has been made obligatory on the Union and State governments to consult the Commission in respect of any policy measures affecting the SCs and STs.

Research and Training

Under the scheme of research and training, financial assistance is provided to universities/organisations/social science-research institutes for conducting action-oriented research and evaluative studies relating to development of scheduled castes. Preference is given to such studies which are for scheduled castes economic development and after practical recommendations suggest taking remedial measures. The studies are undertaken with the approval of research advisory committee of the Ministry constituted for the purpose. A number of evaluation studies in essential areas are being taken up during the current year by engaging reputed research agencies/institutions. Extending assistance to reputed institutions for organizing seminars/conferences on the welfare and development of SCs is also being planned.

Reservation in Services

Article 335 of the Constitution provides that claims of the members of the scheduled castes and scheduled tribes shall be taken into consideration consistently with the maintenance of efficiency of administration in making of appointment in services and posts in connection with affairs of the Union or of a State. Article 16 (4) permits reservation in favour of any backward class of citizens which in the opinion of the state is not adequately represented in services under the State. In pursuance of these provisions, the Government has made reservations for scheduled castes and scheduled tribes in services under its control in proportion to their population.

For scheduled castes, reservation is allowed 15 per cent of the vacancies to which recruitment is made on an all India basis and $16\frac{2}{3}$ per cent of the vacancies to which recruitment is made on all India basis otherwise by open competition. For scheduled tribes, reservation is 7.5 per cent in both the cases. Reservation in direct recruitment to Group C and D posts, which normally attract candidates from one locality or region is fixed in proportion to the population of scheduled castes and scheduled tribes in respective states/union territories. In promotions, reservations of vacancies is allowed at 15 per cent of the vacancies for scheduled castes and 7.5 per cent for scheduled tribes on the result of competitive examinations limited to departmental candidates in Group B,C, and D and in promotion by selection in Group B,C and D and to the lowest rung of Group A in grades or services to which element of direct recruitment, if any, does not exceed 7.5 per cent. Reservation has also been provided for scheduled castes and scheduled tribes in promotions on the basis of seniority subject to fitness in Groups A,B,C and D posts in grades or services to which element of direct recruitment, if any, does not exceed 75 per cent.

In promotion by selection within Group A to posts carrying an ultimate salary of Rs. 5,700 (revised scale Rs. 4,500-5,700) per month or less, scheduled castes and scheduled tribes officers who are senior enough in the zone of consideration for promotion so as to be within the number of vacancies for which the select list has to be drawn up, are included in that list provided they are not considered unfit for promotion.

To facilitate their adequate representation, concessions such as : (i) relaxation of five years in upper age limit; (ii) relaxation in the standards of suitability, for selection provided they are not unfit for the posts; (iii) relaxation of qualification regarding experience in the case of direct recruitment wherever necessary; (iv) exemption from the payment of application fee; (v) inclusion of scientific and technical posts upto the lowest range of Group 'A' posts required for guiding and conducting research in the scheme of reservations, have been provided for; (vi) scheduled castes and scheduled tribe candidates who qualify for direct recruitment without applying relaxed standard are not adjusted against reserved vacancies. Simultaneously, with notification to employment exchanges or advertisements in newspapers, vacancies reserved for scheduled castes and scheduled tribes in Group C and D (Class 111 and IV) posts are announced over All India Radio in areas having a concentration of scheduled castes and scheduled tribes population and are notified to voluntary associations of scheduled castes and scheduled tribes enlisted for the purpose of vacancy circulars as also to Directors of SC/ST Welfare in the states and union territories. Vacancies reserved for SCs and STs filled through Union Public Service Commission otherwise than through examination are advertised on the first occasion exclusively for SCs and STs and on the second occasion along with the other vacancies. Dereservation of vacancies for direct recruitment in Group A, B, C and D has since been banned (with exception in certain rare cases of Group A). If sufficient number of suitable SC/ST candidates are not available against the share of vacancies reserved for them, the shortfall will not be filled up by general category candidates and such vacancies will be kept unfilled till SC/ST candidates become available. There is a provision of indefinite carry-forward of reservations for SCs and STs in direct recruitment. This scheme of reservation is also being followed by public sector undertakings including nationalised public sector banks. Voluntary agencies which are in receipt of substantial grant-in-aid from government, are also required, as a condition, to adopt certain specific features of the reservation scheme in their respective establishments.

To give effect to the reservation, two model rosters of 40 points each have been prescribed for direct recruitment by open competition on all India basis and otherwise than open competition. Hundred point roster is made applicable for recruitment made on local and regional basis outside Delhi. For promotions, 40 point roster used for direct recruitment on all-India basis by open competition is adopted. If the vacancies in a service or cadre are too few for the purpose of applying reservation orders in direct recruitment, isolated posts which are identical in respect of qualifications, pay-scale, etc., are grouped together classification-wise. Annual statements are required to be submitted by recruiting authorities for scrutiny by government. For ensuring implementation of reservation orders, liaison officers have been appointed in each department under different government ministries/departments.

State governments have also framed rules under the powers given to them by item 41 of the State List of the Seventh Schedule to the Constitution for reservation of posts for these classes and have taken steps to increase their representation in State services. Reservation in State government services, however, is under the exclusive jurisdiction of State government. Representation of scheduled castes and scheduled tribes in Central Government services as on 1 January 1994 is given in table 1 below :

TABLE 1

Representation of SCs/STs in Central Government Services (As on 1 January 1994)

Group of posts	Total including	SCs No.	Percentage	STs No.	Percentage
A	59,016	6,046	10.25	1,727	2.92
B	1,03,198	12,443	12.06	2,902	2.81
C	23,81,613	3,74,758	15.73	1,28,228	5.38
D	10,23,285	2,09,423	20.46	62,945	6.15
(Excluding Sweepers)		1,10,569	49.06	15,567	6.90
Total	38,67,112	6,02,670	16.90	1,95,802	5.48

DEVELOPMENT OF SCHEDULED TRIBES

The all-India literacy of scheduled tribes, as per 1981 Census was 16.35 against the national average of 36.23 per cent. The gap between percentage of literacy of tribal women and general women is still wider. It is only 8.04 per cent against 24.82 per cent of general female literacy in the country. The tribal sub-plan (TSP) strategy which was evolved during the Fifth Five Year Plan is based on the twin objectives, namely: (i) protection of interests of tribals through legal and administrative support; and (ii) promotion of developmental efforts through plan schemes to raise their level of living. There are now 193 Integrated Tribal Development Projects (ITDPs). During the Sixth Plan, pockets outside ITDP areas having total population of 10,000 with at least 5,000 STs were covered under TSP under Modified Area Development Approach (MADA). So far 249 pockets have been identified in the country. In addition 77 clusters with a total population of 5,000 of which 50 per cent are STs have also been identified. At present in many states there is no single line administration at the ITDP level. This stands in the way of effective implementation of various schemes and projects for development of tribals. It is desirable that there should be single line administration and unity of command at the ITDP level.

Tribal Research Institutes

Thirteen tribal research institutes (TRIs) have been set up by the states of Andhra Pradesh, Assam, Bihar, Gujarat, Kerala, Madhya Pradesh, Maharashtra, Orissa, Rajasthan, Tamil Nadu, West Bengal, Uttar Pradesh and Manipur. All these institutes, except the ones in Manipur and Uttar Pradesh have museums, exhibiting tribal artifacts. These institutes are being used by states and Central governments for research, evaluation, collection of data, training, seminars/ workshops, professional input in the preparation of Tribal Sub-Plans, publication of tribal literature, codification of tribal customary laws, etc. During 1992-93, an amount of Rs. 105 lakh has been allocated in the budget.

TRIFED

In order to save tribals from exploitation by private traders and to offer them remunerative prices for their minor forest produce and surplus agriculture products Government has set up Tribal Cooperative Marketing Development Federation of India Ltd. (TRIFED), in August 1987 which is registered under the multi-state Co-operative Societies Act, 1984. It started functioning effectively from April 1988. TRIFED handled about 12 items in 1988-89. In almost all the items, the price offered to tribals by TRIFED was higher than the price given to them in the previous years. During 1989-90, it expanded its activities to cover a number of new items. It has been appointed as a canalising agency for export of gum keraya and other seeds of tribal area, and has also been declared as the nodal agency for collection, processing, storage and development of oilseeds of tree and forest origin. TRIFED is also acting as an agent of Food Corporation of India (FCI) for procuring wheat and paddy and as an agent of Department of Agriculture and Cooperation (DAC) for coarse grains, pulses and oilseeds. Its turnover during 1994-95 has gone upto Rs. 215 crore.

OBJECTIVE QUESTIONS BANK

1. Anthropology studies modern countries.

   True False Don't know

2. The materials supplied by anthropologists are widely used by sociologists.

   True False Don't know

3. The term anthropology is derived from the Greek words anthrogios and logas.

   True False Don't know

4. In primitive society, woman was considered as a type of property or wealth.

   True False Don't know

5. Anthropology is a branch of sociology.

   True False Don't know

6. Physical anthropology studies the bodily characteristics of early man.

   True False Don't know

7. Anthropology is the study of man.

   True False Don't know

8. All the races in the world are pure races.

   True False Don't know

9. Negroid is an example of a well known community.

   True False Don't know

10. Racial prejudice is not inborn.

    True False Don't know

11. Race is basically a physiological phenomena.

    True False Don't know

12. A society that inhabits a definite geographical area is known as primitive society.

    True False Don't know

13. Early law and primitive law are not clearly distinguished from religious and moral percepts and doctrines.

True False Don't know

14. The races of the world have been divided into three parts, *viz.*, Caucasoid, Mongoloid and Negroid.

True False Don't know

15. The term race, when properly used, signifies a biological category.

True False Don't know

16. Race is defined as "a group which shares in common a certain set of modern material characters and a political origin within a certain area."

True False Don't know

17. Tribal religion is one of the most primitive forms of religion found in human society.

True False Don't know

18. The tribal society is very strict in regard to the rules and laws of divorce.

True False Don't know

19. Both religion and magic are rooted in objectivity.

True False Don't know

20. According to cultural anthropologists "Privileged relationship" in some societies do not permit premarital and extramarital sexual relations.

True False Don't know

21. According to Margret Mead's finderngs in the Techambuli tribe of New Guinea the sex roles seem to be revised. Their women are dominant, they earn the living, handle business, transactions, take the initiative in courtship, and head the family. Men are submissive, coquettish, graceful, prone to gossip and are expected to be good home makers. The difference is due to

a. Government rules b. Cultural factors
c. Religious code d. School education

22. Racial identity can often lead to :

a. International cooperation b. Ethnocentrism
c. Lack of racial prejudice d. Political disadvantages.

23. Negroid and Mongoloid are the examples of different types of :

a. Castes b. Nationalities
c. Communities d. Races

24. Anthropology is the scientific study of

a. Plants b. Society
c. Men d. Animals

25. Polygamy is a form of marriage in which a woman can have :

a. One husband | b. Two husbands
c. A limited number of husbands | d. Many husbands

26. Levirate means marriages :

a. Between brothers and sisters
b. Of a man with the widow of the deceased mother
c. With the daughter of his sister
d. With the brother's daughter.

27. Totem is a sacred object of :

a. Things or materials | b. Minerals
c. Plants and Animals | d. None of these

28. In patiarchal family the head of the family is :

a. Brother | b. Sister
c. Father | d. Mother

29. In hunting stage, children stayed with the :

a. Father | b. Brother
c. Mother | d. Servants

30. Race is a :

a. Natural category | b. Cultural category
d. Biological category | d. None of these

31. Palaeontology is the study of :

a. Animals | b. Structure
c. Man | d. Fossils

32. Magic was called as the ... sister of science by Frazer :

a. Bastard | b. Half
c. Younger | d. Older

33. Animism is a belief in :

a. Some spiritual power | b. Spirits of dead ancestors
c. Objects having life in them | d. One supernatural being

34. The racial problem is there mainly because race has been correlated with :

a. Physiological traits. | b. superior mental abilities
c. Wealth | d. Politics

35. Totemism is a belief in :
    a. An object believed to have spirit
    b. An object believed to have power
    c. An object believed to have both spirit and power
    d. A deity believed to have power.
36. A man who compares the social significance of tribal rituals in two preliterate societies is most likely :
    a. A sociologist b. A physical anthropologist
    c. A social anthropologist d. An economist
37. The behaviour of human beings is determined according to the culture to which he belongs.
    True False Don't know
38. Animals are having culture in their societies.
    True False Don't know
39. Culture is the modal behaviour of the people in a society.
    True False Don't know
40. Culture is a universal feature found in all societies of living beings.
    True False Don't know
41. The development of culture is a social rather than an individual phenomenon.
    True False Don't know
42. Culture and society mean the same thing.
    True False Don't know
43. Spontaneous origins is a characteristic of folkways.
    True False Don't know
44. Custom can be characterised as a form of social organization.
    True False Don't know
45. Socialization of the Individual is a function of social groups.
    True False Don't know
46. Culture is the complex whole that consists of everything we think and do and have as members of society.
    True False Don't know
47. Culture is found in animal society.
    True False Don't know
48. Culture is what we have and civilization is what we are.
    True False Don't know

49. Cultural lag means that material progress lags behind the cultural progress.

True False Don't know

50. Culture is a human product.

True False Don't know

51. Culture is defined as "the training and refinement of mind, tastes and manners; the condition of being thus trained and refined; the intellectual side of civilization."

True False Don't know

52. Culture is borrowed without chage or loss, but not civilization.

True False Don't know

53. Culture is always advancing but not civilization.

True False Don't know

54. Culture has a precise standard of measurement, but not civilization.

True False Don't know

55. Culture is passed on without effort but not civilization.

True False Don't know

56. Ethnocentrism is the tendency to view other cultures from the perspective of our cultures.

True False Don't know

57. The culture grows out of collective efforts to meet experiences in the environment.

True False Don't know

58. Identical cultural adaptations occur in similar physical surroundings.

True False Don't know

59. Much of the diversity of a culture can be attributed to sub-cultures.

True False Don't know

60. The members of the underworld provide an example of contra culture.

True False Don't know

61. Symbols allow man to add to his knowledge and culture.

True False Don't know

62. Language provides the tools for the transmission of culture.

True False Don't know

63. The civilizational level of a society depends upon its racial composition.

True False Don't know

64. Which of the following comes under mores ?

a. Having three meals a day

b. Shaking hands

c. Weaving clothes

d. Inviting guests to the domestic functions.

65. Greeting a guest with the utterance of "namaste" falls under :

a. Folkways
b. Mores
c. Morals
d. Laws

66. The concept of cultural lag is linked with the name of :

a. Robert E. Park
b. Robert M. MacIver
c. Florian Znaniecki
d. W.F. Ogburn

67. There are a number of types of environments. Customs are an example of:

a. Economic environment
b. Social environment
c. Geographic environment
d. Physical environment

68. Customs are powerful in regulating the conduct of people in :

a. Urban societies
b. Industrialised societies
c. Simple societies
d. Complex Societies

69. That part of the total culture of a society which is shared by most members of the society is called the :

a. Contraculture
b. Subcultue
c. Metaculture
d. Coreculture

70. Which of the following is NOT a characteristic of culture ?

a. It is biologically inherited

b. It is transmitted from generation to generation

c. It is abstract

d. It is changeable.

71. A culture area is a :

a. Segment of a particular society's culture *e.g.* Hoi technology.

b. Segment of culture which cuts across particular societies *e.g.* technology.

c. Geographical area characterised by distinguishing culture traits

d. Geographical area characterised by a high level of cultural development.

72. Which of the following is NOT closely related to cultural change?

a. When societies adopt new ways of doing things.

b. When they pass on skills and information imperfectly.

c. When the factors of their physical environment change.

d. When they borrow discoveries from other societies.

73. Which of the following is NOT an example of types of cultural differences?

a. The relative simplicity of cultural expressions such as music, clothes, dwellings and tools.

b. Differences in variety of knowledge and skills possessed.

c. Differences in biologically inherited traits of people.

d. Differences in systems of social control.

74. The example of a community is :

a. A family | b. A group
c. A town | d. A classroom

75. If the property is transmitted through the mother's brother, the system is :

a. Matrilineal | b. Patrilineal
c. Avunculineal | d. Lineal

76. The institution that is concerned with property is :

a. Family | b. Political institution
c. Economic institution | d. Recreational institution

77. Main function of economic structure is :

a. Replacement of population.

b. Socialization of new population.

c. Maintenance of a sense of purpose.

d. Production and distribution of goods and services.

78. Function of political structure is :

a. Replacement of population.

b. Socialization of new population.

c. Maintenance of a sense of purpose.

d. System maintenance.

79. Main function of Religious Structure is :

a. Replacement of population.

b. Socialization of new population.

c. Maintenance of a sense of purpose.

d. Production and distribution of goods and services.

80. Function of educational structure is :

a. Replacement of population.

b. Socialization of new population.

c. Maintenance of a sense of purpose.

d. System maintenance.

81. Among the Ho community, Anader is a marriage by :

a. Intrusion b. Trial

c. Capture d. Exchange.

82. In Pratiloma type of marriage a man of lower varna marries a woman of higher varna.

True False Don't know

83. In Anuloma type of marriage a man of higher varna marries a woman of lower varna.

True False Don't know

84. Sanskritization is a process by which a low Hindu caste or tribal or other group, changes its customs, rituals, ideology and way of life in the direction of a high and frequently twice born caste.

True False Don't know

CORRECT ANSWERS

1. F.	2. T.	3. T.	4. T.	5. T.
6. T.	7. T.	8. F.	9. T.	10. T.
11. T.	12. F.	13. T.	14. T.	15. T.
16. F.	17. T.	18. F.	19. T.	20. T.
21. b.	22. b.	23. d.	24. c.	25. d.
26. b.	27. c.	28. c.	29. c	30. c.
31. d.	32. b.	33. c.	34. b.	35. c.
36. c.	37. T.	38. F.	39. T.	40. F.
41. T.	42. F.	43. T.	44. T.	45. T.
46. T.	47. F.	48. T.	49. T.	50. T.
51. T.	52. F.	53. F.	54. F.	55. T.
56. T.	57. T.	58. F.	59. T.	60. T.
61. T.	62. T.	63. F.	64. d.	65. b.
66. d.	67 b.	68. c.	69. d.	70. a.
71. a.	72. a.	73. c.	74. T.	75. a.
76. c.	77. d.	78. d.	79. c.	80. b.
81. a.	82. T.	83. T.	84. T.	

SELECTED BIBLIOGRAPHY

(A) ANTHROPOLOGY

Adam, L., *Primitive Art,* Pelican, 1949.

Benedict., R., *Pattern of Culture,* Pelican Books, 1949.

——, *"Folklore" in Encyclopedia of Social Sciences,* Vol. VI, 1931.

Bidney, D., *Theoretical Anthropology,* Columbia, 1953.

Boas, F., *Anthropology and Modern Life*, New York, W.W. Norton and Co., 1928.

Brown G. and B. Hunt., *Anthropology in Action.* Oxford, 1953.

Bouquet, A.C., *Comparative Religion,* Pelican.

Diamond, A.S., *Primitive Law*, London, 1935.

Hodson, T.C., *The Primitive Culture of India,* The Royal Asiatic Society, 1922.

Elvin, V., *The Aboriginals,* O.U.P. pamphlet.

Firth, R., *Human Types,* London, Thomas Neslon & Sons, 1938.

Hadden, A.C., *History of Anthropology*, London, Watts & Co., 1934.

Kluckhohn, C., *Mirror for Man,* London, George G., Harrap and Co., 1950.

Linton, H., *The Science of Man in World Crisis*, Columbia University Press, 1945.

Majumdar, D.N., *Social Anthropology*, Asia, 1957.

——, *The Fortunes of Primitive Tribes,* Lucknow, 1944.

——, *The Affairs of a Tribe,* Lucknow, 1950.

——, *Races and Cultures of India,* Lucknow University, 1957.

Morgan, L.H., *Ancient Society,* New York, 1877.

Murdock, G.P., *Social Structure,* New York, Macmillan, 1949.

Nadel, S.F., *Anthropology and Modern Life*, Canberra, 1953.

Penniman, T.K., *A Hundred Years of Anthropology,* London, G. Duckworth, 1952.

Radcliffe-Brown and Daryll Ford (Ed.), *African System of Kinship and Marriage*, Oxford, 1950.

Smith, E.W., *The Golden Stool*, Edinburgh House Press, 1930.

Thurnwald, R., *Economics in Primitive Cammunities,* 1932.

Tylor, E.B., *Primitive Culture.*

(B) STUDIES ON INDIAN TRIBES

Agro-Economic Research Centre, *Rural Life of Assam Hills* (Case Studies of four villages) edited by P.C. Goswami, Calcutta : Firwa K.L. Mukhopadhyaya, 1969.

Aiyappan, A., *Social Revolution in a Kerala Village,* Bombay : Asia Publishing House, 1963.

Ali, S.A., *Tribal Demography in Madhya Pradesh,* Bhopal, Jai Bharat Publishing House, 1973.

Ambastha, N.K., *A Critical Study of Tribal Education*, Delhi, S. Chand, 1969.

Anthropological Survey of India, *Tribal Map of India,* Calcutta : Anthropological Survey of India, 1967.

Atal, Yogesh, *Adivasi Bharat,* Delhi : Rajkamal Prakashan, 1965.

Bailey, F.G., *Tribe, Caste and Nation,* Oxford University Press, Indian Branch, 1960.

Baine, Sir, A., *Census of India*, 1891 Report, 1891.

Balaratnam, L.K., *Society in India*, Madras, Social Science Association, 1958.

Banerjee, S., *Ethnographic Study of Kuvikandha*, Calcutta : Anthropological Survey of India, 1969.

Berreman, G.D., *Hindus of the Himalayas,* Berkeley, California University Press, 1963.

Bhowmick, P.K., *The Lodhas of West Bengal : A Socio-economic Study,* Calcutta : Punthi Pustak, 1963.

Bingley, A.H., *Jats, Gujars and Ahirs* (Handbooks of the Indian Army), Calcutta, Superintendent, Government Printing Press, 1904.

Biswas, P.C., *the Santhal*, Delhi, Bharatiya Adimjati Sevak Sangh, 1956.

Bose, N.K., "Hindu Method of Tribal Absorption", *Proceedings of the Indian Science Congress,* reprinted in Cultural Anthropology, Calcutta (First Published in 1928), 1944.

——, "Fifty Years of Science in India", *Progress of Anthropology and Archaeology,* Calcutta, Indian Science Congress Association, 64, Dilkhusa Street, 1963.

——, *Culture and Society in India,* Bombay : Asia Publishing House, 1967.

——, *Tribal Life in India*, New Delhi : National Book Trust, 1971.

Bradley-Birt, F.B., *Story of an Indian Upland, Chhota Nagpur : A Little Known Province of the Empire,* London, Smith Elder & Co., 1903.

Brown, A.R., *Andaman Islands : A Social Study,* London.

Buchi, E.C., "The Onge of Little Andaman", *Adivasi*, Delhi : Publication Division (Rev. ed. 1969), 1955.

Burling, *Rengsanggri,* Philadelphia, University of Pennsylvania Press, 1963.

Butler, John., *Travels and Adventure in the Province of Assam During a Residence of Fourteen Years*, London, Smith Elder & Co., S.T. Comhill, 1855.

Chapekar, L.N., *The Thakurs of Sahyadri,* Oxford University Press, University of Bombay Publication, Sociology Series No. 5), 1960.

Chaterjee, S.K., *Balts and Aryan, Simla*, Indian Institute of Advanced Studies, 1968.

Chaudhury, N.C., *Munda and Their Social Structure*, Calcutta, Firm KLM Pvt. Ltd., 1977.

Crooks, W., *The North Western Provinces of India,* Mathury & Co., 36, Essex St. W.C., London.

Dalton, E.T., *Descriptive Ethnology of Bengal,* Calcutta : Superintendent, Government Printing Press, 1872.

Das, A.K., *The Koras and some little known communities of West Bengal,* Calcutta, Cultural Research Institute, Government of West Bengal., 1964.

——, *Trends of Occupational Pattern Through Generation,* Calcutta, Cultural Research Institute, Government of West Bengal, 1968.

——, *The Totos,* Calcutta, Cultural Research Institute, Government of West Bengal, 1969.

Das, A.K. and Banerjee, S.K., *Impact of Industrialisation on the Life of the Tribals of West Bengal,* Calcutta, Cultural Research Institute, Government of West Bengal., 1962-A.

——, *The Lepchas of Darjeeling District,* Calcutta, Cultural Research Institute, Government of West Bengal, 1962-B.

Das, A.K. and Banerjee, H.N., *The Impact of Tea Industry on the Life of the Tribals of West Bengal,* Calcutta, Cultural Research Institute, Government of West Bengal, 1964-B.

Das, A.K. and Raha, M.K., *The Oraons of Sunderbans,* Calcutta, Cultural Research Institute, Government of West Bengal, 1963.

Das, A.K., Raha M.K. and Roychoudhary, B.K., *The Malpaharias of West Bengal,* Calcutta, Cultural Research Institute, Government of West Bengal, 1966-A.

——, *Handbook on Scheduled Castes and Tribes of West Bengal,* Calcutta, Cultural Research Institute, Government of West Bengal., 1966-B.

Deve, P.C. *The Grasias,* Delhi, Bharatiya Adimjati Sevak Sangh, Kingsway, 1960.

Dhir, D.N., "Tribes on the North Western Border of India", Paper read in the seminar on Tribal Situation in India, Indian Institute of Advanced Studies, Simla, 1969.

District Gazetteer : *Gazetteer of the Kangra District;* Vol. I, Kulu, Lahaul and Spiti, Compiled and Published under the authority of Punjab Government, Calcutta.

District Gazetteer : *Punjab Government's Gazetteer of Chamba State,* Part 4, Lahore, Punjab Government, 1904.

District Gazetteer : *Special Gazetteer* (comprising information on Koolo, Saraj, Lahaul and Spiti), Punjab Government, 1918.

Doshi, S.L., *Bhils Between Societal Self-awareness and Cultural Synthesis,* New Delhi : Sterling Publishers, 1971.

Dube, B.K. and Bahadur, F., *A Study of the Tribal People and Tribal Areas of Madhya Pradesh,* Indore, Government Regional Press, 1967.

Dube, S.C., *The Kamar,* Lucknow, Universal Publishers, 1951.

——, "Social Anthropology in India", *Indian Anthropology : Essays in Memory of D.N. Majumdar,* ed. by T.N. Madan & Gopalan Sarana, Bombay, Asia Publishing House, 1962.

Duquensne, S.A., *New Voyage to the East Indians in 1690-91 : Full Description of Isle of Cuces Andaman,* London.

Dutta, Majumdar, N., *The Santhal : A Study in Culture Change,* Delhi : Manager of Publication, Government of India Press, 1956.

Dutta, M.P., *The People of NEFA : The Tangssas of Namchik and Tirap Village,* Shillong, Adviser's Secretariat, 1959.

Ehrenfels, U.R., *Mother Right India,* Oxford University Press, 1941.

——, *Kadar of Cochin,* Madras, University of Madras, 1952.

Ellis, R.H., *A Short Account of the Laccadive and Minicoy*, Madras : 1924.

Elwin, Verrier, *The Baiga*, London, John Murray, 1939.

——, *The Agaria,* Oxford University Press, 1942.

——, *Maria Murder and Suicide,* Bombay, Oxford University Press, 1st ed. 1943 and 2nd ed. 1950, 1943.

——, *The Aboriginals,* Bombay, Oxford University Press, 1943A.

——, *The Muriya and Their Ghotul,* Geoffrey, Cambridge, Oxford University Press, 1947.

——, *Myths of Middle India*, Geoffrey Cambridge, Oxford University Press, 1947.

——, *Bondo Highlanders,* Bombay, Oxford University Press, 1950.

——, *The Tribal Art of Middle India*, Bombay, Oxford University Press, 1951.

——, *The Loss of the Nerves* : A Comparative Study of the contact of people in the aboriginal areas of Baster State, Central Province of India, 1952.

——, *The Tribal Myths of Orissa,* Bombay, Oxford University Press, 1954.

——, *The Religion of an Indian Tribe,* Geoffrey Cambridge, Oxford University Press, 1955.

——, *The Myths of North-East Frontier of India,* Shillong, NEFA, 1958.

——, *India's North-East Frontier Agency in the 19th Century*, Calcutta, Oxford University Press, 1959.

——, *A Philosophy of NEFA*, Shillong, The Adviser to Governor of Assam, 1960A.

——, *Nagaland,* Shillong Research Department, Adviser's Secretariat, 1960.

——, *The Art of NEFA*, Shillong, NEFA, 1962.

Endle, S., *The Katcharis,* Macmillan and Co., 1911.

Enthoven, R.E., *Tribes and Castes of Bombay*, 3 Vols., 1920-22.

Ferriera, J.V., *Totemism in India*, Oxford University Press, 1965.

Fuchs, Stephen, *Social Origins,* Bombay : 1957.

——, *The Gond and Bhumia of Eastern Mandala,* Bombay : Asia Publishing House, 1960.

Furer Haimendorf, *The Chenchus : Jungle Folk of Deccan*, London, Macmillan and Co., 1943.

——, *The Tribal Population of Hyderabad*, Hyderabad Revenue Department (Census), 1945A.

——, *The Reddis of Beson Hills* : *A Study in Acculturation* (with Elizabeth Von C. Furer Haimendorf) in 2 Vols., London, Macmillan & Co., 1945B.

——, *The Raj Gonds of Adilabad : A Peasant Culture of Deccan* (in collaboration with Elizabeth Von. C. Furer Haimendorf), London, Macmillan & Co., 1948.

——, *Himalayan Barbary*, London, John Murray, Albemark, St. W., 1955.

——, *The Apatanis and Their Neighbours : A Primitive Civilization of the Eastern Himalaya,* New York : Routledge and Kegan Paul, 1962.

Gait, E.A., *A History of Assam* (2nd Ed.) Calcutta, Thacker Spink and Co., 1926.

Ghurye, G.S., *The Aborigines* : *So-called and Their Future,* Poona, Ghokhale Institute of Politics and Economics, 1943.

——, *Mahadeo Kollis,* Bombay, Popular Book Dept., 1957.

——, *The Scheduled Tribes,* Bombay, Popular Prakashan (3rd ed., 1963), 1959.

Gorer, G., *Himalayan Village : An Account of the Lepchas of Sikkim,* London : Michael Joseph, 1938.

Griffith, W.G., *The Kol Tribe of Central India,* Calcutta, Royal Asiatic Society of Bengal, 1948.

Guha, B.S., *Racial Element in Indian Population,* Oxford Paper on Indian Affairs, No. 22, Bombay, Oxford University Press, 1944.

——, *The Tribes of India,* 2 Vols. (ed.), New Delhi, Bharatiya Adimjati Sevak Sangh, 1951.

Gurdon, P.R.T., *The Khasis,* London, Macmillan and Co. Ltd. (First Published in 1906).

Harcourt, A.F.P., *The Himalayan Districts of Koolo, Lahaul and Spiti*, London, William A. Hallen, 1871.

Hasan, Amir, *A Bunch of Wild Flowers and Other Essays,* Lucknow, Ethnographic and Folk Culture Society, U.P., 1971.

Hazra, D., *The Dorlas of Bastar,* Calcutta, Anthropological Survey of India, 1970.

Hermanns, M., Study of Magic, Bharwa System, 1952.

Horam, M., *Social and Cultural Life of Nagas*, Delhi, B.R. Publishing Corporation, 1977.

Hunter, W.W., *Orissa*, London, Smith Elder, Calcutta, Thacker Spink, 2 Vols., 1872-73.

Hutton, J.H., *Angami Nagas,* with some notes on the neighbouring tribes, London, Macmillan and Co. 1921.

Hutton, J.H., *The Sema Nagas,* London, Macmillan and Co., 1921.

Ibbetson, D., *Punjab Castes,* Lahore, Superintendent, Government Press, Punjab, 1916.

Ishwaran, K., *Tradition and Economy in Village India,* London, Routledge and Kegan Paul, 1966.

——, *Shivpura, A South Indian Village,* London, Routledge and Kegan Paul, 1968.

——, *Caste in South Indian Village and Other Essays,* Bombay, Asia Publishing House, 1968.

Iyer, L.A. Krishna, *The Travancore Tribes and Castes*, Vol. I, Trivandrum, Government Press, 1937.

——, *The Travancore Tribes and Castes,* Vol. II, Trivandrum : Government Press, 1939.

——, *The Travancore Tribes and Castes,* Vol. III, Trivandrum : Government Press, 1941.

——, *The Coorg Tribes and Castes* (with L.K. Balaratnam), Trivandrum, 1948.

——, *Kerala and Her People,* Palghat, The Educational Supply Depot, 1961.

Iyer, L.K. Ananta, *Cochin Tribes and Castes,* Vol. 2, Government of Cochin, London, Higginbotham and Co. 1908.

——, *The Cochin Tribes and Castes,* Vol. 2, London, Higginbotham and Co., 1912.

——, *The Mysore Tribes and Castes,* Vol. 2, Mysore, Mysore University, 1928.

——, *The Mysore Tribes and Castes,* Vol. 3, Mysore, Mysore University, 1930.

——, *The Mysore Tribes and Castes,* Vol. 4, Mysore, Mysore University, 1931.

——, *The Mysore Tribes and Castes,* Vol. 1, Mysore, Mysore University, 1935.

Izskowitz, K.G., *The Gotr Ceremony of Boro Gadaba,* 1953.

Jay, Edward, J., *Tribal Village of Middle India,* Calcutta, Anthropological Survey of India, 1970.

Joshi, L.D., *the Khasa Family Law in Himalayan Districts of the United Provinces of India*, Allahabad, Government Press, 1929.

Kalia, S.L., "Sanskritisation and Tribalisation", *Changing Tribes* ed. by T.B. Naik, Chhindwara, Tribal Research Institute, 1961.

Lathum, R.G., *Ethnography of India,* London, Voorst, 1859.

Luiz, A.A.D., *Tribes of Kerala,* New Delhi, Bharatiya Adimjati Sevak Sangh (1st ed.), 1962.

Maharashtra Census Office, *Scheduled Tribes in Maharashtra,* Bombay, the Maharasthra Census Office, 1972.

Majumdar, D.N., *A Tribe in Transition : A Study in Culture Pattern*, London, Longmans Green and Co., 1937.

——, *The Affairs of a Tribe : A Study in Tribal Dynamics,* Lucknow, Universal Publishers Ltd., 1950.

——, *Himalayan Polyandry,* Bombay, Asia Publishing House, 1963.

——, *Fortunes of the Primitive Tribe,* Lucknow, The Universal Publishers Ltd., 1963.

Mathur, L.P., *History of the Andaman and Nicobar Islands (1756-1966)*, Delhi, Sterling Publishing (P) Ltd., 1968.

Mathur, P.R.G., *Tribal Situation in Kerala,* Trivandrum, Kerala Historical Society, 1977.

Mills, J.P., *The Lhota Nagas,* London, Macmillan Co., 1922.

——, *The Ao Nagas,* London, Macmillan and Co., 1926.

——, *The Rengma Nagas,* London, Macmillan and Co., 1937.

Mishra, R., *Mullu Kurmumhas of Kaffale*. Calcutta, Anthropological Survey of India, 1974.

Morris, C.J., *Living with the Lepchas : A Book about Sikkim*, Himalayas, London, Torento Heinemann, 1938.

Mukherjee, C.L., *The Santhals,* A.R. Mukherjee, Managing Director, Calcutta-12, 1939.

Nag, D.S., *Tribal Economy* (An Economic Study of the Baiga), Delhi : Bharatiya Adimjati Sevak Sangh, 1958.

Naik, T.B., *The Bhil* : A Study, Delhi, Bharatiya Adimjati Sevak Sangh, 1956.

——, *The Abujh Marias* (ed.), Chhindwara, Tribal Research Institute, 1963.

——, *The Changing Tribes,* Chhindwara, Tribal Research Institute, 1965.

——, *Bara Bhai Binjhwar,* Bhopal, Madhya Pradesh, Hindi Granth Akademy, 1972.

Naik, T.B. and Bhouaskar, K.M., *Changing Tribes,* Chhindwara, Tribal Research Institue, 1961.

——, *Economic Organisation and Market,* Chhindwara Tribal Research Institute, 1964.

Neiggermeyer, H.N., *Khuttia Khond,* Verlog, Klans Renner, 1964.

Newell, W.H., "Goshun : A Goddi Village in the Himalayas", in *India's Village*, ed. by M.N. Srinivas, Bombay, Asia Publishing House (2nd ed.).

Oakley, E.S., *Holy Himalayas,* Edinburgh and London, Oliphan, Anderson and Ferrier.

Perry, N.E., *The Lakkers,* London, Macmillan & Co., 1932.

Pathak, Sushil Madhav, *Vishwa Ki Prachin Sabhyataon Ka Itihas*, Patna, Bihar Hindi Grandh Academy, 1972.

Playfair, A., *The Garos*, London, David and Nutt, 1909.

Portman, M.V., *A History of Our Relation with the Andamanese* (2 Vols.) London : 1899.

Prasad, N., *Land and People of Tribal Bihar,* Ranchi, Bihar Tribal Welfare Research Institute, 1964.

Punekar, V.B., *The Sonkolis of Bombay,* Bombay : Popular Book Depot, 1959.

Radcliff-Brown, A.R., *The Andaman Islanders : A Study of Social Anthropology,* Glencoe, Illinois, Cambridge University Press, The Free Press (also printed in 1948), 1922.

Raghavaiah, V., *Tribal Revolts,* Nellore, Andhra Rashtra Adimjati Sevak Sangh, 1971.

Risley, H.H., *The People of India*, Calcutta, Secretariat Press, 1905.

Rivers, W.H.R., *The Todas,* London, Macmillan & Co. Ltd., 1906.

Robinson, W., *A Descriptive Account of Assam,* London, Ostell and Lepage, 1841.

Roy Burmen, B.K. with Harit, H.L., *A Preliminary Appraisal of the Scheduled Tribe of India*, New Delhi, Office of the Registrar-General, India, 1971.

Roy, S.C., *The Mundas and Their Country,* Calcutta, City Bar Library (Reprint 1972), 1912.

——, *The Oraons of Chotanagpur,* Ranchi Bar Library, 1915A.

——, *The Hill Bhuiyans of Orissa,* Ranchi, Man in India Office, 1935.

Roy, S.C. with R.C. Roy, *The Kharia*, Vol. I and II, Ranchi, Man in India Office, 1937.

Ruhelia, Satyapal, *Godulia Lohars*, Bombay, 1967.

Russel and Hiralal, *Tribes and Castes of Central Provinces of India* (4 Vols.), London, Macmillan & Co., 1916.

Sachidananda, *Culture Change in Tribal Bihar*, Calcutta, Bookland Pvt., 1964.

——, *The Tribal Village in Bihar : A Study in Unity and Extension,* New Delhi, Munshiram Manoharlal, 1968.

——, *The Munda,* 1979.

Sahay, B.N., *Dynamics of Leadership,* New Delhi, Bookhive, 1968.

Saksena, R.N., *Tribal Economy in Central India,* Calcutta, K.L. Mukhopadhyaya, 1964.

Sarkar, S.S., *The Moler of Rajmahal Hills,* Calcutta, The Book Company, 1938.

Save, K.J., *The Warlis : A Study of Aboriginal Tribe of Bombay Presidency*, Padma Publishers and Co., 1945.

Shah, P.G., *Dublas,* Bombay, Gujarat Research Society, 1958.

——, *Naikas-Naikdas,* Bombay, Gujarat Research Society. 1959.

——, *Tribal Life in Gujarat,* Bombay, Gujarat Research Society, 1964.

Shakespeare, J., *The Lushai Kuki Clans*, Part I and II, London, Macmillan and Co., 1912.

Shukla, B.K., *The Dafla,* Shillong, Adviser's Secretariat, 1959.

Singh, K.S., *Tribal Situation in India,* Simla, Indian Institute of Advanced Studies, 1979.

Sinha, D.P., *Culture Change in an Inter-Tribal Market*, Bombay, Asia Publishing House, 1968.

Sinha, R., *The Akas*, Shillong, Adviser's Secretariat, 1963.

Smith, W.C., *The Ao Naga Tribe of Assam : A Study in Ethnology and Sociology*, London, Macmillan and Co., 1925.

Srinivas, M.N., *Marriage and Family in Mysore,* Bombay, 1942.

Srivastava, L.R.N., *The Gullong,* Shillong, Research Department, Adviser's Secretariat, 1962.

Srivastava, S.K., *The Tharu : A Study in Cultural Dynamic*, Agra, Agra University Press, 1958.

Thurston, E., *Ethnographic Notes on Southern India*, Madras, Superintendent, Madras Govt. Museum, 1906.

——, *Castes and Tribes of Southern India,* Vol. 1-7 (assisted by K. Rangachari), Madras Govt. Press, 1906.

Vidyarthi, L.P., *The Maler, A Study in Nature-Man-Spirit Complex of a Hill Tribe*, Calcutta, Bookland Private Ltd., 1963.

——, *Applied Anthropology in India* (ed), Allahabad, Kitab Mahal, 1968.

——, *Cultural Configurations of Ranchi : Study of a Pre-industrial City of Tribal Bihar,* Calcutta, Bookland Private Ltd. 1969.

——, *Social Anthropology in India — A Social Orientation,* Delhi, Concept Publishing Co. 1970.

——, "Tribal Ethnolography in India", A Survey of Researches in Social Anthropology and Sociology, New Delhi : ICSSR, 1972.

——, *Dynamics of Tribal Leadership in Bihar,* Allahabad, Kitab Mahal, 1973.

——, "Report of the Task Force on Development", 1973.

——, *The Kharia : Then and Now,* New Delhi, concept Publishing Company, 1980.

Vyas, M.N., "Banjaras : The Mercantile Nomads of Rajasthan", *Tribe* Vol; III, No. 2, Udaipur, 1967.

——, "The Bhils on the Border of Rajasthan — An Emerging Situation", in *Tribal Situation in India* (ed) K.S. Singh, Indian Institute of Advanced Study, Simla, 1972.

——, "The Kathodis — A tribe in Transition" in *Primitive Tribes : First Step,* (eds) S. Sinha and B.D. Sharma, New Delhi, Ministry of Home Affairs, Govt. of India, 1977.

Vyas, M.N. and N.D. Choudhury, "Forest Co-operative and Change among the Tribes", *Tribe* (Special Number) Vol. 5, No. 4, 1969.

Vyas, S.N., *India in the Ramayan Age,* Delhi Atma Ram and Sons, 1967.

Watts, N.A., *The Half Clad Tribes of Eastern India,* Bombay, Orient Langmans, 1970.

Weling, A., *The Katkaris : A Sociological Study of a Tribe of the Bombay Presidency,* Bombay, Book Dept. 1934.